The Early Medieval World

The Early Medieval World

FROM THE FALL OF ROME TO THE TIME OF CHARLEMAGNE

VOLUME ONE: A–K

Michael Frassetto

ABC-CLIO

Santa Barbara, California • Denver, Colorado • Oxford, England

Library of Congress Cataloging-in-Publication Data

Frassetto, Michael.
  The early medieval world : from the fall of Rome to the time of Charlemagne / Michael Frassetto.
       p. cm.
  Includes bibliographical references and index.
  ISBN 978-1-59884-995-0 (hardcopy : alk. paper) — ISBN 978-1-59884-996-7 (ebook)   1. Europe—History—392-814—Encyclopedias.   2. Middle Ages—Encyclopedias.   3. Civilization, Medieval—Encyclopedias.   I. Title.
  D114.F83 2013
  940.1'2—dc23   2012031995

ISBN: 978-1-59884-995-0
EISBN: 978-1-59884-996-7

17 16 15 14 13   1 2 3 4 5

This book is also available on the World Wide Web as an eBook.
Visit www.abc-clio.com for details.

ABC-CLIO, LLC
130 Cremona Drive, P.O. Box 1911
Santa Barbara, California 93116-1911

This book is printed on acid-free paper ∞
Manufactured in the United States of America

Contents

List of Entries

Guide to Related Topics

Barbarian Peoples and Dynasties

Alans

Alemanni

Anglo-Saxons

Avars

Burgundians

Carolingian Dynasty

Franks

Huns

Jews and Judaism

Lombards

Merovingian Dynasty

Ostrogoths

Vandals

Visigoths

Cultural and Religious Leaders

Alcuin of York

Agobard of Lyons, St.

Ammianus Marcellinus

Ambrose of Milan

Angilbert

Asser

Astronomer, The

Augustine of Canterbury, St.

Augustine of Hippo, St.

Balthild

Basil the Great

Bede

Benedict Biscop

Benedict of Nursia, St.

Boethius

Boniface, St.

Cassian, John St.

Cassiodorus

Caesarius of Arles

Chrodegang of Metz

Columba, St.

Columban, St.

Dhuoda

Einhard

Ermold Nigellus

Genevieve, St.

Gildas

Gottschalk of Orbais

Gregory of Tours

Social and Religious History

Adoptionism

Agriculture

Animals

Arianism

Barbarian Art

Circumcellions

Clothing

Coins and Coinage

Diet and Nutrition

Donatists

Education and Learning

Family

Germanic Religion

Ivories

Jewelry and Gems

Marriage

Monasticism

Peasants

Row-Grave Cemeteries

Saint-Denis, Abbey of

Slaves and Slavery

Sutton Hoo

Tournai

Weapons and Armor

Women

Preface

Examining an often overlooked and little understood period of history, *The Early Medieval World: From the Fall of Rome to the Time of Charlemagne* is an introduction to an important and formative period in European history. Surveying the period from the fourth to the tenth centuries, this two-volume encyclopedia contains almost 250 entries offering the latest scholarship on a wide range of topics. The encyclopedia's alphabetically arranged entries discuss laws, literary works, religion, intellectual and cultural trends, major battles, and important places and institutions. The encyclopedia also examines the great political and religious leaders, influential women, and various peoples who shaped late antique and early medieval civilization. The entries provide cross-references to other related entries as well as bibliographies of additional print and electronic information resources specific to the entry topic.

Written for high school and undergraduate students, as well as for public library patrons and other nonspecialists interested in the period, *The Early Medieval World* includes a variety of useful additional features. A detailed chronology list provides a ready reference guide to the most important events of the period, and an in-depth introduction provides useful social, cultural, and historical context for the entries throughout the two volumes. By using the Guide to Related Topics and following the entry cross-references, a user can trace a broad theme, such as political leadership, laws and government, major battles and military events, through all its major events, ideas, and personalities. An extensive and up-to-date general bibliography provides guidance for further study of this period by listing the most important and accessible general works. An appendix lists all the major rulers of Europe during the period. Finally, the encyclopedia includes excerpts from 30 important primary documents from the period, including works by Bede, Procopius, Einhard, and Saint Augustine. Each excerpt is preceded by a brief introduction putting the document into context for readers. A concise but comprehensive work, *The Early Medieval World* is intended to bring light to what is traditionally understood as a dark age.

Acknowledgments

The completion of this volume has been a long but often pleasant task, and any merit the book may claim is the result of the help that I have received along the way from many sources. I would like to recognize those especially without whom this work would not have appeared. I would like to thank Joyce Salisbury, who introduced me to the editors at ABC-CLIO and encouraged me to take on the project. I received further encouragement and great support from my editor, John Wagner, and Bridget Austiguy-Preschel and Sasikala Rajesh. It has been a great pleasure working with them and the entire staff of editors and researchers at ABC-CLIO who have helped bring this project to a timely end. I should thank especially and dedicate this volume to Jill and Olivia, who have helped me in more ways than they know.

Introduction

Once defined as the "Dark Ages"—a period of unending savagery and ignorance—the era in European history from the fall of Rome to the end of the Carolingian age has now come to be recognized as a time of important social and cultural transformation. Although the great civilization of the ancient Mediterranean gradually faded away during this time, it was replaced by a new and dynamic culture. Despite the very real decline in population, literacy, city life, and economic strength, the leaders of government and society from the fourth to the tenth centuries created a unique culture that drew on a legacy that was at once Christian, German, and Roman. This emerging world laid the foundation for later medieval and modern civilization. Indeed, great leaders refashioned ideas about law and kingship and provided a model of Christian government that remained influential into the modern age (*see* **Alfred the Great; Charlemagne; Justinian**). Early medieval rulers also established the basic outlines of the later medieval and modern nation states (*see* **Verdun, Treaty of**) as they created new kingdoms out of the former Western Empire. Although suffering plague, invasion, and civil and international war, early medieval Europe enjoyed important cultural achievements. During late antiquity and the early Middle Ages, influential thinkers and writers (*see* **Alcuin of York; Augustine of Hippo, St.; Bede; Boethius**) preserved the literary and intellectual traditions of ancient Rome and shaped the theological traditions of the church. Moreover, important church institutions, including monasticism and the papacy (*see* **Benedict of Nursia, St.; Gregory I, the Great, Pope**), underwent significant growth in this period. Europe from the time of Constantine to the age of the Carolingians, therefore, was a period of important transformation from the ancient to the medieval world, and an age that laid the foundation for later medieval and modern civilization.

Overview of the Historiography of the Early Medieval World

Writing in the late 18th century, the great historian Edward Gibbon observed, "If a man were called to fix the period of the history of the world during which the condition of the human race was most happy and prosperous, he would, without hesitation, name that which elapsed from the death of Domitian to the accession of Commodus. The vast extent of the Roman Empire was governed by absolute power, under the guidance of virtue and wisdom" (Gibbon, vol. 1, p. 70). Gibbon then proceeded to outline the subsequent collapse of the Roman Empire, which he believed was the greatest political structure in human history. Beyond the moral corruption that afflicted Rome in the period following what he saw as the golden age, he identified two major causes for the collapse of the empire. One was an internal revolution brought on by the gradual growth of Christianity and its adoption by the emperor and people of Rome. No longer were the Romans willing to fight for the empire because of their adoption of a pacifistic religion that drew them away from their traditional devotion to the service of the state.

The other significant factor contributing to the collapse of this most magnificent empire, according to Gibbon, was the invasion of the barbarians. Large numbers of uncivilized peoples began to put pressure on and then cross over the imperial frontiers. These barbarians entered the empire and destroyed ancient civilization because of their illiteracy and hatred of all things Roman (*see* **Franks; Huns; Vandals; Visigoths**). Moreover, the Romans' inability to provide for their own defense made it necessary that they enroll large numbers of the same barbarians that were invading the empire in the defense of the empire. Internal weakness and the end of traditional civic virtue, along with the invasion of the barbarian peoples, were, for Gibbon, the main factors in the fall of the Roman Empire and the emergence of the Dark Ages.

As a result of Gibbon's remarkable prose, wide knowledge of the original sources in Latin and Greek, and compelling argument, his view of the end of the ancient world and the Middle Ages remained the standard understanding of this period well into the 20th century. Indeed, generations of scholars built upon his fundamental assumption in their studies of Romans and barbarians. In the early 20th century, for example, the English scholar J. B. Bury and the French historian Ferdinand Lot refined and elaborated on the principle arguments of Gibbon. They offered meticulous studies of the movements and character of the various barbarian peoples and the great social and political changes that accompanied the end of the ancient world. The end of the Roman Empire for Gibbon and his successors signaled not only the end of a political entity, but also all of ancient civilization. The causes for this collapse came to be seen as more varied and complex, involving a broad range of factors (economic, social, political, and military), but the consensus remained that the combination of internal Roman weakness and the invasion or migration of peoples led to the demise of the Roman Empire and ancient civilization in the year 476 (*see* **Odovacar**).

During the course of the 20th century and into the 21st century, the view once established by Gibbon was gradually overturned, as scholars brought new methodologies and new insights to the study of ancient and early medieval civilization.

One of the most obvious observations was that the Roman Empire did not cease to exist in 476; only the Western Empire succumbed to the movements of the barbarian peoples. The Eastern Empire (now known as the Byzantine Empire, from its capital of Byzantium, rechristened Constantinople) survived for another thousand years and fell to the Turks only in 1453. The Byzantine Empire clearly enjoyed a long and prosperous life after the "fall" in 476, and Constantinople even ruled again, for a time, over parts of the Western Empire, thanks to the conquests of Justinian and his generals (*see* **Belisarius; Narses**). Moreover, Roman traditions were preserved by the Byzantine state even after the so-called fall of Rome, as they were in the former Western Empire. Indeed, historians have emphasized continuity in a number of areas in the Germanic successor states that emerged after the end of Roman political organization in the West. As the language of law and government, Latin continued, as did economic structures, the machinery of taxation, administrative organization, the religion of the empire—Christianity—and a variety of other social and cultural traditions.

Rather than a time marked by an abrupt and dramatic end of one civilization and the appearance of another, historians now regard the period as one of transformation. The end of the ancient world came gradually, and its continuation can be seen in a number of areas. In the early the 20th century, the great economic historian, Henri Pirenne, argued that the ancient world survived until the time of the expansion of Islam in the seventh and eighth centuries. Peter Brown also demonstrated the survival of ancient civilization into the eighth century, but went beyond Pirenne to consider broader social and cultural developments. Some scholars have even argued that ancient civilization survived until the year 1000, when slavery, the last vestige of classical culture, finally disappeared. Although the exact date remains uncertain, ancient civilization clearly lingered on past the traditional date of its end in 476 in the form of a number of social, cultural, and economic trends that shaped the lives and governments of the Germanic successor kings who ruled over the former Western Empire.

The picture of the "barbarians" also has evolved since the time Gibbon wrote his classic work. The traditional understanding of the peoples who succeeded the Romans was that they were savages and barbarians. Drawing from ancient works by Tacitus, Jordanes, and others, Gibbon and the historians who followed him saw the Germans and other peoples who entered the empire as uncivilized—the noble savage of Tacitus or the barbaric and ugly Hun of Jordanes. The barbarians were seen only as invaders bent on the destruction of the Roman Empire and classical civilization. Citing the examples of Alaric and Gaiseric, who sacked and pillaged the city of Rome in 410 and 455, respectively, the older generation of scholars argued that the intent of the barbarians was destruction of the old order and its replacement with new barbarian kingdoms. Indeed, they saw the great movement of peoples that took place in the fourth and fifth centuries as an invasion of the empire by the barbarians, who then created new kingdoms out of the old political order. The idea that the Germans and other peoples who entered the empire during this time came as conquerors has received vigorous support in the early 21st century from a number of scholars, notably Peter Heather and Bryan Ward-Perkins. They have revived the argument that the Huns and Goths entered the Roman Empire with its conquest as their chief goal. The violent invasions of the Huns and Goths destabilized long-standing economic and political networks that had existed between Rome and tribal groups along the imperial frontier and caused serious destruction to much of the Roman world.

Despite the revisionist scholarship of Heather and Ward-Perkins, scholarship in the 20th and 21st centuries, especially the work of Walter Goffart, has provided a new perspective on the "barbarians" and their relations with the Roman Empire. Although the argument that the increased numbers of barbarians or Germans in the imperial army still carries weight with some scholars, the association of German/barbarian and Roman is seen in a much more positive light. Long-standing contacts between Romans and the peoples outside the empire reshaped both the Romans and the barbarians. There was a gradual transformation on each side, as the Romans and their neighbors traded with each other and intermarried. Many Germans did enter the military and imbibed a better appreciation for the empire, and the leaders came to identify with the empire (*see* **Theodoric the Great**). Although some Germanic and barbarian peoples invaded the empire for spoil and territory, others petitioned for entry into a greater political entity and sought to become part of that entity (*see* **Attila the Hun; Gaiseric**). Furthermore, the traditional identification of the Germans and barbarians with national or tribal groups has been eroded in the new understanding of them. The groups are now seen as less nationally distinct, and there is clear historical discontinuity between the earliest manifestations of the various tribal groups and the groups that established kingdoms in the former Western Empire.

The period of late antiquity and the early Middle Ages has also traditionally been recognized as the "Dark Ages." Indeed, the entire period from the fall of Rome to the start of the Italian Renaissance was once understood as a period of little or no cultural achievement, with the possible exception of the Carolingian Renaissance, which was deemed the one shining moment of that nearly thousand-year period (*see* **Carolingian Renaissance**). As the 20th century progressed, this view came to be revised, so that a smaller and smaller portion of the Middle Ages was deemed "dark." But the notion that the early Middle Ages (c. 400–1000) was a period of cultural stagnation persisted for a longer time, even though the period of "darkness" was narrowed to c. 500–750. Whatever the chronological limits, the "Dark Ages" that followed the fall of Rome in the West have been traditionally understood as a period of limited intellectual and cultural productivity. Both city life and the overall population of Europe had diminished, a decline made all the worse by a devastating plague that swept across the eastern Mediterranean beginning in the age of Justinian (r. 527–565). The great monuments of sculpture and architecture were no longer produced in the cities, and there was also a decline in literacy among the general population. Related to the decline in literacy was the near disappearance of the use of writing in government administration and other public activities. The cultural decline was, it had been argued, related to the general disdain for ancient civilization that many barbarians held, as well as to their own cultural backwardness and the reluctance of some Christian leaders to adopt classical learning—as Tertullian once asked, what has Athens to do with Jerusalem?

Just as the understanding of the barbarians has undergone a revision, so too has the view on the period of "Dark Ages." Although the term itself continues to be used, the period after the fall of the Roman Empire is seen less as a dark age. Indeed, even in the period of 500–750, important cultural developments took place and artistic activity continued. Even though the scale and focus of artistic activity were reduced, they nevertheless continued, as the metalwork of early medieval artisans reveals. Moreover, the Germanic peoples who established themselves throughout the Western Empire are better understood as the heirs of ancient Roman tradition, and in the early Middle Ages the various social and cultural trends that characterized later medieval civilization were taking shape. Important Roman cultural traditions, particularly in law and language, continued into the so-called "Dark Ages" and influenced the shape of government and society after 476. Furthermore, Rome's political successors also adopted Roman religions, specifically Christianity, which would form the essence of early medieval culture. The traditions of learning and letters were preserved by the church, especially in the monasteries. Late antique and early medieval churchmen produced poetry, literature, history, and theology in Latin and preserved the works of the ancient Romans. Clearly, Europe of the early Middle Ages was not the equal of Athens in the fifth-century BC or of Florence in the 15th century, but historians have come to recognize the important cultural developments of the period. And although the Carolingian Renaissance continues to be seen as a great cultural milestone, it is no longer seen as the lone example of early medieval brilliance, and its roots in the sixth and seventh centuries have been identified.

A Brief History of Late Antiquity and the Early Middle Ages

The Later Roman Empire

Although the Roman Empire did not "fall" until the late fifth century, it had undergone a profound change already in the third century, a change that in some ways foreshadowed the transformation of the early Middle Ages. Indeed, during the crisis of the third century, as it is often called, the empire endured many of the difficulties it faced again in the fourth and fifth centuries. The empire suffered a dramatic economic collapse, decline in population and urban life, military disasters, and foreign invasions. The essential strength of Roman civilization and the emergence of several highly talented and determined emperors, however, enabled the empire to survive the crisis. The empire that emerged at the end of the third century and the beginning of the fourth was fundamentally different from the empire of the second century, which was so highly praised by Gibbon.

The empire of the fourth century was shaped by the reforms of two of the greatest rulers in Roman history, Diocletian and Constantine (*see* **Constantine**). Although in one sense they saved the empire, establishing a foundation upon which the Western Empire survived nearly 200 years and the Eastern Empire survived over 1,000 years, in another sense Diocletian and Constantine created something new. Their Rome looked forward to the religious and political structures that characterized the early medieval world. Building on the work of his immediate predecessors, who managed to stop the advance of the Goths and stabilize the government and society, Diocletian reformed the Roman government and military. Organizing imperial administration into four main divisions and establishing a plan of succession, Diocletian saved the empire from ruin and foreshadowed the divisions in the empire that came later, as well as the structure of government and society. He also launched the last major persecution of the Christian church, which failed to destroy it. His religious policy, and much of his imperial settlement, was undermined by his ultimate successor, Constantine.

The first Christian emperor, Constantine seized power in a civil war that followed Diocletian's retirement in 305. Although he accepted baptism only on his deathbed in 337, Constantine legalized the Christian faith in 313 and was the church's greatest benefactor throughout his reign. He granted privileges to bishops, allowed the church to inherit money and property, and made many pious donations of his own. In true Roman fashion, Constantine shepherded the growth of Christianity and presided over one of the most important church councils, the council of Nicaea in 325, which provided the basic definition of the nature of the godhead that remains the cornerstone of Christian teaching. In this way, Constantine offered a model of church–state relations (often termed "caesaropapism") for rulers of later Rome and the early Middle Ages. The emperor's other reforms also paved the way for the future of the Mediterranean basin. His reform of the coinage stabilized the economy and provided the basic unit of money, the *solidus,* for generations to come (*see* **Coins and Coinage**). He also established a new imperial capital at Constantinople, the new Christian city that remained the capital of a "Roman" empire for more than a thousand years.

The reforms of Diocletian and Constantine secured the survival of the empire, and the fourth century appears, on the surface, to have been a time of renewed vitality. Indeed, some emperors resumed wars of expansion, and despite the usual turmoil and dissension in the imperial household, the empire was ably run by Constantine's successors. The house of Constantine maintained united rule of the empire for several generations, and even in the later fourth century cooperation between the emperors in the Eastern and Western Empire was the rule rather than the exception. Indeed, Theodosius ruled over the entire empire for a time before his death in 395; he also protected the empire from the increasing threat from the barbarians and made Christianity the official religion of the empire.

At the same time, however, the fundamental weaknesses of ancient civilization became increasingly evident, especially in the Western Empire. There was clear evidence in the decline of city life in the West, most notably the demise of the original heart of the empire, as Rome was abandoned as the imperial capital and replaced by Milan. Moreover, the increasingly heavy burden of taxation caused the aristocrats to flee the cities for their large plantations, where they could avoid the long arm of government. Flight from paying taxes paralleled the flight from honoring their traditional participation in government. The aristocrats and their plantations also prefigured the estates, or manors, of the Middle Ages, where servile labor farmed as tenants of the lord (*see* **Agriculture**).

These important social changes were accompanied, in the Western Empire, by population and economic decline. The economy remained an agricultural one that failed to develop an industrial component, and as the soils became exhausted, agricultural and economic life collapsed. Unlike the Eastern Empire, the Western did not have long-established urban and commercial traditions to save it in the face of agricultural decline. As a result of economic and demographic decline as well as the widespread reluctance to serve the state, the Romans enrolled more and more Germans in the army. They would defend imperial borders and then retire to farm imperial lands. The underlying weakness of the Western Empire, therefore, was already evident in the fourth century and prepared the way for the so-called fall of Rome in the fifth century.

The Migrations of Peoples

The fall of Rome, or gradual transformation from late antique to early medieval society, was the result of the internal weaknesses of the Western Empire and the empire's inability to respond to the influx of large numbers of Germanic and other barbarian peoples. These peoples, whose origins are obscure, but who are traditionally held to have come from Scandinavia, had long existed along the frontiers of the Roman Empire. They had frequent contact with the empire and as early as the first century had scored great victories against Roman armies, and in the second century the emperor Marcus Aurelius spent much of his reign fighting the Germans along the Danube River. In the third century, these peoples again threatened the empire and violated its frontiers. But the empire survived these repeated threats until the late fourth century, and the Germans saw the empire as a great power whose peace and prosperity they desired to share. Indeed, most Germanic peoples sought not to destroy the empire but to join it, and some did. Germans were enrolled in the army, and significant numbers of them became Roman soldiers by the reforms of Constantine. They often sought entry into the empire to enjoy the better climate and farmlands and the strength and stability of Rome.

In the late fourth century, the traditional relationship that existed between Rome and the peoples on her frontiers was profoundly altered by the entry of a new power, the Huns (*see* **Huns**). These East Asian peoples, for reasons still unknown, began an aggressive movement west in the fourth century. Their great skill on horseback and ferociousness in battle enabled them to create a great empire that stretched across large parts of Europe and Asia. As they moved westward, they absorbed or displaced the peoples settled in their way and initiated a general westward migration of peoples. As a result, the tribes long settled along the imperial frontiers now exerted increasing pressure on the frontiers, in the hopes of entering the empire to find protection against the Huns. Notably, the Hunnish assault on one group of Goths caused another group, traditionally known as the Visigoths, to move toward the empire in the hopes of obtaining protection from the Huns (see **Ostrogoths; Visigoths**). The Goths, like other so-called barbarians, came not as conquerors or invaders, but almost as refugees who sought to join the empire, not to destroy it.

Although many of the tribal groups that entered the empire had great respect for it and did not seek to destroy it, their movements led to the gradual demise of an independent Roman state in the West. Fearing the advance of the Huns and with the permission of the emperor Valens, some 80,000 Goths entered the empire in 376. The failure of the Romans to accommodate this large body of people led to increasing difficulties for both the Goths and Romans. In 378, war broke out between the Goths and Romans, a war that led to the destruction of Roman armies and the death of the emperor and that gave free reign to the Goths, whose movements within the empire further destabilized the situation (*see* **Hadrianople, Battle of**). The independence of the Goths was cut short by the emperor Theodosius, who settled them in the Balkans, where they remained until the death of the emperor in 395. They resumed the warpath in 395 under a new king, Alaric, who assumed a more aggressive stance toward the empire (*see* **Alaric**). His movements were restricted somewhat by the general Stilicho, whose murder in 406 opened the way for Alaric (*see* **Stilicho**). In 410, the unthinkable occurred; Alaric and his followers sacked the city of Rome, the first time it had been sacked in 800 years. This event was a profound shock to the people of the empire, Christian and pagan, and prefigured worse events to come.

The Fall of Rome and the Germanic Successor States

In the fifth century, the pressures on the Roman frontiers increased even more, and the internal weakness of the Western Empire and incompetence of a number of fifth-century emperors made it almost impossible to prevent gradual dismemberment of the Western Empire. Indeed, the Huns, Visigoths, and other peoples continued to pose a threat to the integrity of the empire, as a series of weak emperors were propped up by their generals, some of whom were Germans themselves (*see* **Aëtius; Ricimer; Stilicho**). The Visigoths, for example, continued their wanderings in the western Roman world after the sack of the city, eventually settling in Spain and southern France and creating the first of the Germanic successor states.

The Visigoths, however, were not the only people to undermine the imperial order in the West. The Huns also continued to plague Romans and barbarians alike, especially under their greatest leader, Attila. Although he was unable to replace it, Attila seriously weakened the empire, fighting several major battles against an alliance of Romans and barbarians and threatening to sack the city of Rome in 453 (*see* **Catalaunian Plains, Battle of the; Leo I, the Great, Pope**). At Attila's death, however, the Hunnish empire collapsed, as the various subject peoples revolted against the Huns. While the Huns and Visigoths assaulted the empire, large numbers of other German peoples entered the empire seeking territory, and the empire gradually abandoned its authority in Britain and elsewhere.

Among the other peoples to enter the empire in the fifth century were the Anglo-Saxons and Vandals, who established important successor kingdoms at opposite ends of the Western Empire (*see* **Anglo-Saxons; Vandals**). As the Roman soldiers abandoned Britain, the native population sought aid against raids from tribes to the north and invited the leaders of the Saxons to defend them, an invitation that led to the Anglo-Saxon conquest of the country (*see* **Hengist and Horsa; King Arthur; Vortigern**). The Vandals also carved a successor kingdom out of the Western Empire, settling in much of North Africa, which remained the base for subsequent harassment of the empire by the Vandals and their leader Gaiseric, who sacked Rome for a second time in 455.

The Western Empire was gradually dismembered during the course of the fifth century, as one province after another was transformed into a Germanic successor kingdom. For most of the century, however, Italy remained protected from the onslaught. Indeed, the policy of many of the imperial military commanders was to protect the old heart of the empire. In 476, however, Italy, too, fell to a Germanic conqueror. Leading a mixed band of Germans, the barbarian general Odovacar deposed the reigning emperor, Romulus Augustulus, and killed the power behind the throne, the general Orestes (*see* **Orestes; Romulus Augustulus**). Instead of promoting a puppet emperor as Orestes and others had done, Odovacar sent the imperial insignia and other official seals and symbols back to Zeno, the emperor in Constantinople, and established an independent kingdom in Italy, which lasted until 493 and established the framework for later Italian successor kingdoms (*see* **Zeno**). The deposition of Romulus Augustulus by Odovacar thus is traditionally recognized as the end of the Western Empire, and no emperor reigned in the West again until the ninth century.

The Post-Roman World: Theodoric the Great, Justinian, and the Lombards

Although independent imperial rule was brought to a close by Odovacar in 476, Rome and its influence continued well into the early Middle Ages. Indeed, Odovacar recognized at least the nominal authority of the emperor in Constantinople over Italy, and other Germanic leaders respected the empire and its leaders. Furthermore, Roman traditions were maintained in a number of other areas, including law, religion, and language. Social, economic, and cultural trends that began as early as the fourth century were preserved into the sixth century, as city life was gradually replaced by a more rural society. The institutions of the church that took shape in late antiquity also continued to evolve in the early Middle Ages. Throughout much of the former Western Empire, the bishops, especially the bishop of Rome, assumed many of the administrative duties of the old Roman establishment, as well as responsibility for social welfare. The traditions of monasticism continued to spread throughout the old Western Empire, and the various Germanic peoples either converted to Christianity or continued in their adherence to it.

The abolition of the imperial office in the Western Empire in 476 did not, moreover, end the interest of the emperor in Constantinople in Italian affairs. Indeed, even though he did not recognize Odovacar's usurpation, Zeno granted the German the title of Patricius and remained in uneasy correspondence with him. Zeno also used the uncertain situation in Italy to his advantage when the great Ostrogothic leader, Theodoric, became an increasingly difficult figure in the Eastern Empire. In 488, the emperor commissioned Theodoric to invade Italy and depose Odovacar, thus resolving two problematic issues for the emperor. Theodoric accepted the emperor's offer and led the Ostrogoths to Italy, where they faced strong resistance from Odovacar. In the early 490s, the two leaders fought to a standstill, and in 493 the two came to terms, which were to be celebrated at a banquet held by Theodoric. Upon his arrival, Odovacar was murdered by Theodoric's men, and the Ostrogoth became the sole ruler in Italy.

Theodoric's Italian realm was one of the most dynamic and important of the immediate post-Roman kingdoms, and the king himself was the greatest power in the former Western Empire. Despite his Arianism (a Christian teaching on the godhead rejected at Nicaea), Theodoric enjoyed good relations with the majority Catholic Italian population. Although a "barbarian," Theodoric remained on good terms with the descendants of the Roman citizens in Italy because of his respect for Roman traditions and his promotion of them. He was a patron of the arts and culture, and promoted two of the leading late Roman writers, Boethius and Cassiodorus, to important court positions (*see* **Boethius; Cassiodorus**). He supported Roman traditions in law and education and was a great builder—as all Roman rulers were. Despite Theodoric's early success, the last years of his reign were troubled, as relations with the senatorial aristocracy worsened. His increasing brutality, seen, for example, in his execution of Boethius, soured relations with the Italian population and revived the desire for imperial rule. Theodoric's death in 526, moreover, left the kingdom in an even more difficult situation for his heir, Athalaric, whose mother, Amalaswintha, was Theodoric's daughter. Internal political disputes, in part involving relations with the Eastern Empire, led to the murder of Amalaswintha, which opened the door for the invasion of the emperor Justinian.

The legacy of Rome weighed heavily on Justinian, who was born in a Latin-speaking region of the Eastern Empire and was inspired to rule as a traditional Roman emperor. His actions as emperor reflect the important influence of Roman tradition on him. He is remembered for his magnificent construction projects, most notably the Hagia Sophia in Constantinople, and his reform of Roman law and publication of the *Corpus Iuris Civilis*. A builder and law giver as all Roman rulers were, Justinian felt a true emperor should rule the city of Rome itself. He believed, therefore, that it was his responsibility to rule over both the eastern and western halves of the empire. His conquest of Italy brought about reunification, but at great cost to both the Eastern Empire and Italy. The Gothic Wars devastated the Italian countryside, as Justinian's generals fought great battles against the Ostrogoths for over two decades, from 535 to the late 550s. Although Justinian was not able to restore long-term authority over Italy, Byzantine influence in Italy continued into the eighth century. Indeed, just as the Byzantines under Justinian ended Ostrogothic rule in Italy, so the Lombards ended Byzantine control of much of Italy (*see* **Lombards**). In their turn, the Lombards were replaced in the eighth century by the greatest of the Germanic successors of Rome, the Franks (*see* **Franks**).

The Kingdom of the Franks

Unlike most of the other Germanic peoples that established kingdoms in parts of the former Western Empire, the Franks established a lasting power and came to rule Gaul and much of post-Roman Europe from the late fifth to the late 10th centuries. In two great dynasties, the Franks created a substantial kingdom, and triumphed over several of the other successor peoples to the Romans, and established numerous precedents for later medieval society (*see* **Merovingian Dynasty; Carolingian Dynasty**). The first of the dynasties, the Merovingian, was founded by the great king Clovis, who was an effective warrior and the first of the barbarian kings to accept Catholic Christianity (*see* **Clovis**). Although none of his heirs were his equal, many of them were colorful and effective rulers, especially Chlotar II and Dagobert (*see* **Chlotar II; Dagobert**). Others were involved in bitter civil wars that nearly destroyed the kingdom, and the last of Clovis's heirs were increasingly less effective rulers (*see* **Brunhilde; Fredegund;** *Rois Fainéants*). The dynasty, despite its ultimate demise, managed to secure good relations with the church, protected and promoted important missionaries, and enjoyed the production of important works of history and literature (*see* **Gregory of Tours**).

The Carolingian dynasty, which replaced the Merovingians in 751, was perhaps the most important family in the early Middle Ages. Their rise to power is often seen as a great triumphal march, but neither their success nor Merovingian failure was foreordained. Indeed, they faced numerous setbacks in the seventh and eighth centuries, and even once they secured the royal throne, they were beset by revolts and turmoil. Nonetheless, the great Carolingian kings Pippin and Charlemagne, and to a lesser extent Louis the Pious and Charles the Bald, guided the kingdom and empire of the Franks to great political, military, and cultural heights (*see* **Charlemagne; Charles the Bald; Louis the Pious; Pippin III, Called Pippin the Short**). Under the Carolingian kings, the Frankish state reached its greatest extent, without peer in the former Western Empire and the rival of the Eastern Empire in territorial size. The Carolingians were great conquerors, who expanded the boundaries of the realm into Saxony, Italy, and beyond, and who also spread Christianity into new regions. They also revived imperial rule in the west when Charlemagne, their greatest king, was crowned emperor by Pope Leo III (*see* **Leo III, Pope**). Although Charlemagne is the king most associated with the Carolingian Renaissance, all the Carolingian kings and emperors promoted learning and religious reform throughout their vast realms. Even though the empire forged by Charlemagne collapsed in the two generations following his death, it remained one of the great accomplishments of the early Middle Ages and provided important precedents for the later history of Europe.

The Importance of Early Medieval Europe

Although long recognized as a backward period politically and culturally, early medieval Europe was an important period in history and a critical period in the transition from ancient Roman civilization to medieval and modern civilization. Long associated with the "fall" of the Roman Empire, early medieval Europe accomplished more than the destruction of ancient civilization. Rather, it adopted aspects of classical culture and mixed them with Christian and Germanic traditions to create a unique and impressive new culture. The various kings of the early Middle Ages provided a wide range of legal and governmental precedents for the future. Indeed, the greatest of them, Charlemagne, was a model for kings for centuries after his death, and his empire also provided the highest ideal of government into the 19th century. The church continued to evolve in this period, as did key ecclesiastical institutions. Many kings also promoted cultural life, and most monasteries remained centers of education and learning. Far from being the Dark Ages, the early Middle Ages were a pivotal period in the history of civilization.

Select Bibliography

Becher, Matthias. *Charlemagne*. New Haven, CT: Yale University Press, 2005.

Bois, Guy. *The Transformation of the Year One Thousand: The Village of Lournand from Antiquity to Feudalism*. Trans. Jean Birrell. Manchester, UK: Manchester University Press, 1992.

Brown, Peter. *The World of Late Antiquity, A.D. 150–750*. London: Thames and Hudson, 1971.

Brown, Peter. *The Rise of Western Christendom: Triumph and Adversity*, A.D. *200–1000*. 2nd ed. Cambridge, MA: Blackwell, 2003.

Bury, John B. *The Invasions of Europe by the Barbarians*. 1928. Reprint ed. New York: W. W. Norton, 1967.

Cameron, Alan. *The Last Pagans of Rome*. Oxford: Oxford University Press, 2010.

Collins, Roger. *Early Medieval Europe, 300–1000*. 3rd ed. New York: Palgrave, 2010.

Costambeys, Marios. *The Carolingian World*. Cambridge: Cambridge University Press, 2011.

Fossier, Robert, ed. *The Cambridge Illustrated History of the Middle Ages, 350–950*. Vol. 1. Trans. Janet Sondheimer. Cambridge: Cambridge University Press, 1989.

Geary, Patrick. *Before France and Germany: The Creation and Transformation of the Merovingian World*. Oxford: Oxford University Press, 1988.

Gibbon, Edward. *The Decline and Fall of the Roman Empire*. 1776. 3 vols. Reprint ed. New York: Modern Library, 1983.

Goffart, Walter. *Barbarians and Romans*, A.D. *418–584*. Princeton, NJ: Princeton University Press, 1981.

Goffart, Walter. *The Narrators of Barbarian History (*A.D. *500–800): Jordanes, Gregory of Tours, Bede, and Paul the Deacon*. Princeton, NJ: Princeton University Press, 1988.

Goffart, Walter. *Barbarian Tides: The Migration Age and the Later Roman Empire*. Philadelphia: University of Pennsylvania Press, 2007.

Goldsworthy, Adrian. *How Rome Fell: Death of a Superpower*. New Haven, CT: Yale University Press, 2010.

Heather, Peter. *Empires and Barbarians: The Fall of Rome and the Birth of Europe*. Oxford: Oxford University Press, 2010.

Heather, Peter. *The Fall of the Roman Empire: A New History of Rome and the Barbarians*. Oxford: Oxford University Press, 2007.

Herrin, Judith. *The Formation of Christendom*. Princeton, NJ: Princeton University Press, 1989.

Herrin, Judith. *Byzantium: The Surprising Life of a Medieval Empire*. Princeton, NJ: Princeton University Press, 2009.

Jones, Arnold Hugh Martin. *The Later Roman Empire, 284–602: A Social, Economic, and Administrative Survey*. Norman: University of Oklahoma Press, 1964.

Laistner, Max Ludwig Wolfram. *Thought and Letters in Western Europe*, A.D. *500 to 900*. 2d ed. Ithaca, NY: Cornell University Press, 1976.

Little, Lester K. *Plague and the End of Antiquity: The Pandemic of 541–750*. Cambridge: Cambridge University Press, 2008.

Lot, Ferdinand. *The End of the Ancient World and the Beginnings of the Middle Ages*. 1931. Reprint ed. New York: Harper and Row, 1961.

McCormick, Michael. *Origins of the European Economy: Communications and Commerce*, A.D. *300–900*. Cambridge: Cambridge University Press, 2002.

McKitterick, Rosamond. *Charlemagne: The Formation of a European Identity*. Cambridge: Cambridge University Press, 2008.

McKitterick, Rosamond. *The Uses of Literacy in Early Medieval Europe*. Cambridge: Cambridge University Press, 1992.

Mitchell, Stephen. *A History of the Later Roman Empire, A.D. 284–641*. Oxford: Wiley-Blackwell, 2006.

Murray, Alexander Callander, ed. *After Rome's Fall: Narrators and Sources of Early Medieval History*. Toronto: University of Toronto Press, 1998.

Olson, Lynette. *The Early Middle Ages: The Birth of Europe*. New York: Palgrave, 2007.

Pirenne, Henri. *Mohammed and Charlemagne*. Trans. Bernard Miall. New York: Barnes and Noble, 1992.

Riché, Pierre. *Education and Culture in the Barbarian West: From the Sixth through the Eighth Century*. Trans. John Contreni. Columbia: University of South Carolina Press, 1978.

Smith, Julia. *Europe after Rome: A New Cultural History, 500–1000*. Oxford: Oxford University Press, 2007.

Sullivan, Richard. *Heirs of the Roman Empire*. Ithaca, NY: Cornell University Press, 1974.

Wallace-Hadrill, John Michael. *The Barbarian West, A.D. 400–1000*. New York: Harper and Row, 1962.

Ward-Perkins, Bryan. *The Fall of Rome and the End of Civilization*. Oxford: Oxford University Press, 2006.

Wickham, Christopher. *Framing the Middle Ages: Europe and the Mediterranean, 400–800*. Oxford: Oxford University Press, 2007.

Wolfram, Herwig. *The Roman Empire and Its Germanic Peoples*. Trans. Thomas J. Dunlap. Berkeley: University of California Press, 1997.

Chronology of the Late Antique and Early Medieval World

305	With the retirement of the emperors Diocletian and Maximian, the Roman Empire falls again into civil war, which leads to the eventual triumph of Constantine the Great.
312	Constantine defeats his rival Maxentius at the battle of the Milvian Bridge and takes control of the Western Empire. Before the battle Constantine had a vision that led to his conversion to Christianity.
313	The emperors Constantine and Licinius issue the Edict of Milan, which legalizes Christianity and establishes religious toleration in the Roman Empire.
325	In the year following a victory over Licinius and reunification of the empire under one ruler, Constantine calls the Council of Nicaea to resolve the great dispute over the nature of Christ's relationship to God the Father. The council accepts the Athanasian definition and rejects the teachings of Arius. Although the former lays the foundation for later Christian belief, the latter continues to exercise great influence in the empire and on the barbarians who eventually settle in much of the Roman world.
330	Constantine founds the new imperial capital of Constantinople on the straits of the Bosporus. The city will stand as the capital of the Roman Empire, and its successor the Byzantine Empire for more than 1,000 years before falling to the Ottoman Turks in 1453. Constantine's city will be a Christian city and the political and religious heart of the empire.
337	The great emperor Constantine converts to Christianity, accepting baptism, and dies shortly after on May 22, 337.
341	Ulfilas is consecrated bishop. He will later translate the Bible into the Gothic language and spread an Arian form of Christianity among the Goths.
360	St. Martin of Tours establishes the first monastery in Gaul.

370	First appearance of the Huns in southeastern Europe. Their arrival forces further movement of the peoples living along the empire's frontier, including movement into the empire.
376	Emperor Valens welcomes a large number of Visigoths into the empire to settle a frontier area, which they will cultivate and help defend.
378	After failing to settle the Visigoths, Emperor Valens leads a major Roman army against them and is defeated and killed at the Battle of Hadrianople. The Visigoths are then able to move freely about the empire until forced to settle by Theodosius the Great.
380	Theodosius the Great issues a decree declaring Catholic Christianity the official religion of the Roman Empire.
382	Death of Ulfilas, Gothic missionary, bishop, and translator of the Bible.
391	Alaric I becomes king of the Visigoths.
394	Defeat of Arbogast and the pretender Eugenius by Stilicho, the Roman military commander.
395	Death of Emperor Theodosius the Great, the last ruler of a united Roman Empire. He has divided the realm between his two sons, Honorius and Arcadius. Death of the great Roman historian Ammianus Marcellinus.
402	Stilicho wins major victories over the Visigothic leader Alaric at Pollentia and Verona.
405/406	Major crossing of the Rhine by large numbers of Alans, Franks, Visigoths, and other Germanic peoples. The removal of Roman frontier troops to protect the imperial heartland more effectively has led to this serious breach of the frontier.
406	Burgundians establish kingdom along the Rhine.
408	Murder of Stilicho by Emperor Honorius. Despite questionable relations with the Gothic king Alaric, Stilicho has managed to keep the Goths at bay and preserve the well-being of Italy. After his death, Alaric and the Visigoths invade Italy.
409	Vandals and other barbarian peoples settle in Spain.
410	The city of Rome is sacked by Alaric and the Visigoths. The first major attack on the city in 800 years, the event profoundly shocks both pagan and Christian Romans across the Mediterranean. Pagan Romans blame the Christians for the event, and St. Jerome is so dismayed that he cannot speak. The sack of Rome, however, will

contribute to the composition of one of the great works of Christian literature, Augustine's *City of God,* a response to pagan criticisms of Christianity. Roman armies make final withdrawal from Britain. Death of Alaric.

414	Marriage of the Visigoth king Ataulf and the emperor's sister Galla Placidia, who was captured by the Goths during the sack of Rome.
428	Gaiseric becomes king of the Vandals.
429	Picts and Scots raid British territory. Vandals leave Spain and enter Africa.
430	Death of St. Augustine of Hippo, the year before the city is to fall to the onslaught of the Vandals.
432	St. Patrick begins the mission to Ireland, where he will remain until 461.
433	Attila the Hun takes the throne.
439	Vandals capture Carthage and strengthen their hold on North Africa.
440	Huns begin raiding in the Balkans.
449/450	Traditional date of first Saxon invasions of England at the invitation of the British leader Vortigern. The invasions will provide the context for the origins of the legend of King Arthur.
450	The empress Honoria sends Attila the Hun a ring and possibly a proposal of marriage if the barbarian king would come to her rescue.
451	Aëtius and an army of Roman and barbarian troops win the Battle of the Catalaunian Plains over Attila and the Huns. Council of Chalcedon is held to determine important matters of faith and ecclesiastical organization.
452	Attila the Hun threatens Rome but is persuaded not to sack the city by Pope Leo I.
453	Attila dies, and by 455 his great empire will collapse.
454	Death of Aëtius.
455	The city of Rome is sacked by Gaiseric and the Vandals. Defeat of the Huns at the Battle of Nedao and collapse of their empire.
456	Ricimer, Roman military leader of Germanic descent, defeats Vandal fleet off the coast of Italy.
459	The future Ostrogothic king of Italy, Theodoric, to be known as Theodoric the Great, arrives in Constantinople as a hostage and remains there for 10 years.

461	Ricimer becomes master of the Western Empire and remains so, ruling in the name of puppet emperors of his creation, until his death in 472.
475	Traditional date of the issuance of one of the most influential barbarian law codes, the *Codex Euricianus* (Code of Euric), by the Visigothic king Euric, ruler of a large territory in France and northern Spain.
476	Traditional date of the fall of the Roman Empire. Odovacar, Germanic leader serving in the Roman army, deposes the last Roman emperor in the west, Romulus Augustulus, and rules as king in Italy until his murder by the Ostrogoth Theodoric the Great.
481	Clovis becomes king the Franks and establishes the Merovingian dynasty, which will rule the Franks until 751.
486/487	Victory of Clovis and the Franks over the Roman Syagrius, ruler of the kingdom of Soissons.
488	Theodoric the Great, after long being a thorn in the side of the eastern emperor Zeno, invades Italy at the emperor's behest to deal with the Germanic king Odovacar.
493	Murder of Odovacar by Theodoric, whose reign in Italy begins.
494/495	According to the *Anglo-Saxon Chronicle*, date of the invasion of England by the chieftains Cerdic and Cynric who would found Wessex, the kingdom of the West Saxons.
496	Traditional date of Clovis's victory over the Alemanni. According to Gregory of Tours, Clovis swore that he would abandon the traditional gods and convert to Christianity if God would grant him victory. Pope Gelasius dies. Traditional date of the battle of Badon Hill where the Saxons were defeated by the Britons.
498	Traditional date of the baptism of Clovis as a Catholic Christian by Archbishop Remigius and subsequent conversion of the king's followers. Clovis is the first of the Germanic successor kings to accept Catholic Christianity.
506	On February 2, the Visigothic king Alaric II issues the *Breviarium Alaricianum* (*Breviary of Alaric*) as a complement to the *Codex Euricianus* issued by his father Euric. The Breviary, also called *Lex Romana Visigothorum* (Roman Law of the Visigoths), covers the Romans living under Visigothic rule.
507	Clovis defeats the Visigoths at the Battle of Vouillé, fought, according to Gregory of Tours, by the Catholic king Clovis to expel the Arian Visigoths from Gaul.

511	Clovis provides for the succession, dividing the kingdom of the Franks among his four sons, and dies on November 27.
516	Traditional date of the Battle of Badon Hill, in which King Arthur turns back the invading Anglo-Saxons.
517	Codification and publication of the *Lex Gundobada* or *Liber constitutionem,* which probably appeared in some form already around the year 500, and the *Lex Romana Burgundionum* by the Burgundian king Sigismund.
524	Boethius, the Roman writer and statesman who has served Theodoric the Great, is executed, having written his great work, *The Consolation of Philosophy,* while in prison, suspected of having conspired against Theodoric, during his last year of life.
526	Death of Theodoric the Great, after which the Ostrogothic kingdom in Italy enters a period of unrest caused by conflict concerning the succession and the course of royal policy. His daughter, Amalaswintha, becomes regent and focus of discontent.
527	Justinian becomes Byzantine emperor and begins one of the most important reigns in Byzantine history. During his long reign, which will last until 565, he will rebuild Constantinople, reconquer much of the former Western Empire, and codify Roman law.
529	St. Benedict of Nursia founds the great monastery at Monte Cassino.
531	Franks destroy the kingdom of the Thuringians.
532	Justinian, thanks to his empress Theodora, survives the Nika Revolt and begins construction of the great church, Hagia Sophia.
533	Conquest of the North African kingdom of the Vandals by the great Byzantine general Belisarius, which will be completed in 534. Justinian's codification of Roman law, begun in 527, is completed.
534	Franks, according to Gregory of Tours at the suggestion of Chlotild, destroy the Burgundian kingdom.
535	Murder of Amalaswintha. Her death provides Justinian the pretext for invading Italy, and he begins what will later be known as the Gothic Wars in Italy.
540	Belisarius captures Ravenna in the war against the Ostrogoths in Italy.
548	Death of the empress Theodora.
550	Death of St. Benedict of Nursia, the father of Western monasticism. Approximate time of the appearance of the writings of Gildas, an important writer on the conquest of England by the Anglo-Saxons.

552	Byzantine armies under Narses win the Battle of Busta Gallorum, defeating the Gothic armies and essentially ending the power of the Ostrogoths in Italy, and even their independent existence.
555	Last of the Ostrogoths in Italy surrender to the Byzantines.
565	Death of the great Byzantine emperor, Justinian, who is succeeded by his nephew Justin II.
567	Division of the Frankish kingdom into Austrasia, Neustria, and Burgundy.
568	The Lombards begin the invasion of Italy; according to one tradition, they come at the invitation of the disgruntled Byzantine general, Narses. The Merovingian queen Radegund founds the monastery of the Holy Cross at Poitiers.
575	Murder of the Merovingian king of the Franks, Sigebert, by Chilperic I and Fredegund. Brunhilde assumes the regency and continues her rivalry with Fredegund.
579	Hermenegild revolts against his father, Leovigild, the king of Visigothic Spain, and converts to Catholic Christianity. The revolt will fail, and Hermenegild will die shortly after it ends in 584.
580	Lombards sack Benedict of Nursia's famed monastery of Monte Cassino.
584	Assassination of King Chilperic I, possibly by his wife Fredegund.
587	Reccared, king of Visigothic Spain, converts to Catholic Christianity and renounces his former adherence to Arian Christianity.
589	Marriage of the Lombard king Authari with the Bavarian princess Theudelinda on May 15, which forms an important alliance against the Franks. Theudelinda will remain an important figure in the Lombard kingdom until her death in 628. A Catholic in an Arian kingdom, she will maintain good relations with Pope Gregory the Great.
590	Gregory I, called the Great, becomes pope; he will reign until 604.
591	Death of King Authari. Theudelinda chooses Agilulf as her new husband and successor to Authari.
594	Death of Gregory of Tours, Frankish bishop and author of an important history of the Franks.
595	Gregory the Great sends Augustine of Canterbury on a mission to England to convert the Anglo-Saxons. Augustine will successfully introduce Christianity to England two years later.

597	Death of the Merovingian queen Fredegund. Aethelberht, king of Kent, accepts baptism at the hands of Augustine, to whom the king had granted land in Canterbury. According to tradition, thousands of the king's subjects accept baptism on Christmas day in this year.
613	Brunhilde, queen of the Franks, is overthrown and brutally executed by Chlotar II, who will reign alone until 622, and with his son Dagobert until 629. He will then be succeeded by Dagobert, who will rule until 638. The two kings will represent the high point of Merovingian kingship after Clovis. At some point following the overthrow, Pippin of Landen and St. Arnulf of Metz will form a marriage alliance that lays the foundation for the later Carolingian dynasty.
614	The Irish missionary St. Columban founds the celebrated monastery of Bobbio. Columban dies the following year.
616	The Lombard king Agilulf dies, and his son, Adaloald, succeeds to the throne. Theudelinda, Adaloald's mother, acts as regent.
629	Visigoths expel the last of the Byzantine armies from Spain.
636	Death of the Spanish prelate and scholar Isidore of Seville, a man of great learning and the historian of the Visigoths.
643	Edict of Rothari, an important Lombard legal code, is issued.
652	Benedict Biscop, Anglo-Saxon churchman from the kingdom of Northumbria in northern England, makes his first trip to Rome, where he acquires many important religious manuscripts. The founder of monasteries at Jarrow and Wearmouth, Benedict exercises great influence on the religious and cultural life of northern England, and his trips to Rome will be important in the formation of Northumbrian culture and learning.
656	Death of the Carolingian mayor of the palace, Grimoald, who attempted to usurp the throne but failed.
657	Death of the Merovingian king Clovis II, who is succeeded by his young son Chlotar III. Balthild, Chlothar's mother, assumes the regency and provides wise rule for the kingdom.
664	Synod of Whitby is held, presided over by Oswy, a powerful king in the north of England, and the Anglo-Saxon church accepts Roman Christianity over Irish Christianity. Chlotar III assumes his majority and ends the regency of his mother Balthild, who will die circa 680.
674	Benedict Biscop founds the monastery at Wearmouth.

681	Benedict Biscop founds the important and influential monastery at Jarrow.
687	The mayor of the palace, Pippin of Herstal, wins the Battle of Tertry and establishes Carolingian hegemony in the Frankish kingdom.
688	Caedwalla, king of Wessex, abdicates the throne and departs for Rome to accept baptism at the hands of the pope.
711	Muslims from North Africa invade and begin the conquest of the Visigothic kingdom of Spain, which will fall in 725.
712	Liutprand becomes king of the Lombards and rules until his death in 744.
714	Death of Pippin of Herstal. After some conflict over who will assume the Carolingian mantle, Charles Martel succeeds his father Pippin as mayor of the palace.
717	Leo III, called the Isaurian, ascends the imperial throne in Constantinople and defends the city against an Arab assault that nearly succeeds.
722	The Anglo-Saxon missionary, Boniface, begins his preaching in Germany. Early in his mission, he destroys the sacred oak of the thunder god Thor at Geismar.
730	Leo III officially introduces the policy of iconoclasm in the Byzantine Empire, a policy that will be condemned by Pope Gregory III in the following year.
731	Anglo-Saxon scholar, theologian, and historian Bede, the most famous beneficiary of the revival of letters in Northumbria started by Benedict Biscop, completes his important and influential *History of the English Church and People.*
732	Charles Martel defeats Muslim invaders from Spain at the Battle of Poitiers.
735	The great Anglo-Saxon scholar and monk Bede dies.
737	The Merovingian king, Thierry IV, dies, and no new Merovingian ruler is placed on the throne by Charles Martel, who will rule alone as mayor of the palace until his death in 741.
739	Liutprand, king of the Lombards, lays siege to the city of Rome, and Pope Gregory III appeals to the Carolingian mayor of the palace, Charles Martel, for assistance. Charles is unable to assist because of an alliance with the Lombards that was necessary to protect the southwestern part of the Frankish realm from Muslim raids from Spain.

741	Death of Charles Martel and ascension of Pippin III and Carloman to the office of mayor of the palace. They will rule without a Merovingian figurehead until 743, when they will be forced to raise Childeric III to the throne.
747	The Carolingian mayor, Carloman, retires to the monastery of Monte Cassino, leaving his brother Pippin as the de facto ruler of the Frankish kingdom.
749	Aistulf becomes king of the Lombards and takes up an aggressive policy against the papacy, which will lead to an alliance between the papacy and the Franks.
750	Pippin III, called the Short, writes Pope Zachary asking whether the person with the title or the person with the real power should be king. The pope answers as Pippin hoped.
751	Deposition of Childeric III, the last Merovingian king, by Pippin, who is crowned king of the Franks by the bishops of his realm and founds the Carolingian dynasty. The Lombards, under their king Aistulf, capture the imperial capital in Italy, Ravenna.
753	Pippin welcomes Pope Stephen II to his court and begins negotiations with the pope, which possibly lead to the Donation of Pippin.
754	Pope Stephen II crowns Pippin king of the Franks. Byzantine Emperor Constantine V holds the Council of Hiereia, which supports his iconoclastic policies. Martyrdom of the Anglo-Saxon missionary Boniface while evangelizing in Frisia on June 5. The Donation of Constantine, a forged document giving the papacy great power, appears around this time.
755	Aistulf, king of the Lombards, lays siege to Rome. Pippin undertakes his first Italian campaign to protect the papacy against Lombard advances. Pippin holds an important reform council at Ver.
756	Pippin's second Lombard campaign. Pippin deposits the so-called Donation of Pippin on the altar of St. Peter in Rome, helping to create the Papal States.
757	Offa becomes king of Mercia and rules until 796. His reign will be remembered for the famed dyke he ordered built to protect his kingdom from the Welsh.
763	Publication of the revised version of the Salic Law, a collection of the laws of the Franks first published under the great Merovingian king Clovis.

768	Death of Pippin and succession to the throne of his sons Carloman and Charlemagne.
771	Death of Carloman, whose reign was characterized by strife with his brother that nearly led to a disastrous civil war.
772	Charlemagne campaigns for the first time against the Saxons and destroys the great pagan shrine, the Irminsul. Within the next few years, the campaign will turn into a full-scale effort to conquer and convert the Saxons that will last until 804. Hadrian becomes pope and will reign until 795.
774	Pavia falls to Charlemagne, and the Lombard kingdom is incorporated into the growing Carolingian empire.
778	Charlemagne invades Spain but returns to settle unrest in his own kingdom. While crossing back into his kingdom, his rear guard, led by Roland, is attacked and destroyed by the Basques. The incident will be the foundation for one of the great epics of the Middle Ages, the *Song of Roland.*
782	Charlemagne orders the massacre of 4,500 Saxons at Verdun in retaliation for Saxon defeat of his armies and harassment of the church.
785	Saxon revolt of Widukind, which is put down by Charlemagne, though only with the greatest difficulty. Widukind converts to Christianity, and Charlemagne issues the first Saxon capitulary, a law intended to impose Christianity on the Saxons.
787	Irene and her son Emperor Constantine VI hold the Second Council of Nicaea, the seventh ecumenical council, to resolve the iconoclastic dispute that has raged throughout much of the century in the Byzantine Empire. Deposition of Tassilo, duke of Bavaria, by Charlemagne. The *Royal Frankish Annals* are first written in this year or in 788.
789	Charlemagne issues the capitulary *Admonitio Generalis,* which lays the foundation for the religious and cultural revival known as the Carolingian Renaissance. Around the same time, certainly by 800, Charlemagne issues the Letter to Baugulf, which also encourages learning and the establishment of schools in his realm.
793	First Viking raid on England.
794	Charlemagne holds the Synod of Frankfurt to address the great questions facing the Frankish church, including the issues of Adoptionism and Iconoclasm.
795	Pope Hadrian I dies and is succeeded by Pope Leo III.

796	Charlemagne's armies destroy the Avar kingdom. King Offa of Mercia dies.
797	Irene deposes and blinds her son Constantine VI and assumes the imperial throne. Charlemagne issues the second Saxon capitulary, a Carolingian law that encouraged conversion to Christianity.
799	Pope Leo III is attacked while on procession in Rome and is rescued by Charlemagne's representatives in Rome. Leo goes to Charlemagne's court to explain the situation.
800	Charlemagne visits Rome to resolve the dispute involving Pope Leo III and presides over a council at which the pope swears his innocence. On December 25, Leo crowns Charlemagne emperor of the Romans during Christmas mass. First Viking raids on the continent of Europe.
802	Empress Irene is overthrown by Nikephoros I. Charlemagne issues important reform capitulary and uses his official imperial title.
804	Death of the Anglo-Saxon Alcuin of York, one of Charlemagne's most important advisors and court scholars.
806	Charlemagne introduces succession plan that divides the realm among his sons but does not pass on the imperial title.
811	Charlemagne completes creation of the Spanish March, a militarized border region including territory on the Spanish side of the Pyrenees.
813	Coronation of Louis the Pious as emperor by Charlemagne at a great assembly in Aix-la-Chapelle (modern Aachen, Germany).
814	Death of Charlemagne on January 28 and succession to the throne of his son Louis the Pious.
816	Louis the Pious crowned emperor by Pope Stephen IV. Agobard, a Carolingian scholar and ecclesiastic from Spain, made archbishop of Lyons.
817	Louis the Pious nearly killed in an accident while crossing a bridge. Louis holds a great council and issues his *Ordinatio Imperii,* which provides for the succession to the imperial title by Louis's oldest son, Lothar, and settlement of the other two, Louis the German and Pippin, as kings under the emperor's authority. Louis also issues the *Pactum Ludovicianum,* prepared the previous year, codifying Carolingian relations with the papacy. He promulgates important religious reforms, with the advice of the Visigothic monk and reformer Benedict of Aniane. Revolt of Louis's nephew, Bernard, king of Italy.
823	Birth of Charles the Bald to Louis and his second wife, Judith.

824	Lothar issues the *Constitutio Romana,* which further defines Carolingian relations with Rome.
825	Ecghberht, king of Wessex, defeats the Mercians at the Battle of Ellendum and lays the foundation for the resurgence of the power of Wessex throughout England.
827	Louis the Pious alters his succession plan to include his son Charles the Bald, to the dismay of his older sons.
830	Revolt of Lothar, Louis the German, and Pippin against their father Louis the Pious. Einhard writes *The Life of Charlemagne,* though some historians think it appeared as early as 817. Nennius writes the *Historia Brittonum* (History of the Britons), though it may have appeared as early as 800.
833	Meeting at the "Field of Lies," between Louis the Pious and his sons at which Louis's troops dessert, and beginning of second revolt against Louis the Pious, who is deposed and imprisoned.
834	Restoration of Louis the Pious and disgrace of Lothar, the leader of the revolt.
840	Death of Louis the Pious, succession of Charles the Bald, Lothar, and Louis the German, and beginning of civil war between the three sons of Louis.
841	Battle of Fontenoy on June 25 between Lothar and his brothers Louis the German and Charles the Bald.
842	Louis the German, Charles the Bald, and their followers subscribe to the Oath of Strasbourg, which makes the two leaders allies and which contains the first written examples of early Romance languages and of early Germanic languages.
843	Restoration of the practice of the veneration of icons in the Byzantine Empire. The Carolingian rulers, Charles the Bald, Lothar, and Louis the German, agree to the Treaty of Verdun, which divides the empire equally between them.
845	Vikings attack Paris.
848	Gottschalk of Orbais called before a council at Mainz to defend his views on predestination, starting a controversy that will involve Hincmar of Rheims, John Scottus Erigena, and other leading Carolingian ecclesiastics.
853	Alfred the Great of England makes his first pilgrimage to Rome.

855	Alfred the Great makes his second pilgrimage to Rome and on the return marries Judith, the daughter of Charles the Bald. Emperor Lothar dies and his realm is divided between his two sons.
871	Alfred the Great ascends the throne in the kingdom of Wessex.
875	Death of Emperor Louis II on August 12; imperial coronation of Charles the Bald on December 25.
876	Death of Louis the German on August 28.
877	Death of Charles the Bald on October 6.
878	Danes force Alfred the Great from the kingdom of Wessex to the island of Athelney. Alfred marshals his forces and is able to win a major victory over the Danes at the Battle of Eddington. The Danes withdraw from England.
882	Death of Hincmar of Rheims on December 21.
884	Charles the Fat reunites the Carolingian empire under one ruler.
885	Alfred the Great takes London from the Danes.
888	Death of Charles the Fat, the last Carolingian to rule a united empire, who was deposed from the throne in 887.
890	The *Anglo-Saxon Chronicle* first appears in or around this year.
892	Danes invade England again.
896	Alfred finally expels the Danes after 4 years of fighting.
899	Death of Alfred the Great on October 26.
909	Death of Asser, biographer of Alfred the Great.
911	Charles the Simple grants Normandy to the Viking Rollo. Death of Louis the Child, the last Carolingian to rule in the East Frankish kingdom.
987	Carolingian dynasty replaced by the Capetian dynasty in France.
1000	The sole surviving manuscript of the Anglo-Saxon epic *Beowulf* is written.

GERMANIC SUCCESSOR KINGDOMS
EARLY 6TH CENTURY

Merovingian Kingdom

Thuringia

• Tournai

• Soissons

• Paris   • Trier

Lombards

Vienne•

Italy

• Pavia

Illyricum

Toulous•

•Arles

• Ravenna

Visigothic Kingdom

Septimania

Ostrogothic Kingdom

• Rome

•Palermo

Ostrogothic Kingdom under Theodoric

Maximum extent of Merovingian Kingdom in the 7th century

Merovingian Kingdom under Clovis

Boundaries of Roman dioceses

ORDINATIO IMPERII OF LOUIS THE PIOUS, 817

Francia

Brittany

Neustria

Austrasia

Alemannia

Burgundy

Bavaria

Aquitaine

Gascony

Kingdom of Italy

Pamplona

Provence

Septimania

Spanish March

Pippin I of Aquitaine   Lothar   Louis the German   ·············Kingdom Boundaries

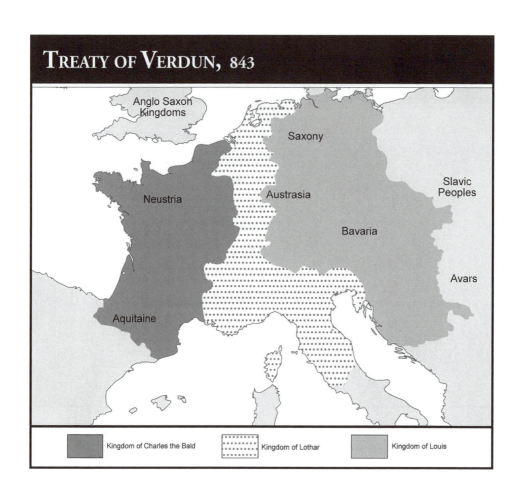

Treaty of Verdun, 843

Anglo Saxon Kingdoms

Saxony

Slavic Peoples

Neustria

Austrasia

Bavaria

Avars

Aquitaine

Kingdom of Charles the Bald Kingdom of Lothar Kingdom of Louis

ENGLAND
8TH AND 9TH CENTURIES

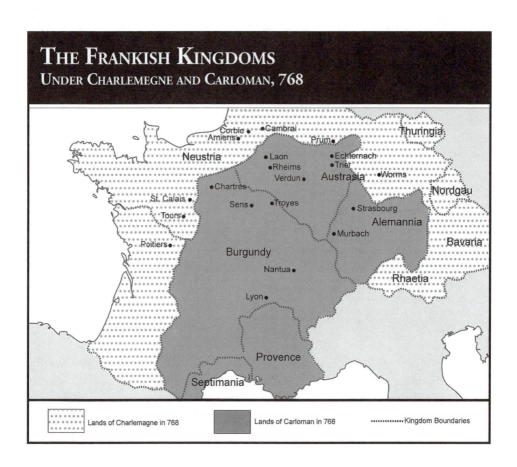

THE FRANKISH KINGDOMS
UNDER CHARLEMEGNE AND CARLOMAN, 768

Corbie • • Cambrai
Amiens • Prüm •
Neustria • Laon Echternach
• Rheims • Trier
Verdun • Austrasia • Worms
Chartres • Nordgau
St. Calais • Sens • Troyes Strasbourg
Tours • Alemannia
Murbach • Bavaria
Poitiers •
Burgundy
Nantua • Rhaetia
Lyon •
Provence
Septimania

Thuringia

Lands of Charlemagne in 768   Lands of Carloman in 768   Kingdom Boundaries

A

Aachen. *See* Aix-la-Chapelle

Admonitio Generalis

The capitulary promulgated by Charlemagne in 789 that established the foundation for the Carolingian Renaissance by announcing the educational and religious goals and ideals of the great Frankish ruler. The *Admonitio Generalis* (General Admonition) consists of 82 chapters. Although 59 of the chapters borrow heavily from the canon law collection, the *Dionysio-Hadriana,* that Charlemagne received from Pope Hadrian I, the capitulary is truly a creation of the king and his advisors. Its extensive use of quotations from Holy Scripture reveals the level of cultural sophistication achieved at Charlemagne's court and points to the greater goals the court sought to achieve.

In this capitulary, Charlemagne asserted his belief that he was a new Josiah, the ancient Hebrew king who reformed Jewish belief and practice, with the responsibility to rule over God's new chosen people and the duty to reform their moral and spiritual lives so that they would be able to achieve salvation. To fulfill his role as the new Josiah, and to create peace and harmony among the Christian people, Charlemagne included chapters concerning the moral reform and discipline of the priesthood in the *Admonitio.* The capitulary also emphasizes the responsibility of the priests in Charlemagne's kingdom to preach "rightly and honestly" and to avoid innovation and teachings contrary to the laws of the church. Priests are expected to live moral lives; they are to teach their flocks to follow the example they set. The priests themselves are to be guided in the performance of their duties by the bishops, who are instructed to obey the accepted beliefs and practices of the church.

Perhaps the most important section of the *Admonitio* is chapter 72, which lays out Charlemagne's program of education. This chapter asserts the responsibility of the bishops and monks of his kingdom to establish schools to teach the psalms, music and singing, and grammar. The schools, in other words, are to teach boys to read and write so that they can help spread the faith of Christianity. The chapter calls on the leaders of the church to set up schools so that those who wish to pray may do so in the proper fashion. Indeed, it was one of Charlemagne's great hopes that all his people would be able to recite the Lord's Prayer and the Apostle's Creed. The *Admonitio* was intended to contribute to that goal by mandating that the schools be established; another purpose was to provide for the correction of books important to the faith. The *Admonitio Generalis* established the religious reform program of Charlemagne's reign, and, with the Letter to Baugulf (*Epistola de litteris colendis*) it promoted the revival of learning associated with his broader reform program.

See also: Capitularies; Carolingian Dynasty; Carolingian Renaissance; Charlemagne

Bibliography

Brown, Giles. "Introduction: the Carolingian Renaissance." In *Carolingian Culture: Emulation and Innovation*, ed. Rosamond McKitterick. Cambridge: Cambridge University Press, 1994.

McKitterick, Rosamond. *The Frankish Church and the Carolingian Reforms, 789–895.* London: Longman, 1977.

Adoptionism

A heresy that emerged in Spain in the eighth century, Adoptionism sought to provide a new understanding of the nature of the godhead. The key figures in the heresy were Felix, bishop of Urgel and Elipandus, bishop of Toledo. Despite providing a simpler explanation of the relationship between God the Father and God the Son, Adoptionism was opposed by Pope Hadrian I and leading Carolingian theologians, notably Alcuin of York, and was formally condemned by the great council of Frankfurt in 794.

Possibly in response to the establishment of Islam throughout the Iberian Peninsula in the eighth century, Adoptionism circulated among the clergy of Spain and may have developed a popular following even though an earlier version of the doctrine had been condemned by a church council in the late seventh century. Elipandus of Toledo revived the teaching of Adoptionism, which could have proved less offensive to Muslim sensibilities, in the early 780s. Although misrepresented by his rivals who asserted that Elipandus taught that Jesus was born human and became the Son of God by his virtue and devotion to God, Elipandus and later Felix of Urgel maintained that Jesus was the incarnate Word. God had sent the Word to the world of humans, but as the Word the fully divine Son emptied himself of his divinity so that he could become fully human all the while remaining fully consubstantial with the Father. As the human Jesus, the son had all the limitations of humanity, except sin, and in this way was able to offer himself as a way to salvation. He was also, in his humanity, the first of the adoptive sons of God and consequently the brother of all of God's adopted children, that is, those who were saved.

The teaching of Elipandus and Felix would have remained a Spanish matter had not the bishopric of Urgel come under Carolingian control as Charlemagne established the Spanish March and extended his authority across the Pyrenees. In part a response to attacks by Beatus of Liebana, an influential Spanish writer, and Charlemagne's own interest in the defense of orthodoxy, Carolingian ecclesiastics turned their attention to Adoptionism in the early 790s. In 793, Felix was ordered by Charlemagne to attend a council at Regensburg, where he was forced to renounce his teachings and go to Rome for a hearing from Pope Hadrian. Adoptionism was officially condemned by Charlemagne's great church council of Frankfurt in 794, and the churchman, Paulinus of Aquilia wrote a treatise against the heresy. Felix, however, began teaching Adoptionism again in 796, and he seemed to generate a following among Spanish clergy. In response, Alcuin, one of Charlemagne's most important advisors, composed two works against Adoptionism in 797–798 and 800, which he sent to Elipanus, and in 799 he debated Felix at Charlemagne's palace at Aix-la-Chapelle. Felix again recanted and was then sent to Lyons where he died in 818 and despite numerous repudiations of Adoptionism seems to have never abandoned this teaching. Other critiques of Adoptionism were written by Benedict of Aniane and Agobard of Lyons, and the teaching of Adoptionism did not long survive the death of its chief advocates, Felix and Elipandus.

See also: Agobard of Lyons, St.; Alcuin of York; Benedict of Aniane; Charlemagne; Carolingian Dynasty; Hadrian I, Pope

Bibliography

Cavadini, J.C. *The Last Christology of the West*: *Adoptionism in Spain and Gaul, 785–820*. Philadelphia: University of Pennsylvania Press, 1993.

Chazelle, Celia. *The Crucified God in the Carolingian Era: Theology and Art of Christ's Passion*. Cambridge: Cambridge University Press, 2001.

McKitterick, Rosamond. *Charlemagne*: *The Formation of a European Identity*. Cambridge: Cambridge University Press, 2008.

Wallace-Hadrill, J.M. *The Frankish Church*. Oxford: Clarendon, 1983.

Aethelberht I of Kent (d. 616)

A powerful and important king of Kent, in southern England. Aethelberht was identified by Bede as one of the bretwaldas ruling over the Anglo-Saxon kingdoms of England. As a king, Aethelberht established important contacts with the Continent, most notably through his marriage to a Merovingian princess. Of greater significance was the king's relationship with Rome and his contact with Pope Gregory I and the pope's representative St. Augustine of Canterbury who preached to Aethelberht who became first king in England to convert to Christianity. He was also the first Anglo-Saxon king to issue a legal code.

Aethelberht was king of the most sophisticated and most populous kingdom of England in the late sixth and early seventh century. Although Bede says that he ruled from 560 to 616, it is more likely that he assumed the throne at some time between 589 and 593 and was born in 560. He was the most powerful ruler of his time, extending his authority across most of southern England, and is identified by Bede as the third king to rule all of England south of the Humber. Perhaps in recognition of his status in England or possibly as a result of his own desires to associate himself with the most powerful family of the continent, Aethelberht married at some point before 588 Bertha, the niece of the Merovingian king Chilperic and the daughter of Charipert, king of Paris. Even though Frankish chroniclers made little of the marriage, it was an important alliance for Aethelberht, and his association with the Frankish dynasty shaped the remainder of his reign.

The closeness of Aethelberht with the Merovingians is, perhaps, revealed in the two great accomplishments of his reign. His most important achievement was his conversion to Christianity. In 595, after having seen angelic boys from England sold as slaves in the market place at Rome, Pope Gregory the Great—who bought and freed them—sent an evangelical mission to England led by St. Augustine of Canterbury. Aethelberht welcomed the mission, although with some hesitation at first, since he feared that they were practitioners of the magical arts who would try to deceive and control him. But after meeting the missionaries, the king gave them permission to preach in his kingdom, and, as Bede notes, Aethelberht was so impressed by their preaching and miracles that he converted and accepted baptism from them. Although he would not compel his subjects to convert, the king did favor Christians in his kingdom and built a number of churches for the missionaries, including St. Paul's Cathedral in London and a church in Rochester. He also allowed them to settle in Canterbury, which later became the most important episcopal see in England.

The king's conversion restored the connection with Rome that had been severed by the invasions of the fifth century. This connection was further confirmed by letters that Aethelberht received from the pope, including one in which Gregory praised the king, compared him with Constantine, and encouraged him to spread the faith throughout his kingdom. Although his son Eadbald (616–640) at first turned his back on Christianity, giving it a temporary setback, Eadbald later converted to the faith and furthered the process of conversion of his people.

Aethelberht's other great achievement was the codification of the law, which was completed between 597 and 616. Although the codification may not have been a thorough one, the king's legal reforms were important nonetheless. His publication of Anglo-Saxon laws reveals the influence of the Merovingians once again, because it recalls the famous codification of the Salic law by Clovis (r. 481–511), the first great Merovingian king. It also suggests Christian or Roman influence, because the great Christian emperor Justinian had codified Roman law a generation before Aethelberht's code. Indeed, the king not only demonstrated the importance he attached to his continental connections with the code but also revealed the sophistication his kingdom had achieved. The code was unique in one regard: unlike the codes of Clovis and the other Germanic kings, which were in Latin, Aethelberht's code was in the Anglo-Saxon tongue making it the earliest code written in any Germanic language and the oldest written work in Old English.

The code did not reflect any advanced legal theory, but it did define the laws of the land and relations among the king's subjects. The code, among other things, established the scale of payment owed for injury, such as the payments (called wergeld) due for killing men and women of various social ranks and for other violations of person and property. The code also established the preeminent place of the king in Kentish society, as well as the important place of the bishops in the kingdom. The laws further established the legal rights and status of the clergy in the kingdom, issued penalties for crimes against the church and clergy, and gave legal expression to the king's new faith. Although Aethelberht is less well known than some other Anglo-Saxon kings, his importance is no less than theirs, as he was the first to reform the law and to convert to Christianity.

See also: Anglo-Saxons; Augustine of Canterbury, St.; Bede; Chilperic I; Clovis; Constantine; Gregory the Great; Justinian; Merovingian Dynasty

Bibliography

Attenborough, Frederick L., ed. and trans. *The Laws of the Earliest English Kings.* Felinfach, Wales: Llanerch Publishers, 2000.

Bede. *Ecclesiastical History of the English Church and People.* Trans. Leo Sherley-Price. Rev. ed. London: Penguin Classics, 1968.

Kirby, David P. *The Earliest English Kings.* London: Unwin Hyman, 1991.

Sawyer, Peter H. *From Roman Britain to Norman England.* 2nd ed. London: Routledge, 1998.

Stenton, Frank M. *Anglo-Saxon England.* 3rd ed. Oxford: Clarendon, 1971.

Yorke, Barbara. *Kings and Kingdoms of Early Anglo-Saxon England.* London: Seaby, 1990.

Æthelflæd, Lady of the Mercians (d. 918)

Daughter of King Alfred, traditionally known as the Great, and wife of the powerful ealdorman (or lord) of Mercia, Ethelred. Although she was described by later historians as too weak to endure the pains of childbirth more than once, despite the powerful motivation of having borne no male heir, Æthelflæd was a strong partner for her husband while he lived and a leader against Viking attacks after his death. After 911, she was recognized as "lady of the Mercians," but not "queen," and was the dominant figure of the kingdom in the first decades of the 10th century. Her marriage forged an important alliance between her native Wessex and Mercia during the critical period of the Viking invasions.

Æthelflæd's career in Mercia began by the end of 889, with her marriage to Ethelred to solidify an alliance between her father and her new husband, an alliance that was to be important in the face of increased Viking pressure. During her entire married life, Æthelflæd exerted influence on her husband's rule, and at least by 900, her name was associated with his in charters confirming grants of land. But it was after her husband's death in 911 that Æthelflæd left her greatest mark as a warrior queen. She assumed control of the kingdom in 911 and was able to keep the loyalty of her husband's vassals. Joining with her brother, King Edward, she led the campaign against the Vikings and enabled her brother to make significant progress against the Danish Vikings in the south. She led her armies personally and achieved smashing victories over the Vikings, victories that enabled her to retake Derby and Leicester. Her victories forced Viking settlers and Welsh kings to recognize her authority. She also built or rebuilt a number of important fortifications, inspired perhaps by her father's example, at places like Stafford and Tamsworth. With her husband, she fortified Worcester. After 911, she embarked on a deliberate program of building to strengthen the defenses of Mercia. She built as many as 10 fortresses, which limited the effectiveness of Viking attacks and allowed her to send out armies against her enemies with increasing success.

She ruled in her own name until her death in 918. She had one daughter, Ælfwyn, who inherited the loyalty of the Mercian nobility. Unfortunately, family ties were not so strong, and her uncle, King Edward, marched into Mercia, seized his niece, and took control of Mercia. Edward, thus, unified Mercia and Wessex. Although Mercia was absorbed by Wessex and the queen failed to secure her daughter's succession to the throne, Æthelflæd was an important figure in Anglo-Saxon England and had a great impact on the struggle against the Vikings.

See also: Alfred the Great; Anglo-Saxons; Mercia; Wessex

Bibliography

Jewell, Helen. *Women in Medieval England.* Manchester: Manchester University Press, 1996.

Leyser, Henrietta. *Medieval Women: A Social History of Women in England, 450–1500.* New York: St. Martin's, 1995.

Stafford, Pauline. *Queens, Concubines, and Dowagers: The King's Wife in the Early Middle Ages.* Athens: University of Georgia Press, 1983.

Stenton, Frank M. *Anglo-Saxon England.* 3rd ed. Oxford: Clarendon, 1971.

Whitelock, Dorothy, ed. *The Anglo-Saxon Chronicle.* Westport, CT: Greenwood, 1986.

Aelfric. *See* Anglo-Saxons

Aëtius (d. 454)

Called "the last of the Romans" by the sixth-century Byzantine historian Procopius, Aëtius was the servant of the emperor Valentinian III, the rival of the empress Galla Placidia, and the military commander who preserved Roman control over Gaul but lost Africa. Like Stilicho before him and Orestes after, Aëtius was the power behind the throne. He maintained the integrity of Western Roman imperial authority in the face of the turmoil and tumult brought on by the Hunnish invasions and movement of various Germanic tribes. A contemporary chronicler called him "the great safety of the western republic" (Marcellinus, *Chronicle,* quoted in Bury 1959, 300) and it can be said that Aëtius's death was a grave misfortune for the Western Empire.

Born in Lower Moesia, a Roman territory in the Balkans, to an Italian mother and Gaudentius, a Roman military commander who served Theodosius, Aëtius was sent as a hostage to Alaric and also to the Huns. His family background and experiences among the Visigoths and Huns were to be of great importance for his future. He learned military techniques from the barbarians that would benefit him in later life and found an ally in the Huns, who helped him gain and hold power once he was an adult. According to Gregory of Tours, Aëtius was described by one contemporary in a panegyric as being of "middle height, of manly condition, well shaped, so that his body was neither too weak nor too weighty, active in mind, vigorous in limb" (Gregory of Tours 1974, 119). The panegyrist notes that he was a skilled horseman and deadly with both an arrow and spear. An "excellent warrior and famous in the arts of peace" (119), Aëtius, our panegyrist continues, was hardworking, able to endure the hardships of the military life, free from greed, and intellectually gifted. Even though it was intended to praise Aëtius, the panegyric offers a good assessment of the Roman leader, as his career would prove.

Aëtius first came to prominence in the 420s during the usurpation of the imperial throne in Ravenna by the civil servant John. At the death of the emperor Honorius in 423, John was elevated to the throne but was opposed by the emperor in Constantinople, Theodosius II, as well as by the widow and son of Honorius, Galla Placidia, and Valentinian III. Aëtius, a rising soldier, recognized the authority of John and went to recruit an army from the Huns to support John. The pretender, however, was captured and executed before Aëtius could return with an army numbering 60,000 Hunnish soldiers. The army was a crucial bargaining chip for Aëtius, who was able to avoid the fate of John and demand a position of authority. Reluctantly, Galla Placidia came in terms with Aëtius and his army. Aëtius was pardoned by the empress and was given the title of count and military command in Gaul.

Although he rose to prominence in an act of rebellion against the Western Empire, Aëtius spent much of his career defending the empire against its various barbarian foes. His command in Gaul brought him great prestige, and the continued enmity of Galla Placidia and her allies. Aëtius's prestige came from his great success in Gaul against the barbarian armies that threatened the empire's hold on the province. He fought a series of successful battles against the Franks, including the one in 428 against one of the first-known kings of the Franks, Chlodio. He also engaged King Theodoric I (419–451) and the Visigoths during his time in Gaul and prevented them from taking the important city of Arles, often using both Frankish and Hunnish allies against the Visigoths. His success brought Aëtius the enthusiastic support of the Roman nobility in Gaul and promotion to the high rank of Master of Both Services (*magister utriusque militum*).

Aëtius's success also brought him the increasing hostility of Galla Placidia, especially after he orchestrated the deposition of her favorite Felix. With her support, Boniface, the military commander of Africa and count, challenged Aëtius in a great battle in Ariminum in 432. Although Aëtius lost the battle and took refuge with his allies, the Huns, he won the contest because Boniface died shortly after their engagement, possibly from wounds he received in the battle. Once again with support from the Hunnish mercenaries, Aëtius was able to reestablish his authority in 433 and remained the most important figure in the Western Empire until his death in 454. The empress now resigned herself to the success of Aëtius, who had defeated her favorites, held important military and civilian rank, and gained great influence over her son Valentinian.

As the real power in the Western Empire, Aëtius took charge of its defense and waged a series of successful and unsuccessful struggles with various barbarian peoples. One of his greatest failures was his inability or unwillingness to prevent Gaiseric and the Vandals from taking control of Roman Africa in the early 430s. The loss of Africa, which was formalized in a treaty of 442 that was cemented by a marriage alliance between the Vandal king and Roman emperor, occurred for several reasons: Aëtius's distaste for the region as the base of power of his vanquished rival Boniface, his lack of an adequate fleet to defeat the Vandals, and his strategic decision to put his efforts toward preserving control of Gaul, an area equally under pressure from barbarian armies during the time of the Vandal invasion. In 436, Aëtius sent an army of Huns against the Burgundian kingdom of Worms. In an event celebrated in the German medieval epic poem the *Nibelungenlied,* the kingdom was destroyed, and as many as 20,000 Burgundians were killed, including the king Gundahar. But the Burgundians themselves were not wiped out and were resettled near modern Geneva, where they remained important allies of the empire. Aëtius also continued his struggle against the Visigoths, who sought to extend their influence into Gaul and who were seen as the greatest threat to the Western Empire. In the late 430s he stopped them at Toulouse, preserving the imperial hold on southern Gaul and restricting the Goths to territories ceded to them by a treaty in 418.

Perhaps his most disappointing struggle with a barbarian people was his war with his long-time allies the Huns. During his rise to power, the Huns were without a king ruling over them, and many of the Huns found employment as mercenaries in the service of Aëtius and the Romans. Changes within the Hunnish nation in the 430s led to the emergence of a king who was eventually succeeded by Attila, the greatest of the Huns who initiated an aggressive policy toward the empire. The invasion of Attila forced Aëtius to respond in the 440s and 450s. Attila's drive into the Western Empire was of great concern to Aëtius, who needed to find new allies to stop his old allies. Somewhat surprised by the Hunnish king's assault, Aëtius mobilized an army of Franks, Burgundians, and Romans and negotiated an alliance with his former enemies, the Visigoths. It was this mixed army that stopped Attila at Orléans and limited his success at Troyes. It was also this army that Aëtius led against Attila at the Battle of the Catalaunian Plains (somewhere between Châlons and Troyes, France). This bloody battle was a near disaster for Attila, who prepared for his own suicide during the fight. Although he defeated them, Aëtius allowed the Huns to leave the battlefield without destroying them, and, according to one tradition, even prevented one of his allies from pursuing the defeated Huns. Aëtius's concerns over the Visigoths and the Huns's earlier service as his allies may have inspired the general to allow their withdrawal. Aëtius was less successful, however, at stopping Attila when he invaded Italy, but the death of the king of the Huns ended their threat to the empire and allowed Aëtius to turn his attention to other problems.

Aëtius, however, had little time to attend to the remaining problems of the empire. Although he faithfully defended the Western Empire and its emperor, Aëtius fell under the suspicion of that emperor, Valentinian III. Perhaps angered by Aëtius's success and attempt to marry his family into the imperial line or influenced by one of Aëtius's rivals, Valentinian ordered the murder of his faithful general. Whatever the case, Aëtius fell to imperial treachery on September 24, 454, when Valentinian accused him of treason and had him killed immediately. After the murder a contemporary is supposed to have said to the emperor, "You have cut off your right hand with your left" (Bury 1959, 299). In fact, the emperor signed his own death warrant, for the following March, loyal followers of Aëtius murdered the emperor. These murders left the Western Empire without a legitimate successor to the throne and, perhaps even worse, without one of its greatest defenders and one who deserved the title of "last of the Romans," at a time when his talents were needed more than ever.

See also: Alans; Alaric; Attila the Hun; Catalaunian Plains, Battle of the; Gaiseric; Galla Placidia; Huns; Procopius; Ravenna; Rome; Stilicho, Flavius; Theodosius; Vandals; Visigoths

Bibliography

Bury, John B. *History of the Later Roman Empire: From the Death of Theodosius I to the Death of Justinian.* Vol. 1. 1923. Reprint, New York: Dover, 1959.

Gregory of Tours. *The History of the Franks.* Trans. Lewis Thorpe. Harmondsworth, UK: Penguin, 1974.

Lot, Ferdinand. *The End of the Ancient World and the Beginnings of the Middle Ages.* New York: Harper and Row, 1961.

Randers-Pehrson, Justine Davis. *Barbarians and Romans: The Birth Struggle of Europe,* A.D. *400–700.* Norman: University of Oklahoma Press, 1983.

Agobard of Lyons, St. (769–840)

Carolingian bishop and religious leader. Agobard's life and career reflect the importance of ecclesiastics in the Frankish kingdom, as well as the tumult that occurred there in the ninth century. As bishop he struggled against clerical abuse and ignorance as well as against the ignorance of the laity. He also strove to enforce clerical discipline and criticized royal abuse of power over the church. Agobard further rejected a number of pious practices approved by the Carolingian church and was a vocal critic of Louis the Pious's policy toward the Jews. He played an important role in the civil wars that shook the reign of Louis, supporting Louis's sons against the emperor, whom he denounced for opposing God's will by violating the *Ordinatio Imperii* (Disposition of the Empire) of 817. His support for the rebels led to his removal from involvement in the daily affairs of his bishopric, although he was eventually restored to his full authority as bishop and resumed his duties for the emperor.

Agobard was probably born in Spain and moved into the Frankish kingdom in 782 at the age of 13. Upon his arrival in Lyons, if not before, Agobard began his ecclesiastical career by joining a monastery near Narbonne. He later moved to Lyons, where he received holy orders and, in 804, was consecrated as a suffragan bishop. In 816 he was elevated to the position of archbishop of Lyons, where he remained, with the exception of a period of exile in the 830s, until his death. As archbishop, he played an important role in the religious and political life of the empire and challenged the emperor, Louis the Pious, on several occasions. He also supported the general reform initiatives of Louis, and he transformed Lyons into one of the centers of learning in the Carolingian world.

In the realm of politics, Agobard remained a staunch supporter of the unity of the empire and believed in its sacrosanct nature. He was an ardent proponent of the *Ordinatio Imperii* of 817, which was Louis's plan of succession. The *Ordinatio* was seen by some, especially in the church, as establishing the essential unity of the empire under God and his divinely appointed ruler. The plan also enhanced the power and status of the church, which could be seen as a guarantor of God's blessings on the realm. Agobard was one of the most adamant supporters of this plan and challenged the emperor for his efforts to undermine the *Ordinatio*, especially when Louis restructured the plan to include Charles the Bald, his youngest son, who was born in 823. Gradually, a group of churchman came to form a sort of "imperialist" party, which advocated the preservation of the original settlement and came to oppose the emperor to the point of rebellion. Indeed, in 830 many churchmen joined the rebellion against the emperor led by his sons. Agobard, however, did not participate in the revolt but remained neutral, even though he had written a letter to Louis the previous year in support of the *Ordinatio* and against Louis's violation of it.

In the mid-830s, however, Agobard underwent a change of heart in regard to Louis. In 833, when Lothar again revolted against his father, Agobard joined with the rebellion. He was among the bishops who called for Louis's abdication, and he wrote in defense of the rebellion. He criticized Judith, the emperor's second wife and the mother of Charles the Bald, and denounced Louis for abandoning his obligations as a Christian emperor and for allowing war and injustice to occur in the empire. Unlike Lothar, Agobard did not flee the empire when Louis was restored to power. He was subsequently stripped of his responsibilities as bishop by a church council in 835. He regained the emperor's favor and was restored to his position in Lyons in 838. He was able to return, in part, because of the unorthodox reforms implemented by his successor. Agobard remained loyal to the empire in his remaining years and died while performing a diplomatic mission for the emperor.

Agobard was also an influential critic of contemporary religious policy and practice. In the Carolingian Empire religion and politics were often mixed, as Louis's succession plan demonstrates, and Agobard frequently called for the proper administration of justice. He criticized secular and religious judges for taking bribes and bending justice to favor the rich over the poor. He was also a harsh critic of the practice of trial by ordeal and the judicial duel. As archbishop, Agobard ruled on more traditional religious issues and participated in debate over religious policy in the empire. He was an active crusader against corruptions of the faith, including ignorance and impiety among the clergy and superstition and pagan practices among the laity. He supported the iconoclastic thinker, Claudius of Turin (d. 827), who rejected the veneration of images in the church. Agobard, Claudius's bishop, wrote a rebuttal to Carolingian thinkers who had attacked Claudius. Agobard also wrote a series of treatises criticizing Louis's Jewish policy. The emperor had favored and protected the Jews, which Agobard thought undermined the unity and integrity of the Christian empire of the Carolingians. Indeed, as with so many other things, Agobard's hostility to the Jews was part of a broader agenda that sought the proper ordering of Christian society.

See also: Carolingian Dynasty; Charles the Bald; Franks; Jews and Judaism; Judith; Lothar; Louis the German; Louis the Pious; *Ordinatio Imperii*

Bibliography

Cabaniss, Allen. *Agobard of Lyons: Churchman and Critic*. Syracuse, NY: Syracuse University Press, 1953.

Cohen, Jeremy. *Living Letters of the Law: Ideas of the Jew in Medieval Christianity*. Berkeley: University of California Press, 1999.

Halphen, Louis. *Charlemagne and the Carolingian Empire*. Trans. Giselle de Nie. Amsterdam: North-Holland, 1977.

Laistner, Max Ludwig Wolfram. *Thought and Letters in Western Europe, A.D. 500 to 900*. 2nd ed. Ithaca, NY: Cornell University Press, 1976.

McKitterick, Rosamond. *The Frankish Kingdoms under the Carolingians, 951–987*. London: Longman, 1983.

Riché, Pierre. *The Carolingians: A Family Who Forged Europe*. Trans. Michael Idomir Allen. Philadelphia: University of Pennsylvania Press, 1993.

Agriculture

In the early Middle Ages the vast majority of the population of Europe was dedicated in some fashion or other to food production, which invariably involved agriculture. In early medieval Europe, as well as in later medieval and modern Europe, agriculture involved both crop farming and animal husbandry—a unique combination compared with agriculture in other parts of the world. In the economy of barbarian Europe, farming and animal husbandry existed in a symbiotic arrangement, in which specific crops were cultivated for animals, which in turn provided food and fertilizer. Despite the attention to agriculture, and the labor put into it, crop yields were generally small—the result of limited technology—and thus the vast majority of the population lived barely at the subsistence level.

In the agricultural villages of early medieval Europe, the agricultural practices of the ancient Romans and their barbarian invaders came together to form the uniquely European agricultural tradition. One aspect of this, perhaps the result of the more pastoral nature of the barbarians who settled in much of the old Western Roman Empire, was animal husbandry. A number of different animals were bred, although not selectively as they were in Roman times, by early medieval peasants. The animals—including cows, oxen, horses, and pigs—provided a supply of both food and ready labor. Although little meat was eaten by the peasants, it was a welcome addition to an otherwise meager diet. But perhaps more important was the labor animals provided in the fields where various cereals were grown. Oxen and, eventually, horses were used to pull the plows that tilled the soil in early medieval villages. Peasants also grew oats specifically for the horses when the horse came into widespread use as a draught animal at the very end of the early medieval period. Cattle were often allowed to graze on the stubble found in the fields after the harvest, and their manure helped revitalize the fields. Also, hay and various grasses grew in the meadows of the villages, and the animals were allowed to wander in those meadows to eat the grasses.

Although animal husbandry was a significant practice of the peasants in barbarian Europe, it was far less important, and provided a much smaller amount of food, than farming. Some distinctive crops were produced in different parts of Europe because of climatic differences. Notably, grapes were grown in the warmer climates but were seldom found in the cooler climate of northern Europe. Despite this variety, the fundamental food crop was some type of cereal, which was often consumed in the form of bread and beer. Various types of wheat were grown in the village fields, as were barley, oats, rye, and spelt. The crop yields were quite poor, averaging a yield of between 2.5 to 1 to 3 to 1 to seeds planted. There were often times when this meager yield was even smaller, and thus famine was not an uncommon phenomenon; hunger was almost constant for the peasants. One means to make up for the poor production of the grains in the fields, however, was to plant small gardens near the home. These gardens often supplied foods that added valuable vitamins and minerals to the diet; the peasants grew root vegetables, peas, beans, and other legumes in their gardens. Thus, even though early medieval peasants spent much of their time cultivating grain, they also found time to grow a variety of vegetables to bring to the table.

Along with hunger, the greatest problem the peasant farmers of the early Middle Ages faced was soil depletion. To produce even the minimal yields they did, the peasants had to find some way to revitalize the fields they planted. One solution, of course, was to manure the fields, which they accomplished by allowing their livestock to graze in the fields and fertilize it while feeding. The early medieval peasant also collected manure from stables and spread it on the fields. But dependence on manure for fertilizer was an inadequate solution because of the smaller size of most farm animals during this period and because most animals were sold or slaughtered every fall (since the peasants did not have enough food to keep the animals through the winter). The most effective way to allow the soil to replenish itself was to let it lie fallow. Peasants in barbarian Europe were forced to leave part of their fields unplanted each year so that the soil could be revitalized and continue to return at least the small harvests that the peasants needed to survive.

Because of the need to let some fields lie fallow each year, the peasants practiced a regimen of crop rotation as well as rotation of fields to be planted. In the drier climates and even in the wetter north the standard practice until the ninth century was a two-field system of crop rotation. In this approach, half of the available land was plowed and half was left fallow, and in the following year the situation was reversed. Although this practice enabled the soil to replenish itself, it did leave much of the farmland uncultivated, which worsened the already difficult problem of food production. A series of Carolingian documents from around the time of Charlemagne (surveys of the great estates called polyptychs) reveal a new three-field rotation system emerging at that time. Even before then, and even in the drier regions, a second planting sometimes occurred; beginning in the ninth century, the new practice of dividing the fields into thirds became more widespread.

The most obvious advantage of this system was that it brought more land under cultivation each year, thus increasing the productivity of the fields; it also enabled the peasants to plant different crops. In this approach one-third of the field was left fallow, another third was planted with winter wheat, and the other third was planted with a spring crop, generally oats or barley and sometimes legumes. The new system of planting did not completely replace the old two-field practice and was used mostly in northern Europe, where the soil was moister and the climate wetter. Although it was not introduced universally, the new three-field planting regimen was a great benefit to those who used it, and they enjoyed better yields of seed to crop than those who did not.

Peasants used a variety of tools in their daily farm labors, but for much of the period were hindered by the simplicity of design and the materials used to make them. The farmer's tools were often made of wood, which was a less durable material than metal. Iron came into more general use only later in the early medieval period; when it did, it offered a great improvement in the quality of farming tools. The most important of all farm implements was perhaps the plow. The most common plow used by peasants in the post-Roman world of Western Europe was the Roman or scratch plow. It was a simple, light tool that could be easily operated by the farmer with a small team of oxen, generally two. The scratch plow, as the name suggests, did little more than break the surface of the soil without turning it over. In areas like Italy where the soil is dry or sandy, this plow was often sufficient for the farmer's needs, but in northern Europe where the soil is moist and heavy, this plow alone was inadequate. Often digging by hand was necessary to supplement the furrow made by the scratch plow.

Probably in the Carolingian age, a new more efficient plow appeared, better suited to till the soil in northern Europe. This plow, known as the *carruca* in contemporary documents, was a wheeled plow that was fitted with a moldboard and needed as many as eight oxen to work it. It was a more complex and expensive tool, but it also was furrowed and turned the soil over, thus aerating the soil and making it more fertile. Although a technological improvement, the *carruca* did not immediately replace the scratch plow even in the north; nevertheless, its gradual spread improved agricultural productivity.

The peasant farmers of early medieval Europe used a number of other tools as well. By the Carolingian period, water and wind mills were coming into more general use to grind the grain that was such an important part of the diet. Even before these mills appeared, hand-operated mills, which were much more labor intensive to operate, enjoyed widespread use by early medieval farmers. Finally, there were several handheld tools that were generally found on early medieval farms, including spades (a useful supplement to the plow for digging in the fields), axes, hoes, sickles, and scythes.

The tools and practices medieval farmers used, especially the plow, dictated the way they farmed and the shape of their fields. Most fields in early medieval villages were long narrow strips because of the difficulty of plowing them, especially when the *carruca* came into more widespread use. It was a difficult and time-consuming job to turn the team of oxen and plow around and so, to accommodate the new plow, the fields were long and narrow instead of short and wide. Also, medieval farmers fenced in their fields or sometimes built wide ditches to manage the livestock that were allowed to graze on the fields. The fences and ditches were intended both to keep livestock in and out so that they would not overgraze some fields or wander off to another village.

Agriculture in the early Middle Ages, therefore, was focused primarily on farming various grains. Peasants also practiced animal husbandry and planted small gardens where they grew beans and leafy vegetables. The level of farming was barely above subsistence and hunger was not unknown. The early medieval peasant, nonetheless, survived in the face of various difficulties through cooperation with other peasants and various techniques developed during that time. Use of animal fertilizer was not uncommon as was the use of animals, especially horses and oxen, as draft animals. Early medieval farmers also gradually developed a

Peasant farmers ploughing in the month of January, from an English calendar, ca. 1025–1050. (The British Library Board)

heavy plow for the rich soils of northern Europe, and they also practiced crop and field rotation.

See also: Animals; Carolingian Dynasty; Charlemagne; Diet and Nutrition

Bibliography

Bloch, Marc. *French Rural History: An Essay on Its Basic Characteristics.* Trans. Janet Sondheimer. Berkeley: University of California Press, 1966.

Duby, Georges. *Rural Economy and Country Life in the Medieval West.* Trans. Cynthia Postan. Columbia: University of South Carolina Press, 1968.

Duby, Georges. *The Early Growth of the European Economy: Warriors and Peasants from the Seventh to the Twelfth Century.* Ithaca, NY: Cornell University Press, 1979.

Finberg, Herbert P. R., ed. *Agrarian History of England and Wales.* Vol. 1. Cambridge: Cambridge University Press, 1972.

Harvey, John. *Mediaeval Gardens.* Beaverton, OR: Timber, 1981.

Lewit, Tamara. *Agricultural Production in the Roman Economy, A.D. 200–400.* Oxford: Tempus Reparatum, 1991.

Riché, Pierre. *Daily Life in the World of Charlemagne.* 1978. Trans. Jo Ann McNamara. 4th Reprint, Philadelphia: University of Pennsylvania Press, 1983.

Slicher van Bath, Bernard H. *The Agrarian History of Western Europe: A.D. 500–1850.* Trans. Olive Ordish. London: Arnold, 1963.

White, Lynn, Jr. *Medieval Technology and Social Change.* Oxford: Oxford University Press, 1964.

Aistulf (d. 756)

Penultimate Lombard king (r. 749–756), and one of the most ruthless and blood-thirsty to wear the iron crown of the Lombard monarchy. Like all the Lombard kings, Aistulf sought to extend his authority over the important central Italian possessions of the papacy and the Byzantine Empire and thereby establish Lombard power over the entire Italian peninsula. Successful against the Byzantines, Aistulf met his match in the protector of the pope, Pippin, king of the Franks. Indeed, it was Aistulf's aggression and repeated violation of diplomatic agreements that forced Pope Stephen II to seek aid from the great power in the north. Stephen's revolutionary act led to the final split between Rome and Constantinople, which in turn led to the formation of the independent papal state, and also brought about the important alliance of the papacy and the kings and, eventually, emperors of the Franks. Aistulf's threats and Stephen's response also provided the conditions in Rome that led to the creation of the greatest forgery of the Middle Ages, the Donation of Constantine.

Aistulf's reign was a difficult time for the papacy because he was determined to unify the Italian peninsula under his authority. Italian unity, however, could be accomplished only at the expense of the pope's vast estates in central Italy, and therefore the official biography of Pope Stephen II contains a very negative picture of the Lombard king. According to the *Book of the Popes* (*Liber Pontificalis*), Aistulf was a "shameless Lombard king" who was "contaminated by the Ancient Enemy's cunning" (Davis 1992, 94.6, 55). He was accused of "pernicious savagery" (Davis 1992, 94.5, 55) and cruelty. Stephen's biographer describes him as an "atrocious king . . . [who] boiled over with mighty rage and, roaring like a lion, kept sending pestilential threats to the Romans" (Davis 1992, 94.10, 56–62). Clearly this account is biased, but other contemporary accounts reveal that Aistulf was a treacherous and ambitious ruler who was not unwilling to violate treaties in pursuit of his goal. And although he was a Catholic king, Aistulf did not let his religion get in the way of conquest.

Aistulf became king in 749 after the death of Liutprand, whose threats to Roman territory and security had already caused the pope to seek Frankish aid. Liutprand, however, was respectful of St. Peter and a less ruthless and duplicitous adversary than Aistulf. From the very outset of his short and terrible reign, Aistulf took the initiative against his rivals in Italy. Within two years of his ascension to the throne, Aistulf captured Ravenna, the imperial stronghold in Italy and seat of the Byzantine emperor's representative in the Latin West, and had begun to issue royal proclamations from the city. The exarch of Ravenna, as the emperor's representative, had been the protector of the pope, and the loss of the imperial city was a blow not only to Constantinople's prestige but also to the safety of Rome and its estates in central Italy.

The Lombard king's success against imperial Italy encouraged him to increase the pressure on papal Italy. Rome was now without its protector and powerless to prevent the expansion of Aistulf, who, according to the *Book of the Popes* (*Liber Pontificalis*), instituted "a great persecution" of Rome (Davis 1992, 94.5, 54). He invaded Roman territory, capturing cities in the northern part of the duchy and increasing pressure on Rome itself. Pope Stephen, following the practice his predecessors had used with other Lombard kings, sought to negotiate peace with Aistulf. Stephen sent his brother and other high-ranking papal officials, along with many gifts, to Aistulf to sign a peace treaty in June 752. Although Aistulf agreed to a peace of 40 years, he violated the treaty in only four months. Tearing up the treaty, Aistulf imposed a heavy tribute on Rome, piled insults on the pope, threatened the Roman people, and claimed that the city was under his jurisdiction.

The difficult position Stephen faced was further complicated by imperial demands that the pope negotiate the return of Ravenna and other imperial territories seized by Aistulf. Shortly after the Lombard resumed hostilities toward Rome, Stephen received an envoy form Emperor Constantine V ordering the pope to secure the return of imperial territory. Stephen now faced the prospect of pleading for his safety and that of the emperor's lands in Italy in the face of a most unfriendly foe. In the summer and fall of 753, Stephen sought to come to terms with his enemy. He had also contacted Pippin, the recently crowned king of the Franks, who had sent his own ambassadors to meet with the pope. Aistulf refused to meet with the pope or begin discussions over lands he had conquered.

In October 753, Stephen began a journey that was to have revolutionary consequences for the papacy, Franks, and Lombards. Contemporary accounts note that his departure was marked by heavenly signs, including a fireball that rose in the sky from the north—over the Frankish kingdom—and set to the south—over the Lombard kingdom. He met Aistulf at the king's residence in the royal capital of Pavia, but the pope's advances were rejected by the king, who demanded that the pope return to Rome rather than continue his trip north. Nevertheless, protection from Frankish allies guaranteed that Stephen could continue to meet the Frankish king in his residence in Ponthion. The meeting was decisive for Frankish-papal relations and was the beginning of the end of Aistulf's dream to unite Italy under his authority.

The fall and winter of 753–754 was spent forging an alliance between Pippin and Stephen. The creation of the alliance was quickened by Aistulf's miscalculation. He sent Pippin's brother, Carloman, who had retired to the monastery of Monte Cassino, to intervene on Aistulf's behalf and convince Pippin not to ally with the pope. Carloman's pleas were rejected, and he was not allowed to return to Italy. At the same time, Pippin grew closer to the pope, who may have used the claims of the Donation of Constantine to support his position. Although it is unlikely that the Donation had been written (most scholars believe it was composed sometime after 755), the basic ideas of the forgery were in evidence in Rome and may have played a role in the negotiations. Stephen confirmed the alliance by crowning Pippin king of the Franks for a second time and bestowing on him the imperial title of Patrician, thus providing the king with the right to intervene in Italy. The discussions between the king and pope did yield a donation from Pippin, one that promised that the lands of St. Peter would be returned to the pope. Pippin agreed to guarantee the return of the lands by an invasion of Italy if necessary and sent repeated demands to Aistulf to return St. Peter's patrimony.

Aistulf refused to submit to Pippin's demands and forced the Frankish king to invade Italy. After convincing the Frankish nobility of the wisdom of his policy, Pippin invaded in the spring of 755 to defend the interests of St. Peter—a focus of Carolingian devotion—and his representative, the pope. Aistulf moved north to stop the advancing Frankish armies, but he was defeated and his army put in disarray. Pippin then laid siege to the Lombard capital of Pavia, and Aistulf sued for peace. He agreed to send hostages to the Frankish court, return cities seized from Rome and Ravenna, and keep the peace, an agreement he broke shortly after Pippin left Italy. Once again Aistulf invaded Roman territory and with three separate armies laid siege to the city of Rome. He violated the cemeteries outside the city by digging up the graves and threatened to kill all the Romans by a single sword if they failed to submit to his authority.

Stephen again sent a letter to the king of the Franks seeking aid in the name of St. Peter. Upon learning of the pope's appeal, Aistulf remarked, "Let the Franks come and get you out of my hands now." In the spring of 756 Pippin did just that, invading Italy, with little of the difficulty from Frankish nobles his first invasion occasioned, and overwhelming Aistulf. The Lombard king was forced to lift his siege and to accept another treaty at the hands of the Frankish king. A list of 22 cities was compiled that were to be returned to the pope, and Pippin's representatives, including Abbot Fulrad, were sent to each of these cities to ensure that Aistulf honored the terms of the treaty. Fulrad accepted the keys of the cities and symbolically laid them on the altar of St. Peter in Rome as a sign of Rome's power.

It is likely that Aistulf would have violated the treaty yet again had he not died in a hunting accident in December 756. He was succeeded by Desiderius, the duke of Tuscany. His repeated assaults on Rome and treaty violations played an important role in the revolution of the eighth century. Aistulf's aggression forced the pope finally to sever ties with the emperor in Constantinople and find a more reliable protector. Stephen's alliance with Pippin and his dynasty had far-reaching repercussions throughout the rest of the Middle Ages and laid the foundation for the creation of a new Western empire. Aistulf's reign was important too because his attempted conquest of Rome helped create the papal states and established the conditions that contributed to the composition of the Donation of Constantine.

See also: Carloman, Mayor of the Palace; Carolingian Dynasty; Desiderius; Donation of Constantine; Liutprand; Lombards; Pippin III, Called Pippin the Short; Ravenna; Rome

Bibliography

Christie, Neil. *The Lombards: The Ancient Langobards.* Oxford: Blackwell, 1998.

Davis, Raymond, trans. *The Lives of the Eighth-Century Popes* (Liber Pontificalis): *The Ancient Biographies of Nine Popes from A.D. 715 to A.D. 817.* Liverpool, UK: Liverpool University Press, 1992.

Herrin, Judith. *The Formation of Christendom.* Princeton, NJ: Princeton University Press, 1987.

Llewellyn, Peter. *Rome in the Dark Ages.* New York: Barnes and Noble, 1996.

Noble, Thomas F. X. *The Republic of St. Peter: The Birth of the Papal State, 680–825.* Philadelphia: University of Pennsylvania Press, 1984.

Riché, Pierre. *The Carolingians: A Family Who Forged Europe.* Trans. Michael Idomir Allen. Philadelphia: University of Pennsylvania Press, 1993.

Aix-la-Chapelle

Located in North-Rhine Westphalia in modern Germany, Aix-la-Chapelle (modern Aachen, Germany) was located in the old heartland of the Carolingian empire in the early Middle Ages. Attracted by its famous hot springs, Charlemagne built a great palace complex there. It would be his primary residence during the latter part of his reign and was the site of his tomb (his relics were later moved to Cologne). It has been regarded by many modern scholars as the capital of his empire. Charlemagne described Aix-la-Chapelle as a "New Rome," and the town came to represent the cultural, political, and religious program of the great Carolingian ruler. Later Carolingian rulers vied for control of the town, recognizing it as a means

Charlemagne's Palatine Chapel (center), now the central element of Aachen (Aix-la-Chapelle) Cathedral in Germany, is the finest surviving example of Carolingian architecture. Charlemagne began construction on his chapel in 786. Construction continued for more than a millennium to form today's Aachen Cathedral. (Jaime Pharr)

to confirm their own imperial authority. Aix-la-Chapelle retained its importance throughout the Middle Ages for German rulers as some 38 German kings were crowned there between 813 and 1531.

Although Aix-la-Chapelle's significance during the Middle Ages emerged only with the arrival of Charlemagne in the 790s, it was a center of modest importance as early as Roman times. Like Charlemagne, the Romans were attracted to the region because of its hot springs, and the modern name itself is derived from the Roman name for the region, Aqua Grani (waters of Granus, reference to the warm baths and a Celtic deity worshipped there). Aix-la-Chapelle formed part of the Roman military and communication structure and was a favorite resort of Roman soldiers who enjoyed the hot springs and the Roman bath built there. By late antiquity, the town had become a Christian center. Remnants of an early church have been identified that was built either by late Gallo-Romans or the Merovingians who took control of the region after the fall of Rome. The Merovingians built a small villa there that was inherited in turn by the Carolingians when they took power. Charlemagne's father Pippin had what contemporary sources call a villa and a *palatium* at Aix-la-Chapelle that he visited on occasion and certainly spent Christmas there with his son in 767.

It was Charlemagne, however, who transformed Aix-la-Chapelle into a town of real cultural and political importance. He was attracted to the region for several reasons, not the least of which according to Charlemagne's biographer Einard, was its hot springs. Once he had built his residence there, Charlemagne would frequent the baths often and even invited friends to join him while bathing. Charlemagne was attracted to the area for more practical reasons, however, including access to Roman roads, Aix-la-Chapelle's proximity to other royal palaces, and its location in the Carolingian heartland of Austrasia. Aix-la-Chapelle also was surrounded by the Ardennes forest, which provided a ready source of game for the royal banquet table.

Along with a series of other building projects, Charlemagne began work on a major palace complex in the 790s, a project that would continue after his death and reach completion in the 820s. The centerpiece of the complex was an octagonal chapel, dedicated to the Virgin Mary, that was completed in 796 and may have been dedicated by Pope Leo III, possibly during his visit in 799 or in 804. The sole remaining part of the complex built by Charlemagne, the chapel was lavishly decorated and suggests that the other building were equally elaborately decorated with mosaics and paintings depicting scenes from the Bible. Built over an existing church, the chapel of Mary was built in two levels, with Charlemagne's throne, built on the model of King Solomon's throne with stone from the Holy Land, on the second level. There was an altar on the first floor dedicated to the Virgin and another altar on the second dedicated to Christ that was directly across from the Carolingian king's throne. The dome covering the chapel was some 110 feet above the main floor and contained a mosaic of Christ in Majesty surrounded by the four symbols of the Evangelists and the 24 elders of the Apocalypse. The chapel was joined by a two-story apse on the east side and on the west side by a three-story entrance that was flanked by semicircular towers on either side. The entrance included a forecourt whose design recalled a Roman triumphal arch.

The chapel gave expression to Charlemagne's main goals as king. It was the focal point of the liturgical reforms Charlemagne promoted during his reign and also announced his political program. The church itself boasted columns from Italy and statues from Rome and was modeled after San Vitale of Ravenna, a church built by the Byzantine emperor Justinian. In this way, the chapel proclaimed the imperial vision of Charlemagne and his advisors. The church also revealed Charlemagne's views on his own place in the divine plan. His throne was placed on the second floor, halfway between the main floor where his subjects worshiped and the dome above, which contained a mosaic of Christ in Majesty. In this way, the great king demonstrated his understanding of his role as an intermediary between God and humankind and expressed his sense of responsibility for the salvation of the souls of his subjects.

Along with his royal chapel, Charlemagne built a number of other structures at Aix-la-Chapelle. There was a two-story great hall that was connected to the chapel by a long covered passageway and a private residence that was situated midway between the great hall and the chapel. Nothing remains of these structures, but literary evidence and the surviving chapel give some indication about the nature of these structures. The great hall, which was inspired by the late Roman great hall in Trier, was used for royal business, receptions of foreign dignitaries and the Carolingian aristocracy, and banquets, and was hundred feet by seventy feet. Literary accounts note that it was decorated with scenes of recent history, including Charlemagne's wars in Spain, and representations of the seven liberal arts. The private residence included Charlemagne's personal chamber, a waiting room for his advisors, and, possibly, a solarium. There were, or course, the baths, including a number of pools, the largest of which could hold a hundred bathers. There was also a large courtyard with a statue of the Gothic king Theodoric the Great, which came from Italy, a park with animals, and two basilicas connected to the chapel of the Virgin. The entire complex was surrounded by a wall with four gates.

Aix-la-Chapelle emerged as one of the great centers of administration and is often identified as Charlemagne's capital in the final part of his reign. As such, it was the location of important assemblies in 797, 802–803, and 809, and Charlemagne issued a number of major capitularies from the town. In 813, Charlemagne crowned his son Louis the Pious emperor and designated him heir before a great assembly of the leading spiritual and secular leaders of the realm. Attracted by Charlemagne, many of his key advisors built homes outside the great complex and contributed to the growth of the town. Among those who built homes there was Charlemagne's biographer, Einhard, whose residence was large enough to include a chapel of its own. By the 820s, Aix-la-Chapelle had a growing population, thriving economy, active marketplace, and many of the essentials of a major town center. It remained an important center in the late Carolingian era, often the focus of imperial claims of Charlemagne's descendants, and beyond as later German rulers sought to identify themselves with the town and its greatest resident.

See also: Capitulary; Carolingian Dynasty; Charlemagne; Justinian; Leo III, Pope, Louis the Pious; Merovingian Dynasty, Pippin III

Bibliography

Einhard and Notker the Stammerer. *Two Lives of Charlemagne.* Trans. David Ganz. London: Penguin Books, 2008.

Fichtenau, Heinrich. *The Carolingian Empire.* Trans. Peter Munz. Toronto: Toronto University Press, 1979.

Lobbedey, U. "Carolingian Royal Palaces: The State of Research from an Architectural Historian's Viewpoint." In *Court Culture in the Early Middle Ages: The Proceedings of the First Alcuin Conference.* Ed. Rosamond McKitterick. Turnhout: Brepols, 2003, pp. 129–54.

McKitterick, Rosamond. *Charlemagne: The Formation of a European Identity.* Cambridge: Cambridge University Press, 2008.

Riché, Pierre. *Daily Life in the World of Charlemagne.* Trans. Jo Ann McNamara. Philadelphia: University of Pennsylvania Press, 1983.

Sullivan, Richard E. *Aix-la-Chapelle in the Age of Charlemagne.* Norman: University of Oklahoma Press, 1974.

Alans

Central Asian people who moved into southern Russia, the Alans participated in the migrations of peoples of the fourth and fifth centuries. Unlike other barbarian groups such as the Huns, the Alans never formed a united hoard, and therefore their impact was felt in various places in the Roman Empire. They were also associated with a number of other groups, including Huns, Vandals, and Visigoths, as well as serving the Roman military commanders Aëtius and Stilicho. Groups of Alans settled in Gaul, Italy, and Spain, with the Spanish contingent joining the Vandals who conquered the empire's North African province. Although active during the fourth and fifth centuries as both allies and enemies of the Roman Empire, the Alans disappeared as an independent people during the sixth century. They were defeated with the Vandals by Justinian's armies in North Africa and gradually absorbed by the surrounding population in both Africa and Europe. Despite their assimilation, the Alans did influence artistic styles in southern France and were known for a special breed of hunting dogs, now extinct, the *canis Alani.*

The Alans were first identified by Roman writers in the first century of the Common Era, but had only limited and minor contact with the Romans until the fourth century. There was, however, one major confrontation before then, and the Alans were often used by the Romans as interpreters. In the late fourth century the Alans, like other peoples of the central steppes of Asia, were forced to move westward by the onslaught of the Huns. Some groups of Alans were defeated by the Huns and incorporated into their army, and one group of Alans joined with the Visigoths who sought entry into the Roman Empire in the 370s. This alliance proved beneficial for the Alans but was nearly fatal to the empire. The Alans joined with the Visigoths at the Battle of Hadrianople in 378, having been promised substantial rewards by the Visigoths for their assistance. After the battle, at which the Roman armies were destroyed and the emperor killed, groups of Alans settled in northern Italy and parts of southeastern Europe. Moreover, many Alans remained with the main Visigothic force and served them into the fifth century. They were part of the force that Alaric led during his rampage in Italy and sack of Rome in 410. They migrated into Gaul with Alaric's successor, where they broke ranks with the Visigoths in exchange for an alliance with the empire and lands from Narbonne to Toulouse.

The greatest number of Alans, however, entered the empire during the mass barbarian crossing of the Rhine River in 406. Led by their kings Goar and Rependial, the Alans entered imperial territory with the Vandals and fought a battle against the Franks, a Germanic people allied with the empire, who attacked the Vandals. After defeating the Franks, the Alans marched across Roman territory and sacked Trier and other cities. The group led by King Goar became an ally of Rome after the king was promised land and gold. His followers were settled around Worms, later supported a rebel Roman general, and were ultimately settled near Orléans by Aëtius. They remained important but untrustworthy allies of the Roman commander during the mid-fifth century and played a significant role in the struggle with Attila. In 451, when the great Hun decided to invade the Western Empire, he hoped to regain control over the Alans. But the Alans of Orléans, led by their King Sangiban, stood with the imperial forces in defense of the Gaul. The king's opposition to Attila slowed his advance. The king also joined with Aëtius in the great Battle of the Catalaunian Plains, but the Roman general placed the Alans between Gothic and Roman troops because of his fear that Sangiban would go over to Attila's side.

Although one group of Alans settled in Gaul, another group remained with the Vandals and entered Spain in 409. After pillaging Gaul, the Alans carved out small kingdoms in Spain and shared land with the native Roman population. Their independent existence in Spain, however, was short lived because the Visigoths, under imperial direction, conquered the Alans, who then joined with the Vandals, losing their political independence at the same time. Although now subject to the Vandals, the Alans continued to play an important role in late imperial history. They joined with the Vandals under King Gaiseric, who was officially styled *rex Vandalorum et Alanorum* (king of the Vandals and Alans), when he led an invasion of North Africa in 429. They were part of the force that gradually displaced Roman rule in the region and established an independent kingdom ruled by Gaiseric and his successors for more than a century. The kingdom fell, however, before the armies of Justinian, led by the great general Belisarius in 533. This defeat, along with the easy assimilation of other Alan tribal units in the old Western Empire and the Alans' conversion to Christianity, brought about the disappearance of the group as an independent people in the sixth century.

See also: Aëtius; Alaric; Attila the Hun; Belisarius; Catalaunian Plains, Battle of the; Gaiseric; Hadrianople, Battle of; Justinian; Vandals; Visigoths

Bibliography

Bachrach, Bernard S. "The Alans in Gaul." *Traditio* 23 (1967): 476–89.

Bachrach, Bernard S. *A History of the Alans in the West, from Their First Appearance in the Sources of Classical Antiquity through the Early Middle Ages.* Minneapolis: University of Minnesota Press, 1973.

Bury, John B. *History of the Later Roman Empire: From the Death of Theodosius I to the Death of Justinian.* 2 Vols. 1923. Reprint, New York: Dover, 1959.

Wolfram, Herwig. *The Roman Empire and Its Germanic Peoples.* Trans. Thomas J. Dunlap. Berkeley: University of California Press, 1997.

Alaric (c. 370–410)

Great Visigothic king and warrior whose sack of the ancient capital city of Rome in 410, following the assassination of his rival Stilicho, profoundly shocked and dismayed the people of the Roman Empire, a shock from which the Western Empire never fully recovered. Alaric's sack of the city was a signal of the declining fortunes of the Western Empire, which finally fell in 476. As king, Alaric revived the challenge the Visigoths had posed for Rome since their entry into the empire in 376 and subsequent stinging defeat of imperial armies at the Battle of Hadrianople, during which the emperor, Valens, died. Ambitious and talented, an Arian Christian who could be most ruthless when necessary, a skilled general who could not achieve a decisive victory over the Romans, Alaric attempted to create a barbarian kingship to rival Roman imperial power and an independent barbarian kingdom in the empire. Although he ultimately failed in his grand design, Alaric's challenge to Roman authorities did set the tone for the way the Romans dealt with other barbarian leaders and the political, military, and territorial arrangements they made with the barbarians in the coming century.

Born around 370, Alaric is first mentioned in the early 390s, and most likely was involved in Gothic actions in the late 380s. In 376, his fellow tribesmen had entered the empire to avoid the westward movement of the Huns—whose activities also shaped the subsequent history of the Goths—defeated imperial armies, killed the emperor in battle in 378, and signed a treaty with the empire in 382 that Alaric spent his career attempting to undo. Alaric's first appearance was as the king of a mixed band of Goths and allied peoples who crossed the Balkans into Thrace in 391. Alaric's advance was stopped by the recently promoted general, Stilicho. It was the first meeting between the two barbarian leaders and the beginning of a long rivalry between them. Stilicho defeated and encircled Alaric at their first meeting but at the order of the emperor, Theodosius, allowed him to go free. Alaric managed to establish the first independent Gothic kingdom on Roman soil on this occasion and was the first barbarian king to be made a general in the Roman army. In this way Alaric broke with tradition, and the empire established important precedents for its future dealings with other barbarian kings. Despite some gains, Alaric was forced to renew the terms of the treaty of 382, which, among other things, required the Goths to serve the Roman military.

In 394, Theodosius called on Alaric to honor the terms of the treaty, as he faced the challenge of the usurper, Eugenius, who had been elevated to the imperial throne in the West after the death of Valentinian II. Failed negotiations between the pretender and the emperor led to open warfare, and although he received a subordinate command and directed no Roman troops, Alaric supplied a sizeable contingent to the imperial army and distinguished himself in battle. The usurper was put down, but only after a terrible battle in which many Goths were killed. To many Goths, it appeared that they had been sacrificed by the imperial generals to secure victory over Eugenius and to reduce the power of the Goths. Indeed, the treatment Alaric received led him to revolt, even though he received a high imperial post.

Alaric's actions were probably motivated by several factors: dissatisfaction over treatment in the suppression of Eugenius; the Hunnish advance in 394–395; and the death of Theodosius in 395, which ended the treaty of 382 because the major party to the treaty dropped out. Of course, the movements of other Goths and the turmoil within the empire allowed Alaric more freedom of action. Whatever the case, he revolted in 395 and spent the next two years on the move throughout the empire. Once again he was opposed by Stilicho, who managed to surround the Goth on occasion but was prohibited from crushing his rival because of imperial restrictions and because of court politics that undermined Stilicho's effectiveness and also threatened his life and position. Alaric plundered Greece during this period, entered into secret negotiations with Stilicho, and, in 397, extracted significant concessions from the empire. He received a new command that gave him regional authority as the *magister militum* for the region of Illyricum, and he also received important territorial concessions. In this way, the empire set further precedents by incorporating a barbarian people more fully into the administrative structure of the empire and placing authority in the hands of that people's king.

Turmoil among some of Alaric's fellow Goths, and their desire to emulate his success, led to a Gothic attempt to take Constantinople, which was suppressed with the aid of the Huns and their leader Uldin. Alaric remained aloof from the struggle, but he did not remain quiet long. In 401, while his rival Stilicho was active against a Vandal force, Alaric invaded Italy and threatened the imperial capital of Milan, an action that so dismayed the emperor, Honorius, that he transferred his residence to Ravenna. Stilicho quickly moved to Italy; he met Alaric in battle at Pollentia, where he inflicted serious damage on the Gothic army, though not able to defeat it outright. Alaric was allowed to return to his lands in the east, but for unknown reasons he stopped at Verona in 402. Stilicho struck at Alaric with great force and handed Alaric his worst defeat. And this time Alaric left Italy for his Balkan homelands.

Having once again escaped destruction, Alaric once again waited for the opportunity to arise to allow him to strike again. It was presented as a result of further turmoil between the Eastern and Western imperial courts and by further pressure from the frontiers. In 404–405, Stilicho fell out with the Eastern authority and may have negotiated with Alaric, making him *magister militum* of Illyricum again. (Alaric received this rank by 407 and may have held it as early as 405, but the record is unclear.) This was a clear violation of relations between East and West because Illyricum was the possession of the Eastern emperor. Stilicho's difficulties were increased by the invasion of the Gothic king Radagaisus, barbarian invasions over the Rhine, and the appearance of the usurper Constantine in Britain. Although he was able to overcome these threats, Stilicho was forced to attempt reconciliation with the Eastern Roman Empire, and he broke the treaty with the Goths. In 408, Alaric rose up in rebellion, occupying important territories and threatening to invade Italy unless he received payment of 4,000 pounds of gold. Alaric's long-time rival, Stilicho, was willing to grant these demands, but he fell from favor and was executed, along with thousands of barbarians living in Italy.

The death of Stilicho opened the final chapter in the life of Alaric. The massacre of so many barbarians caused thousands of Stilicho's supporters to join Alaric, who took the opportunity to invade Italy with a substantially larger army. He reached Rome in 409 and camped outside the city until the following year, threatening to sack it unless Emperor Honorius yielded to his demands. But Honorius refused Alaric's offer of alliance in exchange for the grant of a generalship, payments of gold and grain, and land for the troops. Alaric offered a different arrangement in which he would make an alliance in exchange for land and grain. The emperor again refused, and thus Alaric's attempt to prop up an emperor who would meet his demands failed.

Exasperated with his failure to move Honorius, Alaric ordered the sack of the city on August 24, 410. A Roman noblewoman, according to tradition, opened the city gates for Alaric, and for three days the Goths plundered and burned the city, leaving the churches in peace. The Goths came away with great spoils, including the booty the emperor Titus brought back from the First Jewish War and the destruction of Jerusalem in the first century and Galla Placidia, the sister of the emperor, who was kidnapped by her future husband Ataulf. The sack, the first in 800 years, profoundly shocked the people of the empire, including St. Jerome, who was rendered speechless by the tears he cried, and St. Augustine, who wrote his great work, *City of God,* in response to the sack.

Alaric, however, did not long enjoy the spoils of his victory. After the sack of the city, he moved south with his armies and attempted to cross to Sicily as a first step toward seizing the grain-producing regions of Africa. His fleet was wrecked, and he then turned north, perhaps with designs on Naples or some other city. Along the way he became ill and died in Bruttium. According to tradition, he was buried in the bed of the Busento River while it was temporarily diverted, and the slaves who buried him were killed so that the whereabouts of the tomb would remain unknown. Alaric was succeeded by his brother-in-law, Ataulf.

Although he died shortly after his epoch-making sack of the city of Rome, Alaric had a long-lasting impact on the empire. Indeed, the events of 410 profoundly altered the way the Romans, Christians, and pagans saw themselves. The aura of invincibility and permanence associated with *Roma aeterna* (eternal Rome) had been shattered, and the city suffered further assaults in the course of the fifth century. By the century's end, the Western Roman Empire had disappeared. Alaric also forced the empire to reevaluate its relations with the barbarians and led them to create precedents that affected their dealings with other barbarian tribes that moved into the empire in the coming decades.

See also: Hadrianople, Battle of; Huns; Rome; Stilicho, Flavius; Theodosius; Visigoths

Bibliography

Burns, Thomas S. *Barbarians within the Gates of Rome: A Study of Roman Military Policy and the Barbarians, ca. 375–425 A.D.* Bloomington: Indiana University Press, 1994.

Heather, Peter. *The Goths.* Oxford: Blackwell, 1996.

Lot, Ferdinand. *The End of the Ancient World and the Beginning of the Middle Ages.* New York: Harper and Row, 1961.

Wolfram, Herwig. *History of the Goths.* Trans. Thomas J. Dunlap. Berkeley: University of California Press, 1988.

Wolfram, Herwig. *The Roman Empire and Its Germanic Peoples.* Trans. Thomas J. Dunlap. Berkeley: University of California Press, 1997.

Alaric II (d. 507)

Visigothic king of Toulouse (484–507) who traditionally has been seen as a weak and unworthy successor to his great father Euric, but who more recently has been seen as an important and innovative king. Even by traditional estimates, Alaric is worthy of better treatment than he has received because of his successful military alliance with the most powerful Germanic king of his age, Theodoric the Great. He introduced important legislation during his reign and prepared an important legal codification. He also instituted a new and farsighted religious policy, which laid the foundations for an important church council and would have established an important institutional framework for church-state relations in the Visigothic kingdom had the kingdom not been smashed by the great Frankish king Clovis (r. 481–511). Indeed, it is Alaric's defeat by Clovis that has, most unfairly, shaped his modern reputation.

Although overshadowed by his Ostrogothic father-in-law Theodoric and his Frankish rival Clovis, Alaric was an ambitious and, for much of his reign, successful king. He oversaw the expansion and consolidation of the kingdom of Toulouse that his father Euric may have intended in his attempts to extend the kingdom's boundaries. During Alaric's reign, Visigoths from his kingdom began to migrate in significant numbers into Spain and often fought the local inhabitants to gain control of large estates, military campaigns supported by Alaric.

In the early 490s, Alaric joined Theodoric in his struggles in Italy against the Germanic king Odovacar. Upon Theodoric's victory over Odovacar in 493, Alaric was rewarded by marriage to one of Theodoric's daughters. At the same time Theodoric married one of his daughters to Clovis, so that the new king in Italy could gain the support of the powerful Frank. It is possible that it was for the same reason—to gain the friendship of Clovis—that Alaric handed over Syagrius, the former king of Soissons who had earlier been defeated by Clovis and fled to Toulouse. Although Gregory of Tours in his history places this act earlier and sees it as a sign of weakness, it most likely happened in 493 as part of the broader political strategy involving Theodoric. Indeed, in the early sixth century, when the Franks sought to expand into his territory, Alaric defeated Clovis, who then sought to reestablish their previous amity. But once again the relationship between the two kings changed.

According to Gregory of Tours, Clovis attacked Alaric because the Visigothic king was an Arian Christian and Clovis could not stand the thought of a heretic living as his neighbor. Clovis ignored the warning of Theodoric that he would defend Alaric, and war broke out between Clovis and Alaric in 507. At this point, Alaric may have overextended his resources, and Theodoric himself was concerned about the strength of Alaric's army. In late summer of that year, Alaric and Clovis met in battle at Vouillé, near Poitiers. Alaric was outnumbered by his rival and was defeated. Clovis supposedly killed Alaric himself and then absorbed the kingdom of Toulouse.

Although defeated and killed in battle, Alaric was still a noteworthy king. His success in battle against Clovis, Odovacar, and others before his final defeat testifies to his martial abilities. But more important than his military prowess are the legal and religious reforms he instituted. He promulgated a new legal code, the *Breviarium Alaricianum* (*Breviary of Alaric*), in 506, which had been compiled by a commission of legal experts under the direction of a high-ranking royal official. The code was based upon earlier Roman legal codes and their commentaries and became the official law for the Roman subjects of the kingdom.

The participation of the Roman bishops in the codification of the law laid the foundation for the Council of Agde in 506. The council was Alaric's means to integrate the Roman Catholic bishops and church into the governmental framework of the kingdom ruled by an Arian Christian. His father had been more hostile to the church, but Alaric, recognizing perhaps the wave of the future, sought to incorporate the church into his kingdom. The council at Agde was an important first step in that process, and plans were made at the council to hold a national council in the following year at Toulouse. Although the council was never held because of Alaric's defeat by Clovis, preparation for it foreshadowed church councils in the future. Alaric established an important precedent for later church-state relations with the council at Agde and the proposed council at Toulouse. Although known best for his defeat at Vouillé, Alaric was a successful and innovative king for much of his reign.

See also: Breviary of Alaric; Clovis; Euric; Gregory of Tours; Merovingian Dynasty; Odovacar; Ostrogoths; Theodoric the Great; Visigoths

Bibliography

Bury, John B. *History of the Later Roman Empire: From the Death of Theodosius I to the Death of Justinian.* Vol. 1. 1923. Reprint, New York: Dover, 1958.

Gregory of Tours. *History of the Franks.* Trans. Lewis Thorpe. Harmondsworth, UK: Penguin, 1974.

Heather, Peter. *The Goths.* Oxford: Blackwell, 1996.

Wolfram, Herwig. *History of the Goths.* Trans. Thomas J. Dunlap. Berkeley: University of California Press, 1988.

Wolfram, Herwig. *The Roman Empire and Its Germanic Peoples.* Trans. Thomas J. Dunlap. Berkeley: University of California Press, 1997.

Alboin (d. 572)

According to Paul the Deacon, Alboin was the 10th of the Lombard kings (r. 560/561–574) and the first to rule in Italy. A successful warrior, who defeated a number of rival peoples, including the Gepids, he was also a successful diplomat and enjoyed good relations with the Franks, even marrying a daughter of one of the Merovingian kings. Alboin also enjoyed fairly good relations with the bishops of Italy, even though he and his people were pagans and Arians and the bishops and people of Italy Catholic. Although neither he nor his successors ruled a united Italy, Alboin laid the foundation for an important kingdom in Italy, which survived until it was absorbed by Charlemagne in 774.

Alboin, according to Paul the Deacon, was "a man fitted for wars and energized in all things" (49). And he spent much of his career after succeeding his father Audoin in 560–561 in waging wars. Alboin ascended the throne in traditional Lombard fashion—by election. As proved to be the case throughout Lombard history, Alboin was elected by his people, who usually chose the heir of the former king. He had distinguished himself already during the reign of his father, when he led the Lombards in battle against the Gepids and, according to tradition, killed the Gepid king. Three years after the battle, in 555, Alboin was rewarded with marriage to the daughter of the Merovingian king Chlotar I (r. 511–561), and he maintained good relations with the Franks ever after.

Upon succeeding his father, Alboin led the Lombards against the Gepids and into Italy. His struggles with the Gepids were not always successful; and in 565 he lost a battle against them. Two years later, after forging an alliance with the Avars, Alboin destroyed the Gepids. In the battle, Alboin killed the king and made a drinking cup of his skull, and also seized and married the king's daughter, Rosamund. In 568, according to tradition, Alboin accepted an invitation from the general Narses, who felt slighted by the emperor Justin II, to invade Italy. In thanks for their help, Alboin arranged a treaty with the Avars that gave them control of the old Lombard homeland.

See also: Arianism; Avars; Charlemagne; Franks; Justinian; Lombards; Merovingian Dynasty; Narses; Ostrogoths; Paul the Deacon; Totila

Bibliography

Christie, Neil. *The Lombards: The Ancient Langobards.* Oxford: Blackwell, 1998.

Llewellyn, Peter. *Rome in the Dark Ages.* New York: Barnes and Noble, 1993.

Paul the Deacon. *History of the Lombards.* Trans. William Dudley Foulke. Philadelphia: University of Pennsylvania Press, 1974.

Wolfram, Herwig. *The Roman Empire and Its Germanic Peoples.* Trans. Thomas J. Dunlap. Berkeley: University of California Press, 1997.

Alcuin of York (c. 730/735–804)

An Anglo-Saxon scholar, trained in the tradition of the Venerable Bede, Alcuin was the most important and influential of Charlemagne's court scholars. As one of Charlemagne's most trusted advisors, Alcuin participated in important church councils and advised Charlemagne on some of the critical political issues of the day. Although not a terribly original thinker, he was widely respected for his encyclopedic knowledge. His influence is perhaps demonstrated by the importance and number of his students, including Louis the Pious and Rabanus Maurus, and the warm regard they had for him because of his incomparable talent as a teacher. Indeed Einhard, Charlemagne's biographer and possibly one of Alcuin's students, described him as "the greatest scholar of the day." No longer recognized as the author of the *Libri Carolini* or the creator of the form of writing called Carolingian minuscule, Alcuin remains one of the most important figures in the Carolingian Renaissance because of his teaching and scholarship. He wrote commentaries on various books of the Bible (Genesis, Psalms, Ecclesiastes, the Song of Songs, and the Gospel of John), produced a new edition of the Bible, and wrote hagiography, poems, letters, and works on grammar, rhetoric, and dialectic (the trivium, the three most basic disciplines of the seven liberal arts).

Little is known for certain of Alcuin's early years. He was born in 730/735 to a noble family of York and was a kinsman of the great missionary saint, Willibrord. He entered the cathedral school at York, where he received his education and where he would later teach and serve as deacon. The school at York had recently been founded by Bede's friend and student, Egbert, who introduced the great Anglo-Saxon's love of learning there and invited Aethelberht (or Aelberht) to oversee the creation of a library. It was Aethelberht who taught Alcuin and instilled the love of books and learning that Alcuin bore with him through the rest of his life, an affection that had a strong effect on the Franks and was the foundation of their cultural revival.

Aethelberht evidently recognized Alcuin's talents, for he took his student with him to the continent on two occasions. On these trips Alcuin collected books and met other scholars; he met Charlemagne for the first time on a trip in 768. When Aethelberht succeeded to the position of archbishop of York, Alcuin took over the cathedral school, and when Aethelberht retired in 780, Alcuin also took over direction of the library. The new archbishop, Eanbald, had such confidence in Alcuin that he sent the scholar to Rome to collect the pallium (liturgical vestment granted by the pope to bishops with metropolitan authority), and on Alcuin's return he met Charlemagne at Parma and was invited to take charge of the king's court school. After gaining permission from Eanbald, Alcuin returned to France and spent the rest of his life in the Frankish kingdom, with the exception of two periods, 786 and 790–793, when he returned to his native land.

It was in the service of Charlemagne that Alcuin made his mark on history. From 781 until his retirement in 794, Alcuin was a member of Charlemagne's peripatetic court and one of the king's court scholars. At court, he participated in the cultural and religious revival that Charlemagne promoted and was, no doubt, important in the direction that the revival took. He also led the court school, teaching a broad range of subjects, including astronomy, to Charlemagne, his children, and many others who went on to contribute to the Carolingian Renaissance. He brought the great Anglo-Saxon tradition with him to create, as he once wrote, a new, and better, Athens in the Frankish kingdom, one that honored learning in devotion to God. He was rewarded by Charlemagne with the revenues from several abbeys, and at his retirement was made abbot of the important monastery of St. Martin of Tours, even though he may never have taken monastic vows and took orders no higher than the level of deacon. Even in retirement he continued to influence the cultural and religious life of his adopted homeland. Although not the creator of Carolingian minuscule, he contributed to its development and promoted its use at Tours. He wrote treatises on a variety of religious and secular subjects and produced a new edition of the Bible, now lost, which he presented to Charlemagne on Christmas day 800. On May 19, 804, Alcuin died at Tours, having composed his own epitaph: "Alcuin was my name and wisdom always my love."

A scholar and teacher, Alcuin's influence was felt in many areas during his lifetime, not the least of which was education. He wrote a treatise on the liberal arts and resurrected the system of the seven liberal arts devised by Cassiodorus. The wide range of topics that he taught include chant, grammar, rhetoric, dialectic (logic), mathematics, and astronomy. His method of teaching is preserved in a dialogue with one of Charlemagne's sons and reveals Alcuin's extraordinary pedagogical talents. It is a dialogue in which student and teacher alternate asking and answering questions. He brought encyclopedic learning, which he dispensed to his many students who, in turn, passed it along to their students. Indeed, his active and energetic mind and his comprehensive knowledge were precisely what were needed for the first generation of the Carolingian Renaissance.

Alcuin was more than the teacher to the renaissance; however, he was an important contributor. He supplied the scholars in the Frankish kingdom with numerous books from his native England and rediscovered long neglected works by Boëthius, especially some of his early works on logic, and the pseudo-Augustine. He wrote over 300 letters and over 220 poems that reveal his ability with Latin, his religious and intellectual concerns, and his own attractive personality. His poetry included light verse to students, for example, the *Lament for the Cuckoo* with its echoes of the great Roman poet Virgil, hymns, and acrostic poems to Charlemagne. He also wrote longer, more serious poems, including one on the Viking destruction of Lindisfarne abbey in 793, a life of St. Willibrord, and *The Bishops, Knights, and Saints of York*. He also wrote works of hagiography and treatises on the virtues and vices, the nature of the soul, and confession.

He was a great influence on Carolingian religious life and a staunch defender of religious orthodoxy. He reformed the liturgy of the Frankish church to bring it into line with Roman usage, revised the mass book, and composed a series of masses drawn from the Anglo-Irish tradition of piety. He advised Charlemagne on religious policy and criticized the king's brutal Saxon policy and forced baptisms. Indeed, Alcuin's influence is clearly evident in Charlemagne's second Saxon ca- pitulary of 797, which introduced a less forceful means to converting the pagan Saxons. An ardent foe of Felix of Urgel and the Adoptionist heresy, which denied that Jesus Christ in his humanity was the natural son of God, Alcuin wrote *Libri septem contra Felicem* (Seven books against Felix), which attacked the heresy, and he then presented the case against Adoptionsim at the Synod of Frankfurt in 794. It is likely that he also participated in the debate on the decisions of the Sec- ond Council of Nicaea, 787, approving veneration of icons, which were misun- derstood in the Frankish world because of a faulty translation. Although it is now believed that Theodulf of Orléans wrote the official work, the *Libri Carolini* (the *Caroline Books*), Alcuin may have had an editorial hand in their preparation and influenced their content.

Finally, it should be noted that Alcuin also influenced political life in the Frankish kingdom. He was used by Charlemagne as an ambassador to King Offa of Mercia in 790. He also frequently served on the king's council. Alcuin wrote to Charlemagne on a wide variety of subjects, including Frankish relations with the Saxons and the duties of kings and nobles. His most famous letter, however, was written in 799 and may be understood as encouraging Charlemagne to assume the imperial title. After noting that the imperial throne in Constantinople was vacant, and the holder of the throne of Peter had been attacked and depended on Charlemagne's protection, Alcuin wrote:

> Third, there is the Royal Dignity . . . in power a ruler more excellent than the aforementioned ones, in wisdom more radiant, and in grandeur more sublime. Behold, now in you alone lies the salvation of the churches of Christ. You are the avenger of crimes, the guide of those who err, the consoler of the afflicted, the uplifter of the righteous. (Riché, p. 120)

This letter clearly reveals Alcuin's understanding of both the political realities of the day and Carolingian political ideology. It reflects the discussion Alcuin and others had about the imperial bearing of Charlemagne and further demonstrates Alcuin's importance in the cultural, religious, and political developments of the age of Charlemagne.

See also: Adoptionism; Anglo-Saxons; Bede; Carolingian Dynasty; Carolingian Minus- cule; Carolingian Renaissance; Charlemagne; Einhard; Felix of Urgel; *Libri Carolini*; Louis the Pious; Saxon Capitularies; Theodulf of Orléans; Tours

Bibliography

Bullough, Donald. "Alcuin and the Kingdom of Heaven: Liturgy, Theology, and the Carolingian Age." In *Carolingian Essays,* ed. Uta-Renate Blumenthal. Washington, DC: Catholic University Press, 1983, pp. 1–69.

Duckett, Eleanor Shipley. *Alcuin, Friend of Charlemagne: His World and His Work.* New York: Macmillan, 1951.

Dutton, Paul Edward, ed. *Carolingian Civilization: A Reader.* Peterborough, ON: Broadview, 1993.

Laistner, Max L.W. *Thought and Letters in Western Europe,* A.D. *500–900.* 2nd ed. Ithaca, NY: Cornell University Press, 1957.

Mayvaert, Paul. "The Authorship of the 'Libri Carolini': Observations Prompted by a Recent Book." *Revue bénédictine* 89 (1979): 29–57.

Riché, Pierre. *The Carolingians: A Family Who Forged Europe.* Trans. Michael Idomir Allen. Philadelphia: University of Pennsylvania Press, 1993.

Wallach, Luitpold. *Alcuin and Charlemagne: Studies in Carolingian History and Literature.* Ithaca, NY: Cornell University Press, 1959.

Alemanni

A confederation of Germanic tribes or warrior bands, which may have included the Bucinobantes, Juthungi, Lentienses, and Suevi. The Alemanni first appeared in the third century in a conflict with the Roman Empire. Their name, which they may not have used, means "all men" or "all of mankind" and indicates that they were composed of many different peoples. It was also understood in a pejorative sense by their enemies to mean "half-breeds" or "newcomers." They were distinguished by their long heads, which they created by artificially deforming the skull of newborns with bandages around the head. They were often in conflict with the Roman Empire in the third century and sought to carve out settlements in imperial territory in the fourth. In the fifth century they were able to exploit imperial weakness and enter the empire, but they faced a greater challenge as the century went on from the Franks and their Merovingian dynasty. The Alemanni were ultimately absorbed by their Merovingian rivals, and despite a short period of independence, were subject also to the Carolingian dynasty.

The Alemanni first appeared, according to the Roman historian Cassius Dio, in a conflict with the Roman emperor Caracalla (r. 211–217) in 213. The Alemanni were able to take advantage of the empire during its period of crisis from 234 to 284. They were most likely part of the group of barbarians who crossed the Rhine River and other parts of the imperial frontier in the mid-third century. They were among the first groups of barbarians to take control of Roman territory and settle in parts of the empire. Throughout the mid-third century, even after some settled in the empire, the Alemanni continued to make plundering raids on imperial territory, often reaching Italy. Despite occasional success against them, the Romans were unable to stop the raids of the Alemanni because of their loose organization. They had no central king, but various warlords who led raids of plunder and pillage with loyal war bands. By the late third century, however, the Romans restored order to the empire, and the Alemanni became more settled, acting as more traditional opponents of Rome or as servants of the empire.

In the fourth and fifth centuries, the Alemanni continued their efforts to secure Roman territory. They fought actively along the Rhine and Danube frontiers of the empire, and, on occasion, enjoyed some success. But several emperors during the fourth century inflicted stunning defeats on the Alemanni, including Constantine, Julian the Apostate, and Valentinian I. In fact, Valentinian drove deep into Alemanni territory in 368 to turn back Alemanni advances into the empire. Although the emperors enjoyed victories over the Alemanni in the fourth century, they suffered defeats by their rivals in the fifth century. In 406, a large body of barbarians crossed the Rhine River during a winter freeze, and it is most likely that the Alemanni were part of that group. Their success was limited, however, by the Franks, another Germanic people, which later produced the Merovingian and Carolingian dynasties, and by imperial diplomacy. But with the movement of the Huns under Attila, the Rhine defenses were sufficiently undermined to allow the further incursion of the Alemanni.

The westward movement of the Alemanni into imperial territory was not without negative consequences for these tribes. Although they managed to settle on Roman territory, the Alemanni once again came into contact with the rising power of northern Europe, the Merovingian Franks. The conflict between these two peoples led to the eventual subjugation of the Alemanni by the Merovingians and to the conversion to Christianity of the Merovingians. According to the historian Gregory of Tours, the Alemanni fought a great battle against the Frankish Merovingian king Clovis at Tolbiac (modern Zülpich, Switzerland), which is traditionally dated 495. Gregory informs us that Clovis was losing the battle and promised to convert to Christianity if the Christian God allowed him to win the battle. Clovis won the battle and then converted to Catholic Christianity. Although the date of the battle remains controversial and the entire story of Clovis's conversion is problematic, it is certain that he incorporated the Alemanni into his ever growing kingdom. From the time of Clovis, therefore, the Alemanni were subject to the Franks.

During the sixth and seventh centuries, the Alemanni remained part of the Merovingian kingdom. The exact course of their history, however, remains uncertain because of the lack of written records about them and because of the unclear archeological record. It is likely that they participated in Merovingian military activities, including campaigns in northern Italy. The Alemanni also continued to be ruled by dukes rather than kings, and although loosely organized, codified their laws. They were able to expand their territories of settlement into southern Germany and parts of Switzerland during this period. They also, finally and only gradually, converted to Christianity. This conversion was the result of the missionary activities of St. Columban and his disciples in the later sixth century.

In the later seventh and early eighth centuries, the Alemanni regained their independence from the Merovingians. The Alemanni were able to throw off the Merovingian rule because of the turmoil in the Merovingian kingdom brought on by the decline of Merovingian power and the rise of Carolingian power. Although the Carolingian mayors of the palace Pippin of Herstal and Charles Martel were able to restore Frankish authority over the Alemanni for short periods, the Alemanni remained independent for most of the first half of the eighth century. It was only during the reign of Pippin the Short that the Alemanni were forced once again to submit, permanently this time, to Frankish power. Pippin defeated the Alemanni in two great battles in 744 and 748 and thereby reincorporated them into the kingdom. They remained subjects of the Carolingians thereafter.

See also: Attila the Hun; Carolingian Dynasty; Charles Martel; Clovis; Gregory of Tours; Huns; Merovingian Dynasty; Pippin II, Called Pippin of Herstal; Pippin III, Called Pippin the Short; Vandals

Bibliography

Bachrach, Bernard S. *Merovingian Military Organization, 481–751.* Minneapolis: University of Minnesota Press, 1972.

Bury, John B. *History of the Later Roman Empire: From the Death of Theodosius I to the Death of Justinian.* 2 Vols. 1923. Reprint, New York: Dover, 1959.

Gregory of Tours. *The History of the Franks.* Trans. Lewis Thorpe. Harmondsworth, UK: Penguin, 1974.

Wolfram, Herwig. *The Roman Empire and Its Peoples.* Trans. Thomas J. Dunlap. Berkeley: University of California Press, 1997.

Wood, Ian. *The Merovingian Kingdoms, 450–751.* London: Longman, 1994.

Alfred the Great (849–899)

The most important and influential of the Saxon kings of England, Alfred has been known as "the Great" since the 16th century. As king of Wessex he was involved in a prolonged struggle with the Danes, who invaded England almost annually until the end of Alfred's reign. His victories over the invaders, as well as the navy he created, the network of fortifications he built to defend the country, and his various military reforms greatly curtailed the threat of invasion. He also reformed the law and promoted learning in his kingdom. As the patron of learning in his kingdom, Alfred sponsored the translation of many important Christian texts and even translated some of them himself. As a warrior, legal reformer, and educator, Alfred left an important legacy for his successors.

The youngest of the five sons of the deeply religious but not very effective King Æthelwulf of Wessex—who also had one daughter—and his queen, the noble woman Osburh, Alfred was born in 849 in Wantage, Oxfordshire. Although little is known about his earliest years, it is likely that they were not marked by preparation to succeed to the throne, since Alfred's older brothers would surely have been expected to succeed to the throne before Alfred could. Asser, Alfred's biographer, does offer some information on his hero's earliest years. He says that Alfred was the most beloved of all the children of Æthelwulf and Osburh and was raised at court. In chapter 22 of his life, Asser notes that as a child Alfred was "fairer in all forms than all his brothers, and more pleasing in his looks, his words and ways." He was a skilled hunter who practiced as often as he could, and continued to enjoy hunting as an adult, even though he was afflicted with illness his whole life.

Asser notes too that Alfred was deeply religious and, as a boy and an adult, attended mass daily, prayed often, and gave alms generously. But the most remarkable thing Alfred demonstrated as a youth, and as king, was his great desire for learning. Although he did not learn to read until he was 12 and read Latin when he was older still, Alfred possessed "from his cradle a longing for wisdom." Although he learned to read only in later life, Alfred, according to Asser, "listened attentively" to Saxon poems until he could recite them from memory. Alfred's devotion to learning is revealed in a story his biographer tells of his boyhood. His mother, Osburh, promised her sons that whichever one of them could learn a book of Saxon poetry would receive the book as a prize. Alfred asked if she really meant to give one of them the book, and she replied that she would. Alfred had his master read the book to him and then he repeated it to his mother.

Alfred's zeal for learning may have been inspired by two trips to Rome that he took early in his life. In 853, Alfred paid his first visit to the Holy See, where he was received by Pope Leo IV and underwent a special ceremony of investiture. According to both Asser's life and the *Anglo-Saxon Chronicle,* Alfred was anointed with the kingship by the pope—a most unlikely occurrence because of Alfred's older sons. It is more likely that Alfred was anointed as Leo's godson. In 855 Alfred made a pilgrimage to Rome with his father, who stayed there a year. The journey to Rome and back went, as had the previous trip, through the Carolingian realm. On the return during the second trip, Æthelwulf, whose first wife had died, married Judith, the daughter of Charles the Bald, at whose court the pilgrims stayed. Alfred certainly came into contact with the dazzling culture of the court of Charles the Bald on this trip, which most likely left a lasting impression on a young boy who had a great thirst for knowledge. He may also have become aware of the great legacy of Charlemagne during this visit to the court of the great king's grandson. Charles the Bald had sought to revive the glories of the Carolingian Renaissance, and Alfred's exposure to those glories would surely have reinforced his own interests in learning. When he became king, Alfred attempted to revive learning and letters in his kingdom as the great Frankish rulers had in theirs.

Alfred's path to the kingship was a most indirect one, because his older brothers had precedence over him to the throne. In fact, one of his brothers, Æthelbald, claimed his right to the succession while Æthelwulf was on pilgrimage in 855–856. Æthelwulf submitted to his son's demands by dividing the kingdom and ruling with his eldest son until Æthelwulf died in 858. Two other brothers preceded Alfred to the throne in the 860s. In that decade the Danish threat became increasingly serious and was the major focus of the king's activities. In 868, for example, Alfred joined his brother King Ethelred in support of the king of Mercia, Buhred, in a battle against invading Danes at Nottingham. The Danes continued their raids and had great success against various Saxon rulers, killing Edmund, king of East Anglia, in one engagement.

Alfred succeeded his brother Æthelred on the throne in 871 and began the difficult struggle with Danish invaders that lasted most of his reign. In the first year of his kingship, according to the *Anglo-Saxon Chronicle,* Alfred fought numerous battles against various Danish warrior bands and although he won an important victory at Wilton against a much larger force, in all likelihood he lost most of the battles. In 872, to stem the tide of invasion, Alfred purchased a truce from the Danes, which allowed him time to strengthen his hold on the kingdom and prepare for future attacks. Alfred's truce kept the Danes away from his kingdom for several years, but the surrounding kingdoms were not as fortunate. In the 870s East Anglia, Mercia, and Northumbria were overrun by Danish armies, and at one point the Mercian king was forced to flee to Rome in the face of the onslaught.

The Danes mounted a renewed challenge on Alfred's kingdom in 876. The next few years were the most difficult of Alfred's entire reign, and the Danes nearly took over his kingdom of Wessex. Indeed, in 878 the Danes drove Alfred from his kingdom to the island of Athelney. This was a dark time for Alfred and the English, but it was also the moment (but not the last) that Alfred showed his true greatness. Marshaling his forces from his base on Athelney, Alfred began to attack Danish forces over the course of seven weeks. These attacks culminated in a major victory over the Danes at the Battle of Eddington, breaking their army and driving them from the field. The Danes and their king, Guthrum, agreed to leave Wessex and convert to Christianity. Alfred's great victory saved his kingdom from occupation by the Danes, but it did not end the Danish threat. Guthrum merely turned his attention to other parts of England, and Alfred himself faced further challenges later in his reign.

During the 880s, Alfred strengthened his position in England. He extended his authority over other English kingdoms, most importantly Mercia. In 886 Alfred took control of London, an event of such importance to the English that, as the *Anglo-Saxon Chronicle* notes, "all the English people not under subjection to the Danes submitted to him" (Whitelock). Alfred also reorganized his military, so that he would be better prepared for future attacks by the Danes from land or sea. He reformed the fyrd, the traditional peasant militia of Anglo-Saxon England that was essential for local defense. Useful as the fyrd was for local defense, its greatest weakness was the unwillingness of peasant soldiers to serve outside their county for significant lengths of time. Alfred could not resolve the problem of distance, but he was able to keep the fyrd in the field by dividing service into six-month terms and mobilizing half the peasantry for each term. He also built a series of burghs, fortified settlements throughout the kingdom that could serve as defensive positions or as bases of further operation and counterattack. Situated at key points throughout the realm, the burghs were primarily military garrisons, but some had administrative and financial functions, roles that became more important as time went on. Alfred also built a fleet of ships to meet the Danes on the open sea. The ships were larger than anything the Danes had and were certainly a match for the Danish ships.

Alfred's military reforms were an important precaution, because he faced further attacks in the 890s. In 892 an invasion force crossed the channel from Francia in 250 ships, followed by a second fleet of 80 ships. Over the next several years, Alfred once again was forced to defend his kingdom and once again was successful. From 893 to 896 Alfred waged a series of offensives against the invading Danes, on occasion capturing their camps and forcing them to flee before being totally destroyed. In 896 Alfred's various military reforms served him to good end when he trapped a large Danish navy on the Lea River. Building fortifications and thereby cutting off their escape route, Alfred forced the Danes to abandon their ships and scatter. Although this victory did not end the Danish threat, which continued into the 10th and 11th centuries, it did provide a degree of peace and stability in the kingdom, which Alfred was able to enjoy until his death on October 26, 899.

Alfred's legacy, however, is not limited to his defense against the Danes and military reforms. Indeed, in some ways, his legal and literary contributions are more important than his other achievements. It was probably in the 890s that Alfred issued his compilation of the law. Building on the precedents of kings of Wessex, Kent, and Mercia, Alfred issued a legal code that was intended to cover all the English, even though he referred to himself only as the king of the West Saxons. His use of oaths of loyalty in the code suggests Carolingian influence as well, but it was his genius that gave the code its final shape. He clearly borrowed from his predecessors, but introduced restrictions on the feud, the duty of subjects to their lords, and, as fitting a deeply religious king like Alfred, legislation protecting the church. His religious convictions were evident also in his concerns with learning and literacy in his kingdom. Alfred, lamenting the extreme poverty of learning in his kingdom, undertook the effort to translate a series of important Christian works into the Anglo-Saxon tongue, because many people in his kingdom could read their native tongue but could not read Latin, the language of learning.

With his support translations of various works appeared, including Bede's *History of the English Church and People*, Pope Gregory the Great's *Dialogues*, a martyrology, and a work by St. Augustine of Hippo's supporter, Orosius, *Seven Books against the Pagans*. Alfred himself was responsible for a number of translations, including Pope Gregory's *Pastoral Rule* (*Regula pastoralis*), which Alfred translated as the *Pastoral Care*, Boethius's *Consolation of Philosophy*, and Augustine's *Soliloquies*. The translations by Alfred vary in their loyalty to the original. The work of Gregory was closely translated, but for the works of Boethius and Augustine Alfred took great liberty with the text. He introduced new ideas and questions in the translation of Boethius, and he added material from the Bible, Gregory the Great, and other works by Augustine to the *Soliloquies*. These works reveal the breadth of Alfred's interests, and they continued to be copied into the 12th century. It was also during Alfred's reign that the first compilation of the *Anglo-Saxon Chronicle* was made.

Alfred's contributions to the history of Anglo-Saxon England were numerous and varied. Even though his efforts to revive learning among the people were modest, his translations remain of interest today and had an important impact on

Alfred Jewel, with King Alfred, 849–899, King of Wessex, late ninth century, Somerset. (Ashmolean Museum, University of Oxford, UK/The Bridgeman Art Library)

scholars long after his death. His defense of the kingdom against the Danes provided England important infrastructure to continue the struggle after his death, even though it was to be nearly two centuries before the Danes were finally expelled from England and the threat of invasion ended. Alfred truly was one of the great kings of England.

See also: Anglo-Saxon Chronicle; Anglo-Saxons; Asser; Bede; Boethius; Carolingian Dynasty; Charlemagne; Charles the Bald; Mercia; Offa of Mercia; Wessex

Bibliography

Hodges, Richard. *The Anglo-Saxon Achievement: Archeology and the Beginnings of English Society.* London: Duckworth, 1989.

Keynes, Simon. "The British Isles: England, 700–900." In *The New Cambridge Medieval History,* vol. 2. Ed. Rosamond McKitterick. Cambridge: Cambridge University Press, 1995.

Keynes, Simon, and Michael Lapidge, trans. *Alfred the Great: Asser's Life of King Alfred and Other Contemporary Sources.* Harmondsworth, UK: Penguin, 1983.

Sawyer, Peter H. *From Roman Britain to Norman England.* 2nd ed. London: Routledge, 1998.

Smyth, Alfred. *King Alfred the Great.* Oxford: Oxford University Press, 1995.

Stenton, Frank M. *Anglo-Saxon England.* 3rd ed. Oxford: Clarendon, 1971.

Sturdy, David J. *Alfred the Great.* London: Constable, 1995.

Whitelock, Dorothy, ed. *The Anglo-Saxon Chronicle.* Westport, CT: Greenwood, 1986.

Amalaswintha (d. 535)

Gothic princess and daughter of the important Ostrogothic king of Italy, Theodoric the Great. As regent, Amalaswintha was active in the political life of Italy after Theodoric's death, and she promoted her personal interests and those of her immediate family against enemies in her extended family and among the Gothic nobility in Italy. Her rivalry with other Gothic leaders over control of her son, Athalaric, and then for control of the kingdom after Athalaric's death brought her great difficulties and increased her long-standing pro-Roman political sensibilities. Her relationship with the Byzantine emperor Justinian brought her support in Italy but, if the sixth-century Byzantine historian Procopius is to be believed, the enmity of the great empress Theodora. A possible pawn in Justinian's grand political designs, Amalaswintha drew Justinian further into Italian affairs, and her death led to the Byzantine invasion of the peninsula and the Gothic Wars of Justinian.

The daughter of Theodoric, the most powerful barbarian king of the early sixth century, Amalaswintha was an important figure in Italian political life even before her father's death in 526. Her marriage in 515 to the Spanish Visigoth, Eutharic, was part of Theodoric's efforts to preserve and extend his control over the Goths and in Italy. Eutharic's marriage to Amalaswintha made him part of Theodoric's family and allowed the great king to appoint his son-in-law as his successor, thus eliminating Theodoric's own nephew from the succession and from power in general. Although it caused problems after 526 for Amalaswintha, Eutharic's death in 522–523 hindered Theodoric's plans little, because Eutharic had provided an heir, Athalaric, who, jointly with Amalaswintha, was designated successor to the throne. Moreover, although it was not apparently political, Amalaswintha's first-rate education served her well during her father's lifetime and after. And in fact her education did have political overtones because it was a traditional Roman education; Theodoric may have provided her with a Roman education because of his interest in establishing harmonious Roman-Gothic relations.

Before his death, Theodoric appointed Athalaric as his successor. In 526 Athalaric was still a minor, and his mother assumed the regency. The opening years of Amalaswintha's regency were relatively peaceful, and her abilities were recognized by many, including Procopius, who spoke highly of her courage and intelligence. She sought to restore good relations between Goths and Romans, which had broken down in the last years of her father's reign, especially over Theodoric's imprisonment and execution of Boethius. She restored the confiscated estates of Boethius to his family and sought the counsel of the Roman Senate. To promote good relations with the Romans, she sent a letter to the emperor in Constantinople, seeking to bury old hatreds, and provided her son with a Roman education. To placate the Gothic nobility, she sought to improve relations with other barbarian peoples in the former Western Roman Empire. Ostrogothic armies enjoyed success in 530 against a mixed barbarian force on the northeastern frontier, and Amalaswintha pursued improved relations with the Burgundians. The alliance collapsed, however, in the early 530s as a result of her failure to send the army against the Merovingian Franks when they invaded and conquered the Burgundians. The situation on the kingdom's northern frontier worsened as a result of this failure, and it may also have contributed to her problems with the Gothic nobility in the early 530s.

Despite her early successes and the peace in the kingdom in the opening years of the regency, Amalaswintha faced a grave crisis in 532–533 that nearly ended her power. As her son approached his majority, a rival, possibly anti-Roman, faction in the kingdom attempted to take control of her son and the kingdom. One of the criticisms her enemies raised was that Athalaric was being made "too Roman" and needed to learn good Gothic values. The young king was persuaded by the rebels and supported them against his mother. In the face of this crisis, Amalaswintha sent a letter to Justinian seeking political asylum. The emperor invited the queen to Constantinople and sent a ship with 40,000 pounds of gold to rescue her. Amalaswintha sent the royal treasury to a palace provided by Justinian, but decided to stay and fight for control of her kingdom. The Frankish threat to the frontier provided the queen with the pretext to send the three leaders of the revolt to the frontier. Once they were away from court, she had them killed and as a result saved her position.

Although she secured her hold on power, Amalaswintha faced continued difficulties over the next few years, worsened perhaps by the death of her son in 534. She hoped to resolve the crisis by remarrying, and in 534 she married her hostile family rival, Theodohad, made him coregent, and declared herself queen. Allowed to mint coins and to assume the royal title, Theodohad had to recognize the authority of Amalaswintha and follow her commands. But Theodohad, along with the families of the murdered rebels of 532, had other ideas. They plotted together against Amalaswintha, and in April 535 she was captured and imprisoned on an island in Lake Bolsena.

The rough treatment of the queen brought strong protests from the imperial court at Constantinople, because she had remained neutral during Justinian's invasion of the Vandal kingdom in North Africa and had allowed the Byzantine commander, Belisarius, to use Sicily as a staging ground for his armies. Certainly, too, Justinian's earlier support for Amalaswintha and the long-standing good relations between the two reinforced the emperor's desire to protect her. Moreover, according to Procopius, the emperor was tired of his wife, Theodora, and was highly attracted to the young and intelligent Gothic queen, who would have provided the emperor with great wealth and access to Italy, which he hoped to reattach to imperial control. Procopius further suggested that although Justinian publicly demanded the release of the queen, Theodora secretly plotted her murder with agents in Italy. Although Procopius's version of events is unlikely, Justinian did support the queen against her rivals, and her murder was a public affront to the emperor, especially after Theodohad assured him that no harm would come to her. Her murder provided Justinian with the justification he needed to invade Italy, defeat the Goths, and reunite the old heartland of the empire with the Eastern Empire.

See also: Belisarius; Boethius; Constantinople; Justinian; Ostrogoths; Procopius; Theodora; Theodoric the Great

Bibliography

Bury, John B. *History of the Later Roman Empire: From the Death of Theodosius I to the Death of Justinian.* Vol. 2. 1923. Reprint, New York: Dover, 1959.

Heather, Peter. *The Goths.* Oxford: Blackwell, 1996.

Llewellyn, Peter. *Rome in the Dark Ages.* New York: Barnes and Noble, 1993.

Procopius. *The History of the Wars; Secret History.* 4 Vols. Trans. Henry Bronson Dewing. Cambridge, MA: Harvard University Press, 1914–1924.

Thiébaux, Marcelle, ed. and trans. *The Writings of Medieval Women: An Anthology.* 2nd ed. New York: Garland, 1994.

Wolfram, Herwig. *The Roman Empire and its Germanic Peoples.* Trans. Thomas J. Dunlap. Berkeley: University of California Press, 1997.

Ambrose of Milan (c. 339–397)

One of the Latin Church Fathers, Ambrose was bishop of Milan and a major influence on the political and religious life of his own day. His relations with the emperor Theodosius the Great helped define church-state relations in the late Roman Empire as well as in the centuries to come, and Ambrose himself helped shape the emperor's religious policy. Well versed in Roman administrative traditions, Ambrose was a powerful and effective bishop whose practices as the bishop of Milan provided a model for later church leaders and helped establish Catholic Christianity as the religion of the empire. His personal example of chastity as well as his powerful intellect inspired many in his days, most importantly Augustine of Hippo. Well educated in both the Greek and Latin literary traditions, Ambrose was the author of numerous sermons, exegetical works, and even hymns that contributed greatly to the formation of Christian theology.

Ambrose, the second of three children, was born in Gaul around 339. His father, also named Ambrose, was the praetorian prefect of Gaul and was the descendant of a long line of Roman administrators as well as Christian martyrs. This legacy would shape the younger Ambrose's future as he adopted the Catholic Christianity of his ancestors and inherited a deep appreciation for and understanding of Roman administrative traditions. On his father's death in 354, Ambrose and the rest of his family moved to Rome. In Rome, his older sister, Marcellina, adopted a life of celibacy and prayer, and Ambrose pursued his education. He studied the traditional Roman curriculum, which emphasized the liberal arts, especially rhetoric and grammar—skills necessary for success in the Roman public arena. Unlike some of his contemporaries, Ambrose was deeply immersed in the Greek literary tradition as well as the Latin, preparation that would draw upon when he later turned to theological work. Clearly an excellent student, Ambrose developed a reputation for eloquence that served him well as he began his career in the Roman courts. His ability to argue cases effectively soon attracted the attention of powerful figures, and in 369 the emperor Valentinian (r. 364–375) appointed Ambrose the consular governor of Aemelia-Liguria, with residence in Milan, the western capital of the empire.

At the time of his appointment, Milan was in great turmoil, divided along religious lines between Catholic and Arian Christians. The situation worsened in 374, when the reigning bishop died and a successor had to be found. Responsible for maintaining order during the election, Ambrose was himself popularly acclaimed the new bishop because of his evenhanded rule as governor. Although he held no position in the church and had yet to be baptized (it was not uncommon to put off baptism until later in life at that time), Ambrose reluctantly accepted the office and was baptized and ordained before assuming the post he would hold until his death in 397.

During his long career as bishop, Ambrose had a profound impact on the political and religious developments of his day. Residing in the western imperial capital provided Ambrose great prestige as well as access to the leaders of the empire and often influenced their decisions. He was instrumental in the decision to remove the Altar of Victory from the city of Rome in 382 and encouraged the decision to declare Catholic Christianity the official religion of the empire in 381. At times, however, Ambrose found himself at odds with Roman rulers and was forced to defend himself and his Catholic Christianity. In 386, Justina, the mother of the young emperor Valentinian II (r. 375–392) sent imperial troops against the bishop as part of her effort to impose Arian Christianity in the Western Empire. Besieged in his cathedral, Ambrose refused to back down, upholding his Catholic faith, and the soldiers withdrew rather than massacre the bishop and his flock. He also took a more active approach in his relations with the emperors, supporting Valentinian in his struggles against a usurper. More importantly, he exerted his authority over Theodosius the Great. On one occasion, Ambrose challenged the emperor's decision in regard to the treatment of the Jews in the empire. Following the destruction of a synagogue in Mesopotamia by a group of Christians lead by their bishop in 388, Theodosius decided to punish the bishop and Christians and force them to make restitution for the damage. Ambrose, however, intervened on two separate occasion, threatening the emperor with spiritual penalties and forcing Theodosius to rescind his orders. In a more famous and influential episode, Ambrose again asserted his authority as bishop over Theodosius. In response to a riot in Thessalonica that challenged imperial authority and the local governor, Theodosius ordered the massacre of some 7,000 people in 390. Ambrose humbled the emperor, proclaiming a ban of excommunication against him if he did not perform public penance for his murderous order. A devout Christian, Theodosius submitted to episcopal authority, providing a precedent for later supporters of the powers of the church over the state. Despite these controversies, Ambrose and Theodosius remained on good terms, and the bishop delivered a moving eulogy at the emperor's funeral in 395.

An able administrator and skilled politician, Ambrose was also a leading figure in the development of Christian belief and practice. Along with his efforts to promote Catholic Christianity throughout the empire, Ambrose wrote a number of hymns and sermons, including a series of homilies compiled as the *Hexameron*, a commentary on creation. His writings include an influential guidebook on Christian life and morality, *De Officiis Ministrorum*, modeled on a work of the great Roman writer Cicero (106–43 BC); a commentary on the Gospel of Luke; expositions on the sacraments of baptism and the Eucharist and the mysteries of the faith; and a series of ethical works. He also prepared a work in praise of virginity, which he dedicated to his sister Marcellina; Ambrose himself lived a chaste life, which proved, along with his great rhetorical skills, an inspiration to Augustine of Hippo. And it was Augustine who noted that Ambrose read silently, a most unusual practice in the antiquity when most read aloud.

See also: Arianism; Augustine of Hippo, St.; Milan; Theodosius the Great

Bibliography

Brown, Peter. *The Body and Society: Men, Women, and Sexual Renunciation in Early Christianity.* New York: Columbia University Press, 1988.

Brown, Peter. *The Cult of the Saints: Its Rise and Function in Latin Christianity.* Chicago: University of Chicago Press, 1982.

Liebeschuetz, J.H.W.G., ed., and Wolfe Liebeschuetz, trans. *Ambrose of Milan: Political Letters and Speeches.* Liverpool, UK: Liverpool University Press, 2010.

McLynn, Neil B. *Ambrose of Milan: Church and Court in a Christian Capital.* Berkeley: University of California Press, 1994.

Moorhead, John. *Ambrose: Church and Society in the Late Roman World.* New York: Longman, 1999.

Williams, Daniel H. *Ambrose of Milan and the End of the Arian-Nicene Conflict.* Oxford: Oxford University Press, 1995.

Ammianus Marcellinus (c. 330–395)

Last important pagan historian of Rome, and the first to write a major history since Tacitus (c. 56–120). Although nearly half of his work, the *Res gestae* (Deeds done), has been lost, Ammianus remains one of the most important writers for the history of the Roman Empire and the movement of the Germanic peoples in the fourth century. Inspired by Tacitus, whose work he emulated, Ammianus provides a unique view, especially compared with Christian historians of the time, of the late Roman Empire. In some ways unlike his Christian contemporaries, Ammianus believed that "Rome will last as long as mankind shall endure." Indeed, even though he chronicled the crises of the late fourth century, including the catastrophic defeat of imperial armies by the Visigoths led by Alaric, Ammianus preserved the characteristic faith of the Romans in the empire.

Little is known precisely about Ammianus other than what is revealed in his work of history. He describes himself as a "former soldier and a Greek" in the pages of a history that was written in Latin. He was probably born in Antioch in Syria around 330. He served in the 350s as an officer in both Gaul and Persia under the emperor Constantius II (r. 337–361). His military background enabled him to write effectively about military matters in his history. He later joined the campaigns of the emperor Julian the Apostate (r. 361–363), the nephew of Constantine the Great, against Persia in 363. Julian was raised as a Christian by his uncle but rejected that upbringing in favor of traditional Roman religion, which he actively promoted to the detriment of the Christian church. Although he had earlier enjoyed military success, Julian failed in his attack on Persia and was killed near Baghdad while retreating. Ammianus retired from military service after the failed Persian campaign and traveled widely across the Mediterranean, spending time especially in Egypt and Greece. Sometime in the 380s, he settled in Rome, where he wrote his history, probably in 390.

Written in the last decade of the fourth century, the history of Ammianus began in 96, where Tacitus left off, and covered events down to 378. The work was composed in 31 books, but only books 14 to 31 have survived. This section, however, covered the years 354–378, the period of the author's active military career, and contains much eyewitness reporting. The work is both a personal memoir and testimony and a defense of the career of Emperor Julian. The history contains not only personal observations but also many important observations on military and political affairs, as well as the reflections of a tolerant late Roman pagan. The work of Ammianus is often colorful; it contains numerous details of daily life and scathing accounts of the flaws of Christian and pagan leaders of Rome. Like Tacitus, Ammianus criticized the moral weaknesses and political foolishness of his contemporaries and wrote in a highly rhetorical style. His work reflects the attitudes of a late Roman soldier and noble who valued the traditional Roman virtues of moderation and who believed in the permanence of Roman power. Indeed, his account of the terrible Roman defeat by the Visigoths at Hadrianople in 378 reveals his belief that the empire would recover from this defeat and eventually triumph over its enemies, just as earlier Romans had defeated their great rival Hannibal after his victory at Cannae (216 BC).

Ammianus not only left important information about the Romans and their defeat by the Visigoths but also about the barbarian invaders themselves. He describes the origins and background of the Goths and the extent of their territory. He also describes the origins of the Huns, their nomadic lifestyle, their customs and manners, and their success against the Goths. Although the surviving portion of the history covers only a short period, Ammianus's work is an important source of information on Romans and barbarians in the later fourth century.

See also: Alaric; Hadrianople, Battle of; Huns; Visigoths

Bibliography

Ammianus Marcellinus. *Ammianus Marcellinus.* Trans. John C. Rolfe. Cambridge, MA: Harvard University Press, 1971–1972.

Barnes, Timothy D. *Ammianus Marcellinus and the Representation of Historical Reality.* Ithaca, NY: Cornell University Press, 1998.

Cameron, Averil, and Peter Garnsey, eds. *The Late Empire, A.D. 337–425. Cambridge Ancient History.* Vol. 13. Cambridge: Cambridge University Press, 1998.

Hunt, David, and Jan Willem Drijvers, eds. *The Late Roman World and Its Historian: Interpreting Ammianus Marcellinus.* London: Routledge, 1999.

Matthews, John. *The Roman Empire of Ammianus Marcellinus.* Baltimore, MD: Johns Hopkins University Press, 1989.

Wolfram, Herwig. *The Roman Empire and Its Germanic Peoples.* Trans. Thomas J. Dunlap. Berkeley: University of California Press, 1997.

Angilbert, St. (c. 740–814)

An important figure during the reign of Charlemagne, Angilbert was one of the great king's court scholars and was a central figure in what is called the Carolingian Renaissance. He was given the nickname Homer by Charlemagne and the other court scholars because of his talents as a poet. He also served as an ambassador for the king and was the lay abbot of St. Riquier, which he received from Charlemagne and where he introduced important liturgical reforms. He was also the lover of Charlemagne's daughter, Bertha, with whom he had two sons, Hartnid and the historian Nithard.

Angilbert was a Frank of noble parentage, and he and his family, according to the mid-ninth century historian Nithard, were held in high esteem by Charlemagne. Nithard's view is confirmed by Angilbert's place at Charlemagne's court. Angilbert obtained an excellent education and may have been a student of Alcuin, the leading Carolingian court scholar and close advisor to Charlemagne, at one point. His poetry and liturgical reforms, along with his gift of over 200 manuscripts to the library at St. Riquier, indicate his interest in learning and support for the religious and educational reforms of Charlemagne. His later activities at St. Riquier further demonstrate his concern for learning; he seems to have established, in conformity with Charlemagne's capitulary *Admonitio Generalis,* a school to educate the local boys. He also served as Charlemagne's ambassador to Rome on two occasions. In 792, he was sent to Rome with copies of one of the Saxon capitularies, sections of the *Libri Carolini* (Caroline Books), and the heretical bishop Felix of Urgel, all of which he was to submit to Pope Hadrian I for papal consideration. Angilbert went to Rome a second time in 796 to deliver a great portion of the spoils of the Avar Ring, the Avar capital captured by Carolingian armies in 796, to St. Peter and his representative, Pope Leo III.

As court scholar and abbot of an important monastery, Angilbert assumed a key position in Charlemagne's kingdom and promoted the great ruler's educational and religious ideals. He was a poet of great talent, whose work provided a glimpse into the "court school" of Charlemagne. His poem to the king (*Ad Carolum regem*) portrays the king and his courtiers in discussion with the king, who bestows favors on those around him, especially to his children, and is himself a great lover of poetry. The poem also reveals the hustle and bustle of the court, as well as giving sketches of the court's members. Charlemagne is praised in the poem and his construction of the church at Aix-la-Chapelle is described with reference to Matthew16:18—"On this rock I will build my church." Angilbert's poetry could also be quite personal and touching, as in one short poem sent to the court to inquire about his young son.

Angilbert's activities as abbot of St. Riquier were designed to further the religious goals of Charlemagne. The abbot introduced new wrinkles to the liturgy at the monastery, organized elaborate religious processions, and formed the monks into three shifts to pray continuously for the salvation of the emperor. He also undertook an extensive building program at the monastery and acquired a large number of saints' relics for the community of St. Riquier. His support for the literary, educational, and religious reforms of Charlemagne make Angilbert an important example of the success of the Carolingian Renaissance.

See also: *Admonitio Generalis*; Alcuin of York; Capitularies; Carolingian Dynasty; Carolingian Renaissance; Charlemagne; Franks; Hadrian I, Pope; Leo III, Pope; Nithard

Bibliography

Laistner, Max L. W. *Thought and Letters in Western Europe, A.D. 500 to 900.* 2nd ed. Ithaca, NY: Cornell University Press, 1976.

McKitterick, Rosamond. *Charlemagne: The Formation of a European Identity.* Cambridge: Cambridge University Press, 2008.

Riché, Pierre. *The Carolingians: A Family Who Forged Europe.* Trans. Michael Idomir Allen. Philadelphia: University of Pennsylvania Press, 1993.

Scholz, Bernhard Walter, trans. *Carolingian Chronicles: Royal Frankish Annals and Nithard's History.* Ann Arbor: University of Michigan Press, 1972.

Sullivan, Richard. *Aix-La-Chapelle in the Age of Charlemagne.* Norman: University of Oklahoma Press, 1974.

Anglo-Saxon Chronicle

The most important source for the history of Anglo-Saxon England, especially for the period from the mid-ninth century until the fall of the Anglo-Saxons to William the Conqueror in 1066, the *Anglo-Saxon Chronicle* also provides useful information on the development of the English language. It survives in seven manuscripts, some of which include both Old English and Latin entries, and its accounts are arranged as annals, or year-by-year summaries of events.

The *Chronicle,* including both its earliest versions and most complete later versions, covers the history of England and the Anglo-Saxons from the first-century

BC until 1154. Events covered by the *Chronicle* include Julius Caesar's invasion of England, the Anglo-Saxon invasions, and the deeds of the Anglo-Saxon kings. Although called the *Anglo-Saxon Chronicle,* the focus of the annals is the West Saxon kings, with occasional mention of events in Mercia and on the European continent. The first version, which appeared during the reign of Alfred the Great in the late ninth century and was known to Asser, the biographer of Alfred, focuses on the history of the West Saxon kings, beginning with the fifth-century King Cerdic and ending with King Aethelwulf and his sons. Although the work covers a broad span of time, the period that receives the best and fullest treatment is that after 850.

After the first version, the manuscript tradition divided into several versions, which do not always treat events in the same fashion, some versions of the *Chronicle* treating events more fully than others. Major events, like Alfred's campaigns against invading Vikings, however, often receive similar coverage in all the versions. The continuations of the *Chronicle* lasted until 1154, covering the events of the 10th and early 11th centuries with little detail but offering more depth for the later 11th and 12th centuries. It provides useful discussion of William's conquest in 1066, and one version offers a brief and bitter summary of events of the year.

The sources used by the compilers of the *Chronicle* vary. Works by Jerome and Isidore of Seville were used in the preparation of the early material covered by the annals; also useful for the early period was a Latin translation of the *Ecclesiastical History* of Eusebius. Other sources used for the preparation of the *Chronicle* were the *Liber Pontificalis* (Book of the Popes), genealogies, northern and West Saxon annals, Frankish annals, lists of kings and bishops, and, most probably, oral material. The most important source, and one that helped shape the organizational structure of the annals, was Bede's *History of the English Church and People.*

See also: Alfred the Great; Anglo-Saxons; Bede; Isidore of Seville; Wessex

Bibliography

Whitelock, Dorothy, ed. *The Anglo-Saxon Chronicle.* Westport, CT: Greenwood, 1986.

Anglo-Saxons

Germanic peoples who invaded England in the fifth century, the Anglo-Saxons formed enduring institutions and cultural and religious traditions that remained an important part of English society even after their ultimate defeat by William the Conqueror in 1066. Coming from various points on the European continent, the bands that formed the Anglo-Saxon people entered England during the mid-fifth century. The exact details of the invasions and conquest of England by the Anglo-Saxons, however, remain uncertain and shrouded in legend. Indeed, one of the greatest legends of English history, the legend of King Arthur, is rooted in the history of the invasions. Although the details of the origins of the Anglo-Saxons in England are unclear, the later details of their history are not. In brief, they formed a number of smaller kingdoms that gradually coalesced into a more unified realm. They welcomed Christianity, developed sophisticated political and cultural traditions, faced the challenge from the Danes, and, finally, submitted to the Normans.

According to the Anglo-Saxon historian and monk Bede who wrote in the eighth century, the origins of the Anglo-Saxons are to be found in northern Europe. Bede identifies three main groups of invaders in his history of the English church and people: Angles, Jutes, and Saxons. He notes that the Jutes came from parts of modern Denmark and inhabited the kingdom of Kent and the Isle of Wight. The Saxons were from lands between the Elbe and Ems Rivers and established kingdoms in Essex, Sussex, and Wessex. The Angles settled in the kingdoms of East Anglia, Mercia, and Northumbria and came originally from lands lying between those of the Jutes and Saxons. Although these three groups are traditionally recognized as the conquerors of Roman Britain, they were most likely accompanied by other Germanic peoples. The Frisians, who lived along the coast of northern Europe, were probably among those who joined the invaders. Indeed, it is likely that many people living along the coast from the modern Netherlands to Denmark were involved in the invasions, a group that may have even included the Swedes.

The invasion of Britain began in the confusion that attended the Roman withdrawal from the island and the collapse of the Western Empire. According to the earliest accounts, those of Gildas (d. mid-sixth century) and, especially, Bede, the invasions were part of the religious history of the island. For Gildas the invaders were ignorant barbarians who were to be opposed by faithful Christians, but for Bede, they were punishment sent by God to chastise the natives of Britain. In any event, the invasions most likely began in the mid-fifth century, about a generation after the withdrawal of imperial troops from England in 410. Shortly after that withdrawal, the people of England had become subject to raids by Scots and Picts to the north. To deal with these raids, according to the traditional account, the British leader Vortigern invited groups of Angles or Saxons to come to England to serve as mercenaries in defense of the region from outsiders. But once having expelled the raiders, the Angles and Saxons, led by the brothers Hengist and Horsa, turned against their masters and began the conquest of England.

Over the course of the next century, Angles, Saxons, and other groups gradually took control of the island, despite the possible appearance of a leader of resistance, later to be known as King Arthur. Indeed, by the late fifth century the various tribes had established themselves throughout most of the eastern half of the island, from the Humber River in the north to the Thames in the south. It was at this point that "King Arthur" may have appeared and slowed down the process of Anglo-Saxon penetration of the island. But this was at most a temporary setback for the Anglo-Saxons, who were not only successful warriors but also farmers and shepherds who laid claim to the land and slowly colonized England at the same time that they fought the native population. During the sixth century the various groups of Anglo-Saxons formed what is traditionally termed the heptarchy. The famed seven kingdoms of Anglo-Saxon England—Kent, Sussex, Essex, Wessex, East Anglia, Mercia, and Northumbria—struggled for predominance throughout the Anglo-Saxon period, and from time to time a ruler of one of these kingdoms managed to establish hegemony over the other six. For a time the kingdom of Mercia predominated, and later the kingdom of Wessex provided leadership and unified much of the island, in part due to its most important ruler, Alfred the Great.

Although the traditional designation of heptarchy suggests a degree of equality among the seven kingdoms, such equality seldom existed, and there were smaller units, like the subkingdom of Deira, which formed part of Northumbria, that were greater than some of the kingdoms of the heptarchy. Moreover, the kingdoms of Essex and Sussex were negligible powers, and already in the seventh century, the kingdom of Mercia had become the leading power of the south. Indeed, under its great king, Penda, Mercia undertook a belligerent and expansive policy that culminated in Mercian hegemony in England. He successfully extended Mercian power over parts of central England and even exacted tribute from the king of Northumbria, Oswy. His death in battle against Oswy slowed, but did not stop, the expansion of the kingdom. In the generation after his death, Christianity was established in Mercia, and Northumbrian overlordship was ended.

In the eighth century, Mercia reached its greatest heights of power under the kings Æthelbald (r. 716–757) and, especially, Offa. Although he only gradually established his control in Mercia and the rest of England after the murder of Æthelbald, Offa created the most impressive realm before Alfred. He brought much of England from the Humber River to the English Channel under his control, subjugated lesser kings to his authority, and married daughters to kings in Northumbria and Wessex. He built an extensive dyke along the frontier with Wales, reformed the coinage, issued laws, and enjoyed good relations with and the respect of Charlemagne and Pope Hadrian I. Following his death in 796, however, the kingdom fell into gradual decline under the assault of the Vikings and the rise of the power of Wessex.

As Mercian power declined in the wake of Offa's death, the ascendancy of Wessex began. In the early ninth century, Egbert (r. 802–839) ended Mercian dominance of Wessex and expelled the Mercians from parts of Wessex. He defeated the Mercian king Beornwulf in battle in 825 and broke the power of the rival kingdom. He managed to extend his authority over Essex, Sussex, and Kent, and even conquered and controlled Mercia for a short time. His successors, however, faced an even greater challenge than that posed by the kings of Mercia. Indeed, even before Egbert's death, Danes began raiding the English countryside. Over the next several generations the raids turned into large-scale invasions, and the Danes conquered large sections of England. Wessex withstood the onslaught, and its kings forged marriage pacts with their defeated rivals in Mercia to better withstand the assault. In 865, the situation became critical, as Danish pressure increased and Danish armies seized much of England outside Wessex.

The efforts of Æthelred I (r. 865–871) and, especially, Alfred halted the Danish advance. Indeed, after some initial setbacks, Alfred took back control of much of England below the Humber from the Danes and was recognized as king of all the English not subject to the Danes. In the early 10th century, Edward the Elder completed his father's struggle with the Danes and rid the island of their influence for much of the 10th century. Alfred not only enjoyed success against the Danes but also restructured English defense and military organization. He was a great patron of learning and personally translated a number of important religious texts. He also worked closely with the church and elevated the ideal of kingship. One of the greatest of all English kings, Alfred unified England under the authority of the kingdom of Wessex, and his dynasty ruled England until the Anglo-Saxon defeat at the Battle of Hastings in 1066 and the conquest of England by the Normans.

Political division and eventual unification characterized Anglo-Saxon history before the Norman conquest, and it was matched by division and unification in religion. Like many of the peoples who established kingdoms in the former Roman Empire, the Anglo-Saxons converted to Christianity, but only after an internal struggle between traditional religion and the new faith. They also faced divisions within Christianity, although their division was between Irish and Roman Catholic Christianity instead of the struggle faced by the Franks and Goths between Arian and Catholic Christianity. Although the island had received Christianity while under imperial rule, its loss of contact with the continent contributed to the breakdown of the church. During the sixth and seventh centuries, efforts to Christianize the island were launched from both Rome and Ireland.

The conversion of the Anglo-Saxons was begun in earnest at the end of the sixth century by St. Augustine of Canterbury, who had been sent on his mission by Pope Gregory I, traditionally referred to as the Great. Augustine established himself in Canterbury in 597, where he became archbishop and introduced Roman institutional structures. His greatest success came with the conversion of Aethelberht, the king of Kent, whose wife, Bertha, was a Merovingian Frank and a Christian. In a great outdoor ceremony, Aethelberht, who was greeted by a procession of monks singing psalms and carrying the cross, accepted Christianity and allowed the mission to continue. Bede notes that more churches were built, including one at Canterbury by Aethelberht, and that the king's subjects also came to the faith. The conversion of Aethelberht aided in the conversion of other parts of Anglo-Saxon England, including the northern kingdom of Northumbria, whose king, Edwin, married a daughter of Aethelberht.

Edwin only gradually came to the faith and needed the approval of a royal council before accepting baptism. Although there was a pagan reaction in the generation after Edwin's death, his conversion brought Christianity to the north, and it survived both his death and the pagan reaction. The conversion of Northumbria, however, was further complicated by the influence of Irish Catholic Christianity, which maintained a unique organizational structure; Irish Catholics also calculated the date of Easter and tonsured their clergy in their own way, rather than following the practice of the Roman church. Irish missionaries were active in England and the continent in the seventh century and offered an attractive alternative to Roman Christianity. At the great Synod of Whitby in 664, however, King Oswy accepted the teachings and organization of the Roman church. His decision had a great impact on the church and people of England in the generations to come.

The conversion of Northumbria, which completed the conversion of all of Anglo-Saxon England, was of great and lasting significance. Indeed, until the Reformation England and Rome maintained a special relationship. The Anglo-Saxon church promoted this tie, and as a result the tie greatly influenced cultural and political events in the eighth and ninth centuries. One of the more significant results of the conversion of England was the development of literary culture that followed it. The greatest expression of this culture was the so-called Northumbrian Renaissance of the seventh and eighth centuries. Associated with the monasteries of Wearmouth and Jarrow and their founder, Benedict Biscop, the revival had as its most important figure the man known as Venerable Bede, one of the most influential historians of the Middle Ages as well as a noted Christian scholar. Bede's work on time was very popular among Christian scholars in the Middle Ages; his history of the English church and people was one of the first great national histories and remained an influential work throughout the Middle Ages. The renaissance influenced Carolingian culture because of the numerous books collected by Benedict Biscop, Bede, and others for their monasteries, many of which found their way to the Frankish kingdom through Alcuin. Alcuin also introduced many of the ideals of the renaissance to his fellow Carolingian scholars and ecclesiastics.

The Latin literary tradition of Bede, Alcuin, and others is matched by an equally impressive and important literary tradition in the Anglo-Saxon tongue, which includes both secular and religious materials. The most famous example of Old English literature, of course, is *Beowulf,* which is preserved in a single manuscript from around the year 1000. It is a 3,182-line epic poem that recounts the heroic life and death of its main character, Beowulf, the great king of the Geats, who defeated three terrible monsters and ruled his people wisely after rescuing the king of the Danes from Grendel and his mother. Although Christianized, the poem reveals many of the traditional virtues of the pre-Christian Anglo-Saxons. Other important Old English literary works include *The Battle of Brunanburh* and *The Battle of Maldon. The Battle of Brunanburh* includes dramatic battle scenes and a panegyric to King Æthelstan (r. 924–939); it concerns an important battle in the unification of England. *The Battle of Maldon* exists only as a fragment, but it is celebrated for its depiction of warrior virtues maintained in adversity in its tale of an English loss to Viking invaders. Along with the secular verse tradition, there exists a body of Old English religious poetry. The most important example is *The Dream of the Rood,* in which the Rood, the Cross on which Christ was crucified, speaks of the importance of the crucifixion and of its own role and describes Jesus as a traditional Anglo-Saxon hero.

The Anglo-Saxon literary corpus also contains a number of prose works. The most significant of these is the *Anglo-Saxon Chronicle.* The chronicle, first compiled in the late ninth century, is one of the most valuable sources for the early history of England; it covers the entire period from the arrival of the Anglo-Saxons in England to their defeat by William the Conqueror. Some manuscript traditions of the chronicle continue into the Norman period, extending into the 1150s. Other prose works include the many translations made by King Alfred or his court. Alfred was responsible for translations into English of Boethius's *Consolation of Philosophy,* as well as of various works by St. Augustine of Hippo and Pope Gregory I, known as the Great. He also sponsored translations of Gregory's *Dialogues* and Bede's history. Alfred himself was the subject of a biography, in Latin, by Asser, which is an important part of the Anglo-Saxon tradition of writing history and biography. Finally, in the late Anglo-Saxon period, the ecclesiastics Ælfric and Wulfstan composed a number of sermons in English that advocated reform, lamented the moral decay of the Anglo-Saxons, and expressed the belief that they were living in the Last Days.

See also: Aethelberht I of Kent; Alcuin of York; Alfred the Great; *Anglo-Saxon Chronicle*; Arianism; Asser; Augustine of Canterbury, St.; Augustine of Hippo, St.; Bede; *Beowulf*; Boethius; Franks; Hengist and Horsa; Heptarchy; King Arthur; Mercia; Merovingian Dynasty; Northumbrian Renaissance; Offa of Mercia; Penda; Sutton Hoo; Thegn; Vortigern; Wessex

Bibliography

Arnold, Christopher J. *Roman Britain to Saxon Shore.* Bloomington: Indiana University Press, 1984.

Bassett, Steven, ed. *The Origins of Anglo-Saxon Kingdoms.* Leicester, UK: Leicester University Press, 1989.

Bede. *Ecclesiastical History of the English People with Bede's Letter to Egbert and Cuthbert's Letter on the Death of Bede.* Trans. Leo Sherley-Price. Harmondsworth, UK: Penguin, 1991.

Blair, Peter Hunter. *The World of Bede.* Cambridge: Cambridge University Press, 1990.

Gildas. *The Ruin of Britain and Other Works.* Ed. and trans. Michael Winterbottom. London: Phillimore, 1978.

Heaney, Seamus, trans. *Beowulf: A New Verse Translation.* New York: Farrar Straus and Giroux, 2000.

Higham, Nicholas J. *The Convert Kings: Power and Religious Affiliation in Early Anglo-Saxon England.* Manchester, UK: Manchester University Press, 1997.

Howe, Nicholas. *Migration and Mythmaking in Anglo-Saxon England.* New Haven, CT: Yale University Press, 1989.

Keynes, Simon, and Michael Lapidge, trans. *Alfred the Great: Asser's Life of King Alfred and Other Contemporary Sources.* Harmondsworth, UK: Penguin, 1983.

Myres, John N. L. *The English Settlements.* Oxford: Clarendon, 1986.

Sawyer, Peter H. *From Roman Britain to Norman England.* 2nd ed. London: Routledge, 1998.

Stenton, Frank M. *Anglo-Saxon England.* 3rd ed. Oxford: Clarendon, 1971.

Whitelock, Dorothy, ed. *The Anglo-Saxon Chronicle.* Westport, CT: Greenwood, 1986.

Yorke, Barbara. *Kings and Kingdoms of Early Anglo-Saxon England.* London: Seaby, 1990.

Animals

Domestic animals served a variety of purposes in the early Middle Ages, including farm work and fieldwork, were an important source of food, and, in the case of dogs and horses, were kept for companionship. Among the more important and useful animals was the horse, which was used not only as a draft animal but also for transportation and in war. The other animals used in early medieval society were cattle, sheep, dogs, pigs, geese, and chickens. They provided material for food and clothing, but they were generally smaller than their modern counterparts.

The horse played an important role in daily life in the early Middle Ages and was known to both the ancient Romans and the barbarians who migrated into the empire. There were various breeds of horse bred either by the Romans or the barbarians, and the importance of the horse is revealed in early medieval legislation. The famous Carolingian Capitulary de Villis, which regulated management of the royal estates, contains precise regulations for maintenance of horses, including instructions for overseeing stud horses, mares, and foals. It also rules that foals be brought to the king's palace each year on St. Martin's Day (November 11). Moreover, after the conversion of the barbarians to Christianity, prohibitions against eating horseflesh were enacted by various bishops and popes, including Theodore of Tarsus, archbishop of Canterbury. And in 732, Pope Gregory III ordered Boniface, the missionary and papal legate in Germany, to prohibit consumption of horseflesh.

One of the primary purposes of horses, in peace or war, was transportation. The horse, unlike other large domesticated animals, had a much faster pace than humans and thus provided a fast and reliable source of transportation. The use of horses as riding animals, however, was generally limited to kings and nobles, who could afford them. (Estimates place the cost of a horse as equal to that of four to 10 oxen or 40 to 100 sheep.) Horses were used more generally as draft animals because of their strength and speed and were often used to pull carriages of passengers and heavy loads of produce or other material on wagons. Although they may have been used in Anglo-Saxon England to plow the fields, horses were seldom used for agricultural work in the early Middle Ages. As the result of technological change around the year 1000, however, horses came into more widespread use in agricultural work as plow animals.

The other major use for the horse was in war, and many barbarian peoples used the horse to good effect in war. The Huns were most famous for their use of the horse in war, and the horse was also used in the preparation of food for the Huns and was used in the ceremonies to bury great leaders like Attila. The Lombards and Visigoths were also known for their use of the horse. Among the Franks, both the Merovingian and Carolingian dynasties employed the horse and cavalry in their armies. It must be noted that these horses were not the great warhorses of the later Middle Ages, which could carry a knight in full armor and operate as a sort of premodern tank. Indeed, the horses of barbarian Europe were smaller and lighter, as were most animals, and bore light-armored bowmen. Moreover, Carolingian horses were not used to carry mounted shock troops, as some scholars have suggested. There is no evidence to prove that the Carolingians had the stirrup, which would have been necessary to allow the use of mounted shock troops.

Cattle, both oxen and cows, were important for labor and food. With the arrival of the barbarians and the end of Roman civilization in the old Western Empire, however, the practice of selective breeding—except in the case of horses and dogs—came to an end, and cattle, as well as most other domestic animals, decreased in size. Despite their smaller size, cows and oxen remained vital in daily life. Before the so-called agricultural revolution of the year 1000, the ox was the most important agricultural draft animal. Its size, strength, and docility made the ox an ideal source of power to drive the plows used in cereal production and farm wagons. Although slower than horses, oxen were the preferred draft animal because they were less expensive to feed and keep than horses.

Cows and bulls, although prevalent, were rarely used as draft animals and were used primarily as a food source. Not only was beef the main source of meat for those who could afford it, but cows also provided milk, cheese, and butter, which were prominent in much of the northern European diet. Although the end of selective breeding and the practice of mating before maturity limited the size of the animals and their milk production, cows continued to be a significant part of agricultural life and diet. Cattle had one further use. In the summer they were put out to pasture to graze in farmland left fallow (land that was left unplanted so that it could replenish itself), which they would fertilize naturally with their manure.

Most extra animals were sold before winter because of the scarcity of food to feed them and their human owners.

Along with horses and cattle, a number of other animals were commonplace in early medieval daily life and diet. Sheep provided a source of food and clothing, and pigs also formed a valuable food source. Pigs were raised nearly in the wild, being left in the forest to forage for food, mostly nuts and berries. Written records, such as Charlemagne's capitularies, and archeological evidence reveal the existence of chickens and geese, useful for both eggs and meat, on early medieval farms. Along with these domesticated animals, wild game—including deer, rabbit, and wild boar—was hunted and made part of the diet. At times, these wild animals were confined to specific parts of the forest and even managed. Finally, dogs were a common feature in society. They were selectively bred and used in hunting and to shepherd flocks of animals and were often treated as family pets. Contrary to popular opinion, medieval people, just like modern people, often felt an emotional connection with their dogs.

See also: Agriculture; Attila the Hun; *Capitulare de Villis*; Capitularies; Carolingian Dynasty; Charlemagne; Clothing; Diet and Nutrition; Lombards; Merovingian Dynasty; Visigoths

Bibliography

Bachrach, Bernard S. *Merovingian Military Organization, 481–751.* Minneapolis: University of Minnesota Press, 1972.

Contamine, Philippe. *War in the Middle Ages.* Trans. Michael Jones. Oxford: Basil Blackwell, 1984.

Duby, Georges. *Rural Economy and Country Life in the Medieval West.* Trans. Cynthia Postan. Columbia: University of South Carolina Press, 1968.

Gladitz, Charles. *Horse Breeding in the Medieval World.* Dublin: Four Courts Press, 1997.

Riché, Pierre. *Daily Life in the World of Charlemagne.* Trans. Jo Ann McNamara. Philadelphia: University of Pennsylvania Press, 1983.

Slicher van Bath, Bernard H. *The Agrarian History of Western Europe*: A.D. *500–1850.* Trans. Olive Ordish. London: Arnold, 1963.

Antioch

City (modern Antakaya) on the Orontes that was founded by the Greeks in 300 BC Antioch became an important commercial, military, political, and religious center under the Romans. The city enjoyed a period of great prosperity during the later Roman Empire but suffered decline beginning in the sixth century of the Common Era and remained a town of lesser importance throughout the early Middle

Ages. Despite its decline, Antioch enjoyed an enduring legacy as one of the great centers of early Christianity.

Incorporated into the Roman Empire in 64 BC, Antioch was favored by a series of Roman rulers from Julius Caesar (100–44 BC) to Trajan (53–117 AD) who bestowed privileges on it and built roads and other public works and structures to enhance the city. Antioch's attraction was due to its favorable geographic location, which made it a good choice as a regional capital for the eastern empire. Roman rulers were not the only figures drawn to the city; the apostles Peter and Paul preached in Antioch, which included an important Jewish community. For Paul, Antioch served as the base for later missionary work, and the converts of Antioch were the first be known as *Christians*. Antioch was one of the four original patriarchates, along with Jerusalem, Alexandria, and Rome. In the third century, a series of church councils were held in Antioch to address important matters of the faith.

Antioch enjoyed its greatest prominence in the fourth and fifth centuries. Its population grew significantly and has been estimated at between 150,000 and 300,000, and economic prosperity increased due, in part, to the olive plantations surrounding the city. Emperors continued to build in Antioch; Constantine built the Great Church—its octagonal shape influenced later religious structures including the Dome of the Rock and church of San Vitale of Ravenna—in the early fourth century, and Theodosius II strengthened the walls surrounding the city. Along with the new imperial construction, a long, elegant thoroughfare ran through Antioch that was lined with shops and was the main center of life in the city. Antioch's demographic and economic growth was complimented by its increasing political importance as a result of prolonged war with Persia. Emperors Constantius II (r. 337–350) and Valens (r. 371–378) used the city as a base in their conflict with the Persians. The leading military officers for the east were also based there as was the civilian governor of Syria. Antioch also continued to be a leading center of Christianity. As the seat of the patriarch, Antioch enjoyed special status in the Christian church. Constantius II held a council there in 341 to address lingering questions over the creed and to implement rules of conduct for Christian clergy. One of the most respected and unusual religious figures of the period, Simeon Stylites, adopted his life as a pillar saint in Antioch and attracted large crowds of devotees. During the fourth and fifth centuries, the school of Antioch enjoyed its greatest prominence. One of the last major pagan rhetor, Libanius, taught at Antioch and included a number of leading Christian scholars such John Chyrsostom. Christian scholars developed unique approaches to theology and to reading Scripture that rivaled the work done at Alexandria.

Antioch's fortune declined in the sixth century. In 540 the city was sacked by the Persians, and its citizens were deported. Although recovered for a time by the Roman Empire, the city was again seized by the Persians in the early seventh century, and a major campaign to recover territory led by the emperor Heraklios was stopped outside the walls of Antioch in 611. Imperial forces did retake the city, but it was a more modest place than it had once been. Antioch suffered not only from the violence of warfare but also from repeated earthquakes in the sixth and seventh centuries that undermined its once prominent role. The population was further reduced by plague that swept the region in the sixth century. The once great city was absorbed by Islam in 637 and would remain a relatively small town throughout the rest of the early Middle Ages.

See also: Constantine; Rome; Valens

Bibliography

Brown, Peter. *The World of Late Antiquity* A.D. *150–750*. London: Thames and Hudson, Ltd., 1971.

Cribiore, Raffaella. *The School of Libanius in Late Antique Antioch*. Princeton, NJ: Princeton University Press, 2007.

Downey, Glanville. *A History of Antioch in Syria: From Seleucus to the Arab Conquest*. Princeton, NJ: Princeton University Press, 1961.

Huskinson, Janet and Isabella Sandwell, eds. *Culture and Society in Later Roman Antioch*. Oxford: Oxbow Books, 2003.

Kondoloeon, Christine, ed. *Antioch: The Lost Ancient City*. Princeton, NJ: Princeton University Press, 2000.

Liebeschuetz, J.H.W.G. *Antioch: City and Imperial Administration in the Later Roman Empire*. Oxford: Oxford University Press, 1972.

Arbogast (d. 394)

A Germanic general of Frankish descent, Arbogast was the first in a series of military leaders in the Roman Empire, a list that later included Stilicho, Aëtius, and Ricimer, to appoint a puppet emperor. Although his efforts established a dangerous and important precedent, Arbogast's career as the power behind the throne in the Western Empire was cut short by the arrival of Theodosius the Great. Nonetheless, Arbogast's career foreshadowed many of the events to come and revealed one of the weaknesses of the Western Empire.

Arbogast rose through the military ranks to assume an important leadership position in the Roman army and the Western Empire. He earned the rank of *magister equitum* (master of the horse) in the army of the Western Empire, and, from 380 to 388, served the emperor Theodosius in the east in his struggles against the Goths. In 388 he was sent back to the Western Empire to serve the young emperor Valentinian II (r. 375–392), who had recently been restored to the throne following a period of civil war. Arbogast served Valentinian well and recovered Gaul and strengthened the Rhine frontier. He also imposed a treaty on his fellow Franks who had invaded Gaul. His successes and the death of Bauto, another Frank sent as an adviser by Theodosius, emboldened him to assume the office of *magister militum* (master of the soldiers) without the emperor's consent. Valentinian was outraged and sent his general a letter of dismissal, to which Arbogast replied that since Valentinian had not appointed him the emperor could not dismiss him. Shortly thereafter, in May 392, Valentinian was found dead, and some contemporaries suggested that he was killed by Arbogast.

The death of Valentinian presented Arbogast an opportunity to seize command, but as a barbarian he could not do it personally. He then appointed the teacher of rhetoric Flavius Eugenius emperor, a move that found little favor with Theodosius. Although Theodosius did not strike immediately at Eugenius and Arbogast, he clearly resented the move. Arbogast, a supporter of the pagans of Rome, had hoped to find favor with the Christian Theodosius by his promotion of another Christian. He also attempted to gain Theodosius's support by issuing new coins with the image of Theodosius on them. But these attempts bore little fruit, and Theodosius designated his son Honorius as the heir to the throne in the west. Arbogast and his emperor then promoted the pagan cause more strenuously and restored the famed Altar of Victory to its traditional place in the senate. To further secure his grip on the Western Empire, Arbogast again waged successful campaigns in Gaul during the winter of 393–394. But his efforts proved of little avail when Theodosius led a large force, which included Stilicho and many Germans, against Arbogast and his emperor. In a two-day battle on September 6–8, 394, Arbogast suffered a crushing defeat near the river Frigidus. Eugenius was executed following the defeat, and Arbogast committed suicide.

Although Arbogast was short lived, his career was still significant. His rise to power in the military demonstrated one way to success in the empire, and his use of that power provided a precedent for later military commanders. Indeed, the Western Empire in the fifth century was ruled by several military commanders who had established figureheads on the imperial throne. Arbogast's example was especially important to the many Germans in the military, who could not hold the highest civil office in the empire. His virtual removal of the emperor from military command also had long-lasting consequences by further dividing the civil and military offices in the empire. It also distanced the Western emperors from the army, their most important constituency. The struggles between Theodosius and Arbogast and Eugenius brought further unrest to the empire and drew troops from the frontiers, thus weakening Rome's defense of its borders, which were seriously breached early in the fifth century.

See also: Aëtius; Franks; Ricimer; Stilicho, Flavius; Visigoths

Bibliography

Bury, John B. *The Invasions of Europe by the Barbarians.* New York: W.W. Norton, 1967.

Cameron, Averil, and Peter Garnsey, eds. *The Late Empire, A.D. 337–425. Cambridge Ancient History.* Vol. 13. Cambridge: Cambridge University Press, 1998.

Matthews, John. *Western Aristocracies and Imperial Court, A.D. 364–425.* Oxford: Clarendon, 1998.

Zosimus. *New History.* Trans. Ronald T. Ridley. Canberra: Australian Association for Byzantine Studies, 1982.

Arianism

Arianism is a religious heresy associated with the Alexandrian presbyter Arius (c. 260–336). Arianism offered a concept of the relationship between God the Father and God the Son that differed from that of the Catholic tradition in the late Roman and early medieval period. It was popular throughout the fourth century with several Roman emperors, including Valens (d. 378), as well as with much of the Eastern Roman aristocracy. Although eventually outlawed by the devout Catholic Christian and emperor Theodosius the Great who declared the Catholic faith the official religion of the empire, Arianism had great influence among the barbarian peoples who migrated into the empire. In fact, Arianism had adherents among the Franks, Goths, Lombards, and others into the late seventh century, and was often part of the political and military policies of these peoples. An attractive and in some ways simpler doctrine than Catholic Christianity, Arianism nonetheless was eventually abandoned by its Germanic adherents in favor of the predominant faith of the church of Rome.

Arianism took shape in the early fourth century, after Christianity was legalized in the Roman Empire and supported by the emperor Constantine. It formed in opposition to the Catholic faith, and as a result a great controversy erupted in the empire between supporters of each teaching. Unlike the Catholic faith, which stressed the essential unity of the godhead, the faith of Arius emphasized the superiority of God the Father. Arius taught that God the Son was subordinate and posterior to the Father. According to Arius, the Son, rather than existing from before the beginning of time, was created in time; he argued further that God the Father created the Son as a mediator between himself and fallen humankind. He was divine by grace of the Father, and since he had become like God the Father, others had hope to become like the Father.

The teachings of Arius divided the church in the fourth century. To resolve this controversy Constantine held the first ecumenical council at Nicaea in 325, which was attended by 318 bishops and presided over by the emperor himself.

The council upheld the Catholic view of the essential unity of the godhead, embodying it in the summary of the faith that formed the basis of what is traditionally called the Nicene Creed, but the controversy continued for the next several decades. Even Constantine, in the 330s, became more inclined to the Arian view. His successors often adopted Arianism as the preferred expression of Christianity.

During the reign of Constantius (337–361), the emperor adopted an Arian creed, which became the foundation for the Arianism of the Germanic peoples in the generations to come. The faith of Arius continued to have supporters among the emperors for the next few decades, but it faced a terrible setback under the Arian emperor Valens. His defeat by the Visigoths at the Battle of Hadrianople in 378 was understood as the judgment of God against a heretical ruler. His successor, Theodosius, was a staunch advocate of the Nicene Creed and promoted Catholic Christianity to the rank of state religion at the expense of Arian Christianity, as well as traditional paganism.

The triumph of Catholic Christianity in the empire did not spell the end of Arian Christianity, however. The missionary activities of the Arian Goth Ulfilas from the early 340s until his death in 382–383 and his translation of the Bible into the Gothic language contributed to the acceptance of Arian Christianity by large numbers of Goths. In the 370s, the Gothic leader Fritigern, possibly an ally of Ulfilas, converted to the Arian faith as part of his pro-Roman policy and his rivalry with Athanaric. Of course Fritigern's Arianism did not prevent him from defeating his fellow Arian, the emperor Valens, at the Battle of Hadrianople in 378. It did, however, complicate things for the Visigoths who settled in Spain and other parts of the old Roman Empire where the Roman population was predominantly Catholic. The Arian Visigoths also faced an established Catholic infrastructure of churches, monasteries, and most importantly, bishops, who wielded great power and influence. Ultimately, the Spanish Visigoths converted to Catholic Christianity in 587 when their great king, Reccared I, converted.

Not all Arian Goths had difficulty with their Catholic subjects, however. The Ostrogothic king of Italy, Theodoric the Great, ruled effectively despite religious differences with the majority of his subject population. He benefited from the resistance of the church in Italy to domination by the Eastern church centered in Constantinople, a resistance that made Catholics in Italy more willing to accept local control even if by an Arian. Moreover, Theodoric was a tolerant ruler and took few steps aimed at restricting the rights of Catholics. He was most respectful of the pope during a visit to Rome in 500 and, according to one contemporary, honored the pope just as any Catholic Christian would. As king, Theodoric also presided over a great cultural flourishing. His capital at Ravenna was the beneficiary of a building program that created great monuments of Arian architecture in a baptistery, palace church, and other churches throughout the city. Theodoric also built beautiful Arian

Mosaic of Jesus of Nazareth in the dome of the Arian Baptistry at Ravenna, Italy, which was built by the Ostrogothic king Theodoric the Great (d. 526). (Alinari Archives/ Getty Images)

churches in other Italian cities. Only late in his reign, when Theodoric had brutally crushed an alleged conspiracy, did he lose favor among the Italian population, so that his Arianism became a problem.

Other peoples, including the Burgundians and Vandals, accepted Arian Christianity, and the Lombards in particular used it as part of a grander political scheme. Invading Italy in 568, the Lombards attempted to unify the entire peninsula under their king. This policy met the opposition of various popes, who presided over significant territories in central Italy. Consequently, the Arianism of the Lombards took on political, especially antipapal, and to a lesser extent, anti-imperial connotations. Although the Lombards converted to Catholic Christianity in the late seventh century, their political agenda remained unchanged, although some kings did take a softer stance in relation to the popes.

Arianism had a very different career among the Merovingian Franks under their greatest leader, Clovis (r. 481–511). According to the sixth-century historian Gregory of Tours, Clovis favored Catholic Christianity long before his conversion. His wife, Clotilda, was a Catholic Christian who repeatedly sought to convert her husband to her faith. When Clovis did convert, according to Gregory, he chose

Catholic Christianity, and was described as a new Constantine. Indeed, his conversion during a great battle recalls Constantine's conversion prior to the Battle of the Milvian Bridge. Gregory also describes Clovis's wars against the Visigoths as a sort of crusade, launched because the great Merovingian king could not tolerate Arian heretics living in Gaul. Of course, the situation is not so clear-cut as Gregory presents it. Clovis did ultimately convert to Catholic Christianity, but there is evidence that his conversion may not have been directly from paganism to Catholic faith. Clovis, at the very least, had sympathies with the Arian tradition and may have been an Arian Christian for a time before his final conversion to the Catholic faith.

See also: Athanaric; Burgundians; Clotilda; Clovis; Constantine; Fritigern; Gregory of Tours; Hadrianople, Battle of; Lombards; Merovingian Dynasty; Ostrogoths; Reccared I; Rome; Theodoric the Great; Ulfilas; Theodosius the Great; Visigoths

Bibliography

Geary, Patrick. *Before France and Germany: The Creation and Transformation of the Merovingian World.* Oxford: Oxford University Press, 1988.

Gregory of Tours. *History of the Franks.* Trans. Lewis Thorpe. Harmondsworth, UK: Penguin, 1974.

Hanson, Richard P. C. *The Search for the Christian Doctrine of God: The Arian Controversy, 318–381.* Edinburgh: T & T Clark, Ltd., 1988.

Herrin, Judith. *The Formation of Christendom.* Princeton, NJ: Princeton University Press, 1987.

Pelikan, Jaroslav. *The Emergence of the Catholic Tradition.* Vol. 2 of *The Christian Tradition: A History of the Development of Doctrine.* Chicago: University of Chicago Press, 1978.

Randers-Pehrson, Justine Davis. *Barbarians and Romans: The Birth Struggle of Europe, A.D. 400–700.* Norman: University of Oklahoma Press, 1993.

Wolfram, Herwig. *The Roman Empire and Its Germanic Peoples.* Trans. Thomas Dunlap. Berkeley: University of California Press, 1997.

Arnulf of Metz, St. (580–643/647)

Bishop, saint, and traditionally the founder, with Pippin I, called Pippin of Landen, of the Carolingian family, Arnulf is generally thought to have been an important figure in the political life of the Frankish kingdoms in the seventh century. The marriage of Arnulf's son to one of Pippin's daughters is traditionally thought to have joined two of the most powerful aristocratic factions in Austrasia, the eastern realm of the Merovingian Franks, and Pippin II of Herstal was the product of this marriage. Arnulf's reputation for sanctity, no doubt, strengthened the family's position, and, according to the early ninth-century *Annals of Metz,* Arnulf of "all the Franks is held before God and men to be a special patron" (Fouracre and Gerberding 19976, 352). Much of what is known of Arnulf's life, however, is shrouded in mystery and myth created by later Carolingian writers, and the exact relationship between Arnulf and the two Pippins is uncertain.

According to the traditional account, Arnulf was born in 580 to an aristocratic family with extensive land holding between the Mosel and Meuse Rivers. He early on showed an inclination toward the religious life, possibly inspired by Irish missionaries who established a monastery nearby, and was taught to read and write. He later joined the court of the mayor of the palace (major domo) and then the court of the Merovingian king, Theudebert II. He assumed important administrative duties over royal domains and rose to prominence at court. His youth and early years at court occurred during a time of unrest and often brutal civil war between the queens Fredegund and Brunhilde. After Fredegund died, Brunhilde was the real power in the Merovingian kingdoms, even though she ruled through her sons and grandsons. In 613, Arnulf, along with Pippin and other Austrasian nobles, joined Chlotar II in a revolt that overthrew and savagely executed Brunhilde.

During the reign of Chlotar (613–629), both Arnulf and Pippin played influential roles and were rewarded for their service to the king. Indeed, the alliance they had forged during the revolt had drawn the fortunes of the two ancestral Carolingian leaders closer together. Joined by rebellion, they also were joined by the marriage of Arnulf's son, Ansegisel, and Pippin's daughter, Begga. Moreover, as the *Annals of Metz* note, Arnulf "very often strengthened [Pippin] with sacred admonitions and divine and human learning so that he would be strengthened for more important matters" (Fouracre and Gerberding 1996, 352). Pippin became mayor of the palace, thus acquiring the office that provided the foundation for later Carolingian success. Arnulf was rewarded by Chlotar with the office of bishop of Metz, perhaps as a result of Arnulf's religious inclinations as well as of his administrative talents. As bishop he controlled sizable estates and wealth that would have been important to the king, who allowed Arnulf to retain possession of his administrative posts at the royal court. He was also entrusted with the responsibility of tutor to Chlotar's young son, the future Dagobert I.

In his later years, Arnulf yearned to resign from his official religious and secular duties to take up the life of a monk. He was prohibited from doing so by Chlotar, who valued Arnulf's talents. On the death of Chlotar, however, Arnulf was allowed to retire to a monastery, where he died some time between 643 and 647 after years of pious service. The pious life he led at the monastery contributed to his reputation as a saint, and his feast day is celebrated on August 16 or 19 at his former monastery. Although Arnulf's life may have been subject to Carolingian mythologizing, which makes some of the exact details of his life certain, he was surely an important figure in the early years of the Carolingian family and in the Frankish kingdoms of the seventh century.

See also: Austrasia; Brunhilde; Carolingian Dynasty; Chlotar II; Fredegund; Merovingian Dynasty; Neustria; Pippin I, Called Pippin of Landen; Pippin II, Called Pippin of Herstal

Bibliography

Fouracre, Paul, and Richard A. Gerberding. *Late Merovingian France: History and Hagiography, 640–720.* Manchester, UK: University of Manchester Press, 1996.

Fouracre, Paul. *The Age of Charles Martel.* London: Longman, 2000.

Riché, Pierre. *The Carolingians: A Family Who Forged Europe.* Trans. Michael Idomir Allen. Philadelphia: University of Pennsylvania Press, 1993.

Wood, Ian. *The Merovingian Kingdoms, 450–751.* London: Longman, 1994.

Arthur, King. *See* King Arthur

Asser (d. 909)

Monk, abbot, and bishop of Sherborne (c. 895–909), Asser is best known for his *Life of Alred*, the biography of the Anglo-Saxon king Alfred the Great. Asser, a key figure at the court of King Alfred, was a close friend and confidante of the king and contributed to the cultural revival that took place under the king's direction.

Asser was born in Wales and, as he tells us, was educated, bred, tonsured, and ordained in the "furthest coasts of western Britain." He became a monk of St. David's Abbey in Pembrokeshire and seems to have developed a reputation as a scholar and teacher while there. His renown as a man of learning reached Alfred in Saxon England who sought out the Welsh monk when he needed someone to teach him to read and write in Latin. The two met at Dene, Alfred's estate in Sussex, where the king invited Asser to leave all his possessions and join the royal court. Asser, as he notes in the *Life of Alfred*, was reluctant to leave, and so the king suggested that he spend six months of each year in Wales and six months in Alfred's kingdom. Agreeing to these terms, Asser departed but became very ill and remained without hope for a cure for 53 weeks. He then joined Alfred at his court in Leonaford, where he stayed for eight months reading to Alfred every day. In gratitude for his services, Alfred made Asser abbot of the monasteries at Ambresbury and Banwell and granted him all the possessions of Exeter. Asser continued to serve the king, who by St. Martin's Day, November 11, 887 had mastered reading and writing in Latin. In subsequent years, Alfred with the assistance of Asser translated works by Boethius, Gregory the Great, and Orosius into the Anglo-Saxon language. Along with bestowing Exeter and the monasteries on Asser, Alfred made his friend bishop of Sherborne, a position Asser held until his death.

In 893, Asser began his life of King Alfred, which covered the life of the king from his birth until the year 887. The *Life of Alfred* draws extensively on the *Anglo-Saxon Chronicle* as well as the personal reflections of Asser himself. The biography describes Alfred's personal life, his marriage and children, as well as his life as king. In the *Life*, Asser describes the king's struggles to secure his kingdom and his frequent fights against pagan invaders, notably Vikings from Denmark. He describes as well Alfred's construction and use of a fleet against the Vikings and his important naval and military victories against the Vikings. Asser also comments on Alfred's interest in promoting learning throughout the kingdom as well as the king's own efforts to read or be read to every day. Alfred is portrayed in a most favorable light in the Asser's life. He is depicted as a great Christian ruler, and Asser was inspired in his portrayal. Asser was inspired in his portrayal by great kings such as Charlemagne and, more importantly, Solomon and the kings of the Hebrew Bible. Despite this somewhat one-sided portrait, Asser's *Life of Alfred* remains one of the most important sources for the history of this great king and his reign.

See also: Alfred the Great; *Anglo-Saxon Chronicle*, Anglo-Saxons; Boethius, Anicius Manlius Severinus; Charlemagne; Gregory the Great; Wessex

Bibliography

Keynes, Simon, and Michael Lapidge, trans. *Alfred the Great: Asser's Life of Alfred the Great and Other Contemporary Sources*. Harmondsworth, UK: Penguin Books, 1983.

Astronomer, The (fl. ninth century)

Anonymous author of the *Vita Hludowici imperatoris* (Life of the Emperor Louis), the Astronomer provides an important, contemporary account of the life of the Carolinian emperor Louis the Pious (r. 813–840). Offering a sympathetic but not uncritical portrait of the emperor, the Astronomer also offers commentary on the events of the early ninth century and the fortunes of the Carolingian dynasty.

Most of what is known of the Astronomer is drawn from his biography of the emperor. He has been called "the Astronomer" because of his general interest, which he reveals in his work, and apparent expertise in celestial matters. In the *Vita Hludowici*, the author describes an episode in which Louis called him to court to explain the importance of a passing comet—Halley's Comet—in 837. This incident suggests that the Astronomer had important contacts at court; it is likely that he was a monk who came from the aristocracy and served as an important palace official for Louis. He most likely joined the young ruler when he was sent to Aquitaine, and throughout his biography the Astronomer shows great interest in the south.

His evident dislike for the people of Aquitaine, however, raises the possibility that this was not his homeland, and it may be that he was from Gothic Septimania. Whatever his geographic origins, the Astronomer clearly knew the emperor and had contacts with the emperor's court.

The Astronomer most likely wrote his biography in 841, shortly after the death of the emperor, whose end is movingly described by the author. In preparing the life, the Astronomer drew from a variety of sources, including the *Royal Frankish Annals* and, possibly, official documents of the imperial court. He was also indebted to the information provided by the monk Ademar, who had access to the court and may have been a high-ranking official before entering a monastery. Another source that the Astronomer used was the Life of Charlemagne by Einhard, whom he admired and most likely knew personally. The Astronomer, however, wrote a very different life of Louis than the one that Einhard wrote about Charlemagne. Although firmly in the tradition of imperial biography produced by Carolingian authors and stressing the virtues of the king, the Astronomer's biography is arranged chronologically and is less overtly secular than Einhard's. Less indebted to classical biography, the life of Louis also stresses the important role of the divine in the life and history of the emperor and pays close attention to the religious reforms of the ruler.

The *Vita Hludowici* surveys the life of the emperor Louis the Pious from his youth to his death. The life provides a brief summary of the reign of Louis's father, Charlemagne, and it also emphasizes the character of Louis as Charlemagne's designated heir and strongly endorses Louis's position as the legitimate Carolingian ruler and heir of Charlemagne, who took pains to prepare his son as emperor. The Astronomer also attributes the important imperial virtues to Louis, but is not uncritical of his hero, whom he blames for being a bit too merciful at times. Along with establishing Louis's place as Charlemagne's chosen successor, the Astronomer also asserts the legitimacy of Louis's authority during the troubled times of the 830s when the emperor's sons rebelled against him. The Astronomer was highly critical of Lothar and his brothers and was a staunch defender of the rights of Charles the Bald. In the *Vita Hludowici*, the Astronomer sought to promote the legitimacy Louis and Charles the Bald as well as to promote the integrity of the empire. In this way, the life provides not only a valuable depiction of the period but also an important commentary on Christian kingship.

See also: Carolingian Dynasty; Charlemagne; Charles the Bald; Einhard; Lothar; Louis the Pious

Bibliography

Cabaniss, Allen, trans. *Son of Charlemagne: A Contemporary Life of Louis the Pious.* Syracuse, NY: Syracuse University Press, 1961.

Innes, Matthew, and Rosamond McKitterick. "The Writing of History." In *Carolingian Culture: Emulation and Innovation.* Ed. Rosamond McKitterick. Cambridge: Cambridge University Press, 1994, pp. 193–220.

Laistner, M.L.W. *Thought and Letters in Western Europe,* A.D. *500 to 900.* 2nd ed. Ithaca, NY: Cornell University Press, 1957.

Noble, Thomas F. X. ed. *Charlemagne and Louis the Pious: Lives by Einhard, Notker, Ermoldus, Thegan, and the Astronomer.* University Park, PA: University of Pennsylvania Press, 2009.

Athalaric. *See* Ostrogoths

Athanaric (d. 381)

Gothic warrior leader or judge from 365 to 381, whose reign was marked by prolonged struggles against the Romans and the Huns as well as against other groups of Goths. His reign was later recognized by the Visigoths as the moment of the beginning of that people, and he was deemed their founder king. It was as a result of the pressure of the advancing Huns that Gothic followers of Athanaric abandoned their leader and, with rival Gothic groups, petitioned the Roman emperor Valens for entry into the Roman Empire. The entry of the Visigoths in 376 led to the Battle of Hadrianople, but Athanaric was not involved in that battle and was eventually welcomed to Constantinople and honored there shortly before his death. His reign was characterized also by the indiscriminate persecution of Christians, Catholics, and non-Catholics, living in his territory, which led later Christian historians to blacken his name.

Athanaric was a member of a royal clan among the Gothic Tervingi, and from his youth he had strained relations with the empire. His father, after an apparent failed diplomatic contact with Constantine the Great (r. 306–337), made Athanaric swear an oath never to step foot in the empire. Moreover, although the empire supported Athanaric's dynasty, Goths fought with Rome against Persia, and trade went on between the Goths and Rome, these good relations followed a crushing defeat by Rome and rested on Gothic hostages at the Roman court. In the 360s, when he had come to rule in his own name, Athanaric supported the pretender to the Roman throne, Procopius, against the legitimate emperor, Valens (r. 364–378). Valens massacred the warriors Athanaric sent to support Procopius and prepared for open war against Athanaric.

The Roman campaign against the Goths in the late 360s brought great devastation and suffering to Athanaric's people. From 367 to 369 Valens prosecuted war against Athanaric but, despite considerable advantages, could not defeat the Goth. Athanaric was no match for Roman power and lost battles against Rome, but he managed to avoid the severe defeats his predecessors suffered. In 369, with a growing Persian threat, Valens accepted Athanaric's offer of peace. The treaty was settled, much to the chagrin of Valens, on an island in the Danube, because Athanaric refused to set foot in Roman territory. The treaty freed Athanaric's Goths from Roman hegemony and ended tribute payments to the Romans.

After settling with the Romans, Athanaric turned his attention to affairs in his realm. From 369 to 372 Athanaric, fearing that Christianity would undermine the traditions of Gothic society, conducted a systematic persecution of Christians in his realm, many of whom had converted as a result of the missionary activities of Ulfilas. He forced Christians in his realm to honor a tribal idol and make sacrifices to it, and if they refused they were punished and their houses burned. The idols were probably images of important ancestors or tribal founders, and those who failed to honor them denied the tribe and its divine origins. In other words, they violated the integrity of the community to which they otherwise belonged. In a sense Athanaric, much like the Roman emperors before the conversion of Constantine, was trying to preserve the unity of his realm by forcing Gothic Christians to adhere to the traditional religion. Athanaric's persecutions were also part of his anti-imperial policy, because of the close association of Christianity with the Roman Empire, which had sponsored missionaries north of the Danube River. But Athanaric's efforts backfired because they failed to unite the Goths. In fact, his persecutions led to a division within the community when his rival, Fritigern, agreed to convert to Christianity in exchange for the support of the Roman emperor Valens. Fritigern also challenged Athanaric's authority in the mid-370s, but Athanaric managed to keep control as a greater threat emerged on the horizon.

The Huns' advance followed in the wake of the Gothic war with the Romans and the internal struggle between Athanaric and Fritigern. Although at first modest, the pressure of the Huns became increasingly intense and caused a dramatic realignment of barbarian settlements inside and outside the frontier of the empire. As the Huns moved eastward, various Gothic groups faced them, with generally disastrous consequences. One tribe of Ostrogoths was smashed by the Huns, even though a small group managed to make their way to Athanaric's territory. In the summer of 376, Athanaric was ambushed by an advance force of Huns, from which he managed to escape with his army intact.

In response to the threat of the Huns, Athanaric began a program of building defensive fortifications similar to Roman fortresses along his frontier. Unfortunately for Athanaric and his Goths, this policy of wall building proved ineffective, as Hunnish raiding parties once again fell on him and defeated the Goths in battle near the Danube River. His ability to retreat successfully and regroup failed him after his defeat by the Huns, in part because the Huns took control of important territory and managed to cut off Athanaric's supply lines. As a result of his losses to the Huns and the devastation it caused, Fritigern, Athanaric's old rival, established himself as a leader and, with a majority of the Tervingi, withdrew from Athanaric and received the right from Emperor Valens to settle in the Roman Empire. The division of the Goths had serious consequences for both Athanaric, who had lost most of his followers, and Valens, who was defeated by Fritigern and killed at the Battle of Hadrianople in 378.

Athanaric and his remaining followers did not follow Fritigern into the Roman Empire, but he could not remain where he was because of continued pressure from the Huns. Just as the Huns advanced at Athanaric's expense, Athanaric's successful withdrawal came at the expense of other barbarian peoples. He advanced against another barbarian people who lived across the Carpathian Mountains and settled there for the next four years with his remaining followers. In late 380, Athanaric was forced out in a coup engineered by Fritigern. Despite his long-standing hostility toward the empire, Athanaric sought asylum in Constantinople in January 381. He was welcomed by the emperor Theodosius, who met him at the gates of the city and offered him a lavish reception. The welcome afforded Athanaric was outdone only by the funeral Theodosius provided him two weeks later, after the Goth's death on January 25, 381.

See also: Fritigern; Hadrianople, Battle of; Huns; Ulfilas; Visigoths

Bibliography

Heather, Peter. *The Goths.* Oxford: Blackwell, 1996.

Randers-Pehrson, Justine Davis. *Barbarians and Romans: The Birth Struggle of Europe,* A.D. *40–700.* Norman: University of Oklahoma Press, 1983.

Wolfram, Herwig. *History of the Goths.* Trans. Thomas J. Dunlap. Berkeley: University of California Press, 1988.

Wolfram, Herwig. *The Roman Empire and Its Germanic Peoples.* Trans. Thomas J. Dunlap. Berkeley: University of California Press, 1997.

Attila the Hun (d. 453)

The fifth century king of the Huns, called the scourge of God. Attila was a mighty warrior who extracted great wealth from the Roman Empire and posed a threat to the peace of the late ancient world during his reign from 435 to 453. Although he did not pose a direct challenge to the existence of the Roman Empire, Attila invaded the empire on several occasions and inflicted serious damage on the empire and its armies. His armies threatened both the new Rome, Constantinople, and the original city of Rome. His empire was a rival to the Roman Empire, but despite its size and military power, the empire of the Huns did not long survive Attila, its greatest king.

Several late ancient writers have left descriptions of Attila's physical appearance and personality. The sixth-century historian of the Goths, Jordanes, describes Attila as short of stature but of mighty bearing. Attila had a swarthy complexion, a broad chest, a large head with small eyes, a thin beard, and a flat nose. In his history, Jordanes observes that Attila had a haughty walk, which revealed his proud spirit and abundant self-confidence. A lover of war, he terrified all the world but was gracious to suppliants. The Roman ambassador to Attila's court, Priscus, left an account of diplomacy at the court that complements the account of Jordanes. Priscus describes the favorable treatment he received from the king, who spoke "friendly words" to him and sent warm greetings to the emperor. He also describes a banquet he was invited to by Attila. The king sat on a couch in the middle of the room, surrounded by couches for his guests. The guests were served lavish dishes on silver platters and wine in goblets of silver and gold, but Attila ate meat on a wooden plate and wine from a wooden goblet. His clothing, Priscus notes, was plain but clean. His sword, boots, and bridle were without elaborate ornamentation. Attila had numerous wives and an even larger number of children.

In the year 435, Attila and his brother Bleda ascended to the throne of the Huns, succeeding their uncle Ruga. It was Ruga who enjoyed the first successes against the Roman Empire, invading the empire, threatening the capital, and extracting tribute from the emperor. Ruga, in the 420s, brought cohesion to the disparate bands that made up the Hunnish confederation and imposed unity of purpose on these tribes. Ruga also imposed a treaty on the empire, demanding not only tribute but also the return of Huns who had deserted and joined the imperial army. This was a most serious demand for the empire, which had come to rely on the service of Hunnish soldiers. It also proved critical to Attila, who exploited the terms to his advantage.

As king, Attila immediately took the offensive and negotiated a new treaty—the Treaty of Margus—with the empire, which became the cornerstone for relations with the empire for the rest of his reign. According to the new treaty, the amount of tribute paid to the Huns was doubled from 350 pounds of gold a year to 700 pounds. Huns who had deserted were to be returned to Attila or ransomed at the value of a Roman solider. (The fate of returned deserters was not pleasant, as the example of two royal deserters who were sent back by the Romans and crucified by Attila suggests.) Constantinople was not to make treaties with the enemies of the Huns and had to guarantee that fairs be held along the frontier between the two powers. Attila also extended the size of the empire he inherited by waging war on the barbarian tribes on his northern and eastern frontier during the later 430s.

In response to the refusal of the emperor, Theodosius II, to honor the terms of the Treaty of Margus—he suddenly ceased the payment of tribute—Attila invaded the empire. Seizing the opportunity to harass the empire while Theodosius II was engaged with the Persians, Attila inflicted great damage on imperial territory. He razed a number of important cities, including Singidunum (Belgrade) and Serdica (Sofia). Another city, Naissus (Nis), was badly devastated; the stench of death was so great that no one could enter the city, and human bones filled the Danube River.

He won a series of battles in 443 and threatened the city of Constantinople itself. His numerous victories forced the empire to renegotiate its treaty with the Huns. The annual subsidy was raised to 2,100 pounds of gold, with a one-time payment of 6,000 pounds of gold to cover the missed payments.

The early successes of Attila, however, were suddenly interrupted. The terror inspired by the great Hunnish horsemen no longer seemed so great, and they no longer acquired the spoils of war they once did. Epidemic or rebellion may have struck the empire of the Huns. The armies were no longer successful in battle. And the emperor once again refused to make the tribute payments to the Huns. Following these setbacks, Attila murdered his brother Bleda in 444. It may have been an assassination motivated solely by the lust for power, but it is also possible that Bleda was blamed for the misfortunes that had struck the Huns. Bleda's incompetence may have caused the military setbacks. He was clearly a *rex inutilis,* a "useless king," or even worse, a king who had lost the favor of the gods. Whatever the reason for the assassination, Bleda's murder left Attila in sole control of the empire.

Shortly after the murder of his brother, Attila once again took the offensive and invaded the Eastern Empire a second time. This invasion was even greater than the previous campaign and led to even greater devastation. Although suffering heavy losses himself, Attila inflicted severe defeats on imperial armies. He laid waste to large sections of the Balkans and had led his armies to Thermopylae by 447 when the emperor pleaded for peace. The treaty renewed the terms of the earlier treaties. The Empire was to renew annual payments of 2,100 pounds of gold. It was forced to ransom Roman captives and to promise to return Huns who had deserted and to stop accepting them into the empire and its army. The empire also ceded a significant portion of its Danubian province to Attila.

In 450, Attila was once again on the warpath, but this time it was the Western Empire that felt the wrath of God's scourge. There are several factors that inspired Attila to attack the imperial West, not the least of which was its military weakness. The Vandal king, Gaiseric, fearful of the power of the Visigoths, encouraged Attila's western focus. The death of Theodosius II in 450 also contributed to Attila's decision to attack the empire again, because the new emperor, Marcian, refused to pay the tribute or make any other concessions to the Huns. Finally, there is the interesting case of Honoria, daughter of Galla Placidia and sister of the emperor Valentinian. She had led a dissolute life and was caught with a servant. He was executed, and she was betrothed to a trustworthy senator—that is, one who posed no threat to the emperor. To avoid marrying a senator she detested and to acquire a protector, Honoria sent a ring to Attila. The great king interpreted this as a proposal of marriage and demanded that Honoria be turned over and that she be given half of the territory of the Western Empire. Although there was some interest in turning Honoria over to the king of the Huns, Marcian's refusal to pay the tribute pushed Attila to take his bride by force.

The preparations for the invasion were extensive, and Attila entered Gaul in the Western Empire with a massive army, counted at between 300,000 and 700,000 men by contemporary sources. Although these numbers are probably exaggerated, it is certain that Attila led an army of great size into the Western Empire. His army contained a large number of allied and subject peoples, including Alans, Burgundians, Heruls, Ostrogoths, Ripuarian Franks, Sarmatians, Suevi, and Vandals led by Gaiseric, as well as his own Huns. He faced a great alliance of Romans and Burgundians, Celts, Salian Franks, and Visigoths, all led by the Roman military commander, Aëtius, who had long relied on the Huns for the imperial army. Despite the great alliance against him, Attila enjoyed success early in the campaign and sacked the important cities of Rheims, Metz, Strasbourg, Cologne, and Trier. His efforts to seize Orléans in the summer of 451, however, failed. Aëtius managed to secure the city before Attila's arrival, and rather than waste time and men on a prolonged siege, Attila withdrew. Although a wise tactical move, Attila's withdrawal provided the Romans with a victory and raised their morale.

Attila's own morale was undermined by the loss at Orléans, as well as by a soothsayer who predicted that the impending battle would prove disastrous for the Huns, even though a great rival would die. Nonetheless, Attila prepared for a showdown with his enemy, and on June 20 on the plains between Troyes and Châlons, the two armies fought a great battle that some have seen as one of the decisive battles of world history. The Battle of the Catalaunian Plains (also known as the Battle of Maurica, or of Châlons) was a terrible, bloody battle in which, according to Jordanes, 165,000 men died. The fighting was so ferocious in this battle of nations that the ancients report that a small stream near the field grew to a raging torrent from the blood of the combatants.

The battle for a time went so poorly for the Huns that Attila prepared a funeral pyre for himself should it come to that. But the death of the Visigoth Theodoric staved off the destruction of the Huns, and Attila was able to withdraw from the field of battle and leave Gaul. Aëtius, victorious, decided not to pursue his foe, perhaps because he did not wish to destroy the Huns, who were an important counterbalance to Rome's other barbarian rivals. Aëtius's use of the Huns in his army no doubt also kept him from destroying his rival's army. Attila was like a wounded animal at this point, more ferocious because of his own injury, and any pursuit could have led to a devastating counterattack that would have destroyed the army of Aëtius and opened the Western Empire to Attila.

Attila may have been beaten near Châlons, but he was a determined enemy and planned an even greater invasion in 452. Attila crossed the Alps and led his armies on a grand invasion of Italy that brought devastation to the north of the peninsula and threatened the ancient capital, Rome. Aëtius was unable to rally his allies among the Alans and Visigoths and thus had insufficient forces to challenge the great army of the Huns. As a result much of northern Italy suffered heavy damage from the Huns. Many cities were pillaged and destroyed. The city of Aquileia was razed to the ground, and its inhabitants, according to tradition, fled into the lagoons of the Adriatic and founded Venice. According to one early account, the cities of Milan and Pavia were completely destroyed and left depopulated. Attila's armies sacked Verona and Vicentia as well and extorted a ransom from the people of Ticinum to spare that city. Unchecked by imperial armies, Attila set up court in northern Italy, probably at Milan. He was met there by two Roman senators and Pope Leo I, known as the Great; the eloquence and prestige of the elderly pontiff is alleged to have convinced Attila to withdraw from Italy. According to papal tradition, it was not Leo alone who persuaded the king to leave the peninsula; the heavenly hosts, led by the apostles Peter and Paul, threatened Attila with death if he disobeyed the papal commands. The plague afflicting the army of the Huns and the threat of an imperial army from the east no doubt also influenced Attila's decision to withdraw.

Once again, despite military setbacks, Attila planned further campaigns against the empire, including a massive invasion of the Eastern Empire in 453. His plans, however, were cut short by his own death. He was found dead with his new wife the morning after his wedding. There were rumors that his wife had poisoned him. He may have celebrated his marriage too enthusiastically and, in a drunken stupor, drowned in his own nosebleed. Or he may have suffered a fatal stroke. Whatever the cause, the mighty king was dead, and he was buried in great state. His body was borne by the best horsemen of the Huns into an open field, where it was laid to rest. The body was placed in a tent of the finest Chinese silk, and a great revel, the *strava,* took place around it. The Huns rode around the tent, chanting a dirge, tearing out their hair, and gashing their faces. The body was then placed in three nested coffins bound with gold, silver, and iron. It was buried with great wealth, including gem-encrusted weapons, and the slaves who prepared Attila's tomb were killed so that its whereabouts would remain unknown.

The empire of the Huns did not long survive its greatest king. None of Attila's many sons had the abilities of their father, and fraternal squabbling worsened a bad situation. The many subject peoples revolted and brought down the empire. Rome surely rejoiced. Despite its rapid demise, the empire of Attila had posed a grave threat to the empire of Rome. His ambition and military prowess challenged Rome, and he nearly succeeded in taking control of the Western Empire. His untimely death cut short even greater plans of conquest that could have proved devastating to the Roman Empire, and despite his ultimate failure Attila remains one of the best known and greatest of Rome's foes.

See also: Aëtius; Gaiseric; Galla Placidia; Huns; Rome; Visigoths

Bibliography

Baüml, Franz H., and Marianna Birnbaum. *Attila: The Man and His Image.* Budapest: Corvina, 1993.

Bury, John B. *History of the Later Roman Empire: From the Death of Theodosius I to the Death of Justinian.* Vol. 1. 1923. Reprint, New York: Dover, 1959.

Thompson, Edward A. *A History of Attila and the Huns.* Oxford: Clarendon, 1948.

Thompson, Edward A. *The Huns.* Oxford: Blackwell, 1995.

Wolfram, Herwig. *The Roman Empire and Its Germanic Peoples.* Trans. Thomas J. Dunlap. Berkeley: University of California Press, 1997.

Augustine of Canterbury, St. (d. 604)

Missionary to the Anglo-Saxon people, Augustine was sent to England by Pope Gregory I, called the Great, with forty other missionaries. Much of our knowledge of his evangelical mission comes from two primary sources: the letters sent to Augustine from Gregory, which were preserved, in part, by Bede in *A History of the English Church and People,* and Bede's history itself. Augustine successfully introduced Christianity to the kingdom of Kent, converted the Kentish king, built or restored churches, and introduced monastic life to England. Augustine was not only a successful evangelist, but he was also the first archbishop of Canterbury. Although there was a period of apostasy after the deaths of Augustine and Aethelberht, the Anglo-Saxon king, Augustine can be recognized as restoring contacts between England and Rome that had been broken during the barbarian invasions and also as reestablishing Christianity in Anglo-Saxon England.

According to Bede, the inspiration to evangelize England was the result of an experience Gregory had before he became pope. One day while in the marketplace in Rome, Gregory came upon some merchants who had recently arrived with young boys to sell as slaves. Remarking on their attractive features, Gregory asked the name of their race. He was told they were Angels, and he said that was appropriate because "They have angelic faces" (Bede 1981, 100). He learned too that they were pagan and from the land of Deira, and he hoped to rescue them from the wrath of God (*de ira*). He approached the pope, asking to be sent as a missionary but was refused this request. According to the tradition recorded by Bede, however, he did not forget his hope and as pope sent a mission to England. Although the tale may be apocryphal, it does reveal Gregory's desire to convert the English as well as his possible awareness of the importance of western Europe for the papacy.

Whatever the truth of Bede's tale, Gregory did send an evangelical mission to England, which was led by Augustine. Little is known of Augustine's life before he was chosen to lead the mission to England, other than that he was probably a student of Felix, bishop of Messana, and was a monk and prior of St. Andrew's monastery in Rome. In 596 Augustine was appointed to lead roughly forty monks to England to preach the Christian faith or at least to learn if the people would be receptive to hearing the word. It was a mission of some uncertainty and setbacks but one that ultimately proved successful.

Leaving Rome sometime before July 596, Augustine and his fellow missionaries arrived first in Gaul, bearing letters from Gregory asking the bishops of Gaul to support the missionaries on their way. Augustine's route through Gaul possibly took him to the cities of Arles, Lyons, Marseilles, and Tours. As the letters of Gregory reveal, the missionaries also visited the powerful Merovingian queen Brunhilde and possibly also her grandsons Theudebert, later Theudebert II, and Theuderic, later Theuderic II. The queen was, no doubt, interested in the mission because her niece Bertha was married to the English king Aethelberht. A letter from Gregory in 597 suggests that she was most helpful; the pope thanks her for her efforts and praises her as a new Helena, the mother of the first Christian emperor Constantine. The journey through Gaul, however, was not without incident. At either Lérins or, more likely, Arles, the missionaries sent Augustine back to Rome to ask the pope to reconsider sending the mission because of their fears of going to a barbarous, pagan nation. Gregory promoted Augustine to the rank of abbot and returned him with a letter encouraging the missionaries to proceed to England and another letter seeking support for the missionaries from the bishop of Arles.

The exact date of the arrival of the missionaries in England remains uncertain, but it was probably sometime during the summer of 597. They arrived first on the island of Thanet near the coast of Kent and brought with them Frankish interpreters. Augustine, now a bishop, having been consecrated at Arles, made contact with the king, Aethelberht. Although his wife was a Christian, the king remained a pagan, but he informed Augustine that he would welcome them, even though Augustine was to stay on the island. The king feared that Augustine would use magic to deceive him and ordered an open-air audience to be held, rather than one in a house where Augustine would more easily be able to use magic. The bishop arrived at the head of a procession bearing a silver cross and an icon of Jesus Christ. Although he did not convert, the king welcomed Augustine and offered him a dwelling in the capital of Canterbury, where Augustine settled and restored the ancient church of St. Martin. He thus began the mission, and then his prayers and the miracles he performed convinced the king to convert. This was Augustine's greatest accomplishment, and even though the king did not compel his subjects to convert, many did, and Gregory reported in a letter to the patriarch of Alexandria that Augustine baptized 10,000 people on Christmas Day, 597.

Augustine set about establishing the infrastructure needed for the church in England. In 601 he received the pallium, symbol of full episcopal authority, from Gregory and permission to establish a number of new bishoprics under his authority as archbishop. He was to promote London to the status of archbishopric and also create a new archiepiscopal see in York and twelve new episcopal sees under the authority of York. Augustine's see at Canterbury, was to remain the primatial see in England. Augustine also repaired the cathedral in Canterbury, Christ Church, which was consecrated on June 9, 603, and established a monastery near the cathedral, which served as the burial site for Augustine and his successors as archbishop as well as for the kings of Kent. He received aid from further missionaries in 601, who brought a number of items necessary for worship, including altar covers, books, church ornaments, relics, and vestments. He corresponded often with Gregory in Rome and received instructions on various matters, including an order not to destroy the pagan temples of the English. Gregory approved destruction of pagan idols but recommended purifying existing pagan temples and consecrating them as churches so that the English would flock "more readily to their accustomed resorts, [and] come to know and adore the true God" (Bede 1981, 87). Augustine also received a letter from Gregory cautioning the archbishop against taking pride in the miracles that God was performing through the archbishop in England.

Augustine also organized a council at Augustine Oak in 603, between the church he had established and the British churches that existed outside the Anglo-Saxon kingdoms. These churches had fallen out of communication with Rome, and Augustine hoped to reconcile with them and introduce Roman practices to them. The conference was a failure because the British churches refused to accept his, and Rome's, teaching on the date of Easter and other matters. Even though Augustine miraculously cured a man of blindness as a test of whom God favored, while the British clerics failed at the task, the conference ended without reconciliation between the two churches. A second council was held sometime later, and again the two sides failed to agree. The British priests refused to accept Augustine's compromise of allowing them to continue their traditional practices but requiring them to conform to Roman usage on Easter and baptism because Augustine did not rise from his seat when they approached. Bede records Augustine's prophecy of strife afflicting the British churches, which, Bede notes, was fulfilled.

Despite this failure and the period of apostasy after his death on May 26, 604, and the death of Aethelberht, Augustine's mission was of great importance for the history of Christianity in England. He successfully restored connections between England and Rome. He baptized many Anglo-Saxons, including the king of Kent, established a network of bishops, built a monastery, and restored many churches that had fallen into disuse and disrepair. Indeed, as the epitaph on his tomb notes, the first archbishop of Canterbury "supported by God with miracles guided King Aethelberht and his people from the worship of idols to the faith of Christ." (Bede 1981, 105).

See also: Aethelberht I of Kent; Anglo-Saxons; Bede; Brunhilde; Constantine; Gregory the Great; Merovingian Dynasty; Rome

Bibliography

Bede. *Ecclesiastical History of the English People with Bede's Letter to Egbert and Cuthbert's Letter on the Death of Bede.* Trans. Leo Sherley-Price. Harmondsworth, UK: Penguin, 1991.

Blair, Peter Hunter. *The World of Bede.* Cambridge: Cambridge University Press, 1991.

Mayr-Harting, Henry. *The Coming of Christianity to Anglo-Saxon England.* 3rd ed. University Park: Pennsylvania State University Press, 1991.

Stenton, Frank M. *Anglo-Saxon England.* 3rd ed. Oxford: Clarendon, 1971.

Augustine of Hippo, St. (354–430)

The greatest of the Latin church fathers. Augustine's influence extended from late antiquity into the early Middle Ages and beyond. His voluminous writings, of more than 5 million words, shaped much of the intellectual culture of barbarian Europe. His autobiography, polemical and theological works, sermons, and other treatises shaped how early medieval ecclesiastics from Caesarius of Arles to Alcuin understood the faith. Early medieval writers also looked to Augustine for instruction on how to interpret and teach Scripture. It was not only learned ecclesiastics, but also the barbarian kings of the early Middle Ages who were influenced by Augustine's ideas. If Charlemagne's biographer, Einhard, is to be believed, one of the great king's favorite books was the *City of God,* which, for the king and his advisors, may have offered a model of the just earthly society.

Augustine was born in Thagaste in North Africa (now Souk Ahras, Algeria) in 354 to parents, Patricius and Monnica, who belonged to the lower aristocracy, and was probably their only child. He was educated in the traditional Roman fashion, and was sent to the best schools his father could afford, including those in the great city of the province, Carthage. There was little remarkable about his youth, except, as Augustine notes in his autobiographical work *Confessions,* for his theft of some pears with his friends. As a young adult he acquired a mistress who bore him a son, Adeodatus, and, much to his Christian mother's dismay, he converted to Manichaeanism, a religion that taught the belief in a good god and a bad god and held that the material world was evil because it was created by the bad god. He remained a Manichaean until his conversion to Christianity in Milan in 386.

Having developed a reputation as a teacher in Thagaste and Carthage, Augustine had moved to Milan in 384 to find a position at the imperial court. While there he met the archbishop, Ambrose, and converted to Christianity. After his conversion, he returned to Africa, without his mistress or the woman to whom he had become engaged while in Milan, and hoped to live the quiet life of a Christian scholar. He was ordained a priest in 391 and in 395 made bishop of Hippo, a promotion that

St. Augustine of Hippo. (Library of Congress)

forced him to consider the meaning of his new faith and write *On Christian Doctrine* and *Confessions*. As bishop he was involved with fighting a number of religious heresies, administering the diocese, and preaching. Over his long career, he wrote numerous sermons, which provided an important outlet to develop his theology.

In 413, he began his greatest work, *City of God,* a Christian apology inspired by the Visigoths' sack of Rome in 410. This massive work contains philosophies of history and politics, a defense of Christian belief, and profound Christian theology. It tells, among other things, the history of the tragedies that befell the Roman Empire before the sack of Rome, which the pagans blamed on Christianity, to prove that the pagans were wrong and to comfort Christians who questioned their belief in the face of disaster. Augustine spent his last years administering his diocese, struggling against one final heresy, and reexamining his many written works. He died on August 28, 430, as the Vandals began to threaten Augustine's city of Hippo, which they sacked in 431.

Shortly after his death, Augustine's writings, together with his relics, were moved from his native Africa to Italy and from there continued to shape intellectual life for centuries after. His influence on the cultural life of Europe can be measured by the many ecclesiastics who borrowed from his writings and the libraries where his works were found. Isidore of Seville (c. 560–636), the late Roman bishop and encyclopedist, who was influential in the Visigothic courts of Spain, borrowed heavily from the principles Augustine laid out in his work *On Christian Doctrine,* which advocated the use of classical learning in the service of the Christian faith. In the seventh century, the works of Augustine were deposited in numerous monasteries in the Merovingian kingdom of the Franks. And in the eighth century, the Anglo-Saxon missionary, Boniface, recognized the authority of Augustine as a biblical commentator, and the bishop of Hippo's influence can be detected in the work of the great Anglo-Saxon scholar Bede. But the extent of Augustine's influence is perhaps best revealed in the Carolingian Renaissance.

Manuscript copies of his works were found in most Carolingian libraries, and of particular importance was the library at Lyons, which was a virtual Augustine research center. Augustine's treatise on Christian doctrine was the foundation for Carolingian educational ideas, and his influence can be seen on the works of the greatest Carolingian teacher, the Anglo-Saxon scholar Alcuin. Finally, the great debate over predestination begun by Gottschalk of Orbais in the mid-ninth century involved competing interpretations of Augustine's works.

Augustine's influence was felt beyond the intellectual realm, however, since his ideas also affected the political realm, especially during the Carolingian age. Einhard, in his biography of Charlemagne, noted that the great king of the Franks enjoyed hearing excerpts from the *City of God* read during his banquets. Indeed, it has been suggested that Charlemagne's, or at least his advisors', ideas of government were inspired by a reading of Augustine's works. Although the question of whether Augustine intended to provide a blueprint for the just Christian society in his great work remains open, many of his readers saw such a blueprint and worked to establish it. Political Augustinianism was an important influence in early medieval society and involved a number of key concepts touched on by the great bishop in the *City of God.* The *City of God* describes the existence of two "cities" on earth—the city of God, whose members are virtuous, and the earthly city, whose members are corrupt. Augustine explains that the two societies coexist but that the only true and just city is the heavenly one. Implicit, however, in his discussion is the notion that a society could be just if it were ruled by a Christian monarch, and it is this implication that may have inspired Charlemagne and his advisors, such as Alcuin.

See also: Alaric; Alcuin of York; Bede; Boniface, St.; Caesarius of Arles; Carolingian Renaissance; Charlemagne; Einhard; Gottschalk of Orbais; Isidore of Seville; Merovingian Dynasty; Vandals; Visigoths

Bibliography

Augustine. *Confessions: Books I–XIII.* Trans. Francis J. Sheed. Indianapolis: Hackett, 1993.

Augustine. *Concerning the City of God against the Pagans.* Trans. Henry Bettenson. Harmondsworth, UK: Penguin, 1981.

Augustine. *On Christian Doctrine.* Trans. Donald W. Robertson, Jr. New York: Macmillan, 1958.

Brown, Peter. *Augustine of Hippo: A Biography.* Berkeley: University of California Press, 1967.

Deane, Herbert. *The Political and Social Ideas of Saint Augustine.* New York: Columbia University Press, 1964.

Laistner, Max L. W. *Thought and Letters in Western Europe,* A.D. *500 to 900.* 2nd ed. Ithaca, NY: Cornell University Press, 1976.

O'Donnell, James J. *Augustine.* Boston, MA: Twayne, 1985.

Wills, Gary. *Saint Augustine.* New York: Penguin, 1999.

Austrasia

The "eastern land" or "eastern realm," Austrasia was the northeastern part of the Frankish kingdom and included parts of modern day Belgium, France, Germany and Luxembourg. Its territory stretched from near the Seine to the Rhine and included the Meuse and Moselle River valleys. The capital of the region was Metz and Trier, Cologne, and Mainz were its other major cities and episcopal sees. The homeland of the Ripuarian or Rhineland Franks, Austrasia was the birthplace of the Carolingian dynasty and one of the three major regions that made up the Frankish kingdom.

Austrasia was first established as the core of the kingdom of the Ripuarian Franks in the fifth century and was made part of the growing Merovingian kingdom by Clovis (r. 489–511). After the death of Clovis, Austrasia emerged as one of the kingdoms, along with Neustria and Burgundy, that was divided between Clovis's successors. It had its own king and mayor of the palace and followed a different path of development than the other kingdoms. Austrasia was less Romanized than the other regions and was more Germanic in language and custom. The Austrasians spoke the Germanic Frankish language, rather than Latin or Romance, and possessed their own law code, the *Lex Ripuaria.* It was from Austrasia that the Franks expanded into regions such as Alemannia, Bavaria, and Thuringia.

Throughout much of the sixth and seventh centuries, the Austrasians and Neustrians engaged in bloody conflict for dominance in the larger Frankish realm. Following the overthrow of the queen Brunhilde in 613, Austrasia and Neustria were united under Chlotar II who, in 623, appointed his son Dagobert as king in Austrasia. The office of mayor of the palace emerged at this point, and the roots of the Carolingian dynasty were established in Austrasia in the early seventh century. In 687, the Austrasian mayor, Pippin I of Landen defeated his Neustrian rival at the battle of Tertry and reestablished the preeminence of Austrasia in the Frankish kingdom. In 751, Pippin's grandson, Pippin the Short overthrew the last of the Merovingian kings and was crowned the first king of the Franks. In the late eighth century, Charlemagne built his imperial capital in Austrasia at Aix-la-Chapelle, preserving the importance of the region in the Carolingian empire. Under the later Carolingians, Austrasia was incorporated into the central kingdom of Lotharingia.

See also: Aix-la-Chapelle; Brunhilde; Carolingian Dynasty; Charlemagne; Chlotar II; Clovis I; Dagobert; Merovingian Dynasty; Neustria; Pippin I, Called Pippin of Landen; Pippin II, Called Pippin of Herstal; Tertry, Battle of

Bibliography

Geary, Patrick J. *Before France and Germany the Transformation of the Merovingian World.* Oxford: Oxford University Press, 1988.

James, Edward. *The Franks.* Oxford: Basil Blackwell, 1991.

Riché, Pierre. *The Carolingians: A Family Who Forged Europe.* Trans. Michael Idomir Allen. Philadelphia: University of Pennsylvania Press, 1993.

Wood, Ian. *The Merovingian Kingdoms, 450–751.* London: Longman, 1994.

Avars

An amalgamation of peoples from the central steppes of Europe, the Avars were a late arrival among the barbarian peoples who were the successors of the Western Roman Empire. They were skilled horsemen, who may have had an important impact on the development of military technology in the early Middle Ages, and successful warriors. Although less well known than their relatives the Huns, they had similar success in threatening the established kingdoms of their day and greater success in creating a permanent kingdom. They were seen as a threat by the Byzantine Empire and caused difficulty for the Franks before their great capital was destroyed by Charlemagne's armies.

The exact origins of the Avars remain uncertain. They have been identified with the Juan-Juan, a group of tribes in Mongolia, and with a tribal group of Afghanistan, the Ephthalites. There is, however, general agreement that at some time in the mid-sixth century, the Avars were pushed out of their homeland by the Turks. They appear in the historical record in 558, when an Avar embassy arrived in Constantinople and met with the emperor Justinian. They settled not long after that in the region of modern Hungary.

On their arrival, the Avars were welcomed by the Byzantines, who needed allies along their eastern frontier, but they quickly wore out their welcome. They demanded land and other privileges from Emperor Justinian, who offered them some gifts but insisted they prove themselves before he made any major concessions. They very quickly subdued several nomadic steppe tribes and thus demonstrated their abilities. By 562 they made further demands for territory from Justinian, who agreed to give them land west of modern Belgrade. They had wanted other territory, and the two powers were on the verge of war when the Avars turned their attention for the first time to the Franks. For the next generation they continued their westward efforts. By the 580s, with Slavic subjects and allies, the Avars turned their attention to Byzantine territory in the Balkans. They extended their influence into the Balkans and posed a serious threat to the empire, which they forced out of the region of the Danube River in 602. In 626, with the Slavs and new Persian allies, the Avars pressed on and threatened the city of Constantinople. The siege failed, and the Avars lost ground to the Byzantines, as well as to the Bulgars and other Slavs who were supported by the empire. The Avars showed their first sign of decline in the face of their defeat and the Slavic rebellions. These losses of ground were the first sign of decline for the Avars. They subsequently posed less of a problem for the Byzantines, even though occasional battles took place for decades to come.

The Avars made their mark not only on the Byzantine Empire but also on the kingdom of the Franks and other powers in the former Western Roman Empire. In 562, rather than launch an attack on the Byzantine Empire, the Avars turned their attention westward to make their strength known in that region. They attacked the Merovingian kingdom of Austrasia in 562 but were turned back by the king Sigebert (r. 560/561–575). But in 565 or 566, the Avars attacked Sigebert's kingdom again and defeated him. According to Gregory of Tours, the Avars won the second battle because they "made a number of phantom figures dance before [the Franks'] eyes and so beat them easily" (29). Sigebert gave them many gifts and agreed to a treaty with them. Following this success, the Avars, in 567, joined with the Lombards to destroy the Gepid kingdom. The Lombards, uncertain of Avar intentions, moved into Italy, leaving the Avars the main power along the Danube River.

Although they turned their attention elsewhere, the Avars returned to their struggle with the Franks in the early seventh century. They had some success in the early seventh century, but an alliance of Franks and Saxons led by King Dagobert pushed them out of eastern Frankish territory in the Rhineland. Again in the eighth century, the Avars and the Franks were at war when the Avars invaded the kingdom and destroyed the city of Lorch and its surrounding territory in 711. They launched another campaign into Frankish territories in 740 and were decisively defeated. This marked the end of their period of aggression and the beginning of the end of their kingdom. They now faced the expansionistic policies of the Carolingian dynasty and its greatest member, Charlemagne. He directed an eight-year war against the Avars from 788 to 796 that led to the destruction of the kingdom and its great capital. According to Einhard, the entire Avar "nobility died in this war, all their glory departed" (67). He noted further that the Avars had unjustly acquired their wealth and that Charlemagne justly took it from them in a war that brought the Franks more wealth than any other war.

Although the Avars disappeared in the face of the Carolingian attack, they left an important legacy. According to some historians, the Avars introduced important military technology to Europe. The Avars may have used an iron stirrup. The stirrup improved the fighting ability of soldiers on horseback by making them more secure and steady in the saddle. With the stirrup, they could more effectively wield their lances. The Byzantines, who made contact with them before other peoples around the Mediterranean, adopted the iron stirrup for their cavalry by 600, but the stirrup only gradually made its appearance in the barbarian kingdoms. The Avars also used a composite bow in battle that was more effective than other bows, and skilled Avar riders at full gallop could shoot up to twenty arrows a minute. The arrows had heavy three-winged heads and could be fired up to 1500 feet. The bow was shorter than most other simple bows and was made of layers of horn, sinew, and wood that were glued together and reinforced with bone. Although very effective for the Avars, the bows were not widely used by other peoples because they were difficult to produce.

See also: Carolingian Dynasty; Charlemagne; Dagobert; Einhard; Franks; Gregory of Tours; Huns; Justinian; Lombards; Merovingian Dynasty

Bibliography

Bury, John B. *History of the Later Roman Empire: From the Death of Theodosius I to the Death of Justinian.* 2 Vols. 1923. Reprint, New York: Dover, 1959.

Einhard and Notker the Stammerer. *Two Lives of Charlemagne.* Trans. Lewis Thorpe. Harmondsworth, UK: Penguin, 1981.

Gregory of Tours. *The History of the Franks.* Trans. Lewis Thorpe. Harmondsworth, UK: Penguin, 1982.

Herrin, Judith. *The Formation of Christendom.* Princeton, NJ: Princeton University Press, 1989.

Wallace-Hadrill, John M. *The Barbarian West, A.D. 400–1000.* New York: Harper and Row, 1962.

Wolfram, Herwig. *The Roman Empire and Its Germanic Peoples.* Trans. Thomas J. Dunlap. Berkeley: University of California Press, 1997.

B

Badon Hill, Battle of (fifth century)

Traditionally associated with the legendary King Arthur, the battle of Badon Hill or Mount Badon (*Mons Badonicus*) was an important episode in the invasion of England by the Saxons in the late fifth and early sixth centuries. Although the exact date and location of the battle remain uncertain, the early English sources agree that it was a major battle that slowed the progress of the Saxon invaders. The sixth-century chronicler and cleric, Gildas, notes that the battle was the last in a series of indecisive battles, won sometimes by Britons and sometimes by Saxons, before the Britons inflicted great slaughter on their enemies at Badon Hill. Gildas, however, observes that England remained a troubled land after his battle. Although he does not name the commander directly, Gildas implies that the victor at Badon Hill was not Arthur but rather the late Roman general Ambrosius Aurelianus.

In the eighth century, the great scholar Bede confirmed the account of Gildas and identified Aurelianus as the victorious general. Writing in the eighth century, the chronicler Nennius identified the victor at Badon Hill as Arthur. According to Nennius, the kings of the Britons, lead by Arthur, fought 12 battles against the invading Saxons. The last of these battles was fought at Badon Hill, where Arthur personally slew 960 of the enemy and single-handedly won the battle. Despite his victory at Badon Hill and elsewhere, Arthur was only able to delay the inevitable, and, as Nennius explains, the Saxons continued to attract kings from Germany who would come to rule over the Britons.

See also: Anglo-Saxons; Bede; King Arthur

Bibliography

Barber, Richard. *The Figure of Arthur*. Totowa, NJ: Rowan and Littlefield, 1972.

Bede. *Ecclesiastical History of the English Church and People*. Trans. Leo Sherley-Price. Revised R. E. Latham. Harmondsworth, UK: Penguin Books, 1968.

Gildas. *The Ruin of Britain and Other Works*. Ed. and trans. Michael Winterbottom. London: Phillimore, 1978.

Giles, J. A. ed. *Six Old English Chronicles, of which Two are Now First Translated from the Monkish Latin Originals: Ethelwerd's Chronicle; Asser's Life of Alfred; Geoffrey of Monmouth's British History; Gildas; Nennius; and Richard of Cirencester*. London: H. G. Bohn, 1848.

Balthild, St. (d. 680)

Wife of King Clovis II (639–657) and regent of Chlotar III (657–683), Balthild was an important figure in the Merovingian kingdom of the second half of the seventh century. A saint, whose feast is celebrated on January 30, Balthild was also a shrewd political leader who successfully guided her son's regency and implemented important political and religious reforms. Often compared with the Merovingian queen Brunhilde (d. 613), Balthild could be as ruthless as her predecessor when family interests were at stake, but Balthild was not quite so brutal as the earlier Merovingian queen. Indeed, even when their policies seem most similar, Balthild seems to have been motivated less by simple power politics than Brunhilde. Balthild also seemed genuinely committed to the reform of the Frankish church and, according to her biographer, was a devout and pious member of the convent where she spent her last years. Her hagiography, or saint's life, *The Life of Saint Balthild* or *The Life of the Lady Balthild,* written by a member of her community at Chelles, is the primary source for our knowledge of Balthild's life.

Little is known of Balthild's early life. Her biographer notes that before her marriage to Clovis II she had an "admirable and pious religious way of life" and that she was "kind in her heart, temperate and prudent" (*Vita Domnae Balthildis,* 119). She was described as an Anglo-Saxon slave, who was purchased by a Frankish noble to serve at his court. Indeed, so attractive were her personality and appearance that, as her biographer tell us, the noble desired to marry her, but she resisted. "By the true will of God" (120) she eventually married Clovis, son of the great king Dagobert I, and bore him the future kings Chlotar II (584–629) and Childeric II (662–675). She apparently had little direct influence during her husband's reign and lived a life of piety and religious devotion. Her husband recognized this and granted her as a servant Abbot Genisius, who assisted her in works of charity, including donations of food and clothing to the poor as well as grants of money to churches and monasteries.

After Clovis's death in 657, however, Balthild assumed the regency for her son Chlotar III and exercised much power and influence throughout the kingdom. She may also have been instrumental in the reunification of the three parts of the Merovingian kingdom, Austrasia, Neustria, and Burgundy. Under his mother's regency, Chlotar assumed authority over Neustria, and Balthild's close ties with important abbots and bishops in Burgundy strengthened the connection between Neustria and Burgundy. She also appointed a new mayor of the palace for Neustria, further extending her authority in the realm. She also arranged the marriage of her son Childeric with an important noblewoman in Austrasia in 622. The marriage and Balthild's connection with Austrasian nobles paved the way for Childeric's ascension to the Austrasian throne.

Balthild's political success was due in part to the good relationship she had with the clergy in the Merovingian kingdom. She was by all accounts pious and deeply committed to the reform of the Frankish church. She was an ardent supporter of the cult of the saints, and she also actively collected the relics of the saints, perhaps to gain the saints' support for her family. As regent, Balthild was actively involved in the daily affairs of the church and its hierarchy. She appointed bishops to their sees and to important positions in the regency government.

Although she has been blamed for the death of nine bishops, Balthild should not be compared too closely with Brunhilde in this matter. As regent, Balthild was responsible for executions, but only after the letter of the law had been followed; apparently, she never acted arbitrarily. Indeed, any executions she ordered were to preserve the peace and order of the kingdom. Moreover, despite the suggestion that some of these bishops were martyred, Balthild's relationships with the bishops were not that bad, and the appointments she made were uniformly good bishops. She also, unlike Brunhilde, was an active opponent of simony and a strong supporter of religious reform. She promoted the more stringent monasticism of the Irish missionaries and founded monasteries, including one at Chelles that followed the pattern of Luxeuil, which had been founded by the great Irish saint Columban. To strengthen monasticism in the kingdom, she ordered that certain monasteries be exempted from episcopal jurisdiction, an act that surely alienated some bishops in her kingdom but also found much support from the bishops as a whole.

By the mid-660s, Balthild had ruled effectively and proved a successful regent for her son, Chlotar, who reached his majority in 664. In that year or the year after, 665, Balthild fell from power. According to the author of the saint's life, Balthild lost power because of her opposition to the murder of the bishop of Paris, Sigobrand. Her struggle against the nobles responsible for the murder proved unsuccessful, however, and she was deposed and allowed to enter the woman's monastery she founded at Chelles. She stayed at Chelles until her death in circa 680. Although she may have felt the convent to be a prison, Balthild's hagiographer assures the reader that the queen was a model of pious devotion at the monastery. She exhibited "great humility," "joy," and a "cheerful heart" even when cleaning the kitchen or the latrines (127). Her piety was so great that as her death approached, according to the author of *The Life of Saint Balthild,* she received a vision in which she ascended a stairway leading to Mary. Although she lived her final years secluded in a monastery in a sort of internal exile, Balthild left an important mark on the Merovingian kingdom, its ruling dynasty, and its church.

See also: Anglo-Saxons; Austrasia; Brunhilde; Columban, St.; Dagobert; Merovingian Dynasty; Neustria

Bibliography

Fouracre, Paul, and Richard A. Gerberding. *Vita Domnai Balthildis* (The Life of Lady Balthild, Queen of the Franks). In *Late Merovingian France: History and Hagiography, 640–720.* Manchester, UK: University of Manchester Press, 1996, pp. 47–132.

Nelson, Janet L. "Queens as Jezebels: The Careers of Brunhild and Balthild in Merovingian History." In *Medieval Women.* Ed. Derek Baker. Oxford: Blackwell, 1978, pp. 31–77.

Schulenburg, Jane Tibbetts. *Forgetful of their Sex: Female Sanctity and Society, ca. 500–1100.* Chicago: University of Chicago Press, 1998.

Wemple, Suzanne. *Women in Frankish Society: Marriage and the Cloister, 500 to 900.* Philadelphia: University of Pennsylvania Press, 1981.

Wood, Ian. *The Merovingian Kingdoms, 451–751.* London: Longman, 1994.

Barbarian Art

The product of the various peoples who entered the Roman world in late antiquity and then established successor kingdoms during the early Middle Ages, barbarian art was often highly stylized and quite accomplished. Indeed, the label *barbarian* or *barbarian art* in some ways demeans the quality of the works that Germanic and other peoples created from the fourth to ninth centuries. Works of art were produced in various media. These artists produced works in ivory and precious metals and gems, creating beautiful book covers of carved ivory or metalwork and jewelry of gold and silver. Weapons, too, were created as works of art. Some of the most impressive examples of barbarian or early medieval art, however, are found in the manuscript illuminations that were produced in monasteries throughout Europe. Both the covers and illustrations of early medieval manuscripts reveal a high level of skill and a well-developed aesthetic sensibility. Barbarian art drew its inspiration from various sources and, especially after the initial period of contact and conversion, mixed Christian, Germanic, and Roman influences to create a distinctive and often beautiful artistic style.

The most predominant form of artistic expression of the migration period and into the early post-Roman period was in metalwork. Artists and artisans created exquisite pieces of jewelry—earrings, rings, bracelets, and brooches—and other things, such as belt buckles, to adorn clothing and the body. There were several categories of the design of metalwork during the migration period. Some pieces were simply abstract and geometric in design; other styles were more clearly representational, and the decoration of the jewelry and other metalwork included animal patterns. The representational, animal style is generally classified in one of two categories, Style I or Style II. Style I, which originated in northern Europe and spread into France by the sixth century, arranged parts of animals or complete but compact animals in a decorative pattern in the metalwork. The ribbon animal

Brooch earrings, bracelets, and Visigothic jewelry, 621–672. (The Art Archive/ Archaeological Museum Madrid)

style, Style II, was a Lombard innovation that spread to other peoples, and it placed animal figures in elongated, intertwined, continuous, and symmetrical patterns in the metalwork. These traditional designs mixed and mingled with Roman influences, especially among the Visigoths and Lombards, as the various Germanic peoples settled in the former Western Empire and came into fuller contact with Roman artistic traditions.

Other forms of metalwork include the work done in bronze and other base metals, used for adorning soldiers. A polychrome cloisonné style, which developed by the fourth century and employed gold and precious gems, was also popular. The polychrome style was used in brooches and to decorate the swords and other weapons of kings and nobles. Gold was also employed by late antique and early medieval artisans to decorate book covers, especially of the more important manuscripts in a monastic, cathedral, or royal library. Borrowing the techniques and styles used for jewelry and other metalwork, craftsmen decorated book covers with figures in gold and other metals, and incorporated precious gems to further enhance the beauty and value of the book and its cover. Because many of the covers were for books of the Bible and other religious texts, the scenes on the covers were often drawn from the history of the church and from the religious texts themselves. Especially popular were decorations portraying Christ in majesty, with the four Evangelists represented by their symbols.

Another medium in which early medieval artists were skilled is ivory, which was used for decoration of book covers as well as liturgical objects. The style of the carved miniatures that adorned important books in the early Middle Ages was at first a continuation of ancient Roman styles. The artists borrowed both technique and subject matter from their Roman predecessors, but as time went on, they began to develop their own unique styles. The carvings often displayed scenes from the Gospels, Psalms, and other books of the Bible. The carvings themselves reveal variation in style, technique, and talent. Some ivory carvings are noteworthy for their monumental quality, even though they were done on a miniature scale, and others are characterized by more animated figures that recall the illuminations found inside the books. They also reveal the mingling of Christian, Roman, and Germanic influences. The covers often included scenes from the Christian Scriptures or history that were modeled on Roman or Byzantine precedents. The artists also often included decorative borders with geometric or floral patterns. Ivory carvings also adorned reliquaries and other small containers, various liturgical objects such as crosiers, and even larger architectural items, such as the doors of Santa Sabina in Rome.

Among the most characteristic and magnificent products of early medieval artists are the manuscript illuminations that decorated many of the great books of the period. Although mural painting was practiced, few examples survive—one important exception is the mural from the church of Theodulf of Orléans, which portrays the story of the Ark of the Covenant and reveals Theodulf's sophisticated theory of art—to allow us to judge them, in contrast to the manuscript illuminations. Particularly by the Carolingian period, manuscript illuminators had achieved a highly developed style that merged Christian, Roman, and German traditions, just as the artists in ivory had. Numerous psalters, gospels, and other important texts received luxurious illuminations.

Subjects included Jesus, Mary, the saints and apostles, and other important figures in the history of the church such as the popes. By the Carolingian age, subjects included kings and emperors, including Louis the Pious, Charles the Bald, and Lothar. The illustrations portraying the monarchs stressed key political ideas, emphasizing the religious nature and divine origin of kingship. The illustrations often borrowed from classical models, and some clearly repeat their Roman predecessors, but others reveal a more unique and individual spirit. The illuminations, in many colors and sometimes highlighted with gold, are often dramatic and stately.

Ark of the Covenant from the Oratory of Theodulf (mosaic). (Peter Willi/The Bridgeman Art Library)

Individual letters in the text were sometimes decorated. These letters, the so-called historiated capitals, included images that captured a brief incident or scene or were decorated with abstract designs or floral patterns. The miniatures also included the kind of abstract or geometric ornamentation in the borders and throughout the main image that had been popular in the migration period. Some images as well include the dramatic movement and expression that the migration-period peoples seemed to favor. But Roman styles also shaped the illuminations and defined the way individuals like Louis the Pious or the Evangelist Matthew were portrayed: the former as a Roman ruler, the latter as a classical scribe.

See also: Carolingian Renaissance; Charlemagne; Charles the Bald; Clothing; Franks; Ivories; Jewelry and Gems; Lombards; Lothar; Louis the Pious; Weapons and Armor; Visigoths

Bibliography

Beckwith, John. *Early Medieval Art.* London: Thames and Hudson, 1969.

Grabar, André. *Early Medieval Painting from the Fourth to the Eleventh Century.* Lausanne: Skira, 1957.

Hubert, Jean, Jean Porcher, and Wolfgang Fritz Volbach. *The Carolingian Renaissance.* New York: George Braziller, 1970.

Lasko, Peter. *Ars Sacra 800–1200.* 2nd ed. New Haven, CT: Yale University Press, 1994.

Lasko, Peter. *The Kingdom of the Franks: Northwest Europe before Charlemagne.* London: Thames and Hudson, 1971.

Mütherich, Florentine, and Joachim E. Gaehde. *Carolingian Painting.* New York: George Braziller, 1976.

Ross, Marvin, and Philippe Verdier. *Arts of the Migration Period in the Walters Art Gallery.* Baltimore, MD: Walters Art Gallery, 1961.

Snyder, James. *Medieval Art: Painting, Sculpture, Architecture, 4th–14th Century.* New York: Harry Abrams, 1989.

Basil the Great, St. (330–379)

One of the Cappadocian Fathers and a doctor of the church, Basil the Great, or Basil of Caesarea, played an important role in the development of orthodox Christian belief and practice. A skilled administrator, Basil served as bishop of Caesarea, staunchly opposed Arianism, and left an important body of writings on various religious topics. He was also an ardent supporter of monasticism and made great contributions to its development and dissemination.

Born in Caesarea, the capital of Cappadocia to a prominent Christian family of long standing (his grandfather was forced to flee during the persecutions of the early fourth century), Basil had connections to both the ecclesiastical and literary elite of his day. One uncle was a bishop, and Basil's father, Basil the Elder, was an orator and lawyer. The younger Basil followed in his father's footsteps and was given the best education of late antiquity, studying at Caesarea and then Constantinople and Athens. After beginning a secular career, Basil turned to the religious life, in part influenced by his sister Macrina. In 357–358, Basil visited a number of ascetic communities and colonies of hermits in search of spiritual guidance. Most impressed by the communal monastic life of St. Pachomius, Basil returned home to establish a small monastery on a family estate at Annesi with a number of friends. Although closely associated with the monastic life, Basil had a very public career even after establishing his community. In 360, he was called to assist the bishop of Caesarea at the council of Constantinople, in part because of his deep learning and commitment to the orthodox faith. He was consecrated a presbyter in 362 and, after a breach of a few years, served the bishop from 365 to 370. Becoming bishop himself in 370, Basil defended the Nicene faith against rival ecclesiastics and the pro-Arian emperor Valens, who sought to force Basil's submission to imperial commands. As metropolitan of Cappadocia, Basil promoted other opponents of Arianism to the bishoprics under his authority and strongly advocated Nicene teachings in his own sermons. The death of Valens at the battle of Hadrianople in 378 opened the door for the victory of Nicene teachings, but Basil's strong support for Nicene orthodoxy was critical to its long-term success and his defense of orthodoxy is one of Basil's lasting legacies.

A strong supporter of orthodox teachings, Basil is perhaps best known for his influence on monasticism, and it was at the community of Annesi that Basil first developed his ideas on monastic life and practice. Although not composing a formal rule like the Rule of St. Benedict, Basil did compile the so-called Longer and Shorter Rules, which are collections of his writings on monastic life assembled in response to concerns raised by fellow monks. His vision of the religious life stressed the communal over the eremitical to avoid the excesses of the solitary life of spiritual competition and to stress brotherly love and sociability of humanity. This emphasis on community can be seen in Basil's placement of monasteries in or near cities, rather than in the desert, so that the laity could experience the monastic life. Basil's form of monasticism also shaped the relationship between the head of the community and the monks, stressing the absolute obedience to the abbot as a means to emphasize humility and the imitation of Christ who obeyed God and accepted his Passion. Another influential innovation of Basil was his emphasis on work as a way toward spiritual perfection and as a means to make the monastery self-sufficient.

Along with his monastic writings, Basil left an important body of theological and liturgical works that shaped Christian teaching and further incorporated the Greek cultural and philosophical tradition into Christian thought. His writings include the *Hexameron*, a commentary on the six days of creation, *On the Holy Spirit*, and anti-Arian treatise *Against Eunomius*. His numerous letters—some 300 still exist—address topics of daily living, theology, and ethical behavior, and his epistles on matters of clerical discipline have become part of canon law. Although revised in later days, the *Liturgy of St. Basil*, a eucharistic service, originally compiled by its namesake continues to be used by the Eastern Orthodox churches of the world.

See also: Arianism; Caesarea; Constantinople; Monasticism; Valens

Bibliography

Harmless, J. William. "Monasticism." In *The Oxford Handbook of Early Christian Studies*. Eds. Susan Ashbrook Harvey and David G. Hunter. Oxford: Oxford University Press, 2008, pp. 493–517.

Hildebrand, Stephen M. *The Trinitarian Theology of Basil of Caesarea: A Synthesis of Greek Thought and Biblical Faith.* Washington, DC: Catholic University Press of America, 2009.

Radde-Gallwitz, Andrew. *Basil of Caesarea; Gregory of Nyssa, and the Transformation of Divine Simplicity.* Oxford: Oxford University Press, 2009.

Rousseau, Philip. *Basil of Caesarea.* Berkeley: University of California Press, 1998.

Silvas, Anna M. *The Asketikon of St. Basil the Great.* Oxford: Oxford University Press, 2005.

Bede (c. 673–735)

Traditionally known as the Venerable Bede, Bede is the most important and influential Anglo-Saxon scholar and the most important scholar of the period from the death of Pope Gregory I, called the Great, to the coronation of Charlemagne in 800, a period sometimes known as the Age of Bede. He was a monk at the communities of Wearmouth and Jarrow, which were founded by Benedict Biscop. He was a devout monk who seldom traveled far from his Northumbrian monastery. He was also an accomplished writer and teacher, whose values were transmitted to the Carolingian world by his most famous admirer, Alcuin. He popularized the *anno Domini* dating system and had great influence on the practice of biblical exegesis and history writing. He wrote numerous commentaries on Scripture and other works, but his most famous work is *A History of the English Church and People.*

Much of what is known of Bede comes from an autobiographical note at the end of his history. Born probably in 673 on lands that later belonged to the monastery of Wearmouth, Bede tells us that he was sent to that monastery at the age of seven. He later joined Abbot Ceolfrith at the monastery of Jarrow, which he ruled, together with nearby Wearmouth, after its founder, Benedict Biscop, died. In the anonymous life of Abbot Ceolfrith, we learn that a young boy, generally believed to be Bede, was one of the only survivors, with the abbot, of a plague that struck Jarrow in 686. Bede helped the abbot sing the canonical hours after the disaster and retained a great love for the hours throughout the rest of his life. In a story told by Alcuin, Bede is once supposed to have said, "I know that angels visit the congregation of brethren at the canonical hours, and what if they should not find me among the brethren? Would they not say, 'Where is Bede?'"

Bede himself tells us that he spent his entire life in the monastery, although he did visit the abbey of Lindisfarne and other monasteries, as well as the archbishop of York and King Ceolwulf of Northumbria, who was a patron of learning and who became a monk shortly after Bede's death. He also notes that he became a deacon at age 19 and a priest at age 30 and that he "observed the regular discipline [of a monk] and sung the choir offices daily in church" (Bede 1981, 336). Although devoted to the monastic life, he explains that his greatest pleasure came from "study, teaching, and writing" (336). From the age of 30 until the age of 59 he "worked, both for my own benefit and that of my brethren, to compile short extracts from the works of the venerable Fathers on Holy Scripture and to comment on their meaning and interpretation" (336). He lists these works in his autobiographical note, and they include commentaries on the books of the Hebrew Bible and Christian Scriptures, letters, saints' lives, a history, a martyrology, and a book on hymns.

He continued writing and teaching until his death, four years after writing his autobiographical note. His last work, which he left unfinished when he died on

A page from the Anglo-Saxon theologian Venerable Bede's *Historia Ecclesiastica Gentis Anglorum* (*A History of the English Church and People*), completed around 731. (The British Library Board)

May 25, 735, was an Old English translation of the Gospel of John. He was buried in the south porch of the monastery church but later moved to the main altar. His fame continued long after his death and was the cause of the theft of his relics in 1020. His bones were stolen by a monk of Durham, who buried them at the shrine to

St. Cuthbert in Durham. They were later encased in a gold and silver reliquary, and during the Reformation, when the monasteries were pillaged and closed by Henry VIII, his relics were allegedly transferred to the Holy Land.

Bede's fame rests on his talents as biblical commentator, teacher, and historian. He left a great legacy to the generations that followed and had a marked influence on the Carolingian Renaissance because of his writing and teaching. In the Middle Ages, he was perhaps best known for his biblical commentaries. He wrote some 24 commentaries on the books of the Bible in an elegant, almost classical Latin, mainly line-by-line explanations of biblical texts, which were commissioned by Bishop Acca of Hexham. Most of his exegetical work is on the books of the Hebrew Bible, including commentaries on Genesis, Song of Songs, Isaiah, Daniel, and Job. He wrote commentaries on the Gospels of Mark and John as well as works on the Epistles and Apocalypse of John. His commentaries on the books of the Bible employed allegorical interpretation of the literal events recorded in Scripture. He borrowed from numerous Christian fathers, including St. Augustine of Hippo, St. Ambrose, and Pope Gregory the Great. Although he often read his sources in compendia rather than the original texts, Bede was very familiar with Jerome's Latin translation of the Bible, the Vulgate.

His talents as a teacher are revealed in two ways. First, they are demonstrated by the importance of his students and the students of his students, such as Alcuin. His talents, along with his interest in teaching, are also revealed in numerous works written as instructional aids. In fact, all his works, including the lives of St. Cuthbert and of the abbots of Wearmouth and Jarrow, have a didactic purpose. He wrote three little books designed specifically for teaching students in monastic schools, one book on spelling and two books on poetry. The books on poetry include a collection of commentaries on an ancient Latin book of grammar and a book in which Bede discusses the language of the Bible. He wrote a book on natural phenomena, influenced by Isidore of Seville, which discusses earthquakes, storms, the planets, stars, and the heavens. He was also a master of the important monastic art of *computus,* the science of calculating dates in the calendar, most importantly Easter. His first attempt to explain this science, written in 703, led to charges of heresy against Bede, which he vigorously denounced in a letter to another monk. A second work, *De temporum ratione,* was much less controversial and much more successful. It became the standard introduction to the science of computus, and through it the practice of dating from the birth of Jesus Christ, rather than from the beginning of the world, became commonplace in medieval Europe.

Bede's most important and well-known work, however, is his *History of the English Church and People,* which he completed in 731. True to his concerns as a teacher, Bede wrote his history so that his reader could follow the good examples therein and act in ways pleasing to God. Organized in five books, the *History* traces the events from the time of Roman Britain, through the period of invasions, the deeds of the Anglo-Saxon kings, and the establishment of Roman Christianity in England. The arrival and triumph of Roman Christianity is one of the important themes of the book and includes some of his more memorable stories, including the tale of Gregory the Great's decision to evangelize England, and the tale of the Synod of Whitby in 664.

The work itself is a true history and not a simple chronicle of events, of the kind his predecessors and contemporaries had compiled. It was an immensely popular work throughout the Middle Ages because of Bede's powerful style and command of the Latin language. He also was most skilled at handling his sources, and although he included miraculous events, he was a critical reader of his sources. He sifted through a variety of eyewitness, oral, and written traditions and borrowed from writers such as Orosius and Pliny. His *History* was so popular that it was translated into Old English during the reign of King Alfred the Great, and his talents as a historian so great that he has been called the father of English history.

Bede was truly one of the great teachers and writers of the early Middle Ages. A devout monk and ardent supporter of Roman Christianity, Bede was venerated in his own time and is still venerated in ours for his many talents and faith. In 1899 he was declared a Doctor of the Church, and in 1935 he was declared a saint. His tomb in Durham, pillaged in 1541, remains a site of veneration.

See also: Alcuin of York; Alfred the Great; Anglo-Saxons; Augustine of Hippo, St.; Benedict Biscop; Carolingian Renaissance; Charlemagne; Gregory I, the Great, Pope; Isidore of Seville; Northumbrian Renaissance

Bibliography

Bede. *Commentary on the Acts of the Apostles.* Trans. Lawrence Martin. Kalamazoo, MI: Cistercian Publications, 1989.

Bede. *Ecclesiastical History of the English People with Bede's Letter to Egbert and Cuthbert's Letter on the Death of Bede.* Trans. Leo Sherley-Price. Harmondsworth, UK: Penguin, 1991.

Blair, Peter Hunter. *The World of Bede.* Cambridge: Cambridge University Press, 1990.

Brown, George Hardin. *Bede the Venerable.* Boston, MA: Twayne, 1987.

Farmer, David H. *The Age of Bede.* Harmondsworth, UK: Penguin, 1998.

Laistner, Max L.W. *Thought and Letters in Western Europe, A.D. 500–900.* 2nd ed. Ithaca, NY: Cornell University Press, 1976.

Lapidge, Michael. *Bede and His World: The Jarrow Lectures, 1958–1993.* 2 Vols. Aldershot, UK: Variorum, 1994.

Riché, Pierre. *Education and Culture in the Barbarian West: From the Sixth to the Eighth Century.* Trans. John Contreni. Columbia: University of South Carolina Press, 1978.

Stenton, Frank M. *Anglo-Saxon England.* 3rd ed. Oxford: Clarendon, 1971.

Belisarius (c. 500–565)

Leading general and loyal supporter of Justinian for more than 40 years, Belisarius fought numerous campaigns against the Persians, the Vandals in Africa, and the Goths in Italy. Completely loyal to Justinian throughout his life, despite the suspicions held by the emperor that sent Belisarius into disgrace, the general helped save Justinian during the Nika Revolt and was critical to Justinian's efforts to reconquer Italy and other sections of the Western Empire that were governed at that time by barbarian kings. His successes, however, sometimes worsened Justinian's fears about his powerful and popular general. Indeed, the respect contemporaries felt for Belisarius is best illustrated in the pages of the sixth-century Byzantine historian Procopius, the general's military secretary. Best known for his scandalous accounts of Justinian and Theodora, Procopius portrayed Belisarius in the least unfavorable light in the *Secret History* and in some ways made Belisarius the great hero of *The History of the Wars.*

Born in a village in modern western Bulgaria in circa 500, perhaps as late as 505, Belisarius was a Romanized Thracian, with possible Gothic ancestry, of modest, but not peasant, circumstances. He entered the military as an officer, and his talents and dazzling personality must have quickly come to the attention of Justinian, then Master of Soldiers, who appointed him to his staff. In the mid-520s, Belisarius, still in his early or mid-twenties, was given a military command against Rome's great eastern rival, Persia. His early command met with little success, but in 529, Justinian, now emperor, appointed Belisarius Master of Soldiers with a command over the eastern frontier. Further campaigns in the east met with little success, but Belisarius demonstrated great personal courage and saved an important imperial city from conquest by the Persians. Recognizing his value, Justinian had Belisarius marry Antonina, an old friend of Justinian's wife Theodora. His greatest early accomplishment, however, was the part he played in the Nika Revolt in 532. Belisarius remained loyal to the emperor during this moment of great crisis. He volunteered to lead a garrison to capture the rival emperor, Hypatius, an enterprise that failed because he met some imperial bodyguards. Despite this setback, Belisarius played a part in the final suppression of the revolt and commanded a group of Germanic mercenary soldiers who massacred the rebels in the capital of Constantinople. Belisarius's demonstration of loyalty and military ability revealed his full worth to the emperor.

His presence in Constantinople in 532 was a lucky accident; Justinian had recalled him from the east to give him charge of the forces to be sent against the Vandals of North Africa. The Vandals, previously thought to be a potential ally in Justinian's efforts to recover Italy, were to be the first step in a grand scheme of conquest. In 533 Belisarius invaded the Vandal kingdom and quickly smashed it.

In two great battles, Belisarius and his well-trained imperial armies and cohort of Hunnish auxiliaries overwhelmed their Vandal opponents. At the second battle, Belisarius displayed his abilities for strategy and tactics. By forcing battle he managed to retake the initiative, and his assault forced the Vandals from the field, their camp, and the pages of history. Indeed, the Vandals as a people disappeared after their defeat by Belisarius, and imperial authority was restored in North Africa. His achievement was so highly regarded in Constantinople that he was awarded a triumph—the ancient Roman ceremonial parade accorded to victorious generals—through the capital's streets.

Belisarius provided further service for Justinian's great plan to reconquer the Western Empire, leading imperial armies, although sometimes with inadequate support, into Italy. In the early 530s the Gothic kingdom of the late Theodoric the Great was rent by conflict between his daughter Amalaswintha and much of the Gothic nobility over the management of her regency of her son Athalaric and of relations with Constantinople. Amalaswintha had much support from Justinian, and her murder, accomplished according to Procopius with the complicity of Theodora, provided the emperor with the justification he needed to invade Italy.

In 535, in the midst of the turmoil among the Goths of Italy, Justinian ordered Belisarius to invade. His opening campaigns in Sicily and southern Italy were surprisingly easy, as Roman militias welcomed the imperial armies and Gothic commanders were eager to negotiate. Belisarius reached Rome by the end of 536; in the following year he faced stiffer resistance, from the new Gothic king, Witigis, who had begun to rally the Goths in 536. Witigis laid siege to Rome in 537 and 538, and despite great hardship and starvation Belisarius was able to hold the city. His troops were able to kill many of the besiegers, and their spirits were revived by reinforcements, which allowed Belisarius to take the offensive against Witigis in 538. By 540, after his efforts to attract support from the Franks and Lombards failed, Witigis was forced to submit to Belisarius, who had surrounded and besieged his rival at Ravenna. There is also the suggestion that Belisarius was offered royal and imperial titles at this point by the Goths and his own soldiers, a possibility supported by Justinian's cool reception of his victorious commander. Nonetheless, Belisarius returned to Constantinople after successfully establishing the imperial presence once again.

The Gothic Wars, however, did not end in 540, even if Belisarius decreed that they had. Another new Gothic king, Totila, took the offensive against Justinian, and his successes forced the emperor to recall his loyal general. From 544 to 548, Belisarius was once again leading Roman armies, with only limited support from Constantinople, against the enemy Goths in Italy. Despite Justinian's limited support of his general, Belisarius managed some success against Totila and even took Rome back from the Gothic king and managed to tilt the struggle back in Constantinople's favor. Achieving few victories, Belisarius left Italy in late 548 with the conquest incomplete, leaving it to Narses the Eunuch to ultimately complete the task.

Belisarius had one final moment of glory in the service of Justinian and the empire. In 559 an army of Huns invaded from the north and came within 30 miles of Constantinople. Justinian called on Belisarius to save the city, and, with only a small army, he did just that. Persuading the Huns that his army was much larger than it was, Belisarius convinced them to depart. After that victory Belisarius resumed his retirement, only to fall into disgrace again in 562 for alleged involvement in a plot against Justinian. He was restored to favor the following year and died two years later, after a long career in defense of the empire, still loyal to an emperor who did not always appreciate him.

See also: Amalaswintha; Gothic Wars; Huns; Justinian; Narses; Ostrogoths; Procopius; Theodora; Theodoric the Great; Vandals; Witigis

Bibliography

Browning, Robert. *Justinian and Theodora.* Rev. ed. London: Thames and Hudson, 1987.

Bury, John B. *History of the Later Roman Empire: From the Death of Theodosius I to the Death of Justinian.* Vol. 2. 1923. Reprint, New York: Dover, 1959.

Heather, Peter. *The Goths.* Oxford: Blackwell Publisher, 1996.

Llewellyn, Peter. *Rome in the Dark Ages.* New York: Barnes and Noble, 1993.

Procopius. *The History of the Wars; Secret History.* 4 Vols. Trans. H. B. Dewing. Cambridge, MA: Harvard University Press, 1914–1924.

Randers-Pehrson, Justine Davis. *Barbarians and Romans: The Birth Struggle of Europe, A.D. 400–700.* Norman: University of Oklahoma Press, 1983.

Wolfram, Herwig. *History of the Goths.* Trans. Thomas J. Dunlap. Berkeley: University of California Press, 1988.

Wolfram, Herwig. *The Roman Empire and Its Germanic Peoples.* Trans. Thomas J. Dunlap. Berkeley: University of California Press, 1997.

Benedict Biscop (d. 689)

Founder of the two great Northumbrian monasteries of Wearmouth and Jarrow, Benedict Biscop was a leading intellectual and monastic leader of the later seventh century, who laid the foundation for the so-called Northumbrian Renaissance. A frequent pilgrim to Rome, where he collected relics and other treasures and, most importantly, books, Benedict, known as Biscop Baducing before his monastic conversion, left an important legacy for Anglo-Saxon learning. The libraries he established at the monasteries of Wearmouth and Jarrow provided the books necessary for the work of numerous scholars, including Alcuin, who transferred this great learning—and the desire for books—to the empire of Charlemagne and created the basis for the Carolingian Renaissance.

A Northumbrian noble in the service of King Oswy, Benedict Biscop received numerous estates appropriate to his rank and service, estates that were of great importance later in his life. The kingdom of Northumbria was a meeting place of Celtic and Roman Christianity and the site of the important Synod of Whitby in 664, at which Roman Christianity triumphed. Benedict's experience in Northumbria exposed him to important influences from both forms of Christianity. He was a lifelong supporter of Roman Christianity, as witnessed by his numerous trips to Rome, and he looked to Rome for books, relics, and the proper rule of religious life. But he also was probably influenced by elements of Celtic Christianity, especially the tradition of *peregrinatio,* the tradition of pilgrimage or missionary activity far from home. This influence would help to explain his numerous trips to the Continent, the first of which was a trip to Rome with Wilfrid of Ripon in 652–653, when Benedict was roughly 25 years old.

Although the first trip was not without significance—or controversy, as Wilfrid and Benedict separated at Lyons—Benedict's second trip to Rome was even more critical for the life of Benedict. Sometime after 657, in the company of Alchfirth, son of King Oswy and friend of Wilfrid, Benedict journeyed to the Continent. From Rome he went to the important monastery of Lérins, where he received the tonsure and learned the monastic life. When Benedict later founded his own monasteries, he drew from his experience at Lérins, a place where many of the great ancient and early medieval Irish monastic leaders had stayed and shaped the monastic life. But as important and influential as Lérins was, it could not hold Benedict permanently; he again heard the call of Rome, after probably two years at the monastery. While in Rome, Benedict was sent back to England. He accompanied the new archbishop of Canterbury, Theodore of Tarsus. Departing Rome in the spring of 668 and arriving about a year later, Theodore and Benedict took up residence in Canterbury. Benedict resided in the monastery founded by Augustine of Canterbury in the early years of the century for the next two years, until the arrival of the community's new abbot.

In 671–672, Benedict made another trip to Rome, but this trip may have been taken with the purpose of acquiring the materials necessary to found a new monastic community. Earlier trips to Rome had been taken so that Benedict could improve his understanding of the faith at its capital. But in the early 670s Benedict had absorbed a great deal from his earlier trips and had also had extensive monastic experience at Lérins and Canterbury. While in Rome, Benedict collected books of all sorts that would be useful for the monastic library, and also collected books at Vienne and Rhone Valley. The books, along with relics and other materials collected, provided the foundation for his first great monastic community, Wearmouth.

The foundation at Wearmouth was the first of two important monasteries Benedict established. He founded the monastery on land he had received from his old friend King Ecgfrith, who had succeeded Oswy in 671, and with the collaboration of Ceolfrith, a Northumbrian noble who like Benedict had left the secular life for the monastic. Benedict's many trips and connections on the continent continued to serve him in the construction of the monastery, which began in the year 674. Leaving Ceolfrith in charge, Benedict returned to the continent, where he hired builders and masons from a friend in Francia. He also recruited glassmakers to put windows in the church and other monastic buildings at Wearmouth. When the buildings of the monastery were completed or well on their way, Benedict, joined by Ceolfrith and most likely a large group, returned to Rome yet again to acquire even greater learning in the faith so that he could better prepare a rule for his new community. He also accumulated more books for the library at Wearmouth and received an exemption from the pope that allowed the monks to elect their abbots without outside interference. He was joined on his return to the monastery by Abbot John, the archcantor of the church of St. Peter in Rome, who taught the monks of Wearmouth the Roman method of singing and, possibly, the Roman style of handwriting.

The success of Wearmouth inspired Ecgfrith to grant Benedict more territory at Jarrow, which was some seven miles from the original foundation; the new house was established in 681. It was colonized by a group of monks from Wearmouth, possibly including the great historian and scholar Bede, which was led by Ceolfrith, who became the abbot of the new community. Benedict again went to Rome and appointed a relative as abbot of Wearmouth, but Ceolfrith assumed the superior position in Benedict's absence and oversaw the election of a new abbot for Wearmouth when Benedict's relative died. The two communities were ruled separately at first, but they remained very closely connected. After the second abbot of Wearmouth died, Ceolfrith was elected as abbot and thus ruled both houses, and Benedict declared that the two communities should be ruled by one abbot.

Benedict took one final trip to Rome in the mid-680s to acquire still more books for the monasteries of Wearmouth and Jarrow. He died on January 12, 689, sometime after returning from his final Roman pilgrimage. His legacy in England was a great one. He strengthened English ties to Rome and the continent and passed his devotion to Rome on to his many disciples. He established two of the great monastic communities of medieval England and created a library at Wearmouth and Jarrow that inspired generations of Anglo-Saxon scholars, including the greatest of all, Bede. Benedict's monastic foundations influenced cultural developments in England and, through Alcuin, on the continent for generations to come and contributed to renaissances in Northumbria and the Carolingian kingdom.

See also: Alcuin of York; Anglo-Saxons; Bede; Augustine of Canterbury, St.; Carolingian Renaissance; Northumbrian Renaissance; Rome; Synod of Whitby

Bibliography

Bede. *Ecclesiastical History of the English People with Bede's Letter to Egbert and Cuthbert's Letter on the Death of Bede.* Trans. Leo Sherley-Price. Harmondsworth, UK: Penguin, 1991.

Blair, Peter Hunter. *The World of Bede.* Cambridge: Cambridge University Press, 1990.

Laistner, Max L. W. *Thought and Letters in Western Europe,* A.D. *500 to 900.* 2nd ed. Ithaca, NY: Cornell University Press, 1976.

Riché, Pierre. *Education and Culture in the Barbarian West: From the Sixth through the Eighth Century.* Trans. John Contreni. Columbia: University of South Carolina Press, 1976.

Stenton, Frank M. *Anglo-Saxon England.* 3rd ed. Oxford: Clarendon, 1971.

Benedict of Aniane (c. 750–821)

A Visigothic monk and reformer, Benedict of Aniane was a close advisor of the Carolingian emperor Louis the Pious. He helped establish the Rule of Benedict of Nursia as the official rule of monastic life in the Carolingian Empire in the early years of the reign of Louis. His implementation and interpretation of the Rule, moreover, involved a reform of monastic life that is traditionally seen as the precursor to the great monastic reform movement of Cluny in the 10th and 11th centuries.

The son of a Gothic count of southern Gaul, Benedict, or Witiza as he was originally known, was sent to the court of the Frankish king Charlemagne to be educated and taught the use of arms. While on campaign in Italy with Charlemagne, however, Benedict nearly drowned, and the incident forced him to examine himself. His soul-searching led him to abandon the world for the monastic life, and in 774 he joined the monastery of Saint-Seine, near Dijon, France. His life there was unsatisfactory, and his extreme asceticism led the abbot to criticize him, to which Benedict, according to his biographer, responded, "the Rule of blessed Benedict as for beginners and weak persons, he strove to climb up to the precepts of blessed Basil and the rule of blessed Pachomius" (Ardo 220). Indeed, Benedict revealed his single-minded determination early in his monastic career, as well as his desire for a better, purer monastic life than existed in the "mixed rule" communities of the Carolingian realm. In 780, Benedict left the community of Saint-Seine to found a new monastery on his father's property in Aniane, near Montpellier, France, and probably about that same time changed his name to Benedict. Despite his earlier interest in the great eremitic monks, Benedict established the Rule of Benedict of Nursia at his monastery, but, true to his earlier zeal, strictly followed the rule of his namesake. With his dedication to Benedict's rule, he broke with the contemporary mixed rule traditions of Carolingian monasticism; nevertheless, the devotion and discipline of his house attracted numerous followers. Over the next few decades, Benedict and his followers spread the strict observance of the rule to many monasteries throughout Aquitaine and Septimania in southwestern France. Moreover, in 802 Benedict participated in a council of bishops and abbots meeting at Aix-la-Chapelle to discuss the Rule of Benedict, and in fact the later Benedict was the most important discussant at the council. His activities surely brought him to the attention of the king of Aquitaine, Louis the Pious, whose mentor Benedict became.

Shortly after Louis became sole emperor following his father's death in 814, he called Benedict from Aquitaine because of "the fame of his life and saintliness," according to a contemporary chronicle. Benedict was to be the emperor's religious advisor and was to introduce throughout the entire empire the reforms implemented in Aquitaine. Benedict was installed in a new monastery, which Louis built for him at Inde, near the imperial palace at Aix-la-Chapelle. The monastery, consecrated in 817, was not only the residence of Louis's chief religious advisor but also the model for monastic life in the empire. Benedict welcomed monks and abbots from throughout the realm and instructed them on the Rule of Benedict. Perhaps of even greater importance was Benedict's role at two councils at Aix-la-Chapelle in 816 and 817, at which monastic life in the Carolingian Empire underwent dramatic reform. Under Benedict's direction, and with the support of the emperor, the council reformed the life of all religious in the empire and established the Rule of Benedict as the standard for all monasteries in the empire, ending the long-standing tradition of the mixed rule.

Benedict's career is important for two reasons. First, Benedict successfully imposed the Rule of Benedict of Nursia on all the monasteries (with a few exceptions) in the Carolingian Empire. His activities are important also because the original Benedictine rule was reformed by Benedict, a reform that foreshadowed the reforms at Cluny in the next century. Among other things, Benedict of Aniane's reforms altered the relationship between the abbot and his monks. On the one hand, the reforms limited the abbot's authority, as well as the community's independence, by subjecting both to an overall "abbot-general," whose authority superseded that of the local abbot. The reforms also granted the abbot certain privileges that the original rule had not.

The reforms of 816 and 817 also enforced a stricter rule of cloister, which not only limited the monks' access to the outside world but also severely restricted the access of the outside world to the monastery. Most notably, the reforms eliminated access to the monastery school for the laity or secular clergy. But the most important reform involved the increase in the liturgical duties of the monks. The original Benedict had sought to establish a balance in the lives of the monks between labor and prayer, but Benedict of Aniane dramatically increased the amount of time the monks were expected to pray, chant the Psalms, and perform divine services. Benedict's death in 821 and the civil war and division in the Carolingian Empire beginning in the 830s limited the impact of his reforms, but he remains important for his efforts on behalf of the Rule of Benedict and the foundation he put in place for later monastic reform movements.

See also: Aix-la-Chapelle; Benedict of Nursia, St.; Carolingian Dynasty; Charlemagne; Louis the Pious; Monasticism; Visigoths

Bibliography

Ardo. "The Life of Saint Benedict, Abbot of Aniane and of Inde." Trans. Allen Cabaniss. In *Soldiers of Christ: Saints and Saints' Lives from Late Antiquity to the Early Middle Ages.* Eds. Thomas F. X. Noble and Thomas Head. University Park: Pennsylvania State University Press, 1995, pp. 213–54.

Knowles, David. *Christian Monasticism.* New York: McGraw Hill, 1969.

Lawrence, Clifford H. *Medieval Monasticism: Forms of Religious Life in Western Europe in the Middle Ages.* 2nd ed. London: Longman, 1989.

Riché, Pierre. *The Carolingians: A Family Who Forged Europe.* Trans. Michael Idomir Allen. Philadelphia: University of Pennsylvania Press, 1993.

Riché, Pierre. *Education and Culture in the Barbarian West: From the Sixth through the Eighth Century.* Trans. John Contreni. Columbia: University of South Carolina Press, 1976.

Sullivan, Richard. "What Was Carolingian Monasticism? The Plan of St. Gall and the History of Monasticism." In *After Rome's Fall: Narrators and Sources of Early Medieval History.* Ed. Alexander Callander Murray. Toronto: University of Toronto Press, 1998, pp. 251–87.

Wallace-Hadrill, John M. *The Frankish Church.* Oxford: Clarendon, 1983.

Benedict of Nursia, St. (c. 480–547)

Benedict of Nursia was the founder of Western monasticism. His Rule (code of behavior, spiritual life, and monastic organization) was the most influential rule in the early Middle Ages. Little is known of his life, except what is found in the pages of Pope Gregory the Great's *Dialogues,* which were written nearly a half-century after Benedict's death. Gregory's life was a model of hagiography and remained an important source for later monastic writers. Benedict's personality, however, can best be discerned from his Rule, which reveals the intelligence and humanity of the saint, who made allowances in his code for human weakness. His monastic foundation at Monte Cassino, roughly 80 miles south of Rome, was an influential house until its destruction by the Lombards in 589 (the community was reestablished in 720), but Benedict's influence continued, as his Rule became the basic rule for most monks in the post-Roman world. Indeed, during the reign of the Carolingian dynasty and under their direction, the Benedictine Rule became the primary rule for monks.

St. Benedict of Nursia (ca. 480–543), the founder of Western monasticism, ca. 510. (The British Library Board)

Born, according to tradition, in 480 in Nursia, about 70 miles north of Rome, Benedict, according to Gregory the Great, was "blessed also with God's grace [and] in boyhood he showed mature understanding, for he kept his heart detached from every pleasure with a strength of character far beyond his years" (Geary 1989, 215). Gregory also tells us that Benedict's family sent him to Rome for a liberal education, which suggests that Benedict was from a fairly prosperous family. In Rome, however, Benedict saw that the other students had fallen into vice, and fearing that he might do the same and offend God, he turned his back on worldly learning. He also renounced his family and wealth and took up the religious life in a cave in Subiaco, about 35 miles outside Rome, in circa 500. He was assisted during his stay at Subiaco by a monk from a nearby monastery named

Romanus, who brought Benedict some food on occasion. Moreover, Benedict began to attract the attention of others and gathered numerous disciples. And he was elected abbot by the monks of a nearby abbey. Although called unanimously by the monks, he soon left the community because the monks found his rule too strenuous and tried to poison him. According to Gregory, Benedict was saved by a miracle when the pitcher with the poisoned wine shattered after Benedict made the sign of the cross over it.

After the attempted poisoning, Benedict left the community and took up the path that led to the establishment of his famous rule and community at Monte Cassino. He returned to Subiaco with several companions to establish a new community. He was again the target of poisoning, this time by a jealous local priest, and he also attracted a great number of followers. After the second attempt on his life, Benedict founded his famous monastery on a mountain some 1,500 feet high. He had great success at this monastery, which he built on top of an old pagan shrine, attracting many monks and preaching to the people in the surrounding region. According to Gregory the Great, Benedict performed more than a few miracles while at the monastery, including saving one of the monks of Monte Cassino from drowning. He also sent a group of monks to found another monastery, and he met once a year with his sister Scholastica, who was a nun in a nearby community. After establishing his house and laying the foundation for Western monasticism, Benedict died, according to tradition on March 21, 547.

Benedict's greatest accomplishment was the composition of the Rule of Benedict, a code guiding the life of the monks and the organization and government of the monastery. The Rule evolved over time and was probably composed in its final from, a prologue and 73 chapters, in the later 530s. Although the Rule was once thought to have been an independent creation by Benedict, it is now recognized that he borrowed heavily from several existing rules, most importantly from the Rule of the Master, the anonymously written monastic rule composed around 500. But comparison of the two demonstrates Benedict's practical wisdom, humanity, and organizational ability. The Rule of the Master is a long and often rambling blueprint for monastic life, but Benedict's Rule is much briefer and more focused. Benedict's Rule opens with a discussion promoting the ascetic life and outlining the virtues a monk should cultivate, particularly obedience and humility. The next section outlines the daily routine of divine service, prayer, and readings of Scripture. There are chapters on the election of the abbot and other officers of the community in the next section of the Rule. Benedict also regulated hours of sleep, manual labor, and reading for the monks in his community, and provided guidelines for meals and for monastic discipline.

The daily routine for the monks was clearly outlined by Benedict and was all focused on service to God. But the Rule is important not only for its religious devotionalism but also for its flexibility and humanity. Indeed, it is these last two characteristics that help explain the success of the Rule. Benedict not only included guidelines for the recruitment and training of monks, but also provided guidelines for the duties of the abbot. Benedict's abbot was to be a father figure, who could be stern and demanding when the situation required, but who was also to be consoling and encouraging as circumstances dictated. Benedict intended that the abbot respond to the needs of the monks as well as rule over them. He also recognized that not all monks were on the same level and established different guidelines for different monks. For example, he allowed different measures of wine and food for those who were sick or elderly, as compared to those who were in better physical or spiritual condition.

Although in its early history Benedict's rule would have competition from the Rule of St. Columban and others, the rule of Benedict would come to be the dominant rule in the western church. Benedict and his rule received strong support from Pope Gregory the Great in the late sixth century and the Carolingian rulers Charlemagne and Louis the Pious would establish the Rule of Benedict as the rule of the monasteries of the empire in the ninth century. Benedict's growing importance in the Carolingian period and after is also demonstrated by the claim of the monasteries of Monte Cassino and Fleury to possess Benedict's relics, and both houses boasted a thriving cult of Benedict.

See also: Anglo-Saxons; Augustine of Canterbury, St.; Bede; Benedict of Aniane; Benedict Biscop; Boniface, St.; Caesarius of Arles; Carolingian Dynasty; Charlemagne; Columban, St.; Gregory I, the Great, Pope; Lombards; Louis the Pious; Monasticism; Monte Cassino

Bibliography

Farmer, David Hugh, ed. *Benedict's Disciples.* Leominster, UK: Fowler Wright, 1980.

Fry, Timothy, ed. and trans. *RB 1980: The Rule of Benedict in Latin and English with Notes.* Collegeville, MN: Liturgical Press, 1981.

Gregory the Great. *Life and Miracles of St. Benedict (Book Two of the Dialogues).* Trans. Odo J. Zimmerman and Benedict Avery. Collegeville, MN: St. John's Abbey Press, 1949.

Geary, Patrick J., ed. *Readings in Medieval History.* Peterborough, ON: Broadview Press, 1989.

Knowles, David. *Christian Monasticism.* New York: McGraw Hill, 1969.

Lawrence, Clifford H. *Medieval Monasticism: Forms of Religious Life in Western Europe in the Middle Ages.* 2nd ed. London: Longman, 1989.

Riché, Pierre. *The Carolingians: A Family Who Forged Europe.* Trans. Michael Idomir Allen. Philadelphia: University of Pennsylvania Press, 1993.

Riché, Pierre. *Education and Culture in the Barbarian West: From the Sixth through the Eighth Century.* Trans. John Contreni. Columbia: University of South Carolina Press, 1976.

Sullivan, Richard. "What Was Carolingian Monasticism? The Plan of St. Gall and the History of Monasticism." In *After Rome's Fall: Narrators and Sources of Early Medieval*

History, ed. Alexander Callander Murray. Toronto: University of Toronto Press, 1998, pp. 251–87.

    Wallace-Hadrill, John M. *The Frankish Church.* Oxford: Clarendon, 1983.

Beowulf

The greatest literary work of Anglo-Saxon literature, *Beowulf* is a heroic epic poem of 3,182 lines that contains a mixture of history, legend, and myth. The poem, the earliest extant long poem written in English, describes the legendary feats of the great hero, Beowulf, who, unlike other characters in the poem, is known only from this poem. Divided into two parts, *Beowulf* describes the title character's great victories over Grendel, his mother, and a fire-breathing dragon. The poem addresses the great heroic ideals of courage, loyalty, and service, and also matters of life and death. Although the poem conveys the values of pagan Germanic culture, it was probably written at a Christian court; it expresses belief in the Christian God and upholds the Christian ideals of good against evil.

    The events of the poem take place in the fifth and sixth centuries—Gregory of Tours, the sixth-century historian, describes the raid into Francia by Hygelac, Beowulf's uncle, in his *History of the Franks*—and begins at the court of the Danish king Hrothgar. The poem opens with the genealogy of Hrothgar, the great and good king of the Danes who brought peace and prosperity to the kingdom and built the great hall Heorot. In his mead hall, Hrothgar and his warriors celebrate the good things that Hrothgar has brought, and the king gives his warriors gifts of gold. The good times at Heorot are suddenly disrupted by the monster Grendel, who is of the line of Cain, which has been cursed by God and exiled from humanity. Hearing the sounds of revelry at Heorot, Grendel is enraged and attacks the hall, killing and eating Hrothgar's warriors. Grendel's reign of terror lasts 12 years before the arrival of the great hero Beowulf, who offers his services to the king. Although his talents are questioned by Unferth, one of the king's counselors, Hrothgar welcomes Beowulf as his hero. That evening Grendel returns and devours one of Beowulf's men before reaching for Beowulf himself. But the monster meets the unexpected—a hero whose grip is greater than any man's. A terrible struggle follows, as the two enemies fight each other with their bare hands. Heorot suffers great damage, and the Danes fear for their hero. But Grendel cannot overcome Beowulf. The great warrior's grip holds firm, and Grendel is able to get away only by having his arm torn off. The monster then flees to his home, where he bleeds to death.

    Beowulf's victory is welcomed by Hrothgar, who rewards his hero handsomely, and a great celebration ensues in Heorot, in which Beowulf is praised and songs are sung that foreshadow the dark events to come. Not everyone rejoices at the death of Grendel, however. Upon learning of her son's death, Grendel's mother is enraged and moves quickly to avenge her son's death. She too attacks the great hall of Heorot, and, although she is not as powerful or ferocious as her son, brings great destruction with her and manages to kill and eat one of the Danes before being driven back to her home in a lake. Beowulf is then asked to defend Hrothgar once again.

This time, uncertain of what he will face, Beowulf dons full battle armor and carries a sword offered by Unferth. Beowulf has to dive into a lake and swim a full day to reach his enemy's lair. Before he arrives, the she-monster senses his coming and reaches out to take him, beginning to fight him underwater. She drags him into her lair, where he now can fight without the weight of the water. A mighty struggle again takes place, and Beowulf strikes his foe with the sword from Unferth, but it proves of no use against the monster. Beowulf is in dire straits, as Grendel's mother nearly overwhelms him. He manages to take hold of the giant's sword he sees on the wall and slays Grendel's mother with it. Although the sword kills his enemy, it melts like thawing ice because of the great heat of the monster's blood, which then bubbles up to the surface.

The sight of the blood greatly dismays Beowulf's men, who fear the worst. But these fears are quickly laid to rest by the return of Beowulf, who bears the head of Grendel, which he cut off after his victory over the monster's mother. Once again Beowulf returns to Heorot to receive the thanks and praise of Hrothgar, whose speech carries a warning for the future. After the celebration Beowulf takes leave, in a moving scene with Hrothgar, and departs for his home in Geatland. Once he arrives in his homeland he is warmly received by his king, Hygelac, who learns of Beowulf's great success in Denmark.

The second part of the poem begins some time later, after Beowulf has ruled the Geats for 50 years. Although Beowulf has ruled the Geats well, his path to the throne was marked by the tragic deaths of Hygelac and his son and by bitter wars with the Frisians and Swedes. Under Beowulf there is peace, but that peace is suddenly interrupted by the appearance of a fire-breathing dragon, who terrorizes the kingdom and brings great destruction, burning houses, forts, and Beowulf's own great hall. The dragon has risen in anger because a slave of one of Beowulf's warriors stole a cup of gold from the dragon's great treasure hoard. Once again, the great hero Beowulf prepares to do battle with a powerful foe. Dressing in a suit of armor and bearing a mighty sword and a shield of iron—instead of the traditional shield of wood—Beowulf marches out to meet the dragon. He is joined by 12 warriors, and then by one more (the warrior who forced the slave to steal the cup). After declaring that it is his duty alone to fight the dragon, Beowulf begins his terrible and final battle with the dragon.

Beowulf has finally met his match and is overwhelmed by the dragon, whose breath of fire greatly wounds Beowulf. In the heat of the battle, all but one of his warriors, Wiglaf, abandon Beowulf in his hour of need. Wiglaf denounces the cowardice of his fellow warriors and enters the struggle with the dragon. Together, Beowulf and Wiglaf are able to defeat the horrible creature, but only after Beowulf has been fatally wounded. Beowulf then offers a final speech and looks over the fantastic treasure hoard of the dead dragon. After his death, prophecies are made about the impending destruction of the Geats by their rivals, who will take advantage of the Geats after the death of their great king. The poem concludes with the funeral of Beowulf, whose warriors ride around his tomb singing a dirge and lamenting their loss.

The poem was preserved in one manuscript from about the year 1000, and was first published in a modern edition in 1815. The original composition of the poem is uncertain, but most scholars believe that it was composed in the early eighth century at a court in Bede's Northumbria, although there are those who argue for a late eighth-century composition at the court of King Offa of Mercia. Those who support an early date argue that a Scandinavian hero would not have appeared in an English poem at a time when Viking warriors were invading the island. Of course, others suggest that the poet may have hoped to appeal to the invaders. The date of composition is important for both the understanding of the poet and the poem, but once again there is little agreement among scholars on those matters. Most *Beowulf* scholars are split between those who believe that the poem was composed in a predominantly oral culture or those who believe it was composed in a literate culture.

The values embodied in the poem and its hero provide support for both sides. The nature of the language of the poem, the interest in material wealth—helmets, swords, jewelry—suggest the possibility of an oral environment. The expression of belief in a creator God, references to the Hebrew Bible, especially the line of Cain, and Christian values of good and evil suggest composition in a literate culture. The answer is probably a mixture of both: The poem may well have been composed at a Christian court in an oral culture, which had absorbed the values of the literate culture by the time the poem was committed to parchment. Finally, interpretation of the poem is complicated by its uncertain origins. Despite variety of opinion, it is certain that the meaning of *Beowulf* is shaped by its origins in a superficially Christianized environment. The poem advocates the epic values of bravery, honor, and fidelity, but within the framework of belief in the Christian God and the importance of the struggle against evil.

See also: Anglo-Saxons; Bede; Gregory of Tours; Offa of Mercia

Bibliography

Alexander, Michael, trans. *Beowulf.* Harmondsworth, UK: Penguin, 1983.

Baker, Peter S., ed. *Beowulf: Basic Readings.* New York: Garland, 1995.

Bjork, Robert E., and John D. Niles, eds. *A Beowulf Handbook.* Lincoln: University of Nebraska Press, 1997.

Chambers, Raymond W. *Beowulf: An Introduction to the Study the Poem with a Discussion of the Stories of Offa and Finn.* 3rd ed., supplement by C. L. Wrenn. Cambridge: Cambridge University Press, 1959.

Hasenfratz, Robert J. *Beowulf Scholarship: An Annotated Bibliography, 1979–1990.* New York: Garland, 1993.

Heaney, Seamus, trans. *Beowulf: A New Verse Translation.* New York: Farrar Straus and Giroux, 2000.

Tolkien, J.R.R. "*Beowulf:* The Monsters and the Critics." *Proceedings of the British Academy* 22 (1936): 245–95.

Bernard Hairyfeet (841–886)

The younger son of Bernard of Septimania and Dhuoda, Bernard Hairyfeet or Hairypaws (Plantevelue) was a key figure in the political turmoil of the West Frankish kingdom in late ninth century and the emergence of the medieval duchy of Aquitaine. As his mother Dhuoda notes, Bernard was born in 841, the year following the death of Louis the Pious. He suffered from the familial difficulties brought on by his father's revolt against Charles the Bald and subsequent execution by the Carolingian ruler. Like his brother William, Bernard was rumored to have planned to assassinate Charles to avenge Bernard of Septimania's death, and as a result spent time in exile in Lothar's realm in the late 860s. It seems, however, that Bernard managed to return to the Charles' good graces and was confirmed in his honors in 869.

In the civil unrest following the death of Charles the Bald, Bernard endured loss of territory but saw the restoration and enhancement of his position by the new Carolingian ruler, Louis the Stammerer. Throughout his tumultuous career, Bernard managed to accumulate extensive properties in Berry, the Limousin, Autun, and the Auvergne. These territories were molded into a principality by his son, William I the Pious (875–918), the founder of the monastery of Cluny as well as the founder of the duchy of Aquitaine.

See also: Aquitaine; Bernard of Septimania; Carolingian Dynasty; Charles the Bald; Dhuoda; Lothar; Louis the Pious; Louis the Stammerer

Bibliography
Dhuoda. *Handbook for William: A Carolingian Woman's Counsel for Her Son.* Ed. and trans. Carol Neel. Washington, DC: Catholic University of America Press, 1999.

Nelson, Janet. *Charles the Bald.* London: Longman, 1992.

Riché, Pierre. *The Carolingians: A Family Who Forged Europe.* Trans. Michael Idomir Allen. Philadelphia: University of Pennsylvania Press, 1993.

Bernard of Septimania (795–844)

Duke of Septimania and count of Barcelona and imperial chamberlain, Bernard was an important figure in the Carolingian Empire and, for a time, a close ally of the emperor Louis the Pious. Bernard played an unfortunate role in the civil strife of the 830s and participated in the conflict in the West Frankish kingdom of Charles the Bald in the 840s. He was also the husband of Dhuoda, whose handbook was written for their son William, and the father of Bernard Hairyfeet.

The son of William, count of Toulouse, and a distant cousin of Louis the Pious, Bernard rose to prominence in the 820s. Inheriting his father's position and duties, Bernard was responsible for protecting Aquitaine from the Muslims of Spain. He turned back a ferocious assault by Abd al-Rahman II in the years 824–827, earning the gratitude of Louis, who appointed Bermard chamberlain in 829 and protector of the emperor's son, Charles the Bald. Bernard's rapid rise earned him powerful enemies, who accused him of sorcery and adultery with the emperor's wife, Judith. When revolt broke out against Louis in 830, Bernard fled to Barcelona where he would insert himself at times in the conflict that raged in the 830s but without ever regaining his old position and influence. In the hopes of expanding his power in Septimania, Bernard at times supported and encouraged further rebellion by Pippin, one of Louis the Pious' sons, and Pippin's son, Pippin II. After the death of Louis, Bernard reluctantly accepted the establishment of Charles the Bald as ruler over Aquitaine and the West Frankish kingdom. Following Charles' victory in 841, Bernard swore his loyalty and sent his son William to Charles as a hostage—an act that inspired Dhuoda to write her handbook. Bernard kept his options open and was apparently plotting to increase his own power in 844 when he was captured by Charles the Bald and condemned for treason.

See also: Aquitaine; Bernard Hairyfeet; Carolingian Dynasty; Charles the Bald; Dhuoda; Judith; Louis the Pious

Bibliography

De Jong, Mayke. *The Penitential State: Authority and Atonement in the Age of Louis the Pious, 814–840.* Cambridge: Cambridge University Press, 2005.

Nelson, Janet. *Charles the Bald.* London: Longman, 1992.

Riché, Pierre. *The Carolingians: A Family Who Forged Europe.* Trans. Michael Idomir Allen. Philadelphia: University of Pennsylvania Press, 1993.

Bertrada (d. 783)

The wife of Pippin the Short, the first Carolingian king, and mother of Charlemagne, the first Carolingian emperor, Bertrada surely played an important role in the Carolingian kingdom. At the very least, she fulfilled the traditional role of royal wives by producing an heir; she bore Pippin three sons, two of whom survived, and a daughter. Her activities may well have stretched beyond the traditional to include support for Pippin's religious reforms. She also was involved in diplomacy after her husband's death and strove to maintain peace between her two sons, Charlemagne and Carloman. Her intervention had limited success, but she remained, according to Einhard, the beloved mother of the greatest Carolingian ruler, Charlemagne.

Pippin and Bertrada were married in 744, but the nature of their relationship, at least at the outset, is confused, in part because of the changing marriage traditions of the realm in the mid-eighth century. It was thought at one time that the two were not legitimately married, but that Pippin took Bertrada as a concubine or in the old Frankish marriage practice of *friedelehe*. The marriage was only legitimate, according to this view, once Charlemagne was born, in either 742 or 748. It is now generally recognized that in fact the two were formally married and that Charles was not illegitimate. Even though the marriage is now recognized as legitimate, it was not the most stable one. Pippin married Bertrada, as was often the case, for her connections with a powerful noble family, connections that would allow Pippin, as mayor of the palace, to strengthen his hold on the kingdom after the death of his father, Charles Martel. At some point during their marriage Pippin tried to repudiate Bertrada to marry another woman, but his efforts were stopped by Pope Stephen II (752–757), and the marriage continued until Pippin's death in 768. Despite his attempt to divorce her, Pippin brought Bertrada along with his entourage when he went to meet Stephen on the latter's visit to the kingdom. And Stephen bestowed a special blessing on Bertrada when he crowned and anointed Pippin and his sons in 754.

After Pippin's death, Bertrada continued to influence affairs in the kingdom, and her most important moment came early in the reigns of her sons Charlemagne and Carloman. On the death of their father, tensions between the two brothers broke out that threatened the peace and stability of the realm. The strain was worsened by Carloman's refusal to help his older brother suppress a rebellion in Aquitaine. At this point Bertrada intervened in the hopes of preventing civil war and also to strengthen Carolingian power and her sons' diplomatic ties in Bavaria and Italy. In 770, according to the *Royal Frankish Annals,* Bertrada met with her son Carloman before proceeding to Italy "in the interests of peace" (Scholz 1972, 48). It is possible that she hoped to allay any fears Carloman may have had about his brother or, on the other hand, to upbraid him for his lack of support for his brother. In either event, she went to Italy through Bavaria, where she met with Duke Tassilo.

The duke had commended himself into vassalage to Pippin in 757, but had failed to honor his oath in 763. Bertrada may have attempted to reconcile Tassilo, and his important and powerful duchy, to her two sons. After meeting with Tassilo, Bertrada went to Lombard Italy to meet with King Desiderius. Allies of the Franks before Pippin's campaigns to protect the pope, the Lombards remained a powerful force in Italy and a potential threat to both the pope and, to a lesser extent, the Carolingians. Bertrada arranged a marriage between the king's daughter, Desiderata, and her son Charlemagne. The apparent success of Bertrada's trip was shattered in the following year with the death of Carloman and the disinheritance of his children, as well as Charlemagne's repudiation of Desiderata.

The rejection of Bertrada's diplomatic initiative, however, according to Einhard, was the only example of tension between Bertrada and Charlemagne. Einhard notes that Bertrada lived to a "very great age," was honored by Charlemagne, with whom she lived, and was "treated with every respect" by her son (Einhard 1981, 74). She lived to see the birth of three grandsons and three granddaughters to Charlemagne. She died in 783 and, Einhard notes, was buried by her son "with great honor in the church of Saint-Denis, where his father lay" (74).

See also: Carloman, King of the Franks; Carolingian Dynasty; Charlemagne; Charles Martel; Desiderius; Einhard; Lombards; Pippin III, Called Pippin the Short; *Royal Frankish Annals*; Tassilo

Bibliography

Einhard and Notker the Stammerer. *Two Lives of Charlemagne.* Trans. Lewis Thorpe. Harmondsworth, UK: Penguin, 1981.

McKitterick, Rosamond. *The Frankish Kingdoms under the Carolingians, 751–987.* London: Longman, 1983.

Riché, Pierre. *The Carolingians: A Family Who Forged Europe.* Trans. Michael Idomir Allen. Philadelphia: University of Pennsylvania Press, 1993.

Scholz, Bernhard Walter, trans. *Carolingian Chronicles: Royal Frankish Annals and Nithard's History.* Ann Arbor: University of Michigan Press, 1972.

Wemple, Suzanne. *Women in Frankish Society: Marriage and the Cloister, 500 to 900.* Philadelphia: University of Pennsylvania Press, 1981.

Bleda. *See* Attila the Hun

Boethius, Anicius Manlius Severinus (c. 480–525)

Roman senator and noble, whose family boasted an emperor in its lineage and strong Christian credentials, Boethius was one of the last great philosophers of antiquity. Like most Romans of his class, he also served in government, in his case as advisor of the great Ostrogothic king of Italy, Theodoric. A talented philosopher, theologian, and orator, Boethius is best known for his *Consolation of Philosophy* (*De consolatione philosophiae*), which he wrote while in prison awaiting his execution at the order of Theodoric. Despite this tragic ending, Boethius's memory lived on long after his death, and his greatest work was the perhaps the most widely read text in the Middle Ages after the Bible and influenced many, including the ninth-century Anglo-Saxon king Alfred the Great, who translated it.

Like many traditional Romans, Boethius enjoyed a good education and was set on the path to holding public office. His later writings suggest that he was a particularly good student, who may have traveled to the great schools at Athens and Alexandria to study for a time, and his talents as an orator stood him in good stead in his political career. His father had served as consul, but had died in 487 while Boethius was quite young. The early death of his father, however, had one beneficial result—the important Christian senator Quintus Aurelius Memmius Symmachus assumed Boethius's father's place and raised and educated him. His family background and education prepared him for a career in public service, which he accepted, as he notes in the *Consolation,* in accordance with Plato's endorsement of philosophers serving in government. In 510, he was made consul, and in 522 his two sons were elevated to the consulship, a great honor that suggests Boethius held favor with the imperial government in Constantinople. He was also highly favored by the Ostrogothic king in Italy, Theodoric, who made Boethius his Master of Offices (*magister officiorum*) in 522.

Boethius's career in public service and his relationship with Theodoric are complex, celebrated, and tragic. His focus was plainly on serving the interests of Italy and its people, and at one point he helped resolve an economic crisis in southern Italy. He was also willing to work with Theodoric. Although an Arian ruler of a Catholic population, Theodoric was generally a wise and tolerant king, with whom educated and public-minded senators like Boethius could work. Indeed, Theodoric often called Boethius to his service, and not only in 522 when he was made chief of staff. Theodoric had often requested Boethius to employ his great mathematical and mechanical talents to create objects that the king could use in diplomacy as gifts. At the same time, there is evidence that Boethius was interested in bridging the gap between the eastern and western parts of the Roman Empire. During the Middle Ages his intellectual work remained an important conduit of the teachings of Plato and Aristotle, notably the works on logic, to the Latin West. The theological treatises he wrote in the 510s were designed to reconcile Eastern and Western theology—an attempt, perhaps, to draw Constantinople and Italy closer together at a time when Theodoric's policy was to keep the two far apart. Boethius's efforts, however, were appreciated by the imperial government at Constantinople, which rewarded him and his sons with the consulship. Clearly, Boethius was involved in a complex web of competing political and religious interests.

His political involvement came to a bad end not long after his promotion to Master of the Offices. The aging Theodoric faced serious difficulties in Italy in his last years, which included tensions at his own court over relations with Constantinople, an aggressive and ambitious emperor in Constantinople, and an uncertain succession because of the death of one son-in-law and the conversion to Catholicism of the other. In the early 520s, Theodoric cracked down hard on anti-Semitic rioters and ordered all Romans disarmed. In 522, he learned of a conspiracy headed by the leading senator, Albinus, who was implicated in corresponding with Constantinople against Theodoric. The king quickly ordered Albinus arrested, and Boethius came to his fellow senator's defense. Despite his good service to Theodoric, Boethius had also made enemies of the king's advisors for his promotion of Catholic orthodoxy against Arianism and for exposing corruption in the king's administration.

Standing before the king, Boethius declared "If Albinus is guilty, then so am I, and so is the whole senate" (Wolfram 1997, 224). Although modern scholarship remains divided on whether Boethius was involved in the conspiracy or not, Theodoric had Boethius arrested. Several senators, in need of money, brought evidence against Boethius, who was found guilty of witchcraft and treason. He was imprisoned in Pavia where he wrote his masterpiece, *The Consolation of Philosophy,* and suffered a gruesome execution, most likely after torture, probably in 525.

Revered as a martyr throughout the Middle Ages because of his brutal execution by Theodoric, Boethius is best known for his theological work and the *Consolation.* His earlier treatises included works on mathematics and music, which preserved elements of earlier Greek works on the subjects. Indeed, one of his great goals was his desire to translate all the works of Plato and Aristotle into Greek. Although he was unable to complete this task, he did translate a number of important treatises of Aristotle that would have an important influence on later medieval thought. An important translator of Aristotle, Boethius was heavily influenced by Neoplatonic thought, as seen in his theological works, and believed in the unity of all knowledge even though that knowledge may appear disconnected. His *Consolation of Philosophy* was written as a dialogue between Boethius himself and Lady Philosophy; it reflects on the great questions of human happiness and suffering, and vindicates divine providence and the freedom of the human will. Although sometimes regarded as a work of pagan philosophy, the *Consolation* addresses clearly Christian themes of God's plan and the realization that human fate is associated with that plan as well as the idea that God stands outside of time and so humans are not predestined to certain actions or specific fate. Along with attempting to understand his own situation, the *Consolation* may have been an effort by Boethius to reconcile Greek philosophy with Christian theology, and whatever the intent it was an important source for the preservation of Greek thought for medieval Latin thinkers.

See also: Alfred the Great; Arianism; Ostrogoths; Rome; Theodoric the Great

Bibliography

Boethius. *The Consolation of Philosophy.* Trans. Richard Green. New York: Bobbs-Merrill, 1962.

Chadwick, Henry. *Boethius: The Consolations of Music, Logic, Theology, and Philosophy.* Oxford: Clarendon, 1981.

Gibson, Margaret, ed. *Boethius: His Life, Thought, and Influence.* Oxford: Blackwell, 1981.

Laistner, Max L. W. *Thought and Letters in Western Europe,* A.D. *500–900.* 2nd ed. Ithaca, NY: Cornell University Press, 1976.

Wolfram, Herwig. *The Roman Empire and Its Germanic Peoples.* Trans. Thomas Dunlap. Los Angeles: University of California Press, 1997.

Boniface, St. (c. 675–754)

Most famous and influential of all the Irish and Anglo-Saxon missionaries to the continent in the seventh and eighth centuries, Boniface spread the Christian faith to pagan Saxons and other Germanic peoples. He also founded several bishoprics and the important monastery at Fulda and reorganized numerous dioceses during his career as a missionary and reformer. He was supported early in his missionary work by the Carolingian mayor of the palace, Charles Martel, and also by the pope. His support from the pope was perhaps most important to Boniface, because, like all Anglo-Saxons, he felt a special devotion to the papacy and structured his reforms along models established at Rome. He later played a role in the reform of the Frankish church and was supported by Charles Martel's sons, Pippin the Short and, especially, Carloman. Martyred on June 5, 754, Boniface has been recognized as the Apostle to Germany because of his successful missionary activity, and his feast day is celebrated on June 5.

Born in circa 675 to a noble family in Devonshire, England, and originally called Winfrith (Pope Gregory II gave him the name Boniface in 719), Boniface, according to his biographer, demonstrated great piety and zeal for the monastic life from an early age. While still a boy, according to his biographer, Boniface "subdued the flesh to the spirit and meditated on things eternal" and discussed spiritual matters with priests who visited his father's house (Talbot 1995, 111). Although reluctant to allow his son to take up the monastic life, Boniface's father eventually relented, after a serious illness, and sent him to a Benedictine community near Exeter. He received an excellent education at the community, was ordained a priest at age 30, and developed a reputation as a scholar. Indeed, in 705 he was called on by the archbishop of Canterbury to help resolve a number of issues facing the king of Wessex, which Boniface did successfully.

Despite his success and the possibility of ecclesiastical advancement, Boniface, like many Irish and Anglo-Saxon monks, felt the call to take up missionary work. In 716 he joined his fellow Anglo-Saxon missionary, Willibrord, on the continent and traveled to the region called Frisia (in the modern Low Countries), whose inhabitants had slid back into paganism during the turmoil after the death of the mayor of the palace Pippin of Herstal. His efforts, however, proved unsuccessful because he found no support from the Frisian leader, Radbod. Boniface then returned to England, but would not stay there for long, even though he was elected abbot of his monastery, an honor he declined in favor of further missionary activity.

In 719, Boniface began his second evangelical mission on the continent. He visited Rome first this time and received both a new name and a commission from Gregory II to preach to the pagan Saxons east of the Rhine River and to spread the Roman method of baptism and the Roman liturgy. Returning north, he joined Willibrord again in Frisia and spent three years evangelizing the Frisians, where the death of Radbod, the Frisian king who opposed the Franks, and the rise of Charles Martel offered the opportunity for success. Indeed, in 723 Charles Martel sent an official letter to the ecclesiastical and lay nobility proclaiming Martel's protection of and support for the activities of Boniface. In the previous year, Boniface had been called back to Rome, where Gregory consecrated him bishop, provided him the mandate to preach to the pagan Saxons, and sent a letter to the Carolingian mayor of the palace requesting his support. Boniface returned to the north and began his mission in most aggressive fashion by chopping down one of the pagan Saxons sacred oaks near Fritzlar. This event had great significance, because Boniface suffered no vengeance from the pagan gods and demonstrated that the power of his God was far greater.

Over the next several decades, Boniface continued his missionary activities and remained in frequent contact with the pope in Rome. From 725 to 735 he spent most of his time in Thuringia, where he converted pagans and struggled against rival missionaries whose methods he disliked and termed heretical. As with all things, Boniface sought the support of Rome in his struggles with rival missionaries. His devotion to Rome, his efforts to spread Roman traditions, and his frequent reports to the pope attracted the attention of the new pope, Gregory III, during his years in Thuringia. Gregory welcomed his efforts and raised him to the rank of archbishop, which increased Boniface's authority and reinforced his power and prestige as the official representative of the pope in Germany.

In 735, Boniface was sent to the duchy of Bavaria to reorganize and reform the church, activities that turned out to be important when the duchy was absorbed by the Frankish kingdom. Although supported by the duke, Boniface was often opposed by the bishops and other church leaders in Bavaria, especially after his trip to Rome in 737. There he had been welcomed by Gregory III, who supported his efforts in Germany. Returning to Bavaria, Boniface wholeheartedly began reorganization of the church of Germany, despite frequent opposition. He established numerous new bishoprics, including those at Erfurt, Freising, Regensburg, and Würzburg. He also, in 744, established a monastery at Fulda, which he placed under the protection of the pope and entrusted to his Bavarian convert Sturmi. His activities in Bavaria were an important prelude to his activities in the Frankish kingdom after the death of his patron, Charles Martel.

Until the rise to power of Pippin and Carloman, Boniface had done little with the Frankish church, which was much in need of reform. Indeed, it is from Boniface that we learn of the sorry shape of the Frankish church. Certainly there is some exaggeration, but Boniface complained that there had been no church council in the kingdom in 80 years and that the bishops were "greedy laymen" or "adulterous, undedicated clerical carousers." Moreover, he lamented that the bishops also shed blood and that the lower clergy were often ignorant and had "four, five, or more concubines in their bed each night." With the support of the Carolingian mayors of the palace, particularly Carloman, Boniface instituted reform of the Frankish church. The German Council of 742 or 743 held by Carloman implemented the reform ideas of Boniface, declaring that priests and other clergy must wear distinctive and simple clothes and must not keep arms, hunting dogs, or women in their house. Monks were encouraged to follow the Rule of St. Benedict and were to live chaste and stable lives. Carloman, inspired by Boniface, also established new episcopal sees, which he put under Boniface's authority as archbishop. Finally, Boniface reinforced the pro-Roman tendencies in the Frankish church, inadvertently laying the foundation for a political alliance between the Carolingians and the pope.

After Carloman's retirement to a monastery Boniface's influence at the Carolingian court declined, particularly because of Pippin's close relationship with Chrodegang of Metz, an important bishop and religious reformer, and Boniface returned to missionary work. His influence continued in the kingdom, and he did not completely separate himself from Pippin's affairs, at least according to the *Royal Frankish Annals,* which declare that Boniface anointed Pippin king in 751. There is more than a little uncertainty about his presence at the ceremony, but his importance in the realm even after Carloman's retirement is attested by the assertion that he participated in the coronation. It is certain that Boniface resumed his evangelical activity and remained dedicated to it during the last year of his life. Retiring from his duties as archbishop, he turned the office over to one of his disciples and began preaching to the pagan Frisians. He was attacked on the morning of June 5, 754, and suffered martyrdom, and, according to his biographer, Boniface encouraged his followers not to fear the attackers but to "endure with steadfast mind the sudden onslaught of death, that you may be able to reign evermore with Christ" (Talbot 1995, 136). Boniface's biographer notes further that within a few years great miracles occurred at the spot of the martyrdom.

See also: Anglo-Saxons; Carloman, Mayor of the Palace; Carolingian Dynasty; Charles Martel; Chrodegang of Metz; Gregory II, Pope; Gregory III, Pope; Pippin II, Called Pippin of Herstal; Pippin III, Called Pippin the Short; Rome; *Royal Frankish Annals*

Bibliography

Duckett, Eleanor Shipley. *Anglo-Saxon Saints and Scholars.* New York: Macmillan, 1947.

Emerton, Ephraim, ed. and trans. *The Letters of Saint Boniface.* New York: Columbia University Press, 2000.

Lawrence, Clifford H. *Medieval Monasticism: Forms of Religious Life in Western Europe in the Middle Ages.* 2nd ed. London: Longman, 1984.

Levison, Wilhelm. *England and the Continent in the Eighth Century.* New York: Oxford University Press, 1998.

Reuter, Timothy, ed. *The Greatest Englishman: Essays on St. Boniface and the Church at Crediton.* Exeter: Paternoster Press, 1980.

Riché, Pierre. *The Carolingians: A Family Who Forged Europe.* Trans. Michael Idomir Allen. Philadelphia: University of Pennsylvania Press, 1993.

Scholz, Bernhard Walter, trans. *Carolingian Chronicles: Royal Frankish Annals and Nithard's History.* Ann Arbor: University of Michigan Press, 1972.

Talbot, C. H., trans. "Willibald: The Life of Saint Boniface." In *Soldiers of Christ: Saints and Saints' Lives from Late Antiquity to the Early Middle Ages.* Eds. Thomas F. X. Noble and Thomas Head. University Park, PA: Pennsylvania State University Press, 1995.

Wallace-Hadrill, John M. *The Frankish Church.* Oxford: Clarendon, 1983.

Bretwalda

Term used to designate any Anglo-Saxon king who exercised power over all of southern England, *bretwalda,* or *bretwald,* was probably a scribal correction of the Old English term *Brytenwealda,* which probably meant "Britain ruler" or "ruler of the Britons."

Although often used in modern scholarship, the term *bretwalda* appears only in one manuscript copy of the *Anglo-Saxon Chronicle.* In the year 829, according to the *Chronicle,* King Egbert of Wessex conquered "the kingdom of Mercia and all that was south of the Humber, and he was the eighth king who was Bretwalda." Other manuscripts reporting the event use the Old English word *Brytenwealda,* but even that version of the term was not widely used. However, echoes of the term bretwalda can be heard in a charter of Æthelbald of Mercia from 736, in which the king is called "rex Britanniae," the Latin version of "king of Britain." The *Chronicle* also lists Egbert's predecessors as bretwalda: Aelle of Sussex, Ceawlin of Wessex, Aethelberht of Kent, Raedwald of East Anglia, and Edwin, Oswald, and Oswy of Northumbria. This list of kings is taken from Bede's history, which identifies the kings as ruling over all the lands south of the Humber and thus reinforces the notion that the term meant "Britain ruler."

Although a clear definition of the term seems to have existed among Anglo-Saxon writers, bretwalda was probably not a regular institution. The appearance of bretwalda in the *Chronicle* may reveal the memory of an overall leader of the combined regions of the south from early Anglo-Saxon history. It may also be of poetical origin, emerging in the banquet halls of the kings and used as a term of praise and honor. It may also have emerged from church ideology, and the writing of the church's most famous representative, Bede, to testify to the unity of the English people.

See also: Aethelberht I of Kent; *Anglo-Saxon Chronicle*; Anglo-Saxons; Bede; Heptarchy; Wessex

Bibliography

Bede, *Ecclesiastical History of the English Church and People.* Trans. Leo Sherley-Price. Rev. ed. London: Penguin Classics, 1968.

Loyn, Henry R. *Anglo-Saxon England and the Norman Conquest.* 2nd ed. London: Longmans, 1991.

Sawyer, Peter H. *From Roman Britain to Norman England.* 2nd ed. London: Routledge, 1998.

Stenton, Frank M. *Anglo-Saxon England.* 3rd ed. Oxford: Clarendon, 1971.

Whitelock, Dorothy, ed. *The Anglo-Saxon Chronicle.* Westport, CT: Greenwood, 1986.

Breviary of Alaric

Compiled by the Visigothic king of Toulouse Alaric II (d. 507) in 506, the *Breviary of Alaric* (*Breviarium Alaricianum*) or *Roman Law of the Visigoths* (*Lex Romana Visigothorum*) is a major codification of Roman law. The *Breviary* reflects the influence of Roman imperial administrative and legal traditions on the Visigoths as well as the importance of the Roman population of Alaric's realm. Incorporating some of the more important works of Roman law and jurisprudence, the *Breviary* had a significant impact on both later Germanic law and the Code of Justinian.

Although his father King Euric (r. 466–484) had promulgated a new legal code of mixed German and Roman traditions, Alaric saw the need to compile a more fully Roman legal code for his numerous Roman subjects that was separate from the Germanic legal traditions applicable to his Visigothic subjects. To accomplish this, Alaric drew together a number of legal experts at his court who were put under the direction of a high-ranking royal official. Their task was to upgrade and organize Roman law and to eliminate redundant and obsolete laws. The collection includes major sections of the Theodosian Code of 438, the novels or new laws of the Roman emperors of the fifth century, and the legal commentaries of the great Roman jurists Gaius, Papinian, and Paulus. As a result, the framework of legal thought and practice of the *Breviary* was Roman. Before undertaking this major reform, Alaric consulted with secular and religious leaders of his kingdom to gain their approval. After the legal experts completed their work, Alaric formally presented the *Breviary* to a great council of state for final acceptance. The new code was officially placed in the royal treasury, and Alaric decreed that under penalty of death his counts were to use no other version of Roman law. It received further support at the council of Adge in 506, a national council of bishops that was the first of its kind in the Germanic kingdoms of the post-Roman world.

Illustration of the king, the bishop, the duke, and the count from a ninth-century version of the *Breviary of Alaric*. (Bibliotheque Nationale, Paris, France/ Flammarion/The Bridgeman Art Library)

A major accomplishment intended for all the lands of the Visigoths, the *Breviary* had both a lesser and greater impact than Alaric had intended. The king's death of thee hands of the Merovingian king Clovis in 507 limited the *Breviary*'s influence in Gaul as Frankish control was established over Visigothic territory there. In Visigothic Iberia, the legal tradition returned to the Germanic-Roman model of Euric over the Roman law of Alaric. In the Frankish kingdom and Byzantine Empire, however, the *Breviary* would shape the legal tradition long after the death of Alaric.

See also: Alaric II; Clovis; *Corpus Iuris Civilis*; Euric; Franks; Justinian; Merovingian Dynasty; Visigoths

Bibliography
Heather, Peter. *The Goths*. Oxford: Blackwell, 1996.

King, P. D. *Law and Society in the Visigothic Kingdom*. Cambridge: Cambridge University Press, 2006.

Van Kleffens, E. N. *Hispanic Law until the End of the Middle Ages*. Edinburgh: University of Edinburgh Press, 1968.

Wolfram, Herwig. *History of the Goths*. Trans. Thomas J. Dunlap. Berkeley: University of California Press, 1996.

Brunhilde (d. 613)

Visigothic princess, Merovingian queen, and rival of the queen Fregedund, Brunhilde had great influence on politics in the Frankish kingdoms in the late sixth and the early seventh centuries. Her struggle with Fredegund contributed to the instability and civil war in the Frankish kingdoms in the late sixth century. Despite frequent attempts on her life by her rival, Fredegund, Brunhilde survived and was the power behind the throne in the last decade of the sixth century and the first decade of the seventh. She worked consistently during her reign of more than 30 years to promote the interests of her family, especially her sons and grandsons. Her efforts, however, provoked opposition and led to a revolt that ended in her death and contributed to the rise of the Carolingian dynasty.

According to the sixth-century bishop and historian, Gregory of Tours, Brunhilde was "elegant in all that she did, lovely to look at, chaste and decorous in her behavior, wise in her generation and of good address" (221). Although Gregory may have been biased toward the queen, since there is good evidence to suggest that she secured his appointment as bishop, his opinion seems born out by Brunhilde's successes while a queen of the Franks. She came to the kingdom, again according to Gregory, to marry the Merovingian king

Sigebert I (r. 560/561–575), who saw that his brothers were marrying their servants and decided to seek the hand of a princess. Brunhilde was the daughter of the Visigothic king of Spain, Athanagild, and she was also an Arian Christian, who converted to Catholic Christianity shortly after her arrival in the Frankish kingdoms. She arrived, therefore, with wealth and pedigree unrivaled by any of the other Merovingian queens.

Her arrival inspired jealousy in Sigebert's half-brother, King Chilperic I (560/561–584), who arranged to marry Brunhilde's sister, the princess Galswintha. She too arrived with great wealth and prestige, but not so much that Chilperic hesitated to murder her shortly after her arrival, refusing to return the dowry. He then married, or remarried, the former servant Fredegund, who may have been behind the murder. The murder of Galswintha and promotion of Fredegund surely embittered relations between the two Merovingian queens. Some scholars argue that a blood feud followed the murder of Galswintha, but others maintain that the strife between Brunhilde and Fredegund was simply an example of the violent politics that occasionally plagued the Merovingian dynasty. Whatever the case, the relationship between the two was hostile and led to great civil strife.

In 575, tragedy again struck Brunhilde when Chilperic had Sigebert murdered and then took control of his kingdom and treasure. Brunhilde was captured and exiled to Rouen from her husband's capital at Paris, and her son Childebert was taken from her. Despite this setback, Brunhilde returned to power in the 580s and became increasingly powerful thereafter. The first step in her return was her marriage to Merovech, son of her rival Chilperic. The marriage provided her with supporters and access to power once again, and Merovech had access to control of a kingdom. But Chilperic separated the two and returned Brunhilde to her eastern Frankish kingdom. When Merovech attempted to return to Brunhilde she rebuffed him, and shortly afterward he was captured and killed, possibly, as Gregory suggests, at Fredegund's orders. Although Merovech met a sad fate, his former wife's fortunes climbed in the 580s. This occurred, in part, because of the death of Chilperic and the subsequent weakness of Fredegund, who may have killed him and certainly made attempts to kill Brunhilde. The murders, possibly at the queen's order, of an abbot and a bishop who opposed her strengthened her hand as well. But the most important factor in her improved circumstances was that her son, Childebert, reached his majority and was recognized as a legitimate king by other Merovingian kings.

For the next three decades, Brunhilde dominated the scene in the Frankish kingdoms. Although first her son and then grandsons were the titular rulers, she held the real power in the kingdom and exercised it in both church and state. She arranged important political marriages for her children, alliances with Visigoth rulers in Spain which included the marriage of her daughter, Ingunde, to the prince Hermenegild. She also corresponded with the Byzantine emperor, who had captured her daughter and grandson after Hermenegild revolted. She also conspired to break up marriages of her son and grandsons to limit threats to her position at court.

Within the kingdom, she strengthened her position further by arranging treaties with other Merovingian kings and orchestrating the murders of her rivals. Moreover, she corresponded with Pope Gregory I, known as the Great (590–604), and oversaw the administration of the church and appointment of bishops in the realm. Her relationship with the pope was an important one, for Gregory who hoped that the queen would help reform the Frankish church and aid Augustine of Canterbury's mission to England. In both regards Gregory was not disappointed, and in return he supported the queen's request to elevate one of her favorites to the rank of metropolitan bishop. Her relations with the church, however, were not always happy. She may have ordered the murder of Bishop Desiderius of Vienne and certainly exiled St. Columban because they both questioned the behavior and right to rule of members of her family.

The difficulties she faced with Desiderius and Columban reveal the problems that arose for Brunhilde after the death of her son Childebert in 596. She continued to rule as regent for her grandsons, Theudebert II (596–612) and Theuderic II (596–613), but she faced growing opposition in the kingdoms, especially among the nobility in Austrasia, where Theudebert ruled, and among the clergy who opposed her heavy-handed control of the church. She took up residence with Theuderic, whom she set against his brother, claiming that Theudebert was the son of a gardener. These first efforts failed, but Brunhilde would not be stopped. She broke the engagement of Theuderic, and worked to maintain her influence at court. In 612 she convinced Theuderic to attack his brother's kingdom, and this time Theudebert was defeated, captured, and killed.

In 612, Brunhilde remained at the pinnacle of power, and threatened Fredegund's son, Chlotar. But her fortunes quickly changed when Theuderic died of dysentery in 613. Although she made her great-grandson, Sigebert II, king, she could not put down the successful revolt Chlotar led against her. She was captured by her former rival's son and tried for the murder of 10 kings, including her husband, children, grandchildren, Merovech, and Chilperic. She was found guilty and condemned to death in a most gruesome fashion, tied to the back of a wild horse and dragged to her death. Although she met a most unfortunate end, Brunhilde ruled effectively for more than 30 years, acting as any Merovingian queen would to defend the rights of herself and her family against their rivals.

See also: Augustine of Canterbury, St.; Carolingian Dynasty; Chilperic I; Chlotar II; Columban, St.; Fredegund; Gregory I, the Great, Pope; Gregory of Tours; Merovingian Dynasty; Visigoths

Bibliography

Gregory of Tours. *The History of the Franks.* Trans. Lewis Thorpe. Harmondsworth, UK: Penguin, 1974.

Nelson, Janet L. "Queens as Jezebels: The Careers of Brunhild and Balthild in Merovingian History." In *Medieval Women.* Ed. Derek Baker. Oxford: Blackwell, 1978, pp. 31–77.

Wallace-Hadrill, John M. *The Long-Haired Kings.* Toronto: Toronto University Press, 1982.

Wemple, Suzanne. *Women in Frankish Society: Marriage and the Cloister, 500 to 900.* Philadelphia: University of Pennsylvania Press, 1985.

Wood, Ian. *The Merovingian Kingdoms, 450–751.* London: Longman, 1994.

Burgundian Code

Compiled by the Burgundian king Gundobad (r. 474–516) and officially promulgated by his son Sigismund in 517, the Burgundian Code (*Lex Burgundionum*), also known as *Lex Gundobada* or *Liber Constitutionem* is the formal codification of tribal law or traditional Burgundian custom. The code, which merged Burgundian and Roman traditions, sought to define patterns of daily life, marriage, the wergild, and other matters concerning the Burgundians. A separate law, the *Lex Romana Burdundionum,* defined relations between Burgundians and Romans.

The Burgundians entered the Roman Empire in the early fifth century and established two kingdoms, the first of which lasted from 413 to 436 and the second lasted from 443 to 534. Like many of the Germanic peoples who settled in the empire, the Burgundians faced the challenge of regulating relations with the majority Roman population they governed and of formalizing their own legal traditions. It is possible that already during the first Burgundian kingdom efforts were made to transform custom into formal written law, but the codification of the law waited for the greatest of Burgundian kings, Gundobad. By about 500, the king, drawing on the precedent of the Visigothic code published in 483 by King Euric, began the process of establishing a code of laws divided into 105 titles that was intended to regulate the lives and affairs of the Burgundian people and their relations with the Romans living under Burgundian authority. The effort was furthered by Gundobad's son and successor as king, Sigismund (516–523) who officially published the code in 517 and by Sigismund's successor, Godamar (524–534) who added to the written code. The *Lex Gundobada,* thus, can be divided into three main sections. The first section, titles 2–42, were compiled by Gundobad and seem to be the written version of established Burgundian custom. A second section, titles 43–88, was compiled between 501 and 517 and reflects the new situation facing the Burgundians as rulers of a settled kingdom. The final section, titles 89–105, were new laws issued by Godomar between 524 and 532.

The *Lex Gundobada* addresses a wide range of topics in its 105 titles and reflects the character of Burgundian society. There are passages that are concerned with economic activity, regulating contracts and sales of property; the planting and preservation of vineyards; and the manumission and conduct of slaves. The *Lex* also reveals social distinctions that existed in Burgundian society, which included slaves and semifree, freemen and serfs, as well as nobles and the king and his family. Although there is evidence of social inequities in the code, there is no evidence that Burgundians and Romans were treated differently—their wergeld was valued at the same level. Along with the definition of relations between Burgundians and Romans, the *Lex* focuses extensively on relations between the Burgundians themselves. Some titles consider gender relations, including number 12 which defines the penalties for abducting women. The code regulates marital and family affairs including titles that provide guidelines for the arrangement of marriages and the wedding gift, offer rules for women who seek marriage, and address the issues of adultery and divorce.

Related to the regulation of marriage and family are the many titles concerned with inheritance, and these titles address several specific matters such as rules for sons who die intestate after the death of their father but while their mother still lives and rules for division between a son and his aunt (like many early codes, the *Lex Gundobada* tends to address specific cases rather than establish general legal precedent). There are numerous titles that outline the penalties and procedures for crimes against slaves and free persons and their property. Among these titles are those that concern acts of violence, assault on women, theft, knocking out teeth, violation of crops and other goods and property, bearing false witness, and murder and murder of royal servants. The code also defines the specific rights of the king and obligations owed him. The *Lex Gundobada* regulates a wide range of social, economic, and criminal matters and although lacking a sophisticated legal philosophy is a step toward a more abstract sense or royal and legal authority.

See also: Burgundians; Gundobad; Visigoths

Bibliography

Fisher Drew, Katherine, trans. *The Burgundian Code: Book of Constitutions of Gundobad; Additional Enactments*. Philadelphia: University of Pennsylvania Press, 1972.

Wolfram, Herwig. *The Roman Empire and Its Germanic Peoples*. Trans. Thomas J. Dunlap. Berkeley: University of California Press, 1997.

Burgundians

Among the most Romanized of the barbarians who settled in the Roman Empire, the Burgundians established two kingdoms in succession that came to include parts of modern France, Germany, and Switzerland and that still bears their name. The Burgundians and their kings played an active role in the affairs of Italy and Gaul in the fifth and sixth centuries before their final defeat by the Merovingian Franks and incorporation into the Frankish kingdom. Although their independent reign was relatively short lived, the legacy of the Burgundians is significant; their early history forms the core of the *Nibelungenlied,* and the *Lex Gundobada,* or Burgundian Code, which was published in 517, remained influential into the ninth century.

The origins of the Burgundians remain obscure; a ninth-century tradition identifies their homeland as Scandinavia, but this is unlikely. Late Roman historians suggest that the Burgundians and Romans were long-standing neighbors. Orosius believed that they arrived along the Rhine during the reign of the emperor Tiberius (14–36 AD). Ammianus Marcellinus placed their appearance along the Rhine by the fourth century when they were enlisted against the Alammani and maintained that Romans and Burgundians were biologically related. This long period of contact with the empire may well have affected the attitude of the Burgundians toward the Romans after their crossing into imperial territory, possibly during the mass crossing of the Rhine in 406 and establishment as *foederati* (federated allies).

Shortly after their settlement within the boundaries of the empire, the Burgundians became actively involved in Roman political and military affairs and established the first of two independent kingdoms. In 407 the Burgundians were enlisted to defend the Rhine frontier against other barbains, and in 411 they joined with the Alamanni to support Jovinus' seizure of the imperial throne in the West. Two years later, Jovinus granted the Burgundian leader, Gundahar, the right to found a kingdom, whose capital would be Worms. Despite the fall of Jovinus, the Burgundians remained secure as *foederati* and maintained good relations with the empire. This changed, however, as the Burgundians sought to expand their territory in Gaul in the early 430s. The Roman general Aëtius attacked in 435 and unleashed his Hunnish mercenaries in the next year. The Huns killed Gundahar and virtually wiped out the Burgundians, an event that would be memorialized in the *Nibelungenlied.*

Despite this savage assault, the Burgundians managed to endure. Although they seem not to have had any kings for some two decades after the attack by the Huns, the Burgundians were resettled along the Rhine by Aëtius in 443 and reformed a kingdom that would last until 534. Throughout this period, as they had during the first kingdom, the Burgundians maintained close ties with the empire and were proud of their position as *foederati.* On numerous occasions in the fifth century, the Burgundians and their kings fought on behalf of the empire. In 451, they joined the Romans against Attila and the Huns at the battle of the Catalaunian Plains, and in 456 they fought as allies of the empire and Visigoths against the Suebi in Spain. Although Burgundian efforts to expand were pushed back by the Romans, their ties to the empire remained strong and even deepened when Ricimer, the brother-in-law of the Burgundain king Gundioc, became *magister militum*. Even after Ricimer's fall, the Burgundians continued to defend Roman interests against threats from the Alamanni and Visigoths. The Burgundian king Gundobad served as *magister militum* from 472 to 474, and his son Sigismund forged ties with the emperor in Constantinople and was given the title patrician. The strong ties to the empire were reflected by the relations between Burgundians and Romans in the Burgundian kingdom where the two groups lived side-by-side and were treated as equals before the law.

Along with their active alliance with the empire, the Burgundians were deeply involved with their barbarian neighbors. Under their greatest king, Gundobad (r. 480–516), and compiler of the Burgundian Code (*Lex Gundobada*), the Burgundians were involved in a complex set of affairs involving Franks, Ostrogoths, and Visigoths. In the 490s, as the Ostrogoth Theodoric struggled for control of Italy with Odovacar, Gundobad expanded into Italy and later, by 496–497, was made part of a system of marriage alliances that included Theodoric, Gundobad, the Merovingian king Clovis, and members of their families. It was at this time that Clovis married Clothilde, Gundobad's Catholic niece who shaped her husband's religious and military programs. As Gregory of Tours relates, it was Clothilde who encouraged Clovis to convert and to invade Burgundy, whose kings were Arian Christians. In an alliance with one of the Burgundian subkings, Godigisel, Clovis entered Burgundy and forced Gundobad to flee to Avignon. The Frank withdrew believing the situation was secure, but the Burgundians rose against Godigisel and the Franks, capturing and killing them all. Recognizing the advantages offered by Clovis, Gundobad allied with him and defeated the Visigoths in 507. They also waged a war against the Alemanni that practically destroyed them in 508–509, but Theodoric intervened much to the disadvantage of the Burgundians. Under Gundobad's successor, Sigismund (516–23) and publisher of the *Lex Gundobada*, the situation worsened. In 522, Sigismund's wife and daughter of Theodoric died and Sigismund killed their son. Enraged and intending on avenging his daughter, Theodoric invaded Burgundy and was joined by the Franks who together inflicted a savage defeat on the Burgundians. Sigismund was abandoned by his people and turned over to the Franks, who killed him. In 524, Godomar, Sigismund's brother, became king and presided over the demise of the kingdom. He faced attacks by the Franks in 524 and 532. In 534, the Merovingians invaded for the last time; they defeated Godomar and brought an end to the Burgundian kingdom, which was then incorporated into the Frankish kingdoms.

See also: Aëtius; Burgundian Code; Franks; Gundobad; Merovingian Dynasty; Odovacar; Theodoric the Great; Visigoths

Bibliography

Gregory of Tours. *Gregory of Tours: The History of the Franks*. Trans. Lewis Thorpe. Harmondsworth, UK: Penguin, 1947.

Fisher Drew, Katherine, trans. *The Burgundian Code: Book of Constitutions of Gundobad; Additional Enactments*. Philadelphia: University of Pennsylvania Press, 1972.

Wolfram, Herwig. *The Roman Empire and Its Germanic Peoples*. Trans. Thomas J. Dunlap. Berkeley: University of California Press, 1997.

Wood, Ian. *The Merovingian Kings, 450–751*. London: Longman, 1994.Aelfric.

Caedwalla (c. 659–689)

According to the historian Bede, Caedwalla was "a daring mad young man of the royal house of Gewissae" (232) who began his career as a pagan but converted to Christianity. He was king of the West Saxons for only a few years but initiated the tradition among West Saxon kings, down to Alfred the Great in the ninth century, of attempting to rule all of southeastern England.

Caedwalla was a member of the royal line but had been sent into exile during the reign of his predecessor, King Æthelwalh. In 685, Caedwalla began his struggle for the kingdom, and leaving exile, he attacked and killed Æthelwalh. He was turned away by his dead rival's retainers but managed to return and assume the throne. As king, he was involved in incessant warfare and conquest. He extended his power throughout southeastern England. Almost immediately after becoming king, Caedwalla invaded the Isle of Wight, where he was seriously wounded, and sought to kill all its inhabitants and replace them with people from Wessex. He took control of Sussex and killed one of its leaders and one of his chief rivals there. In 686, he invaded Kent and managed to secure recognition as king there as well. Although he was able to establish his power in several kingdoms, Caedwalla was unable to keep permanent hold on any of them, with the exception of the Isle of Wight.

Although he was a ferocious warrior king and pagan, Caedwalla remained on good terms with the bishops of his kingdom and eventually converted to Christianity. He was a patron of the church in England and may have founded a monastery at Hoo, in Kent between the Thames and Medway estuaries. According to Bede, Caedwalla abdicated the throne after roughly two years as king, 688, "for the sake of our Lord and his eternal kingdom" (279). Although accepting the faith in 688, the king desired the great honor of baptism in Rome and hoped to die shortly after baptism so that he could pass to "everlasting happiness" (279). In the summer of 688, Caedwalla left England. He stopped at Calais and donated money for the building of a church, and he also spent time at the court of the king of the Lombards, Cunipert. He reached Rome by the spring of 689 and was baptized by Pope Sergius on Holy Saturday before Easter, April 10, in that year, and was given the name Peter. As he wished, Caedwalla fell ill and died in Rome 10 days later on April 20, 689. Although his reign and life were short, Caedwalla left an important legacy for his kingdom as king and Christian convert.

See also: Alfred the Great; Anglo-Saxons; Bede; Lombards; Wessex

Bibliography

Bede. *Ecclesiastical History of the English People with Bede's Letter to Egbert and Cuthbert's Letter on the Death of Bede.* Trans. Leo Sherley-Price. Harmondsworth, UK: Penguin, 1991.

Blair, Peter Hunter. *The World of Bede.* Cambridge: Cambridge University Press, 1970.

Stenton, Frank M. *Anglo-Saxon England.* 3rd ed. Oxford: Clarendon, 1971.

Whitelock, Dorothy, ed. *The Anglo-Saxon Chronicle.* Westport, CT: Greenwood, 1986.

Caesarea

Commonly known as Caesarea Maritima or Caesarea Palaestinae to distinguish it from other cities of the same name, Caesarea was an important late Roman port and city along the Mediterranean coast near modern day Tel Aviv. A provincial capital under the Romans, Caeasarea is perhaps best known today for the ongoing undersea archeological excavations that have discovered much of the dynamic and prosperous city of antiquity.

Built in 22–10 BC by the Jewish king Herod the Great (73–4 BC), Caesarea was dedicated to the emperor Caesar Augustus (d. 14 AD) and consisted of a traditional Roman city as well as an important, man-made harbor that would contribute to the city's importance as a commercial center connecting the Roman Empire with Asia. In 6 AD the city was made the capital of the province of Judaea and following the Bar Kokhba or Second Jewish War (132–35 AD) Caesarea served as the capital of province now called Syria Palaestina. Under Byzantine rule, the city would continue as capital of the province Palaestina Prima. During the Roman and Byzantine periods, Caesarea was enriched by extensive trade in cotton, oil, wine, and other commodities, and the city was marked by warehouses and other structures necessary for trade. Excavation in the city has revealed an amphitheater, aqueducts (restored and updated in the sixth century), public baths, temples, and a hippodrome. An inscription was found that identifies Pontius Pilate as procurator of Judaea. An elegant Roman city, Caesarea's most remarkable feature was its harbor, which was built without any natural protective barriers but instead bounded by two breakwaters of concrete and rubble. The harbor underwent restoration under the emperor Anastasius in 500, and in the sixth century new fortifications were established for the still growing population. In the early seventh century, the city fell to the Persinas and then shortly after to the armies of Islam, after which the city declined in importance.

Along with its prominence as a provincial capital, Caesarea was also an important religious and cultural center. A Christian community was established there by St. Peter in the early first century, and the church may have survived without interruption throughout antiquity. It later became the seat of a metropolitan, and a number of churches were built including a great stone, octagonal church, which was built in the year 500. In 231 the great Christian thinker Origen settled in the city and attracted large numbers of students to the school and library he established there. He also compiled the Hexapla, a work of biblical commentary and parallel Greek and Hebrew texts of the Bible, in Caesarea, and later Christian scholars were attracted to the city as a result. In the fourth century, the scholar and historian and confidant of the emperor Constantine, Eusebius was bishop of Caesarea. The flourishing Christian culture was accompanied by traditional Greek learning and literacy and boasted numerous rhetoricians and other classically trained scholars. The Byzantine historian and chronicler of the reign of Justinian, Procopius, was the descendant of aristocrats of Caesarea.

See also: Constantine; Justinian; Procopius

Bibliography

Holum, Kenneth G., Avner Raban, Robert L. Hohlfelder, and Robert J. Bull. *King Herod's Dream: Caesarea on the Sea.* New York: W. W. Norton and Company, 1988.

Levine, Lee. *Caesarea under Roman Rule.* Leiden: Brill, 1975.

Raban, Avner, and Kenneth G. Holum, eds. *Caesarea Maritima: A Retrospective after Two Millenia.* Leiden: Brill, 1996.

Caesarius of Arles (c. 470–542)

An important bishop and monk whose influence on the later barbarian churches was great, Caesarius ruled as bishop during a critical period in the transition from the Roman to barbarian world. During his reign his city of Arles was controlled by several different barbarian kingdoms, ultimately becoming part of the Merovingian kingdom of the Franks. Although he carefully guided his diocese through troubled times, Caesarius is best known for his pastoral efforts and simple but elegant sermons. A talented preacher, Caesarius introduced the ideas of Augustine of Hippo to a broader audience. He was also very much interested in monastic life and composed two monastic rules, one for women and the other for men.

Born to a noble family near Chalon-sur-Saône in circa 470, Caesarius's relatives included his predecessor as archbishop of Arles. Although he later dedicated his life to the church, Caesarius showed interest in classical culture and the arts of rhetoric as a youth. He studied with an acclaimed teacher of rhetoric but, like St. Jerome and others, experienced a dream that persuaded him to devote himself solely to the church. His later sermons revealed the consequences of his decision by their lack of classical allusions. His decision led him to the monastery of Lérins, one of the great centers of monastic life, in 490. He remained there until 497, but was forced to abandon the rigors of the monastic life because of ill health. He left the monastery for the city of Arles, where he was made a deacon and then ordained priest. He later became an abbot of a local monastery and, in 504, archbishop of Arles, a position he held until his death in 542.

His career as archbishop was an important one for the church in Arles and Gaul. He was confirmed in his position as archbishop by the Visigothic king, Alaric II, and in 505 was summoned to the king's court on charges of conspiring with Alaric's enemies. Caesarius was acquitted, but he was forced to deal with the Ostrogothic king Theodoric after Alaric was defeated by the Merovingian king Clovis (r. 481–511). Although the city was to be ceded to Clovis's descendants in 536, in the meantime it remained subject to the Ostrogoths, and Caesarius was called to appear at Theodoric's court in 513 on suspicion of conspiracy. While visiting Theodoric, Caesarius met with the pope, who named him papal vicar to Spain and Gaul. As archbishop and papal legate, Caesarius assumed important duties in the church, including convening church councils. He held six councils during his reign, councils that shaped religious practice and doctrine. The most important council, at Orange in 529, established the interpretation of Augustine's teachings on salvation.

Archbishop in a critical time for the church and society in Gaul (now France), Caesarius is remembered best for his preaching and monastic rules. His sermons, which reveal Caesarius as a theologian of no great originality, are models of elegant simplicity and instruction. He abandoned the rhetoric he had once studied for a simpler style of delivery, using a less studied manner to comment on the Scriptures. His style of delivery made his sermons, of which some 238 still exist, more comprehensible to his flock. The sermons, however, were not overly simplistic but contained important lessons. They disseminated the ideas of Augustine, as well as other church fathers, to the faithful and included admonitions against superstition and immorality. He encouraged his listeners to read the Scriptures at home during dinner and throughout the evening and suggested that those who could not read should have the Scriptures read to them. He also called on his listeners to ponder the message of the sermon and to sing the psalms to reinforce the teachings of the faith.

Caesarius is also known for his monastic rule. Although unable because of health reasons to live as a monk, Caesarius remained dedicated to the monastic ideal during his life. An archbishop, he was also an abbot and the founder of a community of nuns at Arles. It was for this community that he wrote his famous monastic rule. This important rule seems to have been influenced by the Rule of the Master, and Benedict of Nursia seems to have borrowed from Caesarius when composing his monastic rule. Moreover, according to Gregory of Tours, a version of the rule of Caesarius was adopted by the royal nun Radegund for the convent she founded. The rule legislated on such matters as the length of the novitiate, personal property, and stability in the monastery, and set the precedent for monastic life in Gaul for generations to come.

See also: Augustine of Hippo, St.; Benedict of Nursia, St.; Clovis; Franks; Gregory of Tours; Merovingian Dynasty; Monasticism; Ostrogoths; Radegund; Theodoric the Great; Visigoths

Bibliography

Caesarius of Arles. *Caesarius of Arles: Sermons.* Trans. Mary Magdeleine Mueller. 3 Vols. New York: Fathers of the Church, 1956–1973.

Klingshirn, William E. *Caesarius of Arles: The Making of a Christian Community in Late Antique Gaul.* Cambridge: Cambridge University Press, 1994.

Laistner, Max L. W. *Thought and Letters in Western Europe, A.D. 500 to 900.* 2nd ed. Ithaca, NY: Cornell University Press, 1976.

Lawrence, Clifford H. *Medieval Monasticism: Forms of Religious Life in Western Europe in the Middle Ages.* 2nd ed. London: Longman, 1989.

McCarthy, Maria Caritas. *The Rule for Nuns of St. Caesarius of Arles: A Translation with Critical Introduction.* Washington, DC: Catholic University of America Press, 1960.

Riché, Pierre. *Education and Culture in the Barbarian West: From the Sixth through the Eighth Century.* Trans. John Contreni. Columbia: University of South Carolina Press, 1976.

Wood, Ian. *The Merovingian Kingdoms, 450–751.* London: Longman, 1994.

Capitulare de Villis

One of the most famous and significant of Charlemagne's capitularies, the *Capitulare de Villis* (capitulary on the royal estates) provides important insights into Carolingian government and economic life. The capitulary reveals Charlemagne's interest in governing local affairs as well as the need for Carolingian kings to attend to such matters. It also shows the economic resources available to Carolingian kings and the obligations of royal servants to their king.

The *Capitulare de Villis* is traditionally held to have been issued sometime between 771 and 800, and most likely closer to the year 800. A later date, of 807, for the issuance of the capitulary has also been proposed. It was issued by Charlemagne to improve administration in the kingdom and to end the abuses of the royal treasury and of the king's residences throughout his vast realm. The capitulary was also designed to guarantee that certain basic necessities would be found in each of the residences, so that the king and his court could be well provided for when he and his retinue visited the various estates in the kingdom. Indeed, the capitulary was intended to establish the standards by which Charlemagne wanted his estates maintained and was, thus, an important part of his reform of Carolingian government and administration. It was, in fact, one of a number of rulings by the king to improve administration, and it laid the foundation for similar rulings by his son,

Louis the Pious. The depth of detail in the rulings in the capitulary reveal both the king's interest in government and the rudimentary nature of the administration in Charlemagne's day.

The capitulary legislated the day-to-day workings of the royal estates throughout the realm, regulating the materials and laborers found on these estates. In fact, the capitulary laid out instructions for all economic life in the royal estates. It provided rules for making wine, salting food, maintaining buildings, and taking care of animals, as well as a list of the agricultural products to be raised on the estates. The steward of the palace was to provide an annual statement of the revenues derived from the fields farmed by royal plowmen and from tenant farmers, as well as from the number of piglets born, various fines, and payments from mills, forests, fields, boats, and bridges. The steward was also to keep a record of fruits, vegetables, honey, wax, oil, soap, vinegar, beer, wine, wheat, chickens, eggs, geese, and other farm products raised each year. The capitulary also mandated an account of fishermen, smiths, shield makers, and cobblers who worked on the estates as well as the number of workshops in which they worked. The number of tools on each estate was also given, and this account reveals that most of the tools were wood and not iron. Although the *Capitulare de Villis* is no longer used as a tool to understand the entire economic and social structure of the Carolingian world, since it applied only to the royal estates, it remains an important document for understanding Carolingian material culture and political administration.

See also: Capitularies; Carolingian Dynasty; Charlemagne; Louis the Pious

Bibliography

Dutton, Paul. *Carolingian Civilization: A Reader.* Peterborough, ON: Broadview, 1993.

Ganshof, François Louis. *Frankish Institutions under Charlemagne.* Trans. Bryce Lyon and Mary Lyon. Providence, RI: Brown University Press, 1968.

Halphen, Louis. *Charlemagne and the Carolingian Empire.* Trans. Giselle de Nie. Amsterdam: North-Holland, 1977.

McKitterick, Rosamond. *The Carolingians and the Written Word.* Cambridge: Cambridge University Press, 1989.

Riché, Pierre. *The Carolingians: A Family Who Forged Europe.* Trans. Michael Idomir Allen. Philadelphia: University of Pennsylvania Press, 1993.

Capitularies

Carolingian legislative documents, the capitularies were an important tool of government and administration for all Carolingian kings, especially Charlemagne. The capitularies covered a wide range of topics, from economics and estate management to religious and political reforms. The term comes from contemporary usage, which refers to this kind of document as a *capitulare* or in the plural *capitularia,* because the documents were organized into short sections or chapters (in Latin, *capitula*). The capitularies demonstrate the growing importance of writing and the written word for Charlemagne and all Carolingians; even though the documents did not replace the word of the king as the rule or law, they did make known the king's word. The capitularies were sent to the special agents of the king called *missi dominici,* or messengers of the lord king, who were charged with circulating them throughout the realm (unless the capitularies contained specific instructions for the missi).

The earliest of the capitularies were issued by Carloman and Pippin the Short in the 740s, 750s, and 760s, but they were used to a much greater degree under Charlemagne. Indeed, Charlemagne issued a large number of capitularies as part of his broader reform of the Carolingian church and state. Some of the most famous and important Carolingian capitularies were issued by Charlemagne. The Capitulary of Herstal (779) aimed at general reform of society, and the programmatic *Admonitio Generalis* (789) announced the religious goals and ideals of the Frankish king and laid the foundation for the Carolingian Renaissance by mandating teaching and the establishment of schools. Charlemagne also issued a capitulary shortly after his coronation as emperor of the Romans in 800, restating the goals he pursued throughout his reign, as well as capitularies that addressed images, monastic life, and the law. Charlemagne also issued the *Capitulare de Villis,* which regulated management of the royal estates. Charlemagne's successors Louis the Pious and Charles the Bald continued to issue capitularies throughout their reigns, but the documents were not used in other parts of the divided empire. The last capitulary was issued in 877.

See also: Admonitio Generalis; *Capitulare de Villis*; Carloman, Mayor of the Palace; Carolingian Dynasty; Charlemagne; Charles the Bald; Louis the Pious; Pippin III, Called Pippin the Short

Bibliography

Loyn, Henry R., and John Percival. *The Reign of Charlemagne: Documents on Carolingian Government and Administration.* New York: St. Martin's Press, 1975.

McKitterick, Rosamond. *The Carolingians and the Written Word.* Cambridge: Cambridge University Press, 1989.

Riché, Pierre. *The Carolingians: A Family Who Forged Europe.* Trans. Michael Idomir Allen. Philadelphia: University of Pennsylvania Press, 1993.

Carloman, King of the Franks (d. 771)

Son of Pippin III the Short and brother of Charlemagne, Carloman ruled with his brother as king of the Franks from their father's death in 768 until his own death in

771. Although short, his reign was marked by controversy with his brother, which could have led to a destructive civil war had not Carloman suddenly died. His death saved the kingdom from disaster and allowed Charlemagne to rule with a free hand and subsequently forge one of the great empires of the Middle Ages.

The younger son of Pippin—he was about four years younger than Charlemagne—Carloman first appears in the *Royal Frankish Annals* in 754. With his older brother, Carloman received royal unction from Pope Stephen II when the pope traveled to the Frankish kingdom to crown Pippin king of the Franks. He was elevated to joint kingship of the Franks with his brother on their father's death. Pippin had passed the royal crown to his two sons and divided the realm between them. Carloman received a compact and contiguous territory that included Alsace, part of Aquitaine, Burgundy, Provence, and other neighboring regions, and he was crowned king at Soissons in October 768. As king Carloman followed policies similar to those of his father, especially in regard to monastic policy.

Carloman's short reign is best known, however, for the strife that existed between the two brothers. In 769, Charlemagne sought aid from Carloman in the face of a revolt in Aquitaine led by Count Hunald. Only with great difficulty, made worse by Carloman's unwillingness to help, was Charlemagne able to suppress the revolt. Carloman's refusal to help may have been part of his strategy to undermine his brother's authority; certainly it is likely to have contributed to the strains of an already tense relationship. In 770, Carloman met with his mother, Bertrada, who then went to Italy to help establish peace between the two brothers. Arranging a marriage with the Lombard king, Desiderius, for Charlemagne, Bertrada hoped to establish an alliance with the Lombards as a means to promote harmony in the Frankish kingdom. But Charlemagne repudiated his wife within a year, and the situation between the Franks and Lombards, as well as that between Charlemagne and Carloman, worsened. The potentially explosive situation was resolved by the sudden death of Carloman on December 4, 771. Charlemagne, with the approval of Carloman's supporters, dispossessed Carloman's widow, Gerberga, and two sons, who fled to the Lombard court of Desiderius. They received Desiderius's protection until Charlemagne conquered Italy in 774, and they were then turned over to Charlemagne and disappeared from the records at that point.

See also: Carolingian Dynasty; Charlemagne; Desiderius; Lombards; Pippin III, Called Pippin the Short; *Royal Frankish Annals*

Bibliography

Davis, Raymond, trans. *The Lives of the Eighth-Century Popes (*Liber Pontificalis*): The Ancient Biographies of Nine Popes from* A.D. *715 to* A.D. *817.* Liverpool, UK: Liverpool University Press, 1992.

Einhard and Notker the Stammerer. *Two Lives of Charlemagne.* Trans. Lewis Thorpe. Harmondsworth, UK: Penguin, 1981.

Fichtenau, Heinrich. *The Carolingian Empire.* Trans. Peter Munz. Toronto: University of Toronto Press, 1979.

Halphen, Louis. *Charlemagne and the Carolingian Empire.* Trans. Giselle de Nie. Amsterdam: North-Holland, 1977.

McKitterick, Rosamond. *The Frankish Kingdoms under the Carolingians, 751–987.* London: Longman, 1983.

Riché, Pierre. *The Carolingians: A Family Who Forged Europe.* Trans. Michael Idomir Allen. Philadelphia: University of Pennsylvania Press, 1993.

Scholz, Bernhard Walter, trans. *Carolingian Chronicles: Royal Frankish Annals and Nithard's History.* Ann Arbor: University of Michigan Press, 1972.

Carloman, Mayor of the Palace (d. 754)

Son of the Carolingian Mayor of the Palace, Charles Martel, Carloman inherited control of the Frankish kingdoms with his brother, Pippin the Short, on his father's death in 741. Together as mayors of the palace, Carloman and Pippin built upon the legacy of their father and strengthened the position of the Carolingian family in the Frankish kingdoms at the expense of the Merovingian dynasty. Although they placed a Merovingian on the throne, Carloman and Pippin were the real powers in the kingdoms. Carloman was also active in reform of the church, supporting the activities of the Anglo-Saxon missionary Boniface and promoting reform in the Frankish church. Indeed, his interest in the church and religious life was so great that he left worldly power for the monastic life. His abdication paved the way for the establishment of Carolingian royal power by his brother and eventually for the establishment of imperial power by his nephew Charlemagne.

Although perhaps best known for his retirement to a monastery in 747, Carloman was an active and vigorous mayor (r. 741–747), who helped his brother Pippin suppress the many revolts they faced at the outset of their joint rule. Together they squashed the revolt of their half-brother Grifo, who sought to lay claim to part of his father's legacy. They laid siege to Laon and captured Grifo, who was kept in custody by Carloman until his retirement. The two mayors also faced difficulties from their sister, Chiltrude, who fled to the court of the Bavarian duke, Odilo. They eventually defeated Odilo in 743 but were not able to force him from the duchy. Carloman and Pippin also enforced their authority on subject peoples in Aquitaine and Alemannia, where Carloman imposed Carolingian authority with a terror campaign. The new mayors were ultimately able to establish themselves in the kingdom, but only with much difficulty.

The revolts Carloman and his brother faced led them to an important step. Their father had ruled during the last four years of his life without a Merovingian king on the throne. It became apparent to Carloman and Pippin, however, that to secure their position in the Frankish kingdoms, they needed to place a Merovingian monarch on the throne. In 743 they discovered a member of the dynasty in the monastery of St. Bertin, whom they established as King Childeric III. It is likely that Carloman was the prime mover in the reestablishment of the Merovingian dynasty. And although portrayed as a poor and powerless do-nothing king by Einhard, the last Merovingian provided the legitimization that the brothers needed to maintain their control in the kingdoms.

Carloman, and to a lesser extent his brother Pippin, were active supporters of Boniface, and both mayors were equally strong supporters of the reform of the Frankish church, particularly the reform of clerical behavior and education. Boniface, who had been protected by Charles Martel, found particularly strong support for his missionary and reform efforts from Carloman. At one point, the Carolingian mayor granted him the Anglo-Saxon missionary lands around Fulda so that Boniface could establish a monastery. Carloman also worked with Boniface to reform ecclesiastical organization in the Frankish kingdoms, to bring it more fully into cooperation with the papacy. Carloman also presided at several reform councils in the 740s, with, at times, Boniface and Pippin, to improve the life of the church in the Frankish kingdoms. Carloman, among other things, promised to protect the churches from impoverishment and to protect ecclesiastical property rights.

Carloman's religious inclinations, revealed by his active support for Boniface and church reform, were fully displayed in 747 when he announced to Pippin that he had decided to withdraw from his position of power and retire to a monastery. He settled his affairs and made donations to a monastery in his domain before departing for Rome. He received the tonsure from Pope Zachary and then built a monastery in honor of St. Sylvester on Mt. Soracte. In 754, perhaps because too many pilgrims visited him at his monastery, Carloman moved to the monastery at Monte Cassino. Contemporary sources make clear that Carloman departed voluntarily, but his decision did not bode well for his immediate family, especially his son Drogo, who was disposed of by his uncle.

Carloman's public career, however, did not end with his retirement in 747. In fact, his decision indirectly had a profound influence on the fate of his dynasty and of the Frankish kingdoms. As a result of Carloman's abdication, Pippin was left the sole mayor, and for all intents and purposes, the sole power in the realm. In 751, after deposing Childeric III, Pippin assumed the throne of the king of the Franks and founded the Carolingian royal dynasty. In 754, Carloman directly participated in the public affairs of the kingdom. At the request of the Lombard king Aistulf, Carloman left his monastery at Monte Cassino to take part in the debate among Pippin and the Frankish nobility concerning a possible invasion of Italy. Aistulf had been threatening the pope, Stephen II, who had requested aid from the Frankish king. To prevent an invasion by Pippin, Aistulf sent Carloman to oppose the invasion by his brother. Aistulf's plan failed, however, and the invasion followed shortly after the debate. Carloman was not allowed to return to Italy but was sent to a monastery in Vienne, where he died sometime later in the year 754.

See also: Aistulf; Boniface, St.; Carolingian Dynasty; Charlemagne; Charles Martel; Childeric III; Merovingian Dynasty; Monasticism; Pippin III, Called Pippin the Short

Bibliography
McKitterick, Rosamond. *The Frankish Kingdoms under the Carolingians, 751–987.* London: Longman, 1983.

Riché, Pierre. *The Carolingians: A Family Who Forged Europe.* Trans. Michael Idomir Allen. Philadelphia: University of Pennsylvania Press, 1993.

Scholz, Bernhard Walter, trans. *Carolingian Chronicles: Royal Frankish Annals and Nithard's History.* Ann Arbor: University of Michigan Press, 1972.

Wood, Ian. *The Merovingian Kingdoms, 450–751.* London: Longman, 1994.

Caroline Books. *See Libri Carolini*

Caroline Minuscule

A graceful and rounded formal book hand, Caroline or Carolingian minuscule appeared in its mature form during the late eighth century and became the primary writing style of Carolingian scholars. It caught on quickly after its appearance because it was a clear and elegant script that was easy to read and was a useful script for Charlemagne's efforts at promoting learning and literacy.

The creation of Caroline minuscule has traditionally been associated with the monastery of Tours and its abbot, the great Anglo-Saxon scholar Alcuin. Invited to the Frankish realm by Charlemagne to lead his palace school, Alcuin was thought to have devised the script in the 790s to serve the great king's educational reforms. The emergence of the script, however, predates Alcuin's supposed reform, appearing in its mature form first in manuscripts from Corbie and Trier in the 780s, and was most likely not invented by any one scribe or scholar. Caroline minuscule seems to have evolved over several generations, taking shape in various monasteries in the western Frankish kingdom before its final appearance. Based on an earlier cursive and Roman uncial scripts, Caroline minuscule is notable for its elegance, regularity, uniformity, and, perhaps most importantly, clarity.

The new script was so popular, in part, because it was easy to read, compared with other writing styles, and new rules and practices associated with it, including separation of words, contributed to its legibility. The letters in Caroline minuscule were also easier to write than those in other book hands and thus allowed for faster production of manuscripts. Once it assumed its mature form, Caroline minuscule spread through the Carolingian Empire and appeared in Italy in the 820s and in England by the 10th century. In the 15th century, Italian humanist scholars reading manuscripts copied in Caroline minuscule believed the script to have been an ancient Roman hand because of its beauty. Fifteenth-century scholars adopted Caroline minuscule as the basis for their own writing, which formed the basis of modern Roman script.

See also: Alcuin; Carolingian Dynasty; Carolingian Renaissance; Charlemagne

Bibliography

McKitterick, Rosamond. *The Frankish Kingdoms under the Carolingians, 751–987.* London: Longman, 1983.

McKitterick, Rosamond. "Script and Book Production." In Rosamond McKitterick, ed. *Carolingian Culture: Emulation and Innovation.* Cambridge: Cambridge University Press, 1994, pp. 220–47.

Carolingian Dynasty

Ruling nearly all of Christian Europe from the eighth to 10th century, the Carolingians, as they were known from their tradition of naming a son in every generation Charles (*Carolus* in Latin), established a great empire, presided over important religious reforms, expanded the use of writing in government and society, and laid the foundation for many of the cultural and political achievements of later medieval civilization. The Carolingian tradition of royal and imperial coronation and their governmental ideas served as the model for medieval rulers long after the demise of the dynasty and the breakup of the Carolingian Empire had led to the emergence of the medieval kingdoms of France and Germany. Indeed, later medieval kings and emperors looked to Charlemagne, the greatest of the Carolingians, as a source of inspiration, and the Carolingian ruler was the focus of a great epic tradition and canonized at the initiative of Frederick Barbarossa. A great cultural flowering, traditionally called the Carolingian Renaissance, occurred during the reign of these Frankish monarchs.

The dynasty's origins are usually traced to the mid-seventh century, when the Austrasian nobles St. Arnulf, bishop of Metz (d. c. 645), and Pippin I of Landen (also called Pippin the Elder, d. c. 640) joined together in a marriage alliance. The fortunes of the family came from its control of the office of mayor of the palace (*major domus*), a reward that Pippin earned after helping the Merovingian king Chlotar II (584–629) overthrow Queen Brunhilde and assume the Frankish throne in 613. Pippin exploited his position and became one of the most powerful figures in the kingdom. Although his fortunes ebbed and flowed as the throne passed between various Merovingian kings, Pippin was able to establish a secure base of power and wealth, and to pass it on to his son Grimoald (d. 657), who succeeded his father as mayor when the latter suddenly died.

Grimoald's career turned out to be an instructive one for generations to come and a reminder of the vagaries of political power. Grimoald was a popular and ambitious figure, but the family suffered an almost fatal setback as a result of his political ambitions. Shortly after his elevation to power, Grimoald accompanied the Merovingian king ruling Austrasia, Sigebert III (r. 633/634–656), on a military expedition to suppress the revolt of one of the dukes of the kingdom. The campaign was a disaster, and the king survived only because of the actions of Grimoald, who thus was now closer to Sigebert and able to impose his will on the king. Grimoald next expanded his own base of power by acquiring territory and, in what was to become good Carolingian fashion, forging alliances with monasteries and their monks. The mayor also persuaded the king to adopt his son as heir because Sigebert was still without a son of his own. Subsequent to this arrangement, Sigebert did have a son, Dagobert, who was to be his heir. On the king's death, however, Dagobert was entrusted to Grimoald who deposed Dagobert, sent him to a monastery in distant Ireland, and placed his own son, Childebert the Adopted, on the throne. Unfortunately for Grimoald, his coup failed. The Merovingian king in Neustria, Clovis II, who may have assisted in the deposition but was surprised by Grimoald's enthronement of his son, invited the mayor and his son to Neustria where they were captured and executed—a most unhappy end for Grimoald and his family.

Although forced into the political wilderness for a generation, the Carolingian line would see its fortunes revived. Pippin II, of Herstal (r. 687–714), the nephew of Grimoald and grandson of Arnulf and Pippin I, recovered the office of mayor and, with the advice and guidance of his mother Begga, restored the family to prominence. Pippin's chances were aided by the mayor of Neustria, Ebroin, whose ambitions of unifying the realm under his own authority and growing tyranny brought him enemies, which unsettled the kingdom even more at a time when the Merovingian kings were losing power. Many Austrasian nobles who had supported Grimoald rallied to Pippin, who united the Frankish kingdom when he defeated Ebroin at the Battle of Tertry in 687. As sole mayor, Pippin ruled in the name of several Merovingian kings, including Theuderic III, Clovis IV, Childebert III, and Dagobert III. He strengthened his family's hold on power by improving relationships with the church and gaining control of monasteries. He also enforced royal authority over the various parts of the kingdom and expanded the eastern boundaries of the kingdom. For both his family and the kingdom, Pippin's reign was most beneficial.

Despite his successes, the kingdom fell into civil strife after Pippin's death. Desirous that her descendants should assume the office of mayor, Pippin's widow, Plectrude, imprisoned Charles Martel (the Hammer; r. 714–741), Pippin's son with his second wife or concubine. But her plans were undermined by a rebellion of Neustrian nobles and Charles's escape from prison. Although suffering setbacks of his own, Charles, the first of his family to be so named, laid claim to his inheritance as mayor, seized much treasure held by Plectrude, and forced her from power.

Charles Martel's term as mayor brought increasing prestige and power to the family. A ferocious warrior, Charles managed to take control of the kingdom in the 720s when he forced the Neustrians to accept his authority, and he won numerous victories against foreign foes, as his father had done before him. His most important and famous victory took place somewhere between Tours and Poitiers in 732, when he defeated a Muslim army from Spain. Although more battles were necessary to expel the Muslims from the Frankish kingdom, the Battle of Tours confirmed offered Martel the opportunity to expand into the sought and enhanced his reputation as a great warrior. The victory was understood by contemporaries as the demonstration of God's favor on the Carolingian mayor.

Charles's successes were not limited to the military arena, however, because he further strengthened the alliance between his family and the Frankish church. Although he alienated much church land to compensate the nobility and ensure their loyalty, thus seriously weakening the church, Charles supported the church and its missionary activities. He established strong ties with the royal abbey of St. Denis, an important political as well as religious act, because the abbey had long supported the Merovingian dynasty. He promoted the activities of Anglo-Saxon missionaries, including St. Boniface, and received a proposal from Pope Gregory III for an alliance against the Lombards in Italy. So great was Charles's power in the kingdom by the end of his life that he ruled without a Merovingian king from 737 on and, following Frankish royal tradition, divided the succession between his two sons, Pippin III, called Pippin the Short (d. 768) and Carloman (d. 754).

The new mayors faced much opposition at the outset of their reign. They faced resistance from various sections of the nobility and also from their half-brother, Grifo, who had been granted a number of estates by their father and who desired to rule with his half-brothers. Carloman and Pippin, however, dispossessed Grifo from his legacy and imprisoned him. They also suppressed the dissension they faced and extended their power over Aquitaine and Bavaria. One step they thought necessary to take was to appoint a new Merovingian king, Childeric III, as a means to legitimize their rule and restore confidence in the government among the nobility. At the same time, it was the mayors who held the reins of government and who asserted their authority over the kingdom. They led military campaigns, supported the activities of Boniface, held councils attended by nobles and bishops to address matters concerning the kingdom and the church, and promoted needed religious and political reform—until Carloman withdrew to a monastery in 747, an action that left Pippin as sole mayor.

Pippin next took the fateful steps once taken without success by Grimoald. Secure in his power, Pippin sent two trusted advisors with a letter to the pope, Zachary (r. 741–752), asking if he who had the power or he who had the title should be king. Zachary responded as Pippin had hoped. Pippin deposed Childeric, the last Merovingian king, and sent him to a monastery for the rest of his life. In November, 751, Pippin, following traditional Germanic practice, was elected king by the Frankish nobles, and, to demonstrate the new and more powerful charisma he possessed, he was crowned and anointed by the bishops of the realm, possibly including the pope's representative Boniface. Coronation and unction were repeated in 754 by Pope Stephen, who also anointed Pippin's sons, Charles and Carloman, and forbade the Franks from choosing a king from any other family. Stephen's coronation led to the establishment of a firm alliance between Rome and the kingdom of the Franks and the grant of what is called the Donation of Pippin to the pope.

Pippin's reign as king (751–768) was a critical time in the history of the dynasty; it was Pippin who established the foundation of Carolingian royal policy. He continued the program of reform of the church that had begun during his shared rule with Carloman. His efforts included the introduction of Roman liturgical practices to the churches in his kingdom, the reform of religious life, and the reinforcement of ties with the influential monastery of St. Denis. He also strengthened ties with Rome forged in 754. The papacy and its extensive holdings were under constant threat from the Lombards, who sought to unify the Italian peninsula under their authority. Pippin received requests for aid from the pope, and therefore he undertook two invasions to protect the pope from his Lombard enemies. He also undertook the vigorous expansion of the realm, especially in to Aquitaine, and promoted the idea of sacral kingship, the idea that the king is chosen by God to rule and is God's representative on earth. Despite his many achievements, Pippin's reign is often overshadowed by that of his illustrious son, Charlemagne.

When Pippin died in 768 he left the kingdom to his sons Carloman and Charlemagne. Tensions existed between the two brothers, and civil war nearly broke out, but Carloman's death in 771 prevented this and opened the way for the sole rule of his brother, as king until 800 and then as emperor until 814. Charlemagne's success was, in part, the result of his abilities as a warrior, and during his reign the kingdom enjoyed a dramatic expansion of its territory. Shortly after the death of Carloman, Charles began a campaign to conquer and convert the Saxons, which lasted from 772 to 804. This process saw nearly annual campaigns into Saxony, the mass execution of 4,500 Saxons at Verdun, the destruction of pagan shrines, and the deportation of large numbers of Saxons from their homeland. Reviving the efforts of his father Pippin, but with far greater enthusiasm, Charles invaded Italy, defeated the Lombards, and made himself king of the Lombards in 774. He overcame Tassilo, the duke of Bavaria, in 787, and smashed the Avar capital, or ring, in the early 790s. His first campaign into Muslim Spain in 778, at the invitation of the emir of Saragossa, led to the disastrous attack at Roncesvalles, after which Roland and the entire rear guard were massacred, but Charlemagne returned undaunted to create the Spanish March, a militarized border region that included territory in Spain beyond the Pyrenees.

A successful empire builder, Charlemagne was also an innovator in government. The county was the primary administrative governmental unit and was ruled in the king's name by local nobles called counts. The responsibilities of the counts included maintaining peace and order, implementing royal law, and dispensing justice. A new class of judicial officers (called *scabini*) was established to adjudicate local disputes. Special representatives of the king, the *missi dominici,* or messengers of the lord king, were responsible for overseeing the activities of the local officials. Two missi, a noble and a churchman, were generally sent

Fourteenth-century illumination depicts the coronation of Charlemagne by Pope Leo III in 800. (The British Library Board)

out together to ensure the proper administration of justice, hear oaths of loyalty, and publish new laws. Moreover, Charles issued a new kind of law, the capitulary, and increased the use of writing as a tool of administration and government. The capitularies, so-called because they were arranged in chapters (*capitula*), addressed a broad number of issues, including administration of royal palaces, education, standardization of weights and measures, and legal and religious reform. The most famous of the capitularies was the *Admonitio Generalis* of 789, which laid the foundation for the cultural revival known as the Carolingian Renaissance. Charles himself invited scholars from throughout Europe, including Alcuin, Theodulf of Orléans, and Paul the Deacon, to participate in his court, his reforms, and the cultural revival.

Charlemagne was also responsible for reestablishing the imperial dignity in the former Western Empire, a restoration that occurred when Charles visited Rome to investigate an attack on Pope Leo III (r. 795–816). On December 25, 800, Charles attended Christmas mass, and as he rose from prayer, Leo crowned him emperor, and those in the church hailed him as emperor and augustus. Although doubts about Charlemagne's interest in the imperial title were raised by his biographer, Einhard, who declared that Charles would not have entered the church that day had he known what was to happen, many of the court scholars had already asserted Charlemagne's imperial stature in the 790s. They no doubt noted that the imperial authority was vacant in the Byzantine Empire because a woman, Irene, claimed to be emperor. Charlemagne's building program, especially the church and palace complex at Aix-la-Chapelle (now Aachen), which was influenced by similar structures in the former Byzantine imperial capital in Ravenna, Italy, suggests that he was not unaware of his imperial stature. His dismay was likely over the way the imperial crown was bestowed; certainly Charles employed the title in his last years and rededicated himself to his program of renewal with a new "imperial" capitulary in 802.

Charles first understood the title as a special honor for himself alone, but in 813 he passed on the office of emperor to his surviving son, Louis the Pious (778–840). Louis's reign was characterized not only by continued cultural and religious reforms but also by civil war. Louis made the imperial authority the foundation of his power and thus emphasized it in ways that his father, who preserved his royal titles, had not. He also sought to maintain the empire's permanent integrity by implementing a well-thought-out succession plan in 817, shortly after a near-fatal accident. The *Ordinatio Imperii,* as the capitulary that laid out the succession was called, provided a place in the succession for each of Louis's sons; the younger sons, Pippin and Louis the German, were assigned authority over sub-kingdoms, and imperial and sovereign authority was granted to his eldest son, Lothar (795–855), who was to be associated with his father as emperor during his father's life and then become his successor as emperor. Dissatisfaction with the plan emerged almost immediately and led to the revolt of Louis's nephew,

Bernard, in 817. Bernard was blinded, and he died in the forceful suppression of the revolt. Despite this rebellion, Louis's reign during the 810s and 820s saw important achievements, including monastic reform, which was a precursor of later monastic reform, and governmental reform that provided legal and constitutional grounds for Carolingian power in Italy.

Despite these positive developments, Louis faced a number of crises in the late 820s and 830s. The birth of a son, Charles the Bald (823–877), to his second wife Judith, and the reorganization of the succession plan to include Charles, provided the other sons, and many nobles and bishops, reason to revolt against Louis's authority. The 830s was plagued by much turmoil in the empire, brought on by the revolts of Lothar and Pippin and Louis. In 834 Louis was deposed by Lothar, and Charles and Judith were placed in religious houses. But Louis, despite his ill-deserved reputation for weakness, regained his throne and ruled until his death in 840, when he was succeeded by Lothar, Charles, and Louis the German.

Civil war intensified in the years after Louis's death, as his surviving sons struggled for preeminence in the empire. After several battles, including an especially bloody one at Fontenoy, the brothers agreed to the Treaty of Verdun in 843, which divided the realm between them, with Charles getting western Francia, Louis eastern Francia, and Lothar central Francia and Italy as well as the imperial title. Lothar's territory was the least defensible, a problem not only because of the threats he faced from his brothers but also because of the growing threat of Viking, Muslim, and Magyar invasions. His acceptance of the tradition of dividing the inheritance among his own sons further undermined the territorial integrity of the central kingdom. Indeed, the weaknesses of Lothar's portion were revealed in the treaty of Meerssen, 870, which divided the northern parts of Lothar's territory between his brothers Charles the Bald and Louis. Charles survived the wars of the 830s and 840s to establish a strong kingship and resurrect the dynamic court culture of his grandfather. He also assumed the imperial crown and captured Aix-la-Chapelle before his death in 877.

Although the kings of West Francia preserved the line the longest, until 987 when death and betrayal brought an end to the line, Carolingian power and authority underwent a process of decline beginning in the generation after the death of Charles the Bald. From the time of Louis II, the Stammerer (r. 877–879), until the time of the last Carolingian, Louis V (r. 986–987), the dynasty faced a series of great problems that eroded their power base. The west Frankish kingdom faced repeated Viking incursions, which the traditional Frankish military was unable to stop. Instead, local leaders, dukes and counts, began to exercise authority in their own name and took steps to protect their territories from these invaders. Their ability to provide some protection offered them greater political authority, and their gradual acquisition of territory made them increasingly powerful. The civil strife of the later Carolingians also contributed to their decline, as various kings gave away significant amounts of land from the royal treasury to ensure the loyalty of the nobility. This effort accomplished little more than the gradual impoverishment of the dynasty, and the growth of increasingly independent duchies. By their fall in 987 Carolingian kings could only command a small region around Paris, where they held their last important estates.

In East Francia, the dynasty was replaced much sooner, but it nevertheless left an important legacy to its successors and the medieval empire. After the wars of the 840s, Louis the German continued the Carolingian line in East Francia, but he was faced with many challenges. He ruled over a diverse kingdom, comprising Bavaria, Franconia, Saxony, Swabia, and Thuringia. He was plagued by attacks from Slavs and Vikings and faced the rising power of the nobility, especially the Liudolfings, and suffered revolts from within his family, including two by his son Carloman (d. 880). His dependence on the church, especially the monasteries of his realm, was in part the result of the special problems of his kingdom. He divided the realm between his three sons, who succeeded him on his death on August, 28, 876, but it was Louis's son, Charles the Fat (r. 876–887, d. 888), who received the imperial title and, for a short time, reunited the empire.

Despite a strong start to his reign and early success against invaders, Charles's ill health and the growing success of Viking raiders led to his deposition in 887. He was succeeded in East Francia by his brother's illegitimate son, Arnulf of Carinthia (r. 887–899), who ruled with much early success and was crowned emperor in Rome. But Arnulf too was plagued by ill health in his later years, and he was succeeded after his death by his six-year-old son, Louis the Child (r. 899–911). Louis was the last of the Carolingians to rule in East Francia. His reign was marked by destructive Magyar invasions and the deaths of powerful nobles who were critical to the defense of the realm. On the death of Louis, the nobles of East Francia elected Conrad I (r. 911–918) king. Conrad and his successors inherited a realm divided into numerous duchies and threatened by foreign invaders, but they also inherited Carolingian traditions in government and the Carolingian tradition of strong ties with the church, which laid the foundation for the restoration of the empire by Otto I in 962.

See also: Aix-la-Chapelle; Astronomer, The; Austrasia; Bernard of Septimania; Boniface, St.; Brunhilde; Carolingian Minuscule; Carolingian Renaissance; Charlemagne; Charles the Bald; Charles III, the Fat; Charles Martel; Charles III, the Simple; Childeric III; Chlotar II; Dagobert; Ermoldus Nigellus; *Libri Carolini*; Louis the German; Louis the Pious; Louis the Stammerer; Merovingian Dynasty; Neustria; Notker the Stammerer; Pippin I, Called Pippin of Landen; Pippin II, Called Pippin of Herstal; Pippin III, Called Pippin the Short; Plectrude; Saint-Denis, Abbey of; Tertry, Battle of; Tours; Tours, Battle of; *Vita Karoli*

Bibliography

Bachrach, Bernard. *Early Carolingian Warfare: Prelude to Empire.* Philadelphia: University of Pennsylvania Press, 2001.

Becher, Mattias. *Charlemagne.* New Haven, CT: Yale University Press, 2005.

Costambeys, Marios, Matthew Innes, and Simon McaLean. *The Carolingian World.* Cambridge: Cambridge University Press, 2011.

Einhard and Notker the Stammerer. *Two Lives of Charlemagne.* Trans. Lewis Thorpe. Harmondsworth, UK: Penguin, 1981.

Fichtenau, Heinrich. *The Carolingian Empire.* Trans. Peter Munz. Toronto: University of Toronto Press, 1979.

Ganshof, François L. *The Carolingians and the Frankish Monarchy: Studies in Carolingian History.* Trans. Janet L. Sondheimer. London: Longman, 1971.

Halphen, Louis. *Charlemagne and the Carolingian Empire.* Trans. Giselle de Nie. Amsterdam: North-Holland, 1977.

McKitterick, Rosamond. *Charlemagne: The Formation of a European Identity.* Cambridge: Cambridge University Press, 2008.

McKitterick, Rosamond. *The Frankish Kingdoms under the Carolingians, 751–987.* London: Longman, 1983.

Odegaard, Charles E. *Vassi et Fideles in the Carolingian Empire.* Cambridge, MA: Harvard University Press, 1945.

Riché, Pierre. *The Carolingians: A Family Who Forged Europe.* Trans. Michael Idomir Allen. Philadelphia: University of Pennsylvania Press, 1993.

Scholz, Bernhard Walter, trans. *Carolingian Chronicles: Royal Frankish Annals and Nithard's History.* Ann Arbor: University of Michigan Press, 1972.

Sullivan, Richard E. "The Carolingian Age: Reflections on Its Place in the History of the Middle Ages." *Speculum* 64 (1989): 257–306.

Ullmann, Walter. *The Carolingian Renaissance and the Idea of Kingship.* New York: Routledge, 2010.

Carolingian Renaissance

An intellectual and cultural revival of the eighth and ninth centuries, the Carolingian Renaissance was a movement initiated by the Carolingian kings, especially Charlemagne, who sought not only to improve learning in the kingdom but also to improve religious life and practice. Although once understood as an isolated, shining beacon in an otherwise dark age, the Carolingian Renaissance, or *renovatio* (renewal, or renovation) as it is sometimes called, is now understood to have roots in the Merovingian world and influence on later developments. Despite its foundations in an early period, the real impetus for the movement came from Charlemagne, who sought to reform learning and literacy, improve the education of the clergy, and provide at least a basic understanding of the faith to all his subjects. Toward this end, he attracted a large number of scholars from across Europe to assist him. They laid the foundation for even greater accomplishments in the two generations following Charlemagne's death. Indeed, during the reign of Louis the Pious, as well as in that of Charles the Bald, who consciously modeled his reign on his grandfather's, Carolingian scholars produced beautiful manuscript illuminations, copied and wrote numerous books and poems, and involved themselves in theological controversies. Although the renaissance never accomplished the goals Charlemagne intended and reached only the upper levels of society, it did provide an important foundation for cultural and intellectual growth in the centuries to come.

Although the roots of the renaissance can be traced to the reign of Pippin the Short and even back into the seventh century, the movement was inspired by the reforms of Charlemagne. Indeed, the program of reform and renewal that brought about the emergence of the renaissance was one of the fundamental concerns of the great Carolingian ruler. In two pieces of legislation, the capitulary *Admonitio Generalis* (General Admonition) of 789 and the Letter to Baugulf written between 780 and 800, established the foundation for the Carolingian Renaissance. In the *Admonitio* Charlemagne announced the educational and religious goals and ideals of his reign, which involved the improvement of Christian society in his realm and, at the very least, providing all people in the kingdom knowledge of the Lord's Prayer and Apostle's Creed. He sought to improve the moral behavior and knowledge of the Christian faith among both the clergy and laity, and he believed that for people to live good Christian lives they must have an understanding of the faith.

In chapter 72 of the *Admonitio* Charlemagne asserted the responsibility of the bishops and monks of his kingdom to establish schools to teach the psalms, music and singing, and grammar, so that the boys of the kingdom could learn to read and write and so that those who wished to pray could do so properly. This program of religious and educational reform was restated in the circular letter on learning to the abbot Baugulf of Fulda, or *De litteris colendis*. In the letter Charlemagne emphasized the importance of learning and proper knowledge of the faith for living a good Christian life. The letter proclaims the need for the creation of more books and calls on the higher clergy of the realm to establish schools at churches and monasteries to educate young boys. The Carolingian Renaissance thus grew out of Charlemagne's desire to improve the religious life of the clergy and laity of his kingdom.

To accomplish this end, Charlemagne needed scholars and books, and he managed to acquire both with little difficulty. Indeed, his wealth and power and program of religious reform attracted many of the greatest scholars of his age, many of whom received important positions in the Carolingian church. Among the more noteworthy scholars to join the Carolingian court were the grammarian Peter of Pisa and the Lombard Paul the Deacon, who wrote an important history of the

Lombards. Theodulf of Orléans was another important figure, who joined the court from Spain and became a bishop and the author of significant theological treatises and legislation.

Perhaps the greatest of the foreign scholars to join the court was Alcuin of York, whose importance was recognized in his own day. Alcuin brought the great Anglo-Saxon tradition of Bede and the Northumbrian revival of learning to the Carolingian realm. His was not an original mind, but his contribution to learning was exactly what Charlemagne needed; Alcuin's knowledge was encyclopedic, and his talents as a teacher were widely recognized. Indeed, his learning and pedagogy are revealed by the number of great students, such as Rabanus Maurus, the preceptor of Germany, who followed in Alcuin's tradition. Moreover, Alcuin brought books to the continent from England and remained in contact with his homeland throughout his life, which allowed him to import more books needed for the growth of learning under Charlemagne and his descendants. Alcuin also has long been associated with an important reform, the creation of the elegant and highly readable writing style known as Carolingian minuscule. Although his role is now recognized as less central in the creation of the script, he and his monastery at Tours did play some role in the development of Carolingian minuscule, which was to be admired and copied during the Italian Renaissance centuries later.

The arrival of numerous scholars with their books stimulated learning throughout the realm, especially at the highest levels of society, where the renaissance had its greatest impact, as Alcuin and others began to teach and establish schools associated with cathedrals and monasteries. The new emphasis on learning contributed to the increased production of books, so central to the renaissance, and numerous books of Christian and pagan antiquity were copied in Carolingian monasteries. Indeed, one of the great achievements of the renaissance is the preservation of ancient Latin literature, and the earliest versions of many ancient Latin works survive from copies done by the Carolingians. Among the ancient Roman writers whose works were preserved by the Carolingians are Ammianus Marcellinus, Cicero, Pliny the Younger, Tacitus, Suetonius, Ovid, and Sallust. There were also important works of grammar and rhetoric copied in Carolingian scriptoria (writing rooms). But most important to the Carolingian rulers and scholars and central to their reform effort were the works of Christian authors, many of which were copied in the scriptoria.

The most important book copied by the Carolingian scribes was the Bible, which was often divided into different volumes (e.g., collections of the Prophets, historical books, or Gospels), and a new edition of the Bible was one of Alcuin's many achievements. The scribes also copied the works of the great Christian writers of antiquity and the early Middle Ages, including Bede, Isidore of Seville, Cassiodorus, Pope Gregory the Great, St. Jerome, and others. Of course, St. Augustine of Hippo was also copied extensively, and the monastery at Lyons became a great center of Augustine studies.

As important as the preservation of ancient manuscripts was, Carolingian scholars did much more than just have books copied. Indeed, the renaissance was marked by the production of many new books in a variety of disciplines. One noteworthy area of production was in the writing of history, biography, and hagiography. Carolingian authors wrote numerous saints' lives, as well as more traditional works of history and biography. One of the most famous contributions of the renaissance was the life of Charlemagne, written by his friend and advisor Einhard. The biography provides a somewhat idealized portrait of the great ruler, one that borrows heavily from the ancient Roman biographer Suetonius, but still provides important insights into the personality, appearance, and achievements of its subject. A later ninth-century writer, Notker the Stammerer, also wrote a life of Charlemagne for one his descendants that offers an even more idealized version of the great emperor's life. Charlemagne was not the only Carolingian to be immortalized in a biography, however. Louis the Pious was the subject of three biographies written in his own lifetime, including one in verse. Numerous annals were also written at the monasteries throughout the Carolingian realm, along with the semiofficial *Royal Frankish Annals* and the famous history of the civil wars of the mid-ninth century by Nithard.

Carolingian Renaissance authors also wrote numerous commentaries on the books of the Bible, as well as treatises on proper Christian behavior. Alcuin, Theodulf of Orléans, and others wrote a number of treatises defending the Carolingian understanding of the faith against Adoptionists (Christian heretics who taught that Jesus was the son by adoption) in Spain, icon worshippers in the Byzantine Empire, and others who went astray. Manuals of education and Christian learning, an encyclopedic work by Rabanus Maurus, works of law and political practice by Hincmar of Rheims, and epistles of almost classical elegance by Lupus of Ferrieres were among other noteworthy works of Carolingian writers. Carolingian scholars also wrote Latin poetry. Their work may not be the most original or inspired, but it demonstrates the degree of sophistication they achieved, as well as providing great insights into the court of Charlemagne and its values.

Although initiated by Charlemagne, the renaissance enjoyed its greatest achievements in the generations following his death. And there is perhaps no better witness of the intellectual confidence and maturity reached by the Carolingian scholars than the doctrinal controversies that took place in the mid-ninth century. One dispute, which concerned the exact nature of the Eucharist, involved the theologians Paschasius Radbertus and Ratramnus of Corbie. An even greater controversy involved the reluctant monk, Gottschalk of Orbais, and a great number of Carolingian theologians. The dispute revolved around Gottschalk's doctrine of predestination and his interpretation of the teachings of St. Augustine of Hippo. Gottschalk's teachings, which promoted the doctrine of double predestination (i.e., both to hell and heaven), caused concern among the clergy, especially his bishop, Rabanus Maurus. The dispute attracted the attention of Hincmar of Rheims and the court royal of Charles the Bald. The king himself called upon the brilliant theologian, also the only Carolingian scholar with an understanding of Greek, John Scotus Erigena. His response to Gottschalk, however, was misunderstood by those around him and even further complicated the situation. That notwithstanding, the ability of the Carolingians to carry on high-level doctrinal debates demonstrates the maturity and sophistication of the Carolingian Renaissance.

The achievements of the Carolingian Renaissance were not, however, limited to literary and theological works and book production. Carolingian artists and architects created a great number of brilliant works in the plastic arts. The most notable architectural monument of the Carolingian age, and one of the few remaining (because most buildings were made of wood), was the palace complex that Charlemagne, with the help of his chief architect, Einhard, built at Aix-la-Chapelle (modern Aachen, Germany). The palace was a magnificent structure, as the remaining portion, an octagonal chapel inspired by late Roman imperial models in Italy, suggests. Carolingian artists were skilled jewelers and goldsmiths and created beautiful works in ivory, often used as covers for manuscripts. But perhaps the most remarkable Carolingian works of art are the miniatures that illuminated numerous manuscripts of the late eighth and ninth centuries.

Carolingian painting drew from a varied legacy of Roman, Christian, and Germanic influences. It clearly borrowed from ancient Roman models, its themes were often related to Christian themes and scenes from the Scriptures, and it incorporated the geometric designs and animal figures popular in Germanic traditions. Illustrations based on the Gospels and the Book of Revelation were popular, as were scenes depicting King David, an important figure in Carolingian political thought. Carolingian artists also left stunning depictions of the Evangelists, renderings of various Carolingian kings, and numerous representations of Christ in majesty, an image that had both religious and political connotations for the Carolingians. As with all aspects of the renaissance, Carolingian kings promoted painting, and the courts of Charlemagne and Charles the Bald were especially noteworthy for their support of art.

See also: Admonitio Generalis; Agobard of Lyons, St.; Aix-la-Chapelle; Alcuin of York; Ammianus Marcellinus; Astronomer, The; Anglo-Saxons; Augustine of Hippo, St.; Barbarian Art; Bede; Capitularies; Carolingian Dynasty; Carolingian Minuscule; Cassiodorus; Charlemagne; Charles the Bald; Dhuoda; Einhard; Gottschalk of Orbais; Gregory I, the Great, Pope; Hincmar of Rheims; Isidore of Seville; Ivories; John Scotus Erigena; Letter to Baugulf; Louis the Pious; Nithard; Notker the Stammerer; Pippin III, Called Pippin the Short; *Royal Frankish Annals*; Theodulf of Orléans; *Vita Karoli*

Bibliography

Beckwith, John. *Early Medieval Art.* London: Thames and Hudson, 1969.

Brown, Giles. "Introduction: The Carolingian Renaissance." In *Carolingian Culture: Emulation and Innovation,* ed. Rosamond McKitterick. Cambridge: Cambridge University Press, 1994, pp. 1–51.

Cabaniss, Allen, trans. *Son of Charlemagne: A Contemporary Life of Louis the Pious.* Syracuse, NY: Syracuse University Press, 1961.

Contreni, John J. "The Carolingian Renaissance: Education and Literary Culture." In *The New Cambridge Medieval History,* vol. 2, ed. Rosamond McKitterick. Cambridge: Cambridge University Press, 1995, pp. 709–57.

Dutton, Paul. *Carolingian Civilization: A Reader.* Peterborough, ON: Broadview, 1993.

Einhard and Notker the Stammerer. *Two Lives of Charlemagne.* Trans Lewis Thorpe. Harmondsworth, UK: Penguin, 1981.

Henderson, George. "Emulation and Invention in Carolingian Art." In *The New Cambridge Medieval History,* vol. 2, ed. Rosamond McKitterick. Cambridge: Cambridge University Press, 1995, pp. 248–73.

Hubert, Jean, Jean Porcher, and Wolfgang Fritz Volbach. *The Carolingian Renaissance.* New York: George Braziller, 1970.

Laistner, Max L. W. *Thought and Letters in Western Europe, A.D. 500 to 900.* 2nd ed. Ithaca, NY: Cornell University Press, 1976.

McKitterick, Rosamond. *The Carolingians and the Written Word.* Cambridge: Cambridge University Press, 1989.

McKitterick, Rosamond. *Charlemagne: The Formation of a European Identity.* Cambridge: Cambridge University Press, 2008.

McKitterick, Rosamond. *The Frankish Kingdoms under the Carolingians, 751–987.* London: Longman, 1983.

Mütherich, Florentine, and Joachim E. Gaehde. *Carolingian Painting.* New York: George Braziller, 1976.

Nelson, Janet. *Charles the Bald.* London: Longman, 1992.

Riché, Pierre. *Education and Culture in the Barbarian West: From the Sixth to the Eighth Century.* Trans. John Contreni. Columbia: University of South Carolina Press, 1976.

Riché, Pierre. *The Carolingians: A Family Who Forged Europe.* Trans. Michael Idomir Allen. Philadelphia: University of Pennsylvania Press, 1993.

Scholz, Bernhard Walter, trans. *Carolingian Chronicles: Royal Frankish Annals and Nithard's History.* Ann Arbor: University of Michigan Press, 1972.

Carthage

Although best known as the great rival of Rome of the Republic, the city of Carthage was also an important part of Roman North Africa and a vibrant intellectual and cultural center throughout late antiquity. The capital of late Roman North Africa, Carthage emerged as an important city for the Vandals and was again a provincial capital after the reconquest of the Byzantine emperor Justinian. A center of secular administration, Carthage was also the center of the North African Christian church, and the site of several church councils as well as conflict between Catholic and Donatist Christians.

Soundly defeated by the Romans in the Punic Wars (it is held that salt was sowed after the third war so that Carthage would never rise again), Carthage gradually revived in the late first century BC and was the was the site of a colony established by the first emperor Augustus (r. 31 BC–14 AD) in 29 BC. In the early empire, Carthage became an important city for the empire and a favorite location of a series of emperors, who bestowed favors on the city even if none resided there. By the early third century AD, the population of the city had reached some 300,000, making Carthage the second city of the western Roman Empire. It retained its prominence throughout the later imperial and invasion period, in part, because of its importance as an economic hub. North Africa remained remarkably productive in late antiquity, and its agricultural produce supplied large parts of the Mediterranean. Carthage was the main exporter of grain and oil to Rome and then into the sixth century to Constantinople. Carthage remained prosperous as a result and boasted elegant homes decorated with locally produced sculpture and mosaics, public baths, and in both the Roman and Vandal periods a mint. It was also an educational center; the great Christian thinker Augustine of Hippo studied there as a boy and later established a small school in the city. In 425 the first wall around the city was built. This demonstrates the relative peace and stability Carthage enjoyed throughout the late Roman period.

The Christian community at Carthage seems to have been firmly established by the year 200, and shortly after that the community suffered its first persecutions and offered its most famous martyr, Perpetua. Despite this inauspicious beginning and further persecutions during the third and early fourth centuries, the Christian community at Carthage thrived. One of the greatest of Latin Christian apologists and church father, Tertullian (c. 160–220), was from the city. One of he city's bishops, St. Cyprian (r. 249–258), was also an influential theologian and helped establish the primacy of the see of Carthage in Africa. In the early fourth century, Carthage would be the birthplace of the Donatist schism following the consecration of Caecillian as bishop in 311. The new bishop's rivals accused him of being consecrated by a *traditor*, a Christian who succumbed to pressure during the persecutions and sacrificed to the emperor, and was therefore not validly established as bishop. The schism raged for a century, involving Augustine of Hippo, before it was forcibly ended by imperial authorities. The city and its bishop hosted a number of important church councils in the fourth and fifth centuries that addressed matters of church doctrine and the Pelagian controversy and confirmed the canonical structure of the Christian Bible.

The religious schism that long plagued Carthage and indeed all of North Africa may have contributed to the success of the Vandal invasion in the early fifth century. In 439, Carthage itself was taken by the Vandal king Gaiseric who would establish the city as his capital. The Vandal kings introduced Arian Christianity to the city and North Africa and built new Arian churches in their capital. Ruling from Carthage, later Vanrdal kings persecuted the Catholic church in North Africa but also patronized local poets and presided over a literary revival in the late fifth century. As it had been under the Romans, Carthage continued both as an administrative and commercial and economic center under Vandal rule.

In the early sixth century, the Vandals were defeated by the armies of Justinian's reconquest. Carthage was taken by Belisarius in 533 and the last of the Vandal kings, Gelimer, was deposed. The city would serve as the forward staging post for Justinian's conquest of Italy from 535 to 555. In the sixth century, the position Carthage held during earlier Roman rule was restored. Known as Carthago Justiniana, it became the provincial capital and location of an imperial mint again. Renewed construction took place under the Byzantine emperors and a great new basilica was erected during this period. In the late sixth century, the city became the capital of the Exarchate of Carthage, a semiautonomous province headed by a governor appointed by the emperor. In the early seventh century, the exarch Heraklios launched his rebellion from Carthage, and as emperor, Heraklios considered moving the imperial capital to Carthage to avoid the pressure of the Persians. The exarchate remained a center of Byzantine stronghold until late seventh century, but its economic power collapsed by around mid-century. In 695, the city was seized by Muslim armies but was quickly retaken by a Byzantine naval assault. Three years later, in 698, Carthage was taken by Muslim armies and was replaced by Tunis as the major political and economic center of North Africa.

See also: Arianism; Augustine of Hippo, St.; Donatism; Gaiseric; Heraklios; Justinian; Vandals

Bibliography

Brown, Peter. *Religion and Society in the Age of Augustine.* Eugene, OR: Wipf and Stock Publishers, 2007.

Clover, F. M. "Felix Karthago." *Dumbarton Oaks Papers* 40 (1986): 1–16.

Herrin, Judith. *The Formation of Christendom.* Princeton, NJ: Princeton University Press, 1987.

Cassian, St. John (c. 360–435)

Christian theologian, writer, and monk, John Cassian had a profound impact on the development of Western monasticism. Cassian introduced the ideas and practices of the Desert Fathers to Western monks in his foundation at Marseilles and in his greats work on the coenobitical life, the *Institutes Conferences* (or *Collationes*), which greatly influenced St. Benedict of Nursia and other Latin monks. A defender of orthodoxy, Cassian was implicated in the development of the unorthodox doctrine of Semipelagianism.

Although his birthplace remains a point of debate (either Scythia or Provence), Cassian was born around 360 to a good Roman family and was given a traditional Roman education. In the early 380s, Cassian and his older friend Germanus entered the monastic life in Bethlehem, which in coming years would be shaped by the ideas of Jerome. Desiring to learn more about the monastic calling, Cassian and Germanus left Bethlehem to visit the monks of the deserts of Egypt, where the first monks had been established. For seven years, Cassian toured the monasteries of Egypt, listening to the desert fathers and collecting their teachings, which would form the core of his own later writings on the monastic life. He and Germanus returned to Bethlehem for a short while in the early 390s but then returned to the desert for further instruction from the monks there. They fled the desert in 399 because of a theological controversy involving the bishop of Alexandria and the desert monks. Settling in Constantinople, Cassian attracted the attention of John Chrysostom, patriarch of Constantinople, who elevated Cassian to the rank of deacon. In 405, following the forced deposition of Chrysostom, Cassian went to Rome to defend Chrysostom. While in Rome, Cassian was consecrated a priest by the pope, and little is heard of him for some 10 years. In 415, Cassian founded two communities—one male and female—near Marseilles, dedicating the abbey to St. Victor, who suffered during the persecutions of the third century. Cassian served as abbot of the monastery until his death in 435.

Important as a founder of the monastery of St. Victor, Cassian had his greatest influence through his *Insitutes* and *Conferences,* which provide guidance for the monastic life. His *Institutes,* written in the 420s at the request of the bishop of Apt, near Marseilles, is the first monastic rule composed in the Latin West. A framework for the life of the monks based on the life of the monks of Egypt, the *Institutes* emphasizes communal, or coenobitical, living over the eremitical. It provides instruction on daily living, food, and clothing, and also includes commentary on the eight vices and how to defend against them. His *Conferences,* a work composed as a series of dialogues between Cassian and another young monk and the desert fathers in Egypt. Rejecting the spiritual excesses sometimes associated with the hermits, Cassian stressed moderation, dedication to the ascetic life, purity of heart, and frequent communion. Cassian stressed not only the importance of communal living but also the importance of the interior spiritual life and outlined a schedule of daily prayer and thanksgiving for the monks and encouraged the mystical life. Both works had a great impact on the development of Western monasticism, and Benedict of Nursia borrowed from Cassian for the composition of his own Rule, which would replace the *Institutes* as the primary monastic rule in Western Christendom.

Cassian was also involved in several doctrinal controversies in his lifetime and recognized as a skilled but controversial theologian by contemporaries. While in Egypt, he was involved in debate over the teachings of the great theologian and philosopher Origen (c. 185–254). At around 430, Archdeacon Leo, the future pope, requested that Cassian write a treatise on the Incarnation to refute the heretical teachings of Nestorius. Written in some haste, the work is not generally held as one of Cassian's more important or influential works, but it does reveal his devotion to Catholic orthodoxy. More controversial are his writings on free will, which may have been in response to the late works of Augustine of Hippo and are sometimes characterized as Semipelagian, a heresy that asserts the role of the will in the process of salvation. Some passages in Cassian's monastic works have been identified as being Semipelagian, but Cassian has traditionally been seen as a fully orthodox Christian.

See also: Benedict of Nursia, St; Jerome; Leo I, the Great, Pope; Monasticism

Bibliography

Cassian, John. *John Cassian: Conferences*. Trans. Colm Luibheid. Mahwah, NJ: Paulist Press, 1985.

Chadwick, Owen. *John Cassian*. Cambridge: Cambridge University Press, 2008.

Merton, Thomas. *Cassian and the Fathers: Initiation to the Monastic Tradition*. Collegeville, MN: Cistercian Publications, 2005.

Stewart, Columba. *Cassian the Monk*. Oxford: Oxford University Press, 1999.

Cassiodorus (c. 490–585)

One of the great scholars of late antiquity, Cassiodorus, in full Flavius Magnus Aurelius Cassiodorus, wrote one of the most influential works on later barbarian Europe and, like, the senator and scholar Boethius, was an important advisor to the Ostrogothic king of Italy, Theodoric the Great. Like Boethius, Cassiodorus came from a prominent noble family and rose through the ranks of government. He held numerous high offices and was secretary to Theodoric. Unlike Boethius, he left government service to dedicate himself to letters and the religious life. He founded a monastery, Vivarium, where he spent the end of his life quietly and wrote one of the great classics of sacred learning. He also wrote works of history and theology and encouraged his monks to copy important manuscripts. His influence lasted beyond his long life. His great library was dispersed, benefiting many later scholars, including the great Anglo-Saxon scholar of the eighth century, the Venerable Bede, who used a Bible once owned by Cassiodorus.

Born to a noble family of southern Italy, Cassiodorus enjoyed a long and active life. In the footsteps of his grandfather, who served the emperor and was sent on an embassy to Attila the Hun, and his father, who served the king Odovacar, Cassiodorus followed the traditional path of Roman families and devoted himself to service to the state. By his time, however, it was no longer the ancient Roman emperors that he served, but a series of Ostrogothic rulers, most importantly Theodoric the Great and then his daughter Amalaswintha. Before joining the royal court, Cassiodorus served in various imperial offices, including the prestigious office of consul. He was Theodoric's secretary and wrote many of the king's letters to popes, emperors, and kings. He later served as the praetorian prefect of Amalaswintha, whose death precipitated the invasion of Italy by Justinian.

His services throughout his long career were highly valued, and, unlike Boethius, he never lost the confidence of his masters. He also conducted a personal correspondence with various popes in Rome, including Pope Agapetus I (r. 535–536), to whom he suggested establishing a school of higher Christian learning. His service lasted into the 530s at least, and he appears to have retired to his ancestral estates at around 538. There is, however, evidence that he was in Constantinople in 550, possibly in the service of the pope. His retirement from government service, whenever it finally occurred, found him at the monastic community he founded in 540 or 553 on his family land, which was called Vivarium because of the fish ponds (in Latin, *vivaria*) that decorated the estate.

While loyally serving the Gothic rulers of Italy, Cassiodorus began his other lifelong career, the pursuit of learning, especially learning in the service of the faith. It was in this endeavor, which was demonstrated in his letter to Agapetus and in the foundation of his monastery, that Cassiodorus left his greatest legacy.

See also: Amalaswintha; Attila the Hun; Boethius; Huns; Jordanes; Justinian; Odovacar; Ostrogoths; Theodoric the Great

Bibliography

Amory, Patrick. *People and Identity in Ostrogothic Italy, 489–554.* Cambridge: Cambridge University Press, 1997.

Bury, John B. *History of the Later Roman Empire: From the Death of Theodosius I to the Death of Justinian.* 2 vols. 1923. Reprint, New York: Dover, 1959.

Cassiodorus. *The Variae of Magnus Aurelius Cassiodorus.* Trans. S.J.B. Barnish. Liverpool, UK: Liverpool University Press, 1992.

Heather, Peter. *The Goths.* Oxford: Blackwell, 1996.

Hodgkin, Thomas. *Theodoric the Goth: The Barbarian Champion of Civilization.* New York: G. P. Putnam, 1983.

Laistner, Max L. W. *Thought and Letters in Western Europe, A.D. 500 to 900.* 2nd ed. Ithaca, NY: Cornell University Press, 1976.

Llewellyn, Peter. *Rome in the Dark Ages.* New York: Barnes and Noble, 1993.

O'Donnell, James J. *Cassiodorus.* Berkeley: University of California Press, 1979.

Riché, Pierre. *Education and Culture in the Barbarian West: From the Sixth through the Eighth Century.* Trans. John Contreni. Columbia: University of South Carolina Press, 1976.

Wolfram, Herwig. *The Roman Empire and Its Germanic Peoples.* Trans. Thomas J. Dunlap. Berkeley: University of California Press, 1997.

Catalaunian Plains, Battle of the (451)

Major battle in June 451 between Attila the Hun and his Hunnish and allied armies against the Roman imperial forces and their allies, led by the great general Aëtius. Although it is traditionally known as the Battle of the Catalaunian Plains or Battle of Châlons, J. B. Bury has argued that because of the battlefield's proximity to Troyes it should be known as the Battle of Troyes. Whatever the name should be, the battle was the most important of several that Attila fought as part of his invasion of the Western Empire in the early 450s. Although the battle ended in a draw, Attila himself was on the verge of suicide during the fighting and survived only because Aëtius allowed him to escape.

The battle itself was part of Attila's campaign in the Western Empire after several years harassing the Eastern Empire and extracting significant wealth and political concessions from Constantinople. The invasion of 451 may have been brought on by the emperor's sister, Honoria, who, like her aunt Galla Placidia, may have offered her hand in marriage to the barbarian king. Attila's demands for Honoria and other things were rejected, and therefore he invaded Gaul, seizing Metz, Rheims, and numerous other cities before being repulsed at the important city of Orléans. Despite that setback, Attila caused great destruction and bloodshed and threatened Visigothic power in Gaul. The Goths were compelled to assist the imperial armies in defense of Gaul because of the ferocity of Attila's assault.

After leaving Orléans, Attila moved toward Troyes, where he met the imperial armies of Aëtius, which included Alans, Bretons, Franks, Burgundians, and Visigoths. Attila's army was also made up of peoples of numerous nations, including his own Huns, Alans, Franks, Gepids, Heruls, and Ostrogoths. On the eve of the battle, Attila consulted a priest who examined bones of a sheep. The priest proclaimed that the Huns would lose the battle but that a great enemy leader would fall; Attila desired the death of the leader and therefore risked battle. On the day of the battle, Attila arranged his Huns in the center of his lines and the subject peoples on both flanks. On the opposite side, Aëtius, with his Romans, commanded the left flank; Theodoric commanded his Visigoths on the right flank; and the center was held by the Alans. After major skirmishing on the previous night, the battle began at three o'clock in the afternoon and went on into the evening.

It was a ferocious battle, which, according to one contemporary, ended with 165,000 dead, including the Visigothic king Theodoric. The battle went so badly for Attila that he fortified himself in a circle of wagons, preparing for the final assault that would have left him dead from battle or suicide. But the Roman commander, Aëtius, recognized the value of having Attila's Huns as a legitimate threat to other barbarian peoples to preserve the balance of power. Consequently, Attila was allowed to withdraw from the battlefield without being annihilated by the armies of Aëtius. Although the battle ended technically as a draw, Aëtius could claim victory because he stopped Attila's advance and killed a large number of his enemy's troops.

The battle was a major setback for Attila, who was forced to withdraw from his invasion following the contest on the Catalaunian Plains. Although he again invaded Italy in the following year, Attila's aura of invincibility was damaged and his army seriously depleted by the near disaster on the battlefield between Châlons and Troyes. Although the importance of the battle is overstated when it is described as one of the great battles of history, it was an important moment in late imperial history because Attila's virtual defeat left him much less of a threat to the Roman Empire. Never a serious threat to the life of the empire, Attila nonetheless demanded significant tribute from the empire, and anything that weakened his challenge was a benefit to the emperors.

See also: Aëtius; Attila the Hun; Galla Placidia; Huns; Visigoths

Bibliography

Bury, John B. *History of the Later Roman Empire: From the Death of Theodosius I to the Death of Justinian.* Vol. 1. 1923. Reprint, New York: Dover, 1959.

Bury, John B. *The Invasions of Europe by the Barbarians.* New York: W. W. Norton, 1967.

Randers-Pehrson, Justine Davis. *Barbarians and Romans: The Birth Struggle of Europe,* A.D. *400–700.* Norman: University of Oklahoma Press, 1983.

Thompson, Edward A. *A History of Attila and the Huns.* Oxford: Clarendon, 1948.

Thompson, Edward A. *The Huns.* Oxford: Blackwell, 1995.

Wolfram, Herwig. *The Roman Empire and Its Germanic Peoples.* Trans. Thomas J. Dunlap. Berkeley: University of California Press, 1997.

Charlemagne (742–814)

The greatest king of the Middle Ages, Charlemagne forged a powerful empire during his long reign from 768 to 814 and left an indelible mark on his age and the generations to come. The son of Pippin the Short, the first Carolingian king, Charles (called Charles the Great, in Latin Carolus Magnus, whence his commonly used name) inherited an important political and military legacy from his father. He used that inheritance and expanded upon it, creating a political ideal that would influence European history for the next thousand years.

The great king was physically and personally imposing as well. A full seven times the length of his foot in height, according to his biographer Einhard, Charlemagne towered over his contemporaries, of lofty stature and of regal bearing whether seated or standing. Although his neck was thick, his stomach rather pronounced, and his voice a bit higher than his size would suggest, Charles carried himself in such a way as to make these defects unnoticeable. His health was excellent until old age, but even then he refused to eat boiled meat as his doctors recommended. He had long hair, large eyes, and his face was cheerful and full of laughter.

Equestrian statue of Charlemagne (747–814)
(bronze), French. (Louvre, Paris, France/Giraudon/
The Bridgeman Art Library)

In his biography Einhard describes a monarch who was most personable and who loved company. He often had many guests to dinner, where he indulged in food but drank only in moderation, while German epic tales were told or pages from the works of St. Augustine of Hippo were read. Moreover, he built a great palace over a hot spring, where he would swim with many fellow bathers. He seldom went anywhere without his daughters, whom he loved so much that he could not bear to be apart from them. His daughters never married, but they did bear Charles several grandchildren he loved as dearly as he loved his own children. He took great pains to educate his children and often took them riding and hunting, pastimes at which he excelled and he enjoyed greatly. He was also deeply religious, according to the climate of the age, attended mass regularly, and honored the pope, bishops, and abbots. For Einhard, Charlemagne was as great a person as he was a ruler.

The early part of his reign, however, was a time of crisis. In accordance with Frankish tradition, at his death in 768 Pippin divided the realm between his two sons, Charles and Carloman. In some ways the division was more favorable to the younger Carloman, whose kingdom was compact and easier to manage than the territory given to Charles. Moreover, Charles received territory that had only recently been fully incorporated into the kingdom and was more susceptible to revolt at the change of leadership. And in the opening years of his reign Charles did face a serious revolt in his territory, which was suppressed only with difficulty. The situation was made all the worse by Carloman's unwillingness to come to his brother's aid. Despite efforts to prevent civil war by their mother, Bertrada, who had recently arranged a marriage for her older son with the daughter of the Lombard king, tensions ran high between her two sons. The two were on the point of war when Carloman suddenly died, leaving Charles as the sole Carolingian king, a situation he exploited by dispossessing his nephews and repudiating his Lombard wife.

Having survived his brother and a potentially disastrous civil war, Charlemagne was now able to make his mark as king. His success as king rested on his indomitable will and his ability as a warrior, a fact recognized by Einhard, who dedicated much of his tale of the great king to his military campaigns. One of Charlemagne's first actions after Carloman's death was the conquest of Saxony, a process that lasted 30 years and had important consequences in later medieval history. The wars began in 772 as punitive expeditions against Saxon raiders who plundered Frankish territory, but soon after took on a crusading character. Perhaps inspired by the support the Anglo-Saxon missionary St. Boniface received from his father, Pippin the Short, and uncle, Carloman, Charlemagne was determined to convert the pagan Saxons to Christianity. The great king not only sent armies of warriors into Saxony to impose Frankish political authority over the inhabitants but also sent armies of priests to spread the Christian faith. The Saxons, however, refused to accept the great privilege of being subject to the political and religious power of the Franks and resisted mightily.

One contemporary lamented that the Saxons revolted against Carolingian rule annually, and Frankish armies had to return to put down the revolts. Charlemagne would not be refused, however, and he met force with force. He imposed the death penalty for Saxons who harmed priests or practiced pagan religion, as well as for those who violated Christian fasts or burned their dead. His warriors destroyed pagan shrines, massacred 4,500 Saxons at Verdun, and moved many Saxons from their homeland into Frankish territory. His priests imposed baptism before teaching the Saxons the Christian faith and built churches on destroyed pagan shrines. Even the great revolt of Widukind (782–785) did not stop the process of conversion and subjugation of the Saxons. Charles's brutality was tempered by the time of the second Saxon capitulary of 797, which provided the milk and honey of the faith instead of Frankish iron. Charlemagne's conquest and conversion of the Saxons were completed by the early ninth century, a process that bore great fruit in the 10th century.

Charlemagne's activities as a warrior found other theaters as well. He annexed Bavaria after its duke, Tassilo, failed to honor an oath he had sworn to attend the court of the Frankish king. Breaking an oath was seen as a violation of God's will, and thus again Charlemagne could be seen doing God's work and ensuring God's justice. In the early 790s, in part as a result of the annexation of Bavaria, he was forced to secure his southeastern frontier. He sent his armies against the remnants of the Hunnish tribes that had plundered Europe savagely and smashed the central stronghold of the Huns. Huge wagonloads of treasures were taken from the Huns, and a good portion was diverted to the pope in Rome.

Great conqueror though he was, Charlemagne's military record is not without failure. In the last years of his reign he was unable to respond successfully to the attacks of the Danes, whose lands abutted the Carolingian Empire as a result of the conquest of the Saxons. He also suffered a serious defeat in 778. In that year, responding to the invitation of the Muslim leader of Barcelona to assist him in a struggle against the Spanish emir, Charlemagne invaded Spain. He found his allies in disarray and was able to accomplish little in Spain, but worse was to come. As he crossed the Pyrenees back into France his rearguard was attacked, and it and its commander, Roland, were destroyed. The memory of the event later provided the foundation for one of the most enduring epics of the Middle Ages, the *Song of Roland,* but this could provide little consolation for Charlemagne, who left Spain early to respond to unrest in the kingdom and to another in the series of Saxon revolts. Indeed, the great king not only faced the occasional military setback, he also faced a number of revolts during his long reign, including the one led by his favorite illegitimate son, Pippin the Hunchback.

Despite the occasional failure and revolt, Charlemagne was a warlord to be reckoned with. He did suppress the revolts he faced, and he extended the boundaries of the empire with the creation of the Spanish March, a militarized border region that included territory on the Spanish side of the Pyrenees. But his most important military campaign, after the conquest of Saxony, was his conquest of the kingdom of the Lombards in Italy. This was also one of his earliest victories (773–774), following shortly after the death of his brother Carloman in 771. It signaled a dramatic reversal of a Carolingian policy of close ties with the Lombards that had been in effect, in some ways, since the time of Charlemagne's grandfather, Charles Martel. Even though his father, Pippin the Younger, invaded Italy twice, he did so without the force or the desire that Charlemagne had. Moreover, it was also a dramatic change in the personal life of the king himself. His mother, hoping to keep the peace among her sons and with traditional Frankish allies, had arranged a marriage between her older son and Desiderata, the daughter of the Lombard king in Italy, Desiderius. But Charles repudiated his wife and broke with the Lombards, preferring to ally himself with a far greater power, the pope in Rome. His invasion quickly brought about the defeat of the Lombards and the capture of their capital at Pavia. His invasion also brought much new territory to the growing empire, as Charles not only defeated Desiderius but deposed him and usurped his crown.

The conquest of the Lombards was important for a number of reasons. It brought Charlemagne into close contact with Rome, provided him the legal right to exercise authority in Italy as the king of the Lombards, brought under his control the heartland of the old Roman Empire, and gave him the opportunity to visit Rome as a pilgrim. The first of several visits to the city, his pilgrimage in 774 strengthened the devotion that Charles and his line had for St. Peter and reinforced the family's relationship with Peter's successor, the pope. Although relationships with the reigning pope, Hadrian, were sometimes strained, they were of great importance to Charles, who wept openly when Hadrian died. Rome supplied Carolingian ecclesiastics and their king with a great deal of material essential to Carolingian church reform, including numerous legal and liturgical texts. But more than a source for religious reform and spiritual inspiration, Rome provided Charles with the political justification of his power as an anointed ruler.

One of his most important legacies was his idea of kingship. His father before him had been crowned and anointed by the pope, an act that consciously recalled the ceremonies at the crowning of the ancient kings of Israel. The influence of the Hebrew Bible on the Carolingians was great, and the biblical king David was the model king for the new Frankish dynasty. Charlemagne himself, inspired by his court scholars, saw himself as a "new David" ruling a new chosen people and was given the nickname of David by those at court. He saw himself as God's anointed, with responsibilities over God's church and people, a belief that manifested itself in his relationships with the church in his kingdom and in Rome. In his capitularies, he instituted moral reform of the clergy, encouraging them to know the mass, to live a chaste life, and to avoid frequenting taverns. He also reformed the organization of the Frankish church. He introduced liturgical reforms, appointed bishops and abbots, and employed ecclesiastics in the highest levels of his government. He felt an obligation to defend the faith from heresy and moral corruption and to extend the boundaries of Christendom. His conquests accomplished the goal of extending the faith, and he presided over church councils to protect the faith from internal enemies. At his most famous council, at Frankfurt in 794, he and the assembled clerics denounced the Spanish heresy of Adoptionism (teaching that Jesus was the son of God by adoption), struggled to find the appropriate response to the Iconoclastic Controversy in the Byzantine Empire, and instituted a series of organizational and disciplinary reforms.

As an anointed Christian king, Charles felt obligated to ensure justice throughout his realm, and to accomplish this end he implemented several new administrative practices and reformed existing ones. The use of writing in government increased dramatically during Charlemagne's reign, and the most important instrument in his administration was the capitulary, a written decree divided into chapters *(capitula).* These laws addressed a broad range of topics, and the greatest of them, the *Admonitio Generalis* of 789, outlined Charlemagne's program of government. Other capitularies addressed matters of secular and ecclesiastical administration, religious reform, religious belief and orthodoxy, legal jurisdiction, the price of bread, weights and measures, and general economic matters. The capitularies were issued, often orally (to be afterward written down), from the effective center of government, Charlemagne's court, which moved from place to place and was attended by the leading religious and secular figures of the kingdom.

On the local level Charlemagne's will and desire for justice were implemented by a number of officers. The most important regional officer was the count, who ruled over a specific territorial unit. The count was the king's deputy and received the authority to govern from the king. He was responsible for protecting the interests of the king and disseminating his laws. The count had the right to punish criminals and was expected to maintain peace and order. He also owed military and court service to the king, and could be called on to serve as the king's special envoy. Another area of committal responsibility was the administration of justice, and included in that was the appointment of the *scabini.* The *scabini* were a new class of permanent judges established by Charlemagne to render judgment of legal disputes at the local level. The most important of the royal officials, however, were the *missi dominici,* or messengers of the lord king. These officials, eventually sent out in pairs of one secular and one ecclesiastical noble, were charged with ensuring the proper application of royal laws and justice. They were to guarantee that legal cases were resolved without corruption and that the king's other representatives—counts, judges, and the like—enforced the law honorably.

Charlemagne's sense of responsibility as an anointed Christian king was perhaps the source of inspiration for his promotion of what is called Carolingian Renaissance. Although not the decisive break with an earlier "dark age" it has traditionally been considered, the renaissance did see a quickening of intellectual pace and a dramatic increase in the use of writing in government and the church. Charlemagne's goal was to create an educated clergy that could properly say the mass and teach the fundamentals of the faith to his people. As God's chosen king, he felt responsible for the salvation of his people and desired that all his subjects know the Lord's Prayer and the Apostles' Creed. To do this he needed learned priests and books. He attracted some of the best minds of his day, including Theodulf of Orléans, Paul the Deacon, Peter of Pisa, and, most importantly, the great Anglo-Saxon scholar and teacher, Alcuin of York. These scholars brought with them a devotion to Charlemagne's reforms and a devotion to Christian learning, which they shared with their students, who then contributed to the increasing sophistication of Carolingian government and society. They brought great learning with them, as well as numerous books, especially books of the Bible, and they oversaw the production of new copies of these books. And, beginning in Charlemagne's day, his efforts at cultural reform led to the production of a new edition of the Bible, heightened theological discussion, works of history and poetry, and numerous magnificently illuminated manuscripts.

By the last decade of the eighth century, Charlemagne was the preeminent figure of Western Europe. He ruled over the greatest kingdom, presided over councils and governmental and religious reform, and in many ways rivaled the Byzantine emperor in status and prestige. Indeed, there was the sense among some of his court scholars that Charles was more than a king. A letter from Charlemagne to the pope in 795, a letter from Alcuin to Charlemagne in 799, and the palace complex at Aachen, which was modeled on an imperial palace in Ravenna, all suggest that Charlemagne, or at least those around him, had imperial pretensions. Whether Charles did harbor the desire to be recognized as an emperor in the 790s is unknowable, but the opportunity to become an emperor presented itself shortly after the ascension of Leo III to the papal throne.

The chain of events that led to Charlemagne's elevation to the imperial dignity began in a crisis early in the reign of Pope Leo III. Elected pope in 795 after the death of the powerful and well-connected Hadrian, Leo faced the challenge of ruling the church with significant enemies in Rome, especially relatives of the former pope who were dissatisfied by the election of Leo. Although Charlemagne supported the new pope and called on him to raise his arms in prayer like Moses to support the success in battle of the king, Leo's position remained tenuous. On April 25, 799, Leo was attacked by Hadrian's nephews, Paschal and Campulus, while leading a religious procession through the streets of Rome. He was dragged from his horse and, according to some reports, was blinded and had his tongue cut out. He was then imprisoned in the monastery of St. Erasmus, and his attackers alleged that he was corrupt and guilty of adultery and perjury. He escaped from the monastery and was escorted to the Frankish court by one of Charlemagne's dukes in Italy, where he regained the powers of sight and speech. He was welcomed by the king and returned to Rome, where he awaited the arrival of the king to resolve the dispute.

In November 800, Charles and a sizeable entourage ventured to Rome to determine the fate of the rebels and the pope. After several weeks of meeting with the pope and the nobility, a great council was held on December 23 where the rebels were found guilty and condemned to death, a sentence which was commuted to exile at Leo's request. Leo himself swore an oath of his innocence, which was accepted by all. On Christmas day, Charles attended a mass presided over by the pope, who placed a crown on the king's head when he rose from kneeling at the altar. The assembled crowd then arose and proclaimed Charles emperor and augustus.

The empire had been revived and a new emperor crowned, but according to Einhard, had Charlemagne known what was going to happen he would not have attended mass that day. Einhard's remark has troubled historians ever since. It is most unlikely that Charles did not know and approve of what was going to happen. Although the imperial crown offered him little real new power, it surely brought great prestige. His conquests, his creation of an empire, and his protection of the church qualified him for the position in the eyes of his contemporaries and most likely in his own eyes. The construction of the palace and church in Aachen demonstrated his sense of his imperial authority, and his court scholars had spoken of him in imperial terms throughout the decade. Moreover, a letter from his most important advisor, Alcuin of York, identified Charlemagne as the greatest power in Christendom, given the attack on Leo and the vacancy of the imperial throne in Constantinople (vacant in eighth-century eyes because it was held by a woman). Indeed, it is quite likely that Charlemagne knew that he was to be crowned emperor and welcomed the imperial crown, but perhaps he was troubled by the way the coronation itself took place.

The coronation opened the final phase of Charlemagne's career, a period of diminished activity for the emperor, during which the strains of empire began to show. The emperor was less active on the military front and faced an increasing Viking threat, one that his armies had difficulty stopping. He was also less peripatetic than he had been earlier in his reign, settling primarily at the palace at Aachen. He continued to pass new laws, however, including a capitulary in 802 that restated the religious and political program he had long promoted, now presented as the program of an emperor. By 802 he had also decided on his official title and had come to accept and appreciate the honor bestowed on Christmas day 800. In 806 he issued a succession decree, in which he divided the empire among his three sons but did not bestow the imperial title, which he may have regarded as a personal honor, on any of them. In 813 he altered the decree because two of his sons had died, leaving only his son Louis as his eventual successor. Charlemagne crowned Louis emperor in a great ceremony at Aachen, which was attended by members of the secular and religious aristocracy but not the pope. Having settled his affairs, dividing his wealth among his children and the church, Charlemagne died on January 28, 814.

Although the empire dissolved in little more than a generation after his death, Charlemagne left an indelible mark on his age and the later Middle Ages. His model of Christian kingship remained the ideal for much of the rest of the Middle Ages, and the imperial dignity he created was regarded as the ultimate expression of political power into the modern era. The close ties he forged with the popes in Rome influenced political events long after his death, and his reform of the church in his kingdom revived a sagging institution. The efforts at cultural and religious renewal that created the Carolingian Renaissance established an important foundation for later cultural growth in the Middle Ages. Indeed, Charlemagne's achievement was unsurpassed in the early Middle Ages, and he was the greatest king of the entire Middle Ages.

See also: Admonitio Generalis; Aix-la-Chapelle; Capitularies; Carolingian Dynasty; Einhard; Irminsul; Louis the Pious; Notker the Stammerer; Pippin III, Called Pippin the Short; *Vita Karoli*

Bibliography

Becher, Matthias. *Charlemagne*. New Haven, CT: Yale University Press, 2005.

Bullough, Donald. "*Europae Pater:* Charlemagne and His Achievement in the Light of Recent Scholarship." *English Historical Review* 75 (1970): 59–105.

Collins, Roger. *Charlemagne.* Toronto: University of Toronto Press, 1998.

Davis, Raymond, trans. *The Lives of the Eighth-Century Popes* (Liber Pontificalis): *The Ancient Biographies of Nine Popes from A.D. 715 to A.D. 817.* Liverpool, UK: Liverpool University Press, 1992.

Dutton, Paul. *Carolingian Civilization: A Reader.* Peterborough, ON: Broadview, 1993.

Einhard and Notker the Stammerer. *Two Lives of Charlemagne.* Trans. Lewis Thorpe. Harmondsworth, UK: Penguin, 1981.

Fichtenau, Heinrich. *The Carolingian Empire.* Trans. Peter Munz. Toronto: University of Toronto Press, 1979.

Ganshof, François Louis. *The Carolingians and the Frankish Monarchy: Studies in Carolingian History.* Trans. Janet Sondheimer. London: Longman, 1971.

Ganshof, François Louis. *Frankish Institutions under Charlemagne.* Trans. Bryce Lyon and Mary Lyon. Providence, RI: Brown University Press, 1968.

Halphen, Louis. *Charlemagne and the Carolingian Empire.* Trans. Giselle de Nie. Amsterdam: North-Holland, 1977.

McKitterick, Rosamond. *The Frankish Kingdoms under the Carolingians, 751–987.* London: Longman, 1983.

McKitterick, Rosamond, ed. *Carolingian Culture: Emulation and Innovation.* Cambridge: Cambridge University Press, 1994.

McKitterick, Rosamond. *Charlemagne: The Formation of a European Identity.* Cambridge: Cambridge University Press, 2008.

Riché, Pierre. *The Carolingians: A Family Who Forged Europe.* Trans. Michael Idomir Allen. Philadelphia: University of Pennsylvania Press, 1993.

Scholz, Bernhard Walter, trans. *Carolingian Chronicles: Royal Frankish Annals and Nithard's History.* Ann Arbor: University of Michigan Press, 1972.

Sullivan, Richard E. *Aix-la-Chapelle in the Age of Charlemagne.* Norman: University of Oklahoma Press, 1963.

Charles Martel (d. 741)

Son of Pippin II of Herstal and father of Pippin III the Short, Charles, later known as Martel (the Hammer), was an important Carolingian mayor of the palace, whose reign, after a difficult beginning, marked a significant step in the growth of his family's power and the erosion of the power of the Merovingian dynasty. His reign as mayor witnessed important changes in relationships between his line and the Frankish church, not all of which were positive from the church's point of view. He did, however, support the activities of missionaries, including the great Anglo-Saxon St. Boniface, in the kingdom and along the realm's frontier, and was seen as a champion of the church by the pope in Rome, who sought his aid. Charles is best known for his victory over invading Muslims from Spain at the Battle of Tours, a significant, although generally overemphasized, military victory.

Although he eventually came to command the entire Frankish kingdom and was able to pass this power on to his sons Carloman and Pippin, Charles Martel had few advantages at the time of the death of his own father, Pippin II, in December 714. Overlooked in the plan of succession to the office of mayor of the palace, which had come to rival the authority of the office of king in the early eighth century, Charles was in fact imprisoned by Pippin's widow, Plectrude. Charles, whose mother was one of Pippin's mistresses and so despised by Plectrude, was rejected for the office of mayor of the palace in Neustria by Plectrude in favor of her young grandson, Theodoald, whose father had been designated heir but who was murdered while praying at a religious shrine several months before Pippin's death. Despite these disadvantages, Charles managed to break out of prison and organize a warrior band to support his claims to power.

The next few years were critical for Charles, who faced rivals from within his own family and from other Frankish nobles. His first attempt to acquire power, in fact, was a failure. He was defeated by the mayor, Ragamfred, who had defeated and deposed Theodoald, and the Frisian ruler, Radbod, in 715, and forced to withdraw to his private estates. In the following year Ragamfred, who was supported by the newly crowned Merovingian king Chilperic II, turned against Plectrude, who had retired to Cologne and seized a large part of the treasure of Pippin. Charles, in the meanwhile, had organized a new band of soldiers and fell on Ragamfred as he left Cologne, inflicting heavy losses on his rival. In 717, Ragamfred and Charles again met in battle at Vinchy, where Charles again won a major victory over his rival. At this point Charles felt secure enough to promote his own Merovingian king, Chlotar IV (d. 718), and he seized Pippin's fortune from Plectrude. He next faced battle in 719 from Ragamfred and Duke Eudo of Aquitaine, and once again emerged victorious, pushing the Aquitainians out of the kingdom and taking control of Ragamfred's king. Clearly, Charles was now the dominant figure in the kingdom and was able to appoint a true do-nothing king (as the last Merovingian kings are often called). Theuderic IV, on Chilperic's death in 721.

Although he had secured his position as mayor of the palace by the early 720s, Charles's authority was not guaranteed, and he continued to expand his power in the kingdom throughout the 720s and 730s. During the next two decades, Charles imposed his authority over his fellow Franks and over tributary peoples along the frontier of the kingdom. In 723 he fought and defeated Ragamfred again, but Ragamfred remained in control of Angers until his death in 731. In the following years, Charles defeated the Saxons, Alemanni, Bavarians, and, in the later 730s, the Burgundians, whose territory he subjugated all the way to the Mediterranean. His personal resolve and military skill enabled Charles to assume such great stature in the kingdom that he was able to rule without a Merovingian puppet after the death of Theuderic in 737.

Charles also extended Carolingian power into Aquitaine, where his former rival, Eudo, continued to rule until his death in 735. Charles was able to take over Aquitaine after Eudo's death, in part because the duke had sought Charles's aid against the Muslim invaders from Spain. Indeed, Eudo faced not only the growing power of his rival to the north in the 720s but also the encroachment of the Muslims. Eudo managed, on occasion, to beat back the Muslim invaders with a mixed army of Aquitainians and Franks, but was clearly on the defensive in the face of successive successful raids in the early 730s. He had little choice but to seek aid from Charles, whose willingness to join with Eudo occasioned his most famous military victory. The raids of the Spanish Muslims had become so serious in the early 730s that they had begun to enter Frankish territory. One raid reached especially deep into Frankish territory, and on October 25, 732, somewhere between Tours and Poitiers, Charles and his ally fought a great battle that stopped the Saracen advance.

Although perhaps a bit exaggerated because it was merely a victory over a raiding party and not an invading army, Charles's victory at the Battle of Tours was an important victory and was followed by his continued action against the Muslims, whom he pushed from Aquitaine by the end of the 730s. His victory and continued success against Muslim raiders were central to his subsequent reputation and his acquisition of Aquitaine.

Charles established his control in the Frankish kingdom by his military victories, but he was able to maintain that control by introducing new means to rule, including the appointment of family members to key positions in the church and the establishment of important new ties between his family and the church. He made numerous appointments to episcopal and abbatial office, sometimes deposing the supporter of a rival from the offices to make his appointment. He deposed one of Ragamfred's supporters as abbot of Fontanelle and replaced him with his nephew Hugo, who was later made bishop of Rouen and Paris. He appointed his lay supporter, Carivius, as bishop of Le Mans, and made another noble follower bishop of Redon. These appointments were made repeatedly throughout Charles's reign, and were made in both the heartland of the kingdom and regions like Aquitaine that were a new or restored part of the realm.

Many of the appointments were secular nobles with little training or inclination for the job, who often did more harm than good to the church. Indeed, by the ninth century, his reputation for secularizing church lands found him consigned to hell by religious writers. They did, however, strengthen Charles's position in the kingdom, improve his ties with noble families in newly acquired territories, and, ironically considering the lack of concern for things spiritual the appointments showed, strengthened his ties with the church. At the very least, appointment of lay followers to important ecclesiastical offices brought access to the church's wealth and lands to Charles.

Despite a poor record of appointments, Charles was not completely neglectful of the church, and his reputation for secularizing church property is generally exaggerated. Perhaps his most important connection with the church was his support and protection of the Anglo-Saxon missionary Boniface. The great apostle to the Germans, Boniface was allowed to introduce reform to the Frankish church and was afforded protection by Charles during his evangelical missions among the pagan Saxons. Boniface also reinforced Frankish attention to Rome and St. Peter. The Anglo-Saxon missionary visited Rome, received approval to preach from the pope, and was made the pope's representative in the Frankish kingdom. Boniface's devotion to Rome was reflected by the Franks, who came to the attention of the papacy during the time of Charles Martel. So great had Charles's reputation become that when Pope Gregory III needed help against the Lombards in the 730s he turned to Charles. The Carolingian mayor could not help the pope at the time, but the invitation foreshadowed similar communication between Pippin the Short and

Pope Stephen II in the 750s. Indeed, the connection between Rome and the Carolingians that began to form during the reign of Charles was to be essential to the ultimate triumph of the dynasty.

By the end of his life Charles was clearly the dominant figure in the Frankish kingdom, and he could afford to rule without a Merovingian figurehead during the last four years of his life. Like a traditional Frankish king, he divided the realm between his two sons, who both ascended to the office of mayor on their father's death in 741. Charles's reign was critical to the ultimate success of his family. His military victories and ability to attract supporters from the aristocracy strengthened his family, and his recognition by the pope elevated Charles and his dynasty above the other families of the realm. Although the achievement of the kingship had to wait a generation, the groundwork for Carolingian succession to the throne was laid by Charles Martel.

See also: Boniface, St.; Carolingian Dynasty; Charlemagne; Eudes of Aquitaine; Gregory III; Lombards; Merovingian Dynasty; Pippin II, Called Pippin of Herstal; Pippin III, Called Pippin the Short; Plectrude; Tours, Battle of

Bibliography

Bachrach, Bernard S. *Merovingian Military Organization, 481–751.* Minneapolis: University of Minnesota Press, 1972.

Fouracre, Paul, and Richard A. Gerberding. *Late Merovingian France: History and Hagiography, 640–720.* Manchester, UK: University of Manchester Press, 1996.

Riché, Pierre. *The Carolingians: A Family Who Forged Europe.* Trans. Michael Idomir Allen. Philadelphia: University of Pennsylvania Press, 1993.

Wallace-Hadrill, John M., ed. and trans. *The Fourth Book of the Chronicle of Fredegar with Its Continuations.* London: Nelson, 1960.

Wood, Ian. *The Merovingian Kingdoms, 450–751.* London: Longman, 1994.

Charles the Bald (823–877)

Carolingian king and emperor, Charles the Bald, reigned during a time of great unrest for the Carolingian Empire. As fourth son of Louis the Pious and only son of Louis with his second wife Judith, Charles was forced to endure the challenges of his brothers to his father's authority and to his own legitimate rights of inheritance. After his father's death, Charles faced the rivalry of his brothers and participated in a terrible civil war that led to the division of the empire among Louis's three surviving sons. Charles came to rule the western part of the kingdom, the region that later became France. Although Charles did not receive the imperial title at the division of the empire, he actively sought after it and laid claim to it in 875. His pursuit of the imperial title was, in part, the result of his devotion to the memory of his grandfather, Charlemagne, and the greatness of his reign. Charles, like his grandfather, actively promoted cultural life in the kingdom and was the friend and patron of some of the most important scholars of the Carolingian Renaissance, including Hincmar of Rheims, Rabanus Maurus, and John Scotus Erigena.

The birth of Charles the Bald in 823 was met with great joy, but also with some consternation because of the questions it raised about the succession to the throne after his father's death. Several years earlier, in 817, Louis the Pious had held a great council of the leading churchmen and nobles of the empire to determine the matter of the succession. He devised a system in which the realm was divided between his three sons, with the eldest, Lothar, recognized as coemperor and, eventually, sole emperor. Louis's other two sons, Louis the German and Pippin, were made subkings and were granted authority within their own kingdoms but were subject to Louis and then Lothar. The birth of Charles complicated this settlement, a problem made worse because many believed that the settlement was divinely inspired and to undo it would be an offense against God. But this is precisely, under the influence of his wife Judith, what Louis did in the late 820s, with the consequence being revolts of his older sons in 830 and 833–834. During both the revolts, Charles was packed off to a monastery, where he was to remain without claim to his inheritance. Charles was rescued both times by his father, who managed to regain, after some difficulty, control of the empire on both occasions. In 837 Charles was granted as his inheritance a sizeable kingdom that included much of modern France. In the following year, after the death of Charles's brother Pippin, Louis disinherited Pippin's sons and granted Aquitaine to his youngest son. Charles also benefited from the reconciliation his father made with Lothar, who had been Charles's godfather, and as a result Lothar and Charles forged an alliance in their father's last year.

After the death of Louis the Pious in 840, the alliances forged by Louis broke down, and the empire fell into civil war. Lothar, who had promised to protect Charles, now turned against him in an effort to take control of the entire empire. Charles quickly turned to his other brother, Louis the German, to forge an alliance against their mutual foe, and for the next three years the three brothers fought for control of the empire. In 841, Charles and Louis inflicted a stinging defeat on Lothar at the Battle of Fontenoy, which Nithard, the chronicler of the civil wars, notes was interpreted as God's judgment against Lothar, delivered by Charles and Louis. Firm in their conviction that God was on their side, and in the face of Lothar's continuing attempts to draw Charles away from Louis, Charles and Louis swore an oath to one another in 842. The so-called Oath of Strasbourg was an important moment in the civil wars, but important also because it contains the first recorded examples of the Romance and Germanic languages. The alliance held, and in 843, Lothar submitted and the three brothers accepted the Treaty of Verdun, which assigned the western kingdom to Charles; the eastern kingdom to Louis; and the central kingdom, Italy, and the imperial title to Lothar.

Over the next two decades and more Charles was involved in continued conflict with his brothers for preeminence in the empire and with the sons of Pippin for control of the west Frankish kingdom. In an effort to safeguard his position in his kingdom, Charles held a council in Coulaines, near Le Mans, in 843, in which he promised to protect the property of the church and the nobility and to secure peace and justice in the realm in exchange for the aid and counsel of the nobility. This was an important step in the relationships of the king and nobles, in which Charles sought to establish a reciprocal working relationship. Although he was not always successful, Charles restructured government and administration in his kingdom in meaningful ways. Of course, he did not always have the support of the nobility, but Charles did manage to secure some support for his authority despite the nobility's ambitions. Notably, in Aquitaine he managed to find support despite local patriotism and support for the heirs of Pippin. Indeed, one of Louis the Pious's former allies now struggled against Charles, but because of some local support Charles was able to defeat him and also Pippin's heir. But, like his grandfather before him, Charles was forced to recognize Aquitainian uniqueness, and he appointed his son, Charles the Child, king of Aquitaine. Moreover, although he had only mixed support from the nobility, Charles could count on the full support of the church in his kingdom, particularly from the indomitable bishop, Hincmar of Rheims. The church and bishops played a critical role in preserving Charles's authority in the face of invasion by his brother Louis the German in 858.

Relationships with his brothers ebbed and flowed after the treaty of Verdun. At times, relationships were better with Lothar and at others better with Louis the German. Indeed, warming relationships between Lothar and Charles may have precipitated the invasion by Louis in 858. There were also examples, however, of cooperation between the three, best exemplified in the meeting at Meerssen in 847 to respond to the assaults by the Northmen. But as Charles became increasingly secure in his kingdom, and his brothers and nephews became less of a threat, Charles turned his attention to the kingdom of his nephew Lothar II, son of the emperor Lothar. Particularly after 860, Charles was in a position to expand his authority at the expense of his brothers. He was interested in the dynastic problems of his older brother's son and successor, who was unable to provide an heir or to gain the divorce he desired, and in 862, Charles and Louis agreed to share their nephew's territory, Lotharingia, on Lothar II's death. In 870, the year after Lothar's death, Louis and Charles signed the Treaty of Meerssen, in which they agreed to share their nephew's kingdom and ignored the claims of Louis II, the emperor who ruled in Italy. In 872, Pope Hadrian II wrote to Charles and expressed his support for the king's claim to the imperial title. Indeed, Charles's ambitions grew as his control of the west Frankish kingdom increased.

Seeking to expand his authority and resurrect the glory of his grandfather Char-lemagne, Charles awaited the proper moment. When Louis II died without an heir in 875, Charles seized the opportunity to become emperor, and on Christmas day of that year he was crowned by the pope, John VIII, in Rome. He was opposed by Louis the German, who sent troops to impede Charles's progress in Italy and invaded the western Frankish kingdom. Once again, Charles was saved by Hincmar and returned secure in his kingdom. Charles clearly intended to rule the entire empire, not just his kingdom, after the coronation. After the death of Louis the German in 876, Charles marched into Lothar's old kingdom to take control of Aachen, the imperial capital. He also threatened to invade the eastern Frankish kingdom of his late brother Louis, but became ill and was easily repulsed by the new king, his nephew Louis the Younger. Despite this setback, Charles remained dedicated to the imperial ideal and his responsibilities as emperor, and thus willingly accepted a call by the pope to come to the defense of Rome.

Carolingian king and emperor Charles the Bald (823–877) enthroned. After an illumination in the *First Bible of Charles the Bald*. (Paul Lacroix. *Science and Literature of the Middle Ages and the Renaissance*, 1878)

Preparing for his departure, Charles held a council at Quierzy in 877, and his proclamations at the council have long been seen as a concession to the nobility and the confirmation of the rights of hereditary succession. The capitulary of Quierzy, however, was intended to strengthen royal authority by reinforcing the king's right to recognize the successor to the office of count. He departed for Italy soon after the council but was forced to return when he learned of a revolt by the nobility and the invasion by Carloman, the eldest son of Louis the German. Worn out by overexertion, Charles died on his return to the kingdom on October 6, 877. Although his reign as emperor was short and tumultuous, Charles was one of the great Carolingian kings and a worthy heir of his namesake Charlemagne.

See also: Carolingian Dynasty; Charlemagne; Fontenoy, Battle of; Judith; Lothar; Louis the German; Louis the Pious; Nithard; Strasbourg, Oath of; Verdun, Treaty of

Bibliography

Gibson, Margaret, and Janet Nelson, eds. *Charles the Bald: Court and Kingdom.* Oxford: British Archaeological Reports, 1981.

Laistner, Max L.W. *Thought and Letters in Western Europe, A.D. 500 to 900.* 2nd ed. Ithaca, NY: Cornell University Press, 1976.

McKitterick, Rosamond. *The Frankish Kingdoms under the Carolingians, 751–987.* London: Longman, 1983.

Nelson, Janet. *Charles the Bald.* London: Longman, 1992.

Riché, Pierre. *The Carolingians: A Family Who Forged Europe.* Trans. Michael Idomir Allen. Philadelphia: University of Pennsylvania Press, 1993.

Scholz, Bernhard Walter, trans. *Carolingian Chronicles: Royal Frankish Annals and Nithard's History.* Ann Arbor: University of Michigan Press, 1972.

Charles III, the Fat (839–888)

The third son of Louis the German (r. 840–876), Charles the Fat was the last Carolingian to rule over a united empire. Although his reign began with great promise, ill health and a variety of other problems cut short the emperor's tenure. His failure illustrated some of the fundamental problems of Carolingian power and opened the way for continued decentralization.

Charles became king of Alemmannia on his father's death in 876 and in 879 he became king of Italy. After some negotiation, Charles and his wife, Richardis, were crowned emperor and empress by Pope John VIII (872–882) in Rome in 881. Hopeful that Charles would remain in Italy to protect the region, especially the Papal States, from Muslim raiders from the south, the pope was disappointed when the new emperor returned north to strengthen his hold on Carolingian lands. In 882 his claim to power was expanded as he inherited control of Bavaria, Franconia, and

Saxony on the death of his younger brother, Louis the Younger (r. 876–882). Ruling over the entire east Frankish kingdom, Charles turned his attention to the most pressing problem of the day, the Vikings. His siege of an encampment of Northmen was broken off, but Charles won a diplomatic victory by convincing the leader of the Northmen to convert to Christianity and to accept the emperor's niece in marriage. Recognizing his success, the nobles of the West Frankish kingdom offered Charles the crown on the death of Carloman (r. 879–884), and when the nobility and bishops pledged their loyalty to Charles at Ponthion in 885 he completed the reintegration of the empire of Charlemagne.

With increasing authority came greater responsibility, and Charles was faced with the growing menace of the Northmen in his new kingdom. In July 885, Northmen took Rouen and began the siege of Paris. Although heroically defended by the count of Paris, the city fell by the summer of 886. The people of the region sent an urgent request to Charles for aid, and in response he sent one of his most skilled and trusted military advisors, who was killed by the Vikings shortly after his arrival. Charles himself marched on Paris in October 886 and ransomed the city with a payment of 700 pounds of silver and allowed the Vikings to ravage Burgundy in the following winter.

The emperor's problems were not limited to his difficulties with the Northmen but included a serious health problem: he experienced seizures and suffered headaches that made it nearly impossible for him to rule. Efforts to relieve the condition proved fruitless, and Charles's failure to provide an heir further eroded his support throughout the empire. In 887, a general rebellion broke out against him and forced Charles to move to Tribur where he tried unsuccessfully to rally support. Abandoned even by his loyal supporters, Charles agreed to abdicate in November 887, retiring to estates in Swabia where he would die on January 13, 888. The empire he had recreated dissolved on his abdication as regional kings assumed his position.

Despite the dissolution of the empire and his military failures, Charles did make a positive impact on his own and subsequent generations. Contemporaries regarded him as a good Christian king who gave generously to the poor, prayed often, and put his trust in God. One writer even compared Charles with his illustrious ancestor, Charlemagne. Of more lasting significance was the emperor's impact on literary history. He commissioned Notker the Stammerer, a monk of St. Gall, to write a biography of Charlemagne, which provides important commentary on Christian kingship and moral lessons drawn from a somewhat idealized version of its subject's life. Charles the Fat himself was also the subject of the *Vision of Charles the Fat,* an anonymous tract written at Rheims. In the work, Charles is visited by a serious of ancestors who warn him of the impending collapse of the dynasty and encourage him to seek divine favor.

See also: Carolingian Dynasty; Charlemagne; Louis the German; Notker the Stammerer

Bibliography

Dutton, Paul Edward. *The Politics of Dreaming in the Carolingian Empire.* Lincoln: University of Nebraska Press, 1994.

McLean, Simon. *Politics and Kingship in the Late Ninth Century: Charles the Fat and the End of the Carolingian Empire.* Cambridge: Cambridge University Press, 2007.

Riché, Pierre. *The Carolingians: A Family Who Forged Europe.* Trans. Michael Idomir Allen. Philadelphia: University of Pennsylvania Press, 1993.

Charles III, the Simple (879–929)

Ruler of the West Frankish Kingdom, Charles called "the Simple" (*simplex*: "straightforward" or "without guile") embodied the strengths and weaknesses of the later Carolingian kings. Although respected by the clergy of his realm and by the Saxon ruler of the East Frankish kingdom, Henry I, Charles endured major challenges to his authority by the nobility of his realm and from invaders from the north.

Born some five months after the death of his father, Louis II the Stammerer, and two years after the death of his grandfather, Charles the Bald, Charles the Simple's path to the kingship was a difficult one. His two half-brothers and heirs to the throne died young, and the emperor, Charles the Fat, welcomed him as successor to the West Frankish throne but abdicated before he could enforce the succession. Even when supported at around 892 by a faction of the nobility upset by the reign of King Odo, the son of Robert the Strong, Charles was forced to wait until 898 to take the throne. Once established as king of the West Franks, Charles pursued the traditional Carolingian policy of imposing his authority throughout the realm. He sought to revive royal authority over Aquitaine, forging close ties with leading nobles of the region, issuing charters confirming royal estates, and involving himself with ecclesiastical appointments. He extended his power into the northern part of his kingdom and was recognized as the king of Lotharingia in 921.

Perhaps Charles's greatest achievement came in 911 when he defeated the invading Northmen and agreed to a treaty with them. According to the terms of the agreement, the leader of the Northmen, Rollo, was to become the count of Rouen and preside over a province that would become the duchy of Normandy. In return for this grant, Rollo and his followers were to convert to Christianity and defend their new home and the kingdom from further invasions. Despite this success, Charles's reign would not be a happy one, and royal authority would be seriously eroded. Dissatisfied by his focus on Lotharingian affairs, the nobles of the West Frankish kingdom revolted against Charles in the 920s. In 923, Charles was captured and imprisoned until the end of his life in 929, leaving behind a kingdom that was increasingly fragmented and decentralized.

See also: Carolingian Dynasty; Charles the Bald; Charles III, the Fat; Louis the Stammerer

Bibliography

Nelson, Janet. *Charles the Bald*. London: Longman, 1992.

Riché, Pierre. *The Carolingians: A Family Who Forged Europe*. Trans. Michael Idomir Allen. Philadelphia: University of Pennsylvania Press, 1993.

Childeric III (d. 754)

The last ruler of the Merovingian dynasty, Childeric was king from 743 to 751, but the real power in the Frankish kingdom was held by the Carolingian mayors of the palace, Pippin the Short and Carloman. Drawn from obscurity and hailed as the heir to the dynasty after a six-year interregnum, Childeric was a "do-nothing king" (one of the *rois fainéants,* as the later Merovingians are traditionally called), the puppet of the real rulers of Francia. In a memorable passage by Charlemagne's biographer, Einhard, Childeric is portrayed in most unsympathetic, almost ridiculous, terms. According to the biography, Childeric had little more than the empty title of king and had no influence on government beyond his annual visits to court. Arriving in a rustic oxcart led by a peasant, Childeric would play the role of king, sitting on his throne with his beard and long flowing hair (long hair was the symbol of Merovingian royal power), where he would receive ambassadors from other kingdoms. The answers he gave these ambassadors had been thoroughly rehearsed with the Carolingian mayors. Childeric was not only without political power but he was also without economic power. He owned only a single estate with a house and few servants. The estate itself brought him a meager income, and he was dependent upon the good graces of the mayors of the palace for his economic support. Childeric, thus, was a mere shadow of his illustrious ancestor Clovis (r. 481–511), the first Merovingian king.

Despite his alleged economic and political weakness, Childeric was not a completely useless king. It is likely, first of all, that Einhard exaggerated Childeric's inadequacies to enhance the reputation of the new Carolingian dynasty, and there is evidence that he issued charters and possessed more than a single estate. Clearly, the Merovingian monarch was highly dependent on his Carolingian patrons, but at his enthronement he declared that he was pleased to be restored to the kingship and pleased to allow the Carolingians help rule the kingdom. Moreover, he possessed a certain charisma as a member of the royal line that Pippin and Carloman did not possess. Indeed, it was that very charisma that the Carolingian mayors needed to secure their positions in the kingdom. Childeric was raised to the throne to establish continuity in the kingdom, or at least give the appearance that the traditional dynasty remained in control of the kingdom and that the good fortune of the dynasty would preserve the kingdom. The Carolingian mayors had faced widespread opposition within the Frankish kingdom that was, perhaps, worsened by the absence of a legitimate king. Their father, Charles Martel, had ruled as mayor without a king on the throne during his last years, and Pippin and Carloman inherited this situation. To reduce internal opposition, they put Childeric on the throne, and thus he performed an important political function.

Childeric's utility, however, came to an end by the close of the 740s. In 747 Carloman withdrew from the world and retired to a monastery. Pippin was thus the sole mayor of the Frankish kingdom and much more secure in that role than he had been at the beginning of the 740s. In 750, he sent messengers to the pope in Rome asking if the person with the title or the person with the power should rule as king. The pope answered as Pippin had hoped, and in the following year Childeric was deposed, and Pippin assumed the throne. Childeric was tonsured and placed in a monastery, where he quietly lived out his days.

See also: Carolingian Dynasty; Charlemagne; Charles Martel; Einhard; Merovingian Dynasty; Pippin III, Called Pippin the Short

Bibliography

Einhard and Notker the Stammerer. *Two Lives of Charlemagne.* Trans. Lewis Thorpe. Harmondsworth, UK: Penguin, 1981.

Wallace-Hadrill, J.M. *The Long-Haired Kings.* Toronto: University of Toronto Press, 1982.

Wood, Ian. *The Merovingian Kings, 450–751.* London: Longman, 1994.

Chilperic I (c. 537–584)

Merovingian king from 561 to 584, Chilperic was the son of Chlotar I (d. 561) and grandson of the great king Clovis (r. 481–511). His reign as king was marred by almost constant warfare with his brothers, especially Sigebert, for control of the kingdom. The relationship between Sigebert and Chilperic was further complicated by their marriage practices and the enmity between Sigebert's wife, Brunhilde, and Chilperic's wife, Fredegund. Indeed, after the death of the two kings, Brunhilde and Fredegund continued the feud until Fredegund's death in 597. Chilperic's ambition, brutality, and corrupt ways are highlighted by his contemporary Gregory of Tours in Gregory's *History of the Franks.*

Chilperic, according to Gregory of Tours, was "the Nero and Herod of our time" (379), and it is from Gregory that Chilperic's reputation for violence and deceit comes. Gregory notes that Chilperic destroyed many villages and brought many unjust charges against his subjects to seize their wealth. The king persecuted the bishops, whom he accused of taking all the wealth of the kingdom. According to

Gregory, Chilperic's "god was in his belly" (380), and the king practiced all forms of vice and debauchery. Chilperic declared to his judges, "If anyone disobeys my orders, he must be punished by having his eyes torn out" (380–381). Although Gregory provides a memorable portrait of Chilperic, he was not the only one to do so, and other evidence provides a less brutal image of the king. The great poet Venantius Fortunatus wrote a panegyric praising the king for his authority and intellectual talents. Indeed, even Gregory recognizes that Chilperic had some literary talent and notes that the king wrote two books of poetry and composed hymns and other pieces for the mass. Chilperic also wrote a book of theology on the doctrine of Christ, added several Greek letters to the alphabet to reflect pronunciation of Frankish better, and added to the Salic law.

Although he was more than the brutal king portrayed by Gregory, Chilperic is best known for the civil wars with his brothers, particularly the blood feud involving his wife, Fredegund, and his brother Sigebert and his brother's wife, Brunhilde. Hostilities did, however, precede his marriage with Fredegund, when Chilperic, who had inherited part of the kingdom with its capital at Soissons, attacked Sigebert's kingdom in 562. The attack began 13 years of war between the two brothers, war that nearly led to the defeat and destruction of Chilperic. He was aided throughout the struggle by his ambitious and ruthless wife, Fredegund. She was not Chilperic's first wife, however. Indeed, Chilperic had previously married the Visigothic princess Galswintha. This had constituted a break with the usual practice of the Merovingian kings, who had married lowborn women. Indeed, even before his marriage to Galswintha, Chilperic took the serving maid Fredegund as a concubine and, possibly, wife. His marriage to Galswintha was inspired by Sigebert, who had previously married Galswintha's sister Brunhilde. Shortly after the marriage to Galswintha, who brought a sizeable dowry to the marriage, Chilperic had her murdered, possibly at Fredegund's request, and then married Fredegund. The murder of Galswintha may have worsened an already difficult situation between Sigebert and Chilperic.

The civil wars between the two brothers were quite fierce. They may have been the worst wars in Merovingian history. After Chilperic's initial attack, Sigebert was able to counterattack and seize Chilperic's capital of Soissons. Chilperic was driven from his kingdom and eventually he took refuge with his brother Guntram, who also faced invasion by Sigebert. In the mid-570s, Chilperic, allied with Guntram, and Sigebert once again came to blows. The situation was quite grave for Chilperic, because Guntram had made peace with Sigebert and Chilperic's son had been killed in battle by supporters of Sigebert. On the point of destruction, Chilperic learned that Sigebert had been killed. It is generally held that the murder was committed by agents of Chilperic's queen, Fredegund.

Chilperic exploited his opportunity after the death of Sigebert and invaded his late brother's territory. He seized several cities formerly ruled by Sigebert and nearly disinherited Sigebert's heir, Childebert (d. 596). But the intervention of Guntram saved Childebert and stopped Chilperic's advance. At the same time, Chilperic faced the ambitions of Merovech, his son by one of his concubines. Merovech, having reached his majority and eager to rule as king, sought out and married Chilperic's rival Brunhilde. The marriage gave Merovech claim to a kingdom and returned Brunhilde to the game of Merovingian power politics. But the couple was no match for the ruthlessness of Chilperic and Fredegund, and Merovech, failing to secure power, asked a servant to kill him. Gregory, however, suggests that Merovech was murdered by Fredegund. Whatever the case, Chilperic survived the challenge and was now, in 581, bereft of any heirs. At that point, he made peace with Childebert, adopted him, and named him as heir. For the next three years, Childebert, Chilperic, and Guntram were involved in a complicated diplomatic and military struggle for predominance in the kingdom. Although Chilperic acquired the largest share of the kingdom, he was abandoned by Childebert, who once again allied with Guntram, putting Chilperic on the defensive. Before much further turmoil between the three occurred, Chilperic was murdered while hunting. He was succeeded by an infant son, Chlotar II, who was protected by his mother Fredegund and supported by an important segment of the nobility. It was in fact Chlotar II who ended the civil strife that had existed since the beginning of his father's reign when he overthrew Brunhilde in 613 and unified the kingdom.

See also: Brunhilde; Chlotar II; Clovis; Fredegund; Galswintha; Gregory of Tours; Guntram; Merovingian Dynasty; Salic Law

Bibliography

Gregory of Tours. *History of the Franks.* Trans. Lewis Thorpe. Harmondsworth, UK: Penguin, 1974.

James, Edward. *The Franks.* Oxford: Blackwell, 1988.

Lasko, Peter. *The Kingdom of the Franks: North-West Europe before Charlemagne.* New York: McGraw-Hill, 1971.

Wallace-Hadrill, J.M. *The Long-Haired Kings.* Toronto: University of Toronto Press, 1982.

Wemple, Suzanne. *Women in Frankish Society: Marriage and the Cloister, 500 to 900.* Philadelphia: University of Pennsylvania Press, 1985.

Wood, Ian. *The Merovingian Kingdoms, 450–751.* London: Longman, 1994.

Chlotar II (584–629)

Merovingian king from 613 to 629 and the first monarch to rule a united kingdom since the first Merovingian king of the Franks, Clovis, in the late fifth and early sixth centuries, Chlotar was a successful king who restored the integrity of the dynasty and laid the foundation for the high point in the dynasty's history. The son of Chilperic I and Fredegund, Chlotar established a period of peace and prosperity for the kingdom and ended generations of civil strife and fraternal violence that had plagued the realm since the early sixth century. Chlotar improved relationships with the nobility and the church, reformed the law, established a rudimentary chancery that was to develop in the generations to follow, and emphasized the king's stature as a sacred figure. The peace and prosperity enjoyed by the kingdom during his reign continued during that of the reign of his son, Dagobert, because of important foundations laid by Chlotar and because of the talents of his successor.

Chlotar was born during a time of great civil strife in the kingdom that was the result of the competition between his parents, Chilperic and Fredegund, and their rivals King Sigebert (r. 560/561–575) and his queen Brunhilde. He ascended to the throne in 584 when his father was murdered by his mother and immediately faced numerous difficulties that threatened his claim to the throne. One of the most serious problems was the question of his legitimacy and right to inherit. Many leaders in the kingdom, including the historian Gregory of Tours and King Guntram, the pious and highly respected Merovingian ruler, expressed doubts about his parentage. Only after Fredegund gathered the sworn oaths of three bishops and 300 nobles was Chlotar's claim preserved, with the aid of his uncle, King Guntram. He faced further challenges, however, in the 590s, including the ascendancy of his mother's rival, Brunhilde, attacks on his own part of the kingdom, and the loss of important territories. Growing dissatisfaction among the nobility with Brunhilde and her sons, however, provided Chlotar with the opportunity not only to secure his place in his own part of the kingdom but to establish his authority over the entire Frankish realm. He led a revolt against Brunhilde that led to her deposition and brutal execution in 613.

The opening years of Chlotar's reign, known mainly from the garbled pages of the chronicle of Fredegar, were marked by an attack on the reign of his predecessor. The condemnation and savage execution of Brunhilde for numerous murders were only the start of Chlotar's war on his predecessor's memory. To further denigrate the reputation of his predecessor, Chlotar promoted the memory and saint's cult of one of the bishops that Brunhilde had murdered. He also made contact with the Irish missionary St. Columban, who had been exiled by the queen. Although Columban did not return, his foundation at Luxeuil received protection from Chlotar. These actions not only worsened Brunhilde's reputation, they also improved Chlotar's relationship with the church in his realm.

Chlotar made significant overtures to the nobility during the early years of his reign. His success against Brunhilde was due to the support of the nobility, particularly to the founders of what later became the Carolingian dynasty, Arnulf of Metz and Pippin of Landen. They were made important advisors of the king and rewarded with prominent religious and political offices, Arnulf with the see of Metz and Pippin with the office of mayor of the palace (*major domus*). The support of the Frankish nobility was essential for the success of the king, particularly because of the shifting alliances of various noble families. During his entire reign and that of his son Dagobert's, Chlotar sought to manage these unstable alliances. His creation of a subkingdom in Austrasia in 622 for Dagobert may have been an attempt to appease regional interests and draw powerful families in the region closer to the ruling dynasty. Marriage alliances were also made to maintain good relationships with various noble factions. Dagobert's mother, Berthetrude, may have been Burgundian, which would have preserved ties between Chlotar and that part of the kingdom. After Berthetrude's death, Chlotar married again, and Dagobert married Chlotar's new wife's sister, both marriages attempted to gain the support of the wives' family for the two kings.

Chlotar throughout his entire reign introduced significant legal reforms and issued numerous charters and diplomas. One of his most important pieces of legislation came very early in his reign, when he pronounced the Edict of Paris of 614. Once seen as a concession to the nobility, the edict bound the king and nobility closer together and provided them the shared purpose of ruling a great kingdom and maintaining peace and order throughout the realm. The edict also addressed tolls, ecclesiastical property, and the restitution of property lost under Chlotar's predecessor Brunhilde; in this way Chlotar further denigrated Brunhilde's memory and enhanced his own image before the nobility. His activity as a lawgiver had two further consequences. It forced him to establish a writing office, which in generations to come evolved into an official chancery, an office that attracted skilled men, often from the church, who would support his power. The office also enhanced his reputation as king and reinforced his image as an almost sacred figure, a result that distinguished him from the nobles who served him and needed him to continue to act as lawgiver.

By the end of his reign in 629, Chlotar had reestablished the authority of the Merovingian dynasty and laid the foundation for even greater successes by his son Dagobert. Chlotar had reunited the kingdom under his sole authority and maintained good relationships with the nobility. He reordered and improved relationships with the church in his kingdom, which offered a valuable counterweight to the nobility should he need it. He reformed the law and enhanced his reputation as king through his role as lawgiver. Chlotar also redefined the status of the king in the Merovingian realm—all of which aided his son and established an era of prosperity for the dynasty.

See also: Arnulf of Metz, St.; Brunhilde; Carolingian Dynasty; Clovis; Columban, St.; Dagobert; Fredegund; Gregory of Tours; Guntram; Merovingian Dynasty; Pippin I, Called Pippin of Landen

Bibliography

Bachrach, Bernard S. *Merovingian Military Organization, 481–751.* Minneapolis: University of Minnesota Press, 1972.

Geary, Patrick. *Before France and Germany: The Creation and Transformation of the Merovingian World.* Oxford: Oxford University Press, 1988.

Gregory of Tours. *The History of the Franks.* Trans. Lewis Thorpe. Harmondsworth, UK: Penguin, 1974.

James, Edward. *The Franks.* Oxford: Blackwell, 1991.

Lasko, Peter. *The Kingdom of the Franks: North-West Europe before Charlemagne.* New York: McGraw Hill, 1971.

Lasko, Peter. *The Frankish Church.* Oxford: Clarendon, 1983.

Wallace-Hadrill, J. M. *The Long-Haired Kings.* Toronto: Toronto University Press, 1982.

Wallace-Hadrill, J. M., ed. and trans. *The Fourth Book of the Chronicle of Fredegar with Its Continuations.* London: Nelson, 1960.

Wemple, Suzanne. *Women in Frankish Society: Marriage and the Cloister, 500 to 900.* Philadelphia: University of Pennsylvania Press, 1985.

Wood, Ian. *The Merovingian Kingdoms, 450–751.* London: Longman, 1994.

Chrodegang of Metz (c. 712–766)

Perhaps the most important ecclesiastic in the Carolingian kingdom in the first half of the eighth century, after the Anglo-Saxon missionary Boniface, Chrodegang was a committed church reformer and a close ally of the Carolingian mayor of the palace and later king, Pippin the Short. He assumed the important see of Metz, which one of the founders of the Carolingian line, Arnulf of Metz, once held. Although not as zealous in his commitment to Roman-focused reform as Boniface, Chrodegang nonetheless became papal legate, introduced Roman liturgical forms to the kingdom, visited Rome, and collected important relics from Rome. He helped Pippin with his reforms of the Frankish church and composed an important rule for canons.

Born into a noble family, Chrodegang had many important family connections throughout the kingdom, including prominent ecclesiastics and aristocrats. His uncle may have been a supporter of the mayor of the palace, Charles Martel, and Chrodegang himself served in the chancery at Martel's court. In 742, the year after Pippin and his brother Carloman succeeded their father, Chrodegang was made bishop of Metz by Pippin and with the Carolingian mayor began the reform of the Frankish church. Over the next several decades, in association with Pippin, Chrodegang introduced improvements to religious life and practice at Metz. He also expanded the size of his church at Metz and built several new episcopal buildings, which could accommodate the Roman liturgical practices and chant that he introduced to the church in the Frankish kingdom. In 748, with Pippin's help,

Chrodegang founded the monastery of Gorze near his see of Metz; the new monastery was guided by the bishop's reform principles, and monks from Gorze helped to found new monasteries. While on a trip to Rome sometime between 753 and 755, Chrodegang was made archbishop and papal legate by Pope Stephen II to replace the recently martyred Boniface. He also participated in several church councils held by Pippin that implemented spiritual and institutional reform of church life in the kingdom.

Chrodegang is best known, however, for the rule of canons (*Regula canonicorum*) he wrote between 754 and 756. The rule, inspired by and based on the monastic rule of St. Benedict of Nursia, was intended to improve the religious life of the canons at the cathedral church in Metz and was widely adopted throughout the Frankish kingdom in the coming years. The rule, which received official sanction at the Council of Aachen in 816, reflected Chrodegang's monastic temperament. Chrodegang's rule ordered that the canons, clergy serving at a bishop's cathedral church, live in a community with a common place to eat and sleep. They were to care for the sick, possess no personal wealth, and perform the daily round of prayers. The canons were also expected to spend time reading and studying so that they could better perform their preaching duties. Chrodegang's rule was widely copied in his day and remained the most important rule for canons for several centuries after his death.

See also: Anglo-Saxons; Arnulf of Metz, St.; Benedict of Aniane; Benedict of Nursia, St.; Boniface, St.; Carolingian Dynasty; Charles Martel; Louis the Pious; Pippin III, Called Pippin the Short

Bibliography

Knowles, David. *Christian Monasticism.* New York: McGraw Hill, 1969.

Lawrence, Clifford H. *Medieval Monasticism: Forms of Religious Life in Western Europe in the Middle Ages.* 2nd ed. London: Longman, 1989.

McKitterick, Rosamond. *The Frankish Kingdoms under the Carolingians, 751–987.* London: Longman, 1983.

Riché, Pierre. *The Carolingians: A Family Who Forged Europe.* Trans. Michael Idomir Allen. Philadelphia: University of Pennsylvania Press, 1993.

Riché, Pierre. *Education and Culture in the Barbarian West: From the Sixth through the Eighth Century.* Trans. John Contreni. Columbia: University of South Carolina Press, 1976.

Wallace-Hadrill, J. M. *The Frankish Church.* Oxford: Clarendon, 1983.

Circumcellions

A militant religious group of North Africa, the Circumcellions were closely allied with the Donatist movement, which rejected the Catholic church alleging that it failed its role during the persecutions, and emerged as a serious threat to the political and religious order of Roman Africa in the fourth and early fifth centuries. Sometimes regarded as members of a nationalist as well as religious movement, the Circumcellions are known mainly from the accounts of orthodox opponents like Augustine of Hippo, who described the Circumcellions' ferocious opposition to the Catholic church and its imperial supporters. To prove their devotion to the faith and membership in the true church, they sought out martyrdom—demanding to be executed by Roman soldiers or attacking pagan temples to inspire assaults by pagans. Following the inspiration of the Donatist, the Circumcellions openly fought with Catholics for control of church buildings and the clergy.

Along with their Donatist allies, the Circumcellions would purify churches they seized and destroy Catholic sacred items to demonstrate the impurity of the Catholics. In the later fourth century, the Circumcellions became even more aggressive and violent, staging brutal kidnappings and beatings of Catholic bishops and priests. They were notorious as well for the vicious blinding of their rivals, which they justified by reference to Scripture. Their savagery and extreme violence led some Donatist leaders to reject the Circumcellions and contributed to the empire's equally harsh suppression of the Donatist church and the Circumcellion movement. By the time of the arrival of the Vandals in 429, the Circumcellions seem to have been eradicated.

See also: Augustine of Hippo, St.; Donatists

Bibliography

Brown, Peter. *Augustine of Hippo: A Biography*. Berkeley: University of California Press, 2000.

Frend, W.H.C. "Circumcellions and Monks." *Journal of Theological Studies*, new series, 20 (1969): 542–49.

Clothing

The dress in barbarian Europe was most likely a combination of traditional Germanic clothing and imported Roman fashions. Clothing was relatively uniform throughout the Roman and post-Roman world, although there was variation across Europe in style and fabric, including cotton, linen, wool, and, after the seventh century, silk. There was also some variation, especially in quality, between the peasantry and upper classes. The latter were obviously able to afford higher quality clothing and often adorned themselves with jewelry. In general, though, clothing was simple and functional and was adapted to the prevailing climate, with people in colder regions wearing warmer, heavier clothing.

As with many things, the Roman historian and moralist Tacitus (c. 56–120) provides a useful description of the clothing of premigration Germans. Although

Tacitus's *Germania* must be treated carefully since its praise of the Germans is often simply a means of veiled criticism, its treatment of dress seems relatively accurate, especially when the information it gives is compared with what is known of some later barbarian practices. Tacitus notes that the Germans wear a cloak fastened with a clasp, and the wealthiest wear a close-fitting garment underneath that is "tight and exhibits each limb" (115) (in other words, trousers, never worn by the Romans). They also wear the skins of animals, which are carefully chosen and include, among others, the skins of spotted beasts. He says that they wear animal skins, a practice disdained in Roman society, because they cannot acquire other material through trade. Women, according to Tacitus, dress in the same fashion as men, except that they wear linen garments embroidered in purple and do not extend the garment into sleeves, leaving the lower arm bare.

Under the influence of their contact with Rome, various barbarian peoples wore more loose-fitting and flowing clothes along with their furs and tight-fitting garments. The peasants, whose fashions changed little throughout the Middle Ages, wore heavy shoes, often of wood, a leather belt, and a simple, short tunic with narrow long sleeves or half-long sleeves. The wealthier classes wore more elaborate and expensive versions of this basic outfit, and Carolingian princes and possibly other nobles changed their clothes every Saturday. Perhaps the best-known literary depiction of barbarian dress is Einhard's description of Charlemagne's clothing. He notes that the great king wore "a linen shirt and linen breeches, and above these a tunic fringed with silk" (77). Charlemagne covered his legs with hose and wore shoes on his feet. He also wore an otter or ermine coat to protect himself against the cold and covered everything with a blue cloak. Einhard explains that this was traditional Frankish dress, which differed little from that of the common people. A similar outfit was given to King Harold the Dane by Louis the Pious and included white gloves, a cloak set with a pin, and a tunic with straight sleeves and jewels.

The standard dress of men during much of the early Middle Ages, therefore, included a tunic that reached to the knees and could be gathered with a belt. More than one tunic was often worn, with the sleeves of the undertunic, the *tunica,* extending the full length of the arm and the sleeves of the outertunic, the *dalmatica,* extending only part way down the arm. The Franks and other barbarian folk wrapped their legs with hose or pants, and they wore shoes of wood or boots of leather to cover their feet. A full-length cloak, the *lacerna,* covered their clothes. The cloak was open in the front and held together by a brooch. The primary fabrics were linen and wool, but silk was popular with those who could afford it. The garments were also trimmed with embroidery. In the cold weather, a coat of animal fur was worn, with the fur side turned inward to insulate better and to keep from appearing too animal-like. Women's dress was similar. They too wore an undertunic, and covered it with an outertunic, a full-length gown that reached to the ankles and had long sleeves.

The outertunic was either held up by chains or open in front to make walking easier, and over their clothing women wore a cloak, the *paenula,* which was held closed in the front by a fibula. Women covered their heads, pulling up a mantle to cover their head or wearing or headdress. They also wore necklaces, rings, bracelets, brooches, and jewels with their clothing. By the Carolingian era, women generally wore long veils, but, as they had earlier, they wore their hair long and braided, laced with gold thread or ribbon.

Even though a standard form of dress existed throughout most of the early Middle Ages, there was some variety among peoples. As Einhard again demonstrates, there were differences in fashion preferences between various peoples. Indeed, he notes that Charlemagne hated foreign clothing, but wore it twice out of his respect for Popes Hadrian and Leo III. On two occasions in Rome, Charlemagne wore Roman dress, including local styles of shoes and tunic and the Greek chlamys. The great king also wore more elaborate clothes on feast days and other occasions of state that included embroidered clothes and shoes along with a bejeweled sword.

See also: Animals; Carolingian Dynasty; Charlemagne; Einhard; Franks; Hadrian I, Pope; Jewelry and Gems; Leo III, Pope; Women

Bibliography

Einhard and Notker the Stammerer. *Two Lives of Charlemagne.* Trans. Lewis Thorpe. Harmondsworth, UK: Penguin, 1981.

Riché, Pierre. *Daily Life in the World of Charlemagne.* Trans. Jo Ann McNamara. Philadelphia: University of Pennsylvania Press, 1983.

Tacitus, Cornelius. *Agricola and Germany.* Trans. Anthony R. Birley. Oxford: Oxford University Press, 1999.

Veyne, Paul. *A History of Private Life.* Vol. 1, *From Pagan Rome to Byzantium.* Trans. Arthur Goldhammer. Cambridge, MA: Harvard University Press, 1987.

Clotilda, St. (d. 544)

The wife of the great Merovingian king Clovis, Clotilda is traditionally thought to have played a key role in the conversion of her husband to Catholic Christianity. She may also have influenced his foreign policy by encouraging a war of conquest against her uncle in Burgundy. She fulfilled her primary obligation as a Merovingian queen by providing Clovis with four sons, three of whom survived their father (Chlodomer, Childebert I, and Chlotar I), and a daughter, Clotilda. After the death of Clovis, Clotilda took the veil and entered a convent. She was later recognized as a saint because of her religious life and her influence on her husband.

Clotilda was the daughter of the king of Burgundy, Chilperic, and his Gallo-Roman Catholic wife, Caretena. As a result of her mother's influence, Clotilda was raised as a Catholic Christian, even though most of the Burgundian royal family was Arian Christian. It is possible that Clotilda's Catholic faith attracted Clovis to her because he hoped it would smooth relationships with the powerful Catholic bishops of his kingdom. Late sixth and early seventh century sources, however, offer a less mundane picture of the courtship. Clotilda was orphaned and in exile by the time she came to Clovis's attention, her mother and father having been murdered by her uncle Gundobad. Clovis sent his envoys to secretly observe the exiled princess, and they informed him of her beauty, elegance, and intelligence. He then sent her a ring inscribed with his name, a portrait of himself, and a proposal of marriage. She hesitated because Clovis was still a pagan, but the following year, when he approached Gundobad to ask for her hand, Clotilda's uncle would not refuse the powerful Frank, and she married Clovis.

As queen, Clotilda desired nothing more than the conversion of her husband to Catholic Christianity, and according to the late sixth-century bishop and historian Gregory of Tours, she was pivotal to that conversion. She encouraged Clovis to accept Christianity and denounced the immorality and belief in the pagan gods. She argued that her God was the creator of all things and that her husband's gods were nothing more than idols of wood or metal. When their first son, Ingomer, was born Clotilda had him baptized. The child died shortly after the baptism, which angered Clovis, who claimed the baptism caused his son's death. But Clotilda held firm and thanked God that he chose to take Ingomer after baptism, ensuring the child's entry into heaven. Clotilda baptized their second son, Chlodomer, who became ill shortly after the baptism. Clovis blamed Christ again, but Clotilda prayed for her son's recovery, and Chlodomer regained his health. She continued to urge Clovis to convert, and when faced with certain defeat against the Alemanni, Clovis agreed to accept baptism should he emerge victorious. Winning the battle, he accepted instruction and baptism from St. Remigius, bishop of Rheims, who had been ordered to the court by Clotilda. Although it is a wonderful story, most historians generally discount Gregory's version of events and note that Clovis probably converted to Arian Christianity before finally accepting the Catholic faith. It is still likely, however, that his decision was influenced by Clotilda and her domestic proselytizing.

Clotilda's influence on Merovingian affairs extended beyond her likely influence on the conversion of Clovis. According to work praising her sanctity, Clothild encouraged Clovis to destroy pagan shrines and to build churches, and also to support the poor, widows, and orphans. She also influenced affairs in the kingdom during the reigns of her sons. Gregory of Tours notes that she called on her sons to make war against the Burgundians, allegedly to avenge the murder of her parents. Her son Chlodomer led the war, which ended with the defeat of the Burgundians and the death of Chlodomer, whose children were then raised by Clotilda.

See also: Alemanni; Clovis; Gregory of Tours; Merovingian Dynasty

Bibliography

Gregory of Tours. *History of the Franks.* Trans. Lewis Thorpe. Harmondsworth, UK: Penguin, 1974.

Schulenburg, Jane Tibbetts. *Forgetful of Their Sex: Female Sanctity and Society, ca. 500–1100.* Chicago: University of Chicago Press, 1998.

Wemple, Suzanne. *Women in Frankish Society: Marriage and the Cloister, 500 to 900.* Philadelphia: University of Pennsylvania Press, 1985.

Wood, Ian. *The Merovingian Kingdoms, 450–751.* London: Longman, 1994.

Clovis (c. 466–511)

The most important king (r. 481–511) and founder of the Merovingian dynasty, Clovis was a "*magnus et egregius pugnator*" (a great and distinguished warrior) according to the bishop and historian Gregory of Tours. At times a brutal and treacherous warrior, he unified the Frankish kingdoms and laid a foundation for later Frankish power and influence that was in part drawn from the more advanced traditions of the late Roman Empire. He cultivated good relationships with the bishops in his realm and was the first Frankish king to convert to Christianity.

Clovis waged a series of wars to expand the boundaries of his realm. Although there exists much debate over the exact chronology of these events and even over the extent of Clovis's war making, it is likely that he pursued an aggressive policy against other Germanic tribes and other Frankish groups that led to the enlargement of his kingdom. One of his most famous victories was his victory over Syagrius, the late Roman ruler of the kingdom of Soissons, in 486. He also enjoyed a series of other victories during his reign over other foes, including the Alemanni at the Battle of Tolbiac in 496, the Burgundians in 500, the Visigoths in 507, and various lesser Frankish kings in his last years.

Although Clovis fought a great number of wars during his reign, he was careful, even before his conversion, to maintain the support of the Catholic bishops of Gaul that he had enjoyed from the beginning of his reign. He took great care to guarantee the support of the bishops by ruling that his soldiers should not harm the clergy or despoil the lands of the bishops, the tombs of the saints, or other sacred or church ground. An even greater example of the importance of the Catholic bishops to Clovis can be found in the story of the chalice of Soissons.

According to Gregory, Clovis was approached after his victory by the bishop of Soissons, who asked that a precious chalice used for Mass be returned to him. Clovis promised he would return the chalice should it come to him during the division of spoils, and when he requested it all his warriors, save one, proclaimed he should have it. The lone warrior refused and cut the chalice in half, offering the king his share. Later, while Clovis was reviewing the troops, he came upon this same warrior. Clovis denounced the warrior as a bad example and threw the latter's sword to the ground. As the warrior bent to pick it up, Clovis brought his great axe down on the soldier's head, reminding him that he had done the same thing to the chalice at Soissons. Although it is a most unlikely story, the tale of the chalice of Soissons reveals the importance of the Catholic bishops to Clovis.

The wars against Syagrius, the Alemanni, and the Visigoths were given religious significance by Gregory, and, although an unlikely interpretation, it reveals the importance of the conversion of Clovis to this Gallo-Roman bishop. Moreover, there may have been some truth to Gregory's view of the king, because Clovis did convert to Christianity. Traditionally, the king's conversion was due to the influence of his wife Clotilda, who was a Catholic from the kingdom of Burgundy. In fact, as Gregory tells us, Clotilda baptized their first son, who shortly thereafter died. For Clovis this was a sign of the power of the traditional Frankish gods, but Clotilda remained undaunted. She baptized the second child as well, who in turn became deathly ill, but her prayers saved the child. Clovis remained devoted to his traditional gods, nonetheless, until the Battle of Tolbiac. According to Gregory, the battle was going poorly for Clovis and the king feared defeat. He vowed to the Christian god that should he win the battle he would then convert to the Christian faith. And, of course, he won the battle and, eventually, accepted baptism, along with 3,000 of his followers, at the hands of St. Remigius, the bishop of Rheims.

Both of these stories are probably little more than pious legend, but Clovis did convert to Catholic Christianity at some point between 496 and 508. It is no longer generally held that Clovis converted directly to Catholic Christianity from paganism but that he converted first to Arian Christianity or at least was sympathetic to the Arian confession. His conversion did not greatly influence Frankish belief, nor should Clovis's Christianity be understood in very sophisticated terms. Clovis's conversion remains, however, one of his great accomplishments, because he was the first German ruler to adopt Catholic Christianity rather than the Arian form. Thus his conversion solidified relationships with the Catholic hierarchy in his realm and provided his dynasty with an important source of political and religious support for generations to come.

In his last years, his power came to be recognized by the emperor in Constantinople, who may have granted Clovis an honorary consulship—perhaps as part

Medieval manuscript illumination of the baptism of Clovis, from the *Grandes Chroniques de France* (13th–15th century). (The British Library Board)

of diplomatic struggles with the Ostrogoth, Theodoric—and even in Theodoric's kingdom in Italy. Also in his last years, he focused more on domestic policy by holding a church council at Orléans and by issuing the Salic law. This codification of the law—putting it into organized, written form rather than simply expecting people to follow the unwritten, customary law—was an act of some sophistication, one that reveals the influence of Roman legal and administrative traditions on the king and suggests that Clovis was a more "civilized" ruler than the traditional understanding of him implies. Roman influence can also be seen in Clovis's adoption of several imperial administrative structures, including the system of tax collection.

At his death, the kingdom was divided among Clovis's sons, Theuderic I, Chlodomer, Childebert I, and Chlotar I. Traditionally, the partition of the realm has been seen as a consequence of the Frankish patrimonial view of kingship, in which the kingdom was understood as the king's personal possession to be shared among his family. The division, however, followed the established administrative boundaries of the Roman Empire, suggesting further Roman influence on Clovis. Whatever the precise meaning of the partition of the realm, it established a tradition that continued throughout Merovingian history.

See also: Alaric II; Clotilda, St.; Genevieve, St.; Merovingian Dynasty; Salic Law; Theodoric the Great

Bibliography

Bachrach, Bernard S. *Merovingian Military Organization, 481–751.* Minneapolis: University of Minnesota Press, 1972.

Daly, William M. "Clovis: How Barbaric, How Pagan?" *Speculum* 69 (1994): 619–64.

Geary, *Before France and Germany.* New York,: Oxford University Press USA, 1988.

Gregory of Tours. *History of the Franks.* Trans. Lewis Thorpe. Harmondsworth, UK: Penguin, 1974.

Wallace-Hadrill, J. M. *The Long-Haired Kings.* Toronto: Medieval Academy Reprints, 1982.

Wood, Ian. *The Merovingian Kingdoms, 450–751.* London: Longman, 1994.

Coins and Coinage

An important method of exchange, coins were minted by the Roman emperors and the various barbarian kings that succeeded them. Coins were minted in gold, silver, and bronze, and their values and uses varied from time to time and place to place. They were used as a medium of exchange between kingdoms, bishoprics, duchies, and counties. Control of the coinage was a great concern for the barbarian rulers of the early Middle Ages, as it had been of the emperors, but the successor kings had less success than their imperial predecessors. Later kings, however, did manage to assume greater control of the coinage and instituted important reforms to make their coins more stable and useful. The gold coin continued to be the standard, but its use was limited to large-scale exchange; it was not used for local commerce. The introduction of the silver coin by Carolingian monarchs and others facilitated local trade and contributed to, and reveals the existence of, economic growth.

The Romans, as in many other areas, established important precedents for the Germanic successor kingdoms in terms of coins and coinage. The Germanic successor kings learned much from the Romans about coinage, which underwent important reforms during the reigns of Diocletian (284–305) and Constantine. Although he met with little success in his efforts to institute a major reform of the coin because of a lack of precious metals, Diocletian did introduced new copper and silver coins. He also established a significant change in the production of coins by bringing a number of regional mints under imperial control. His reforms strengthened the coin and made its value, which had suffered a dramatic political and economic collapse in the generations before Diocletian's reign, more uniform across the empire.

Even more significant for the future of Roman, Byzantine, and German coinage was the reform of Constantine, who introduced a coin that became the standard for centuries to come. Building upon Diocletian's efforts, Constantine produced a new gold coin, the solidus, which retained its value and purity well into the Middle Ages; it was minted at 72 coins to the pound of gold. This coin was an important tool of the government, which used it to pay the soldiers' salaries, and archeological discoveries reveal that it was widely circulated. Another popular and commonly used coin was the *triens* or *tremissis,* which was based on the solidus. The triens valued at one-third of the solidus and was originally minted in gold and later minted in a mixture of gold and silver. The Romans also used coins of bronze and, for a time in the second half of the fourth century, silver. The bronze coins were plentiful, but often debased in value. Roman coinage is noted for its symbolism, consisting of striking images of the emperors as well as Christian symbols, which thus conveyed the central political and religious ideologies of the empire.

The various Germanic kings who assumed control over parts of the Western Empire inherited the tradition of coinage from the Romans, even though their coins lacked the stability and uniformity of the Roman precedents. These kings not only inherited the practice of coinage from the Romans, but until the sixth century they continued to mint coins in the name of the emperor, now resident in Constantinople. Among the various peoples that took control of the Western Empire, the Vandals and Ostrogoths most closely adhered to imperial traditions, minting in gold, silver, and bronze, and issuing their version of the *triens.* The Vandal kings who issued coins include Gunthamund (r. 484–496) and Hilderic (r. 523–530), who issued silver and bronze coins with their own names on the coins but using imperial models. The greatest of Vandal kings, Gaiseric (428–477), may also have issued gold coins.

The Ostrogoths of Italy minted coins that imitated imperial models most closely, and Theodoric issued some fine coins based on Roman models. Other Germanic rulers of Italy also minted coins in imitation of their imperial predecessors. Odovacar minted coins in silver and bronze, and the Lombards issued highly imitative coins until the reforms of Cuncipert (r. 680–688 coruler, 688–700) established a uniquely Lombard version. In Spain, Visigothic kings, beginning with Leovigild, minted coins, issuing a thin, gold version of the triens, and they came to include their own names and the name of the town in which the coin was struck. The most important Spanish mints until the early eighth-century Islamic invasion were in Córdoba, Seville, Tarragona, and Toledo. The coins themselves in the sixth and seventh centuries were of relatively high value and used primarily for large-scale trade and government purposes. They were generally not used in local commerce, which contributed to the development of a barter economy at the local level.

The history of coinage in the Anglo-Saxon kingdoms of England followed a different path than that in the early continental Germanic kingdoms. In Roman

Britain, coins were minted into the fourth century at London, but in the later fourth century the mint was closed down, and Britain depended upon mints in Gaul. In 395, the mints supplying Britain were closed, and no coins were imported for the next two centuries. By the seventh century, however, Merovingian coins began to appear in England and became the model for the *thrymas,* the Anglo-Saxon version of the triens. The solidus was also minted, but neither coin was minted in great number or had circulation beyond the kingdom of Kent. As the gold supply rapidly dwindled, Anglo-Saxon kings turned to a thick silver coin, the *sceattas,* which was very similar to Frankish issues on the continent. Further reforms of the coinage were undertaken in the eighth and ninth centuries by various Anglo-Saxon kings. Inspired by the Carolingian coins of Pippin III the Short, Offa of Mercia produced a silver coin that became the basis of the later English penny. Brilliantly decorated in an innovative style, the penny bore the image of Offa and his wife, Cynethryth, and other patterns not dependent on Roman models. Offa's penny, which came to be valued at 12 to the shilling and 240 to the pound, was copied by the rulers of the other Anglo-Saxon kingdoms as well as the Viking conquerors of the ninth and tenth centuries.

In the Frankish lands, Merovingian and Carolingian kings issued a number of coins and introduced important reforms of the coin. Merovingian kings, beginning with Clovis (r. 481–511), minted coins based on late Roman and Byzantine models. Clovis and his successors issued both the solidus and triens; the former was the standard coin, but the latter was more common. Merovingian coins were mainly minted in gold, but issues in silver and copper existed in small numbers. The Salic law, for example, lists fines that describe a silver coin, the denarius, 40 of which equaled a solidus. The coins were originally issued with the image of a current or previous emperor and the Byzantine symbol of victory, but by the mid-sixth century Merovingian kings had begun to impress their own names on their coins, rather than that of the emperor. Merovingian coinage increasingly diverged from late Roman imperial models after the mid-sixth century, and the coin itself was increasingly debased, in part because of the proliferation of mints and the lack of control over them exercised by the kings. By the end of the Merovingian dynasty in the eighth century, the gold coinage was virtually replaced by a silver coinage.

Frankish coinage underwent a major reform just as Frankish society did in the mid-eighth century, as a new dynasty, the Carolingian, took the throne. The first Carolingian king, Pippin the Short, reasserted royal control over the numerous mints in the kingdom, eliminated private mints, reduced the number of mints in the kingdom, and made the production of coinage solely a royal right. He also replaced the much debased gold coinage with a new silver coin, the *denarius,* and struck them with the king's name. Even greater and more influential reforms of the coinage were undertaken by Pippin's son, Charlemagne. In the 790s, Charlemagne reformed the coinage throughout the realm and increased the weight of the coin. The basic coin was the denarius, or penny; it was of pure silver and measured roughly three-quarters of an inch in diameter, with a weight of 1.7 grams. The coins were struck in some 50 mints in such towns as Aachen, Cologne, and Mainz and bore one of three designs: a stylized version of the king's name in Latin (Carolus), a temple, and, rarely, a portrait. Charlemagne also developed an accounting system for the coinage in which 12 pennies equaled a solidus or shilling and 20 shillings equaled a libra, or pound. His coin and accounting system remained the basis for European coinage until the 13th century.

Although it remained the standard, Charlemagne's coinage suffered somewhat during the ninth century. During the reign of Louis the Pious a small number of private mints appeared, and later Carolingian kings granted the right to mint to archbishops and other ecclesiastical leaders. And in Italy, even in Charlemagne's time, the coinage was not always consistent with Carolingian models. It was during the reign of Charlemagne's good friend, Pope Hadrian I, that the papacy began to strike coins. Papal coins followed Roman and Byzantine imperial models, but after Charlemagne's first visit to Rome included the Carolingian king or emperor's name along with the papal monogram. Papal and Carolingian symbols appeared together until 904, when only the name of the pope appeared on the coin.

See also: Anglo-Saxons; Carolingian Dynasty; Charlemagne; Constantine; Leovigild; Lombards; Merovingian Dynasty; Odovacar; Offa of Mercia; Ostrogoths; Pippin III, Called Pippin the Short; Vandals; Visigoths

Bibliography

Blackburn, Mark A. S., ed. *Anglo-Saxon Monetary History: Essays in Memory of Michael Dolley.* Leicester, UK: Leicester University Press, 1986.

Bursche, Aleksander. *Later Roman-Barbarian Contacts in Central Europe: Numismatic Evidence.* Berlin: Gebr. Mann Verlag, 1996.

Dolley, Reginald H. Michael ed. *Anglo-Saxon Coins: Studies Presented to F. M. Stenton.* London: Methuen, 1961.

Grierson, Philip, and Mark Blackburn. *Medieval European Coinage.* Vol. 1, *The Early Middle Ages (5th–10th Centuries).* Cambridge: Cambridge University Press, 1986.

Herrin, Judith. *The Formation of Christendom.* Princeton, NJ: Princeton University Press, 1989.

Morrison, Karl F., and Henry Grunthal. *Carolingian Coinage.* New York: American Numismatic Society, 1967.

Pirenne, Henri. *Mohammed and Charlemagne.* Trans. Bernard Miall. New York: Barnes and Noble, 1992.

Columba, St. (ca. 521–597)

An Irish monk and missionary, Columba was an important force in the evangelization of the Picts in Scotland and the Angles in northern England. He may also have had followers from among the southern Anglo-Saxons, and thus have introduced Christianity to them before the arrival of St. Augustine of Canterbury. Bede notes that Columba was "distinguished by his monastic habit and life," and that "whatever type of man he may have been, we know for certain that he left successors distinguished for their purity of life, their love of God, and their loyalty to the monastic rule" (147).

Columba was an Irish monk born in circa 521 to the Ui Neill line, one of the most powerful ruling families in Ireland. He was raised fully in the Irish Celtic Christian tradition, which emphasized the role of the monastery and its abbot in the institutional structure and religious life of the church. He was also influenced by the missionary tradition, as was his younger contemporary St. Columban, and undertook a pilgrimage to spread the faith. In Ireland, he founded a monastery at Durrow or, as Bede notes, Dearmach, or Field of Oaks. He is best known, however, for his missionary activity in Scotland, where he converted the Picts to Celtic Christianity. He left Ireland with several companions in 563 and converted the people by his personal example of sanctity, his preaching, and his performance of numerous miracles. As thanks for his good work, Columba was granted the island of Iona, where he founded a monastery that was known for its piety and learning. It was the royal Scottish monastery and may have been the site of the Northumbrian king Oswald's conversion. At the very least, Oswald sought aid from Iona to reform the monasteries in Northumbria.

The community at Iona was organized according to the Celtic, rather than the Roman Christian, model in which the abbot was the leading figure and all, including the bishop, were subject to his authority. And although he notes that Columba erred on the matter of Easter and other things, Bede clearly honored the piety and memory of St. Columba.

See also: Anglo-Saxons; Augustine of Canterbury, St.; Bede; Columban, St.; Monasticism

Bibliography

Adomnan. *Adomnan's Life of Columba.* Ed. and trans. Alan O. Anderson and Marjorie O. Anderson. London: T. Nelson, 1961.

Bede. *Ecclesiastical History of the English People with Bede's Letter to Egbert and Cuthbert's Letter on the Death of Bede.* Trans. Leo Sherley-Price. Harmondsworth, UK: Penguin, 1991.

Blair, Peter Hunter. *The World of Bede.* Cambridge: Cambridge University Press, 1971.

Laistner, Max L. W. *Thought and Letters in Western Europe, A.D. 500 to 900.* 2nd ed. Ithaca, NY: Cornell University Press, 1976.

Lawrence, C. H. *Medieval Monasticism: Forms of Religious Life in Western Europe in the Middle Ages.* 2nd ed. London: Longman, 1989.

Stenton, Frank M. *Anglo-Saxon England.* 3rd ed. Oxford: Clarendon, 1971.

Columban, St. (d. 615)

Irish monk and missionary of the late sixth and early seventh century who left an important legacy on the continent with his establishment of the monastery of Bobbio in Lombard Italy and of other monastic communities in the Merovingian kingdoms. His missionary activities were part of the Celtic tradition of *peregrinatio,* or pilgrimage, and foreshadowed the missionary activities on the continent of Anglo-Saxon monks like Boniface. A man of learning as well as piety, Columban is the earliest Irish monk whose writings survive in any quantity, and whose piety and learning had a profound impact on the cultural and religious life of Merovingian Gaul.

Although his date of birth is uncertain, Columban may have been born around 560 in Leinster in Ireland. He received some education while young and later entered the monastic community at Bangor, where he acquired an excellent education and developed a command of Latin. He was introduced to a wide range of Christian authors, but probably few if any classical writers. As was true of all monastery students, Columban studied the Bible extensively and was introduced to the works of the great Christian fathers, including St. Augustine of Hippo, Eusebius of Caesarea, and Jerome, among others. He also was introduced to the rigorous practices of Irish monasticism, which included extreme mortification of the flesh, such as standing in the icy waters of the North Sea, hour after hour, arms outstretched in a cross, in prayer to God. He learned, accordingly, that humbling of the self was the key to salvation. He also absorbed the Irish tradition of missionary work—leaving home and family behind to spread the gospel in strange lands.

It was this tradition that led him to the continent in 590 with a group of disciples. And upon his arrival in Merovingian Gaul he began the work of a missionary, reforming the flawed practices of the Frankish church and establishing important new religious institutions to improve religious life. He was granted territory by the Merovingian king of Burgundy, Guntram, and used this grant to establish a famous monastery at Luxeuil, as well as monasteries at Annegray and Fontaines. These houses, especially Luxeuil, soon attracted numerous converts, particularly from the Frankish aristocracy, because of the rigor of the monastic life there. Columban's disciples were not all men, however, but included numerous Frankish aristocratic women, because the Irish monk cultivated friendships with women and recognized their spiritual equality. As a result, Frankish noble men and women supported his monastic reforms and founded monasteries, including so-called double monasteries of monks and nuns. He introduced Celtic Christian religious practices, including the practice of private penance.

His community was not just a center of disciplined religious life but also a center of learning, focusing on the study of the Scriptures and the church fathers. He reinvigorated a tradition of learning in the Frankish kingdom that had lain dormant and encouraged his monks to read and improve their rudimentary Latin skills. Although it is uncertain whether he encouraged the study of classical authors, his own writings show clear influence of Virgil and other Roman literary greats. Columban himself left an important literary legacy with his monasteries. Perhaps most important was his monastic rule, the earliest Irish monastic rule known to us. The rule instructs the monks on matters of silence, food and drink, religious duties, and monastic perfection, and it is infused with Columban's ethical teaching and religious rigor. His literary corpus also includes sermons, poems, and letters, including one to Pope Gregory I, called the Great, in which he defends the Irish means of determining the date of Easter.

Although well received by many Frankish nobles, Columban was not so well received by the Frankish clergy. His indictment of the lax ways of the Frankish church and his efforts at reform alienated a number of native church leaders. He also ran afoul of Frankish religious leaders for his continued endorsement of Irish practices that differed from those of the Roman church, including the Irish way to tonsure and way of reckoning Easter. Perhaps even worse, Columban refused to recognize the authority of the bishops, because in the Irish tradition the authority of the abbot was supreme over monks, priests, and bishops. His strict discipline also caused difficulties with the powerful queen Brunhilde. He frequently criticized her way of life. In 611, he visited the court of Brunhilde and her grandson Theuderic and refused to bless Theuderic's children because, Columban said, their mothers were prostitutes. Enraged, Brunhilde chased Columban from the kingdom.

After his expulsion from the Frankish kingdom, Columban wandered the continent for a while before settling in the Lombard kingdom in Italy. He received a grant of land from the Lombard king and founded another very important monastery at Bobbio in 614. Like Luxeuil, Bobbio was a center of learning and religious life and attracted converts from the local population as well as other Irish missionaries. Although Columban died in the following year, 615, he left an important legacy in Italy and the Frankish kingdom as a result of his learning and dedication to the monastic life, and his work prefigured the activities of later Irish and Anglo-Saxon missionaries on the continent.

See also: Anglo-Saxons; Boniface, St.; Brunhilde; Gregory the Great; Lombards; Merovingian Dynasty; Monasticism

Bibliography

Bede. *Ecclesiastical History of the English People with Bede's Letter to Egbert and Cuthbert's Letter on the Death of Bede.* Trans. Leo Sherley-Price. Harmondsworth, UK: Penguin, 1991.

Blair, Peter Hunter. *The World of Bede.* Cambridge: Cambridge University Press, 1971.

Clarke, Howard B., and Mary Brennen, eds. *Columban and Merovingian Monasticism.* Oxford: British Archeological Reports, 1981.

Laistner, Max L. W. *Thought and Letters in Western Europe, A.D. 500 to 900.* 2nd ed. Ithaca, NY: Cornell University Press, 1976.

Lawrence, Clifford H. *Medieval Monasticism: Forms of Religious Life in Western Europe in the Middle Ages.* 2nd ed. London: Longman, 1989.

Riché, Pierre. *Education and Culture in the Barbarian West: From the Sixth through the Eighth Century.* Trans. John Contreni. Columbia: University of South Carolina Press, 1978.

Stenton, Frank M. *Anglo-Saxon England.* 3rd ed. Oxford: Clarendon, 1971.

Wood, Ian. *The Merovingian Kingdoms, 450–751.* London: Longman, 1994.

Comitatus

A Latin term meaning "retinue" or "war band," *comitatus* was coined by the Roman historian and moralist Tacitus (56–117) in the *Germania,* his account of early Germanic society. The *comitatus* was a social grouping in early Germanic society that existed from the first century to the migration period and into the early Middle Ages. It was primarily a military institution involving a warrior chieftain and his retainers. The group was bound together by mutual obligation between the war leader and his follower: warriors offered absolute personal loyalty and service to the warrior chief who in return extended special protection to his warriors. The *comitatus*, with its central principle of loyalty and service, was traditionally regarded as one of the building blocks of the later medieval institution of feudalism, a view that has been challenged in recent times.

The term *comitatus* was also used to describe imperial Roman institutions. In the first century CE it referred to the personal associates of the emperor. By the third century it came to mean the entire military and civilian entourage that travelled with the emperor. Under Constantine (r. 306–370), the term was used specifically for the military corps that surrounded the emperor. *Comitatus* or its variant *comitatenses* was also used from the fourth century, especially after the military reforms of Constantine, to identify the mobile force that was led by the emperor on military expeditions, distinguishing that force from the stationary frontier guard.

See also: Constantine; Leudes

Bibliography

Southern, Pat and Karen Ramsey Dixon. *The Late Roman Army*. New Haven, CT: Yale University Press, 1996.

Tacitus. *Agricola and the Germania*. Ed. James Rivers. Trans. Garrett Mattingly. London: Penguin Classics, 2010.

Wolfram, Hewig. *The Roman Empire and Its Gertmanic Peoples*. Trans. Thomas Dunlap. Berkeley: University of California Press, 1997.

Constantine (d. 337)

Roman emperor (r. 306–337) who, with Diocletian (r. 284–305), restored order to the Roman world and laid the foundation for the empire's success for centuries to come. His achievements were numerous, including the establishment of a new capital at Constantinople and reform of the coinage. He is important also for his military reforms and his introduction of many Germans into the Roman military, beginning a process known as the barbarization of the Roman army. He is particularly important for his conversion to Christianity and for becoming the first Christian emperor of the Roman Empire. Indeed, his activities as a Christian emperor had great consequences for the church and for the Germanic peoples who inherited the empire in the fifth and sixth centuries.

Constantine rose to power in the early fourth century in the wake of his father's death and the retirement of the leading Roman emperor, Diocletian, and his colleague Maximian. Diocletian had spent the preceding 20 years creating a delicate system of shared government that was designed to prevent the political and military collapse of the preceding half century. After he retired in 305, with the hope that his succession plan would succeed, he instead witnessed the rapid destruction of that system. It was in the civil wars that followed the retirement of Diocletian that Constantine rose to power.

One of the most critical moments in Constantine's struggle for power came in the year 312, when he fought his rival Maxentius, Maximian's son, for control of the Western Empire. The Battle of the Milvian Bridge, one of the bridges across the Tiber River to Rome, was won by Constantine, and it brought him possession of the ancient capital and the Western imperial title. His victory was preceded by a great vision that was the starting point, if not actual cause, of Constantine's conversion to Christianity. In his biography of the emperor, the bishop and church historian Eusebius of Caesarea reports that Constantine himself told the bishop of the miraculous events that preceded his victory. As Eusebius wrote, the emperor explained that, he saw the sign of the cross in the heavens bearing the inscription "In this sign conquer," and later that night Jesus visited Constantine in his dreams and confirmed the meaning of the vision. The emperor's victory confirmed the validity of the vision and led him to accept Christianity. And it was indeed in the following year that, with the Eastern emperor Galerius, Constantine issued the Edict of Milan, which legalized Christianity in the empire. He then ruled the empire with a colleague in the east, first Galerius and then Licinius, until 324, when he defeated Licinius in battle and reunited the empire. He founded a new capital, Constantinople (now Istanbul, Turkey) in 330 and ruled as sole emperor, although often with his sons as Caesars (subordinate co-emperors), until his death in 337.

Constantine's reign had significant consequences for the Germanic successor kingdoms that emerged in the wake of the collapse of the Western Empire, as well as for much of early medieval Europe in general. As the first Christian emperor he established an important model for numerous kings and emperors, including the

Head of Constantine the Great (d. 337), the first Christian Roman emperor, from a colossal statue, dating from about 325 to 337. (Allan T. Kohl/Art Images for College Teaching)

great Frankish rulers Clovis and Charlemagne, as well as for early medieval writers like Gregory of Tours. His relationships with the church set an important precedent for later rulers in both the barbarian kingdoms and the Byzantine Empire (as the Eastern Empire came to be called). On two occasions, both interestingly after military victories, one that brought him control over the western half of the empire and the other over the entire empire, Constantine convened church councils to decide major issues of the faith. The second of the councils, at Nicaea in 325, was the first ecumenical council of the church and included representatives from throughout the empire. Constantine presided over the council and participated in debate, and his presence set the model for the involvement of the emperor in the affairs of the church and asserted the right and responsibility of the emperor to convene church councils. The most important concern of the council involved the debate initiated by the presbyter Arius over one of the fundamental tenets of the Christian faith, the relationship between God the Father and God the Son. Rejecting the ideas of Arius, the council proclaimed the essential unity of God the Father and the Son, or as the Nicene Creed declares "We believe in our Lord Jesus Christ, the only Son of God, eternally begotten of the Father, God from God, Light from Light, true God from true God, begotten not made, one in being with the Father."

Constantine's involvement in the Council of Nicaea may also have led to the denunciation of the teachings of Arius and the declaration of Arianism as a heresy. Constantine, however, wavered in his support for orthodoxy and allowed the growth of Arianism in the empire. Consequently, the Germanic tribes living along the imperial frontier were evangelized by Arian Christians, and many of the tribes that converted to Christianity accepted the Arian version. Constantine's religious legacy, therefore, was mixed. He provided a positive model of Christian rulership for later kings and emperors, but also contributed to the conversion of many barbarians to Arian Christianity, a process that later caused difficulties for Arian Christian kings, like Theodoric the Great, who ruled over Catholic Christian subjects in the post-Roman world.

Constantine's other legacy to the late Roman and early medieval world was his recruitment of Germans into the Roman army. It is one of the paradoxes of Constantine's reign that he was criticized by contemporaries and has been remembered by historians for the so-called barbarization of the army when he strove to identify himself as a conqueror of the barbarians and the "Triumpher over the barbarian races" (*Triumfator, Debellator, Gentium barbararum*). But, indeed, he both waged war against the Germans and other peoples along the frontier and expanded the existing policy of promoting Germans to high-ranking military posts.

His wars against the Germans were intended to stabilize a frontier that had proved particularly porous during the crisis the empire faced in third century and to provide Constantine a glorious military record to parallel his successes in the civil wars. Toward those ends, he waged wars against a number of Germanic peoples along the frontiers. He fought border wars with the Alemanni along the Rhine River in an attempt to preserve the integrity of that frontier, which had been an important point of entry for the Germans in the third century. The emperor also faced the Visigoths along the Danubian border in the late 310s and early 320s. Here again he sought to restore the stability of the old frontier and even extend Roman power to the limits established by the emperor Trajan in the early second century. Constantine responded to Visigothic incursions into Roman territory with a series of battles that allowed the emperor to repel the invaders and extend Roman authority. Constantine's victories forced the Visigoths to surrender. The extent of his expansion beyond the Danube remains uncertain, however, and the Visigoths launched another attack in the mid-320s. Constantine sent his son against them, who successfully defeated them and extracted a treaty that required the Visigoths to defend the empire. Unfortunately for the empire, Constantine's successes were short lived, and by the end of the fourth century, at the latest, his settlements had broken down, and various Germanic tribes had crossed into the empire.

Despite actively fighting the barbarians, Constantine also enrolled many of them in the army. Although this policy was not new, Constantine included larger numbers of Germans than any of his predecessors, which caused serious problems for the empire in the following century. The army itself had increased in size to meet internal and external threats, and in Constantine's time may have numbered as many as 600,000 men, a number that included traditional Roman legionnaires as well as auxiliary soldiers (*auxiliae*). The auxiliaries were more numerous in Constantine's army than they had traditionally been, in fact more numerous than the legionnaires. It was this contingent that was made up mostly of Germans, so that the army was nearly half immigrant. And the Germans found places at all levels of the Roman army. The highest-ranking officers and Constantine's personal bodyguard were Germans. Constantine also reorganized the army, dividing it into a frontier force and a central strike force, and German soldiers were in both units. Constantine's use of Germans thus did contribute to what has been called the barbarization of the army, a process that, in some ways, undermined Rome's ability to defend itself against other Germanic invaders. On the other hand, it allowed the barbarians to identify themselves with the empire and its values and thus become Romanized.

See also: Arianism; Charlemagne; Clovis; Constantinople; Gregory of Tours; Theodoric the Great; Visigoths

Bibliography

Barnes, Timothy D. *Constantine and Eusebius*. Cambridge, MA: Harvard University Press, 1981.

Brown, Peter. *The World of Late Antiquity*, A.D. *150–750*. London: Thames and Hudson, 1971.

Burckhardt, Jacob. *The Age of Constantine the Great.* Trans. Moses Hadas. Berkeley: University of California Press, 1983.

Grant, Michael. *Constantine the Great: The Man and His Times.* New York: Charles Scribner's Sons, 1994.

Constantinople

The modern day Istanbul, Constantinople was the capital of the Roman and Byzantine Empire. Founded on the old town of Byzantium on the straits of the Bosphorus, Constantinople would become the greatest city of the Mediterranean throughout late antiquity and the early Middle Ages. The center of imperial government and administration, Constantinople was also the seat of the patriarch of Constantinople, the head of the Byzantine church. Constantinople also boasted some of the most influential architectural and artistic monuments of the early Middle Ages, most notably the magnificent church, the Hagia Sophia.

Responding to changing political and cultural needs and recognizing the growing importance and wealth of the eastern half of the empire, the Roman emperor Constantine founded his capital, the "New Rome," on May 11, 330. The emperor established the city on the site of Byzantium, which had been founded as a Greek colony in 658 BC, for a number of reasons. It was better placed strategically to exploit the wealth and population of the eastern Mediterranean and offered other important geographic advantages—it was situated on a hilly peninsula and surrounded on three sides by water. It was both easily defensible and open to trade between Europe and Asia. Perhaps of more significance for Constantine was that the new city would be free of the pagan associations of the old capital of Rome in Italy; Constantinople would be a great new Christian city and the capital of a Christian Roman empire.

Although its population was modest at first, Constantine's city had all the trappings of a major imperial center. The emperor expanded the size of the old city and built extensive new walls around the city. He also imported statuary from throughout the empire to decorate his capital and exploited the two harbors on the peninsula. Along with these features, Constantine built or completed many of the structures traditionally found in imperial cities. Constantinople included a number or broad elegant streets, such as the Via Egnatia, which moved from the southwest gate into the heart of the city and connected with other major thoroughfares. The greatest of these was the Mese, a colonnaded avenue lined with shops and statues. The city center, the Augusteum, was a vast open forum surrounded by the great public buildings, including the Senate House, a hippodrome, and public baths. It was also the site of the imperial of Great Palace, a complex including residence, courtyards, gardens, and rooms for public business.

Under Constantine and his successors Constantinople emerged as the religious heart of the eastern and later Byzantine Empire. In 381 it was declared the seat of a patriarch and, beginning with Constantine, was the location of a number of church councils. Constantine built the first churches in the city, including the Hagia Irene, and he and his son built the Hagia Sophia, which would come to symbolize the city.

Despite the growing threat of the barbarian invasions—the city would face challenges from Avars, Huns, and Visigoths—Constantinople grew in size and importance over the course of the later fourth and fifth centuries. The population surged dramatically during this period, reaching between 500,000 and a million by the end of the fifth century and beginning of the sixth, and forced the construction of new walls to accommodate the growing numbers and to provide further protection from the threats posed by the barbarians. In 418–419, the emperor Theodosius II erected 60-foot high triple-walled fortifications that endured throughout the history of the city and whose ruins remain today. Emperors throughout the fifth century built public monuments, including aqueducts and an elaborate water system to supply the numerous public fountains, baths, and private water needs of the city and its population. Other construction during the century included roads, three new forums, and a new residence, converted from a pagan temple, for the praetorian prefect. The public building was matched by the construction of private homes by the nobility that were lavishly decorated with marble and mosaics and gold and ivory, which kept the numerous artisans that inhabited the city very busy. Tenement housing of timber was built for the less wealthy that not only accommodated their growing numbers but also contributed significantly to the risk of fire.

The extensive construction reflected Constantinople's increasing prominence in the Mediterranean. By the year 500, it was clearly the largest and most important city and was the unrivaled leader of the empire, especially after the fall of the Western Empire in 476. Even before the loss of the west, Constantinople had surpassed the cities of the west in size and importance, a process that was accelerated after the defeat of Roman armies at Hadrianople in 378. It was also during this period that the status of Constantinople as a Christian capital was fully realized by further construction of religious monuments. In the late fourth century, Theodosius built a church dedicated to St. John the Baptist which housed the skull of the saint. Numerous other churches and urban monasteries, including the influential monastery of St. John Stoudios, were built in the fifth century. From Constantinople, the emperor and patriarch worked to maintain orthodoxy and restrict the growth of heresy.

By the opening decades of the sixth century, Constantinople had reached its peak but events in the century would profoundly alter the fates of the city. In 532 the capital endured a terrible riot against the emperor Justinian that nearly toppled the emperor and destroyed large sections of the city. The Nika Revolt exploded as rival factions in the city joined forces and sought to overthrow Justinian, who was on the verge of flight before ordering the brutal suppression of the rebellion and killing some 30,000 people. During the revolt, however, rebels had set fire to the palace of the city prefect and the imperial palace. The fires spread rapidly and led to widespread devastation throughout the city and the destruction of its most prized building, the church of Hagia Sophia. Having survived the Nika Revolt, Justinian and city administrators energetically undertook the reconstruction of the city, rebuilding the great public sites destroyed in the violence. Justinian oversaw the restoration of the imperial palace and the addition of a beautiful new church of Sts. Sergius and Bacchus at the palace complex. He also ordered the reconstruction of the Church of the Holy Apostle, but his most enduring and important work involved the rebuilding of the church of Hagia Sophia, which reemerged as the central church of the empire and testified to the Christian character of the empire and its capital. Commissioning Anthemius of Tralles and Isidore of Miletus, academic geometricians rather than master builders, Justinian intended to build something innovative and majestic. The church was unlike anything seen before. Consecrated in 537, the church was built with four massive piers joined by four arches and topped by a great dome 100 feet across. The interior was even more spectacular; the nave consisted of a vast open space with walls and columns of multicolored marble and adorned with mosaics of gold and silver and precious gems depicting scenes from the Bible. Justinian's construction projects revived the city and assured its continued existence as a place of beauty and majesty and as a center of religious and secular authority. A second disaster, however, would prove more devastating than the Nika Revolt. In 542 bubonic plague struck the empire, and Constantinople lost up to 40 percent of its population and only in the 10th century would the population again reach as much as 500,000.

The disasters of the sixth century had a lasting impact on Constantinople and contributed to its decline in the coming centuries, a decline worsened by a number of internal and external events over the next several centuries. In the early seventh century, the empire was involved in a major war with its old rival, the Persian Empire. In 626 the Persians laid siege to the city, forcing the emperor Heraklios to consider flight to Carthage. He stayed in Constantinople, however, and managed to turn to tide against the Persians and eventually seizing their capital at Ctesiphon. The Persian conflict did lasting damage as it contributed to disruptions of trade with Egypt, the source of the grain that fed the people of Constantinople. For a time, the population of the city plummeted to between 40,000 and 70,000 people. While the empire was busy with the Persians, the Balkans were overtaken first by the Avars and then by the Bulgars, who added to Constantinople's woes by laying siege in 626, 813, and 913. An even greater challenge arose in the seventh century in the deserts of Arabia as Muhammad spread the faith of Islam and Muslim armies marched into Byzantine territory and across North Africa. Muslim conquests further isolated Constantinople from its old trade contacts, and Muslim armies laid siege to Constantinople twice in the seventh century, in 674 and 678.

The most serious threat to the existence of the city and the entire empire, however, came during the Muslim siege of 717–718 and signaled the Muslim desire to make Constantinople their capital (a desire finally realized in 1453). The fear that the Muslim advance caused in the city is revealed by the widespread belief in the city that it was a sign of the apocalypse and that a Muslim victory would secure the rise of the Antichrist. Armies from Syria and Asia Minor joined with a fleet sailing up the Aegean in a three-pronged attack designed to overwhelm the city and its defenders. The emperor, Leo III the Isaurian, however, devised a successful plan of defense that was aided by one of the most severe winters the city ever faced and by the support of the church and the Virgin Mary, whose icon was paraded around the city walls during the height of the siege and felt to have secured the victory. Leo pursued a more mundane defense, organizing a flotilla of ships to attack the Muslim navy with "Greek fire," a substance that would burn even under water and was devastatingly effective weapon. He also coordinated military attacks against the Muslim with the Bulgars and ultimately saved the city, even if Muslim armies continued to harass the empire throughout the century. After turning the Muslims away, Leo restored and strengthened the walls of Constantinople to provide added security, but he also pursued a policy of iconoclasm that divided the city's population and contributed to the growing schism between Constantinople and Rome. Despite the difficulties brought on by the Iconoclastic controversy, Leo assured the survival of Constantinople as the head of a Christian empire for centuries to come and laid the foundation for a renaissance in Constantinople in the ninth and tenth centuries.

See also: Avars, Constantine; Hadrianople, Battle of; Huns; Justinian; Leo III, the Isaurian; Visigoths

Bibliography

Browning, Robert. *Justinian and Theodora*. London: Thames and Hudson, 1987.

Freely, John, and Ahmet S. Cakmak. *Byzantine Monuments of Constantinople*. Cambridge: Cambridge University Press, 2009.

Harris, Jonathan. *Constantinople: Capital of Byzantium*. Oxford: Continuum Books, 2007.

Procopius. *Procopius, Vol. 7: On Buildings*. Trans. H. B. Dewing and Glanville Downey. Cambridge, MA: Loeb Classical Library, 1940.

Sherrard, Philip. *Constantinople: Iconography of a Sacred City*. Oxford: Oxford University Press, 1965.

Trumbull, Stephen. *The Walls of Constantinople A.D. 324–1453*. Oxford: Osprey Publishing, 2004.

Corpus Iuris Civilis

The most exhaustive codification of Roman law, the *Corpus Iuris Civilis* (Body of Civil Law) was published by the Byantine emperor Justinian beginning in 529 and would have a lasting impact on the development of medieval and even modern European law. The result of several years of intense work, the *Corpus* was composed in Latin and published in three main groups—Code of Justinian, the Digest or Pandects, and the Institutes—and was intended to bind the empire together. A fourth work, the Novels, was issued later in Greek by Justinian and included the new laws of the emperor. Along with the great church of Constantinople, the Hagia Sophia, the *Corpus Iuris Civilis* remains Justinian's most enduring accomplishment.

Upon assuming the office of sole emperor in 527, Justinian was faced with a number of challenges concerning the unity and integrity of the empire, the place of the emperor over his subjects, and relationships between the emperor and the church. Justinian realized that one of the greatest achievements of the Roman and Byzantine empires was the law, but he also understood that the law needed serious reform if it were to maintain its place in binding the empire together. Although Roman law had undergone previous codification, most notably the Theodosian Code of the early fifth century, it was in significant disrepair. Even the Theodosian Code proved inadequate by the age of Justinian, in many places the code was out of date and was little more than a compilation of Roman laws. Beyond that, Romans had issued laws for a Republic and an Empire and for a society that was once pagan and then Christian, and as a consequence the legal code was riddled with contradictory and antiquated laws. Justinian understood that more needed to be done to bring the law up to date and to make it applicable to the needs of his day. He turned to the government official and scholar Tribonian to head a committee of lawyers and scholars whose responsibility would be to issue a new and up-to-date legal code for the Empire. The emperor issued a decree on February 13, 528 that initiated the process and by 534 the main elements of the *Corpus* had been published. In the eighth century, an abridgement of the Code in Greek was published so that it could be understood by a Byzantine population that no longer knew Latin, and the emperor Leo IV (r. 886–912) issued the *Basilica,* the translation into Greek of the entire *Corpus Iuris*.

Work on the *Corpus Iuris Civilis* began in 528 and continued until 534 when the final work of the codification of the law was completed. The first part of the *Corpus Iuris Civilis,* the Code of Justinian, was published on April 8, 529. Divided into 12 books, the Code drew on the Theodosian Code as well as private legal codification and contained the constitutions of the Roman emperors from Hadrian (r. 117–138) to Justinian himself. The Code, which had the force of law from the will of Justinian, became the official law of the empire and no imperial law not included in the Code could be cited in the courts. New laws from Justinian necessitated further work, and a second edition of the Code was published in 534. The second part to be published, the Digest or Pandects, was the largest of the three and was divided into 50 books. Begun in 530 and published in 534 the Digest was a work of jurisprudence and contained the commentaries of the great Roman legal scholars from the second to the fourth centuries. It was designed to eliminate obsolete and contradictory explanation of the law and provided an orderly and systematic approach to Roman law. As with the Code, the Digest was the authoritative commentary on the law and no new commentaries were permitted. Along with the Code and Digest Tribonian and his committee issued a shorter work, the Institutes, which was an introductory textbook for students of the law. Based largely on the work of the second-century legal scholar Gaius, the Institutes was divided into four books and formally established as law in 533. The main work of the *Corpus Iuris* was supplemented by a number of new laws, the Novels, that Justinian issued mainly in Greek until his death in 565 but most of which were issued between 535 and 539. A collection of 159 of these new laws and nine constitutions of his successors was compiled in 580.

The *Corpus Iuris Civilis* with its vast collection of law and legal principle would have a lasting influence on Byzantine and later medieval and early modern European laws. The *Corpus* provided the essential text of the law as well as an approach to the scientific study of the law for lawyers and government administrators for centuries to come. Throughout Justinian's great codification, important and influential guidelines were established. The *Corpus* preserved the basic division in the Roman tradition between public and private law. Laws for the transfer of property were reformed, and a new definition of the family and its internal relationships and relationship with society was instituted. The *Corpus* asserted the guiding theory of imperial government, which stated that all power is derived from God and is entrusted by God to the emperor, whose laws, in turn, are sacred. In a famous passage, the *Corpus* declared that whatever concerns the prince has the force of law. Paradoxically, the codification also defined the source of authority as the people, with all power deriving from the consent of the governed. The *Corpus* preserved the distinction between the sacred and secular but further defined the relationships between the emperor and the church and asserted the Christian nature of the empire.

See also: Justinian

Bibliography

Browning, Robert. *Justinian and Theodora*. London: Thames and Hudson, 1987.

The Digest of Justinian. Ed. Alan Watson. Philadelphia: University of Pennsylvania Press, 1997.

Honoré, Tony. *Justinian's Digest: Character and Compilation*. Oxford: Oxford University Press, 2010.

Justinian's Institutes. Trans. Peter Birks and Grant Mcleod. Ithaca, NY: Cornell University Press, 1987.

Metzger, Ernest, ed. *A Companion to Justinian's Institutes*. Ithaca, NY: Cornell University Press, 1999.

Radding, Charles, and Antonio Ciaralli. *The Corpus Iuris Civilis in the Middle Ages*. Brill: Leiden, 2006.

D

Dagobert (608–638/639)

The son of Chlotar II and grandson of Fredegund, Dagobert was the last great and effective king of the Merovingian dynasty. Indeed, under Dagobert, the dynasty reached its high point, only to begin a gradual decline in the generation after his death. Despite the dynasty's misfortunes after his death, under Dagobert the kingdom enjoyed internal peace and prosperity and success against foreign foes. Like his father, Dagobert was active in the administration of law and may have promulgated two law codes for the Franks. He also, like Chlotar, maintained good relations with the church and its missionaries and also founded the important monastery of St. Denis in Paris, which came to serve as a royal tomb and the burial place of Dagobert himself.

Dagobert benefited from the successes of his father, Chlotar II, who had restored the unity and peace of the kingdom after years of civil strife involving Brunhilde and Fredegund. Dagobert also played an important role in his father's efforts to preserve the authority of the dynasty over the entire kingdom. In 622, Dagobert was made subking of Austrasia, possibly as a concession to the local aristocracy and certainly at least to bind the Austrasian nobility closer to the ruling dynasty. Although it is slim, the evidence that exists suggests that Dagobert ruled the region well during his father's lifetime and was aided and greatly influenced by Chlotar's ally and mayor of the palace, Pippin of Landen, the ancestor of the Carolingian dynasty. At his father's death in 629, Dagobert assumed control of the entire kingdom. According to Fredegar, this was a poor time in Dagobert's reign, when the king sank into debauchery and avarice, exploiting particularly the resources of the church. It was Pippin, according to Fredegar, who reprimanded the king and turned him back on the proper path. Indeed, Pippin was one of Dagobert's most important and trusted advisors and joined the king when he moved his capital from Metz in Austrasia to Paris in Neustria. Dagobert moved to establish himself as the ruler of Neustria, and thus of the entire realm as well as Austrasia, which he had ruled since 622. Although he managed to secure his place in his father's kingdom in Neustria, Dagobert's move unsettled the nobility in Austrasia and forced Dagobert to address the concerns of the nobility, including perhaps the regionalism that may have motivated the nobles. As his father had done, Dagobert appointed his five- or six-year-old son Sigebert III (d. 656) as subking of Austrasia in 634. He also appointed his younger brother Charibert (d. 632) subking in Aquitaine, a very independent region that the Merovingians had yet to bring completely under their authority. Although he may have been making concessions to regionalism, Dagobert may also have intended the creation of subkings as a means to bind the kingdom more securely under his authority.

Whatever his goal, Dagobert seems to have succeeded in binding the kingdom more fully together under his authority; he was also, like his father before him, an active lawgiver. The king took tours throughout his kingdom—itinerancy was a key to the success of most early medieval rulers—dispensing justice. Fredegar notes that Dagobert "struck terror" into the hearts of the people of Burgundy when he toured that region in the late 620s. He also toured Austrasia with similar effect in 630. He resolved legal disputes on these tours and dispensed high justice from the royal court, and the proceedings were guided by specific ritual and written texts. After 631, however, it seems that Dagobert ceased taking judicial tours and dispensed justice from his capital in Paris, a testimony to the sophistication of Merovingian legal practices and the peace and order of Dagobert's reign. Moreover, the king may also have codified Frankish legal codes. His name is associated with several legal codes of the early seventh century, including the *Lex Ribuaria* (Law of the Ripuarian Franks) for the Austrasian kingdom. He also may have been involved in the codification of the laws of the Alemanni and the Bavarians. Like his father before him, Dagobert's activities as a lawgiver were intended to enhance his stature as king and to set him apart from the nobility, which needed the king all the more because he dispensed justice.

Dagobert also built upon his father's legacy of good relations with the church, an association important as a counterbalance to potential trouble from the nobility and as a support for his increasingly elevated conception of kingship. Like Chlotar, Dagobert consulted with the bishops and accepted their advice. He also, of course, oversaw the appointment of bishops and took steps to ensure the good quality of his appointments. The king promoted the activities of missionaries and, in general, oversaw the administration and well-being of the church in his kingdom. His most important relationship, however, was with the monasteries of his kingdom, especially the monastery of St. Denis near Paris. Dagobert developed a special relationship with the community, which he founded in 624, and he often made lavish donations to it. According to a late, and probably unreliable tradition, Dagobert felt especially indebted to St. Denis because the saint had protected him from Chlotar's anger during a quarrel Dagobert and his father had. According to Fredegar, Dagobert embellished the church at the monastery with gold and many precious stones. The king also made numerous grants of land to the monastery and in a charter granted the abbey the right to hold a fair on the saint's feast day, October 5. The fair brought great economic benefit to the monastery and attracted increasingly larger crowds as the saint's popularity grew. St. Denis gradually became the patron of the dynasty, and Dagobert and many of his descendants were buried at the monastery.

At his death in 638/639, Dagobert was succeeded by his sons Sigebert III (d. 656), who had ruled as subking in Austrasia since 632, and Clovis II (d. 657). They inherited a kingdom that was at peace and enjoyed much prosperity, as well as close relations between the king and a very powerful church. The office of king had been greatly enhanced, and law and administration had been improved by Dagobert and Chlotar before him. Both Sigebert and Clovis enjoyed some success, and Clovis and his wife Balthild further strengthened ties with the church. But the growing power and ambition of the aristocracy was a bad omen, and signs of trouble began to emerge. Within a few generations of Dagobert's death, the dynasty began its irrevocable decline, and the so-called do-nothing kings (*rois fainéants*) began to assume the throne. Dagobert's reign, however, was the high point of the history of the Merovingian dynasty, and Dagobert was one of the greatest kings of the line.

See also: Austrasia; Balthild, St.; Brunhilde; Carolingian Dynasty; Chlotar II; Fredegund; Merovingian Dynasty; Neustria; Pippin I, Called Pippin of Landen; *Rois Fainéants*; Saint-Denis, Abbey of

Bibliography

Bachrach, Bernard S. *Merovingian Military Organization, 481–751.* Minneapolis: University of Minnesota Press, 1972.

Bachrach, Bernard S., trans. *Liber historiae Francorum.* Lawrence, KS: Coronado, 1973.

Fouracre, Paul, and Richard A. Gerberding. *Late Merovingian France: History and Hagiography, 640–720.* Manchester, UK: University of Manchester Press, 1996.

Geary, Patrick. *Before France and Germany: The Creation and Transformation of the Merovingian World.* Oxford: Oxford University Press, 1988.

James, Edward. *The Franks.* Oxford: Blackwell, 1991.

Lasko, Peter. *The Kingdom of the Franks: North-West Europe before Charlemagne.* New York: McGraw Hill, 1971.

Wallace-Hadrill, J. M. *The Long-Haired Kings.* Toronto: Toronto University Press, 1982.

Wallace-Hadrill, J. M. *The Frankish Church.* Oxford: Clarendon, 1983.

Wallace-Hadrill, J. M., ed. and trans. *The Fourth Book of the Chronicle of Fredegar with Its Continuations.* London: Nelson, 1960.

Wemple, Suzanne. *Women in Frankish Society: Marriage and the Cloister, 500 to 900.* Philadelphia: University of Pennsylvania Press, 1985.

Wood, Ian. *The Merovingian Kingdoms, 450–751.* London: Longman, 1994.

Desiderius (eighth century)

Successor of Aistulf and king from 757 to 774, Desiderius was the last of the kings of the Lombards. His fate was linked with the rise of the Carolingian dynasty and the complex diplomatic relations between the Carolingians, Lombards, and popes in Rome. He pursued the traditional, aggressive policy of Lombard kings and attempted, with some success, to unify Italy under Lombard rule. His threatening posture toward Rome and the papal territories led to his conflict with the popes, who sought aid from the Carolingian dynasty. Pippin the Short intervened diplomatically on the pope's behalf, and his son Charlemagne invaded in defense of the papacy, absorbed the kingdom of the Lombards into the growing Carolingian Empire, and deposed Desiderius as king and exiled him to a Frankish monastery.

Although he eventually suffered defeat as a result of his bad relations with Rome, Desiderius began his reign as king in the good graces of Rome. His election as king of the Lombards on March 3 or 4, 757, in fact, was supported by the pope, Stephen II (r. 752–757). The succession to Aistulf was a complicated affair: Desiderius, a former official in Aistulf's government and duke of Tuscany, appears to have been a likely candidate, but he faced strong opposition from another Lombard noble, Ratchis. Desiderius, however, appealed to the pope for support in his efforts to obtain the crown and met with representatives of the pope. In exchange for promises to return papal cities seized by Aistulf, Desiderius received military backing from the pope. Stephen also secured for Desiderius the support of the Carolingian king Pippin, who had already invaded Italy twice in the 750s to punish Aistulf for harassing the pope. This important backing from Rome secured the election of Desiderius and the retirement of Ratchis.

The reign of the new king opened with the promise of good relations between Rome and the Lombards. In 758, Desiderius visited Rome as a pilgrim and prayed at the tomb of St. Peter, indicating his devotion to the Apostle and to his successor, the pope. But matters changed quickly for the pope, now Paul (r. 757–767), as Desiderius returned to the aggressive and expansive policy of his predecessors. The new king imposed his will on the southern Lombard duchies of Benevento and Spoleto. Even worse, Desiderius refused to return the papal cities as he had promised, despite repeated requests from the pope, and he even seized new territory near Rome. He also negotiated with representatives of the Byzantine emperor in southern Italy, entering into an arrangement that would have seen the further erosion of papal authority in Italy and the further loss of papal territory. In response, Pope Paul sent numerous letters over the next several years to King Pippin for aid against Desiderius. Pippin was no longer interested in military involvement in Italy and was content to intervene diplomatically. In 760, Pippin's envoys convinced Desiderius to agree to return cities to the pope, but the Lombard king still did not follow through on the agreement, and the situation worsened for the pope.

During the reigns of Paul and his successor Stephen III (r. 767–772), the situation deteriorated for Rome, as Desiderius increased his power throughout Italy and benefited from a tumultuous papal election in 767. Moreover, Desiderius benefited from the turmoil in the Carolingian kingdom at the death of Pippin and succession of his sons Carloman and Charlemagne in 768. Charlemagne faced a revolt in part of his kingdom and received little help from his brother, and the two were on the point of civil war after Charlemagne suppressed the revolt. The tensions between the two brothers made intervention in Italy unlikely, but Desiderius, now at the height of his power, benefited further by the diplomatic initiative of Pippin's widow, Bertrada. In an attempt to resolve the crisis between her sons and improve their international standing, Bertrada negotiated a marriage alliance between her dynasty and the Lombard. Desiderata, the daughter of Desiderius, was married to Bertrada's son Charlemagne. The alliance bound the Carolingians with the Lombards and the powerful duke of Bavaria, Tassilo, who was married to another daughter of Desiderius. Clearly a coup for Desiderius, whose greatest rival, the pope, lost his most important ally, the king of the Franks. Although forced by the agreement to return territory to the pope, Desiderius surely gained more than he lost in the agreement. Indeed, the letters of complaint sent by the pope to the Carolingians reveal the great dissatisfaction Rome felt over the treaty.

Desiderius's triumph did not last long, as the alliance collapsed and an aggressive Carolingian king took sole control of the throne. In 771, Carloman died and his widow and sons fled to the Lombard capital of Pavia. Desiderius pressured the pope, now Hadrian (772–795) to recognize Carloman's heirs as king, but the pope felt less threatened by Desiderius because of other changes in the Carolingian kingdom. Charlemagne, now free of the threat of his brother, repudiated the marriage alliance and expressed greater support for the pope than even his father had. The new pope, mindful that Desiderius had not fulfilled his side of the agreement with Bertrada, was willing to strike at the king's allies in the papal administration and establish a stronger alliance with Charlemagne. Desiderius, with Carloman's sons at his side, marched on Rome, threatening a siege and demanding the coronation of the Carolingian princes. Hadrian threatened Desiderius with excommunication, which stopped his advance, and wrote to Charlemagne for aid.

The new king first attempted to negotiate a settlement with Desiderius, but the Lombard's refusal forced Charlemagne to invade in 773. His armies quickly broke the Lombard forces, which preferred flight to battle in the face of the powerful Carolingian army. Desiderius's kingdom quickly collapsed, as the southern duchies detached themselves from his authority and surrendered to the pope. Charlemagne laid siege to the capital of Pavia, where Desiderius had taken up residence, and captured the city in six months. The Carolingian king also took the city of Verona, Lombard Italy's second most important city, where Desiderius's son, Adelchis, had gone with Carloman's family. The invasion of Italy brought Carloman's family and Desiderius into Charlemagne's control. We hear little of either after 774. Desiderius was sent into exile in a monastery in Charlemagne's kingdom. Despite his many talents and early success, Desiderius overplayed his hand in the struggle with Charlemagne, who could not allow Desiderius to ensure the coronation of his nephews or to harass the pope. Desiderius's ambition brought about the end of the independent Lombard kingdom and the coronation of Charlemagne as king of the Lombards in 774.

See also: Aistulf; Bertrada; Carloman, King of the Franks; Carolingian Dynasty; Charlemagne; Lombards; Pippin III, Called Pippin the Short; Rome; Tassilo

Bibliography

Christie, Neil. *The Lombards: The Ancient Langobards.* Oxford: Blackwell, 1998.

Davis, Raymond, trans. *The Lives of the Eighth-Century Popes* (Liber Pontificalis): *The Ancient Biographies of Nine Popes from* A.D. *715 to* A.D. *817.* Liverpool, UK: Liverpool University Press, 1992.

Einhard and Notker the Stammerer. *Two Lives of Charlemagne.* Trans. Lewis Thorpe. Harmondsworth, UK: Penguin, 1981.

Llewellyn, Peter. *Rome in the Dark Ages.* New York: Barnes and Noble, 1993.

Noble, Thomas F. X. *The Republic of St. Peter: The Birth of the Papal State, 680–825.* Philadelphia: University of Pennsylvania Press, 1984.

Riché, Pierre. *The Carolingians: A Family Who Forged Europe.* Trans. Michael Idomir Allen. Philadelphia: University of Pennsylvania Press, 1993.

Scholz, Bernhard Walter, trans. *Carolingian Chronicles: Royal Frankish Annals and Nithard's History.* Ann Arbor: University of Michigan Press, 1972.

Dhuoda (c. 803–845)

Carolingian noble and wife of the powerful Bernard of Septimania, Dhuoda is best known for the *Liber manualis* (Handbook), which she wrote for her son William. The text is the only known work by a female Carolingian author and is an example of the mirror for princes, a literary genre defining the proper duties of the nobility. The *Liber* calls on William to do his duty to God and his father and country. It also reveals much about the character and desires of Dhuoda, as well as her deep longing for her son, who had been separated from her by her husband. Long discounted for its unconventional Latin, Dhuoda's work is now generally recognized for its emotional and spiritual content and is a held to be a great contribution to medieval women's literature.

Little is known of Dhuoda's life, other than what she reveals in the *Liber,* but other things can be discerned about her life from her husband's career. She was born, probably in 803, into the higher nobility, but the exact location is uncertain. It is generally assumed that she was born in the northern part of the Carolingian Empire, an area where her name is common. It is possible, however, that she was born in the south, where her husband later sent her to oversee his estates, something he would have been more likely to do if she was from the south and had relatives in the region, which would have increased her chances for success in administering her husband's possessions. She married Bernard, as she tells us, on June 29, 824, at the imperial palace at Aachen. Her husband was a high-ranking noble who was closely related to the Carolingian family and who was an important ally of the emperor Louis the Pious. Bernard was sent to oversee the Spanish March, a border region between Islamic Spain and Christian Europe. Dhuoda accompanied her husband on his travels until the birth of their first son, William, on November 29, 826. She was then sent to Uzès, where she remained apart from her husband and her son for most of the rest of their married life.

Dhuoda's stay in Uzès was lonely and troubled. Bernard was generally away, and was the focus of the rumor that he was involved in an affair with the emperor's wife, Judith. Although the rumor remained unsubstantiated, Dhuoda surely heard of it and was surely bothered by it. She was surely also discomfited by the civil wars of the 830s between the emperor and his sons, which also involved her husband. He did, however, survive the contest and rumors of the 820s and 830s, and he visited her in Uzès shortly after the death of Louis the Pious in 840. The visit was long enough to bring about the birth of their second child, Bernard, on March 22, 841. Her husband's participation on the losing side in the Battle of Fontenoy on June 25, 841, brought further heartbreak for Dhuoda. Her son William was sent to Charles the Bald as a hostage to secure Bernard's loyalty after the battle. Shortly thereafter, her other son, not yet baptized, was sent to her husband's side in Aquitaine.

In late 841, without either of her two beloved sons with her and abandoned by her husband yet again, Dhuoda began work on her *Liber,* which she completed on February 2, 843. She may have faced even more unhappiness after completion of the book. Her husband was executed by Charles the Bald for treason in 844, and her son William, joining with the rebels to avenge his father, was captured and executed in 849. It is likely that Dhuoda witnessed her husband's execution, but less likely that she lived to see her son's death, since she probably died within a year or so of the completion of the book for William. She mentions her illnesses throughout the book, and she left detailed information for her funeral, including the epitaph for her tomb.

Dhuoda's surviving son, Bernard, may have been an influential figure in the history of later Aquitaine as well as the father of the founder of the great monastery of Cluny. Although she had a most illustrious descendant, Dhuoda's own claim to fame is her *Liber manualis,* translated as *Handbook for William,* a work of 73 chapters plus introduction, prologue, and epitaph (Thiébaux 1994, 161–162). The work was intended as a guidebook for William at the royal court of Charles the Bald. It was clearly influenced in style and content by the Bible, the works of the church fathers, various Christian writers and poets (e.g., Venantius Fortunatus and Isidore of Seville), Roman grammarians, and the Roman poet Ovid. It is a deeply personal work that reveals Dhuoda's loneliness and longing and love for her son; the love is shown in the poem in the prologue, "Dhuoda greets her beloved son William. Read." She hoped that her book would be one that William turned to often for advice and as a means to maintain a connection with his mother. Dhuoda outlined his duties as a prince, particularly his obligations to his lord. In a possible reference to the turmoil of the 830s, she tells her son not to show disloyalty to his lord. She also reminded him of his spiritual responsibilities and encouraged him to love God, pray, and accept the gifts of the Holy Spirit. For Dhuoda her son's worldly and spiritual duties were closely intertwined. Indeed, she saw a heavenly reward for her son if he fulfilled his duties as a virtuous prince in this world. She also stressed family obligations. William should honor and obey his father and look after his younger brother. Dhuoda also asks her son to pray for her and to honor the financial obligations she has incurred as a result of maintaining her husband's estates. With this most human and humble request, Dhuoda closes her book, and, despite the hardships of her life, seems at peace with the world and ready to find her heavenly reward.

See also: Bernard Hairyfeet; Bernard of Septimania; Carolingian Dynasty; Charles the Bald; Fontenoy, Battle of; Isidore of Seville; Judith; Louis the Pious

Bibliography

Dhuoda. *Handbook for William: A Carolingian Woman's Counsel for Her Son.* Ed. and trans. Carol Neel. Washington, DC: Catholic University of America Press, 1999.

Dronke, Peter. *Women Writers of the Middle Ages: A Critical Study of Texts from Perpetua (d. 203) to Marguerite Porete (d. 1310).* Cambridge: Cambridge University Press, 1984.

Nelson, Janet. *Charles the Bald.* London: Longman, 1992.

Riché, Pierre. *The Carolingians: A Family Who Forged Europe.* Trans. Michael Idomir Allen. Philadelphia: University of Pennsylvania Press, 1993.

Scholz, Bernhard Walter, trans. *Carolingian Chronicles: Royal Frankish Annals and Nithard's History.* Ann Arbor: University of Michigan Press, 1972.

Thiébaux, Marcelle, ed. and trans. *The Writings of Medieval Women: An Anthology.* 2nd ed. New York: Garland, 1994.

Wemple, Suzanne. *Women in Frankish Society: Marriage and the Cloister, 500 to 900.* Philadelphia: University of Pennsylvania Press, 1981.

Diet and Nutrition

The early medieval diet, particularly for the peasant class, was a notoriously poor one. Many of the fruits and vegetables popular in the modern world were unknown in the early Middle Ages, and some vegetables, such as celery, were known only for medicinal purposes. The majority of the calories in the early medieval diet were made up of carbohydrates, but there were occasions when meat, mostly chicken or pork, was eaten. The diet of the wealthy and powerful, of course, was much better than that of the peasants, who lived barely above the subsistence level.

The evidence for the diet can be found in a variety of written sources, but unfortunately not from any contemporary cookbooks, examples of which are known from ancient Roman and late medieval times. One valuable source for diet is the Rule of Benedict, which, although valuable only for understanding the restricted diet of monks, does provide examples of the things found on early medieval dinner tables. Benedict, who was more sympathetic to human weakness than some monastic regulators, allowed the monks two meals a day; at the "sixth and ninth hour" the monks were offered two cooked dishes. And, when available, a third dish was allowed that contained apples or vegetables. The monks could have a one-pound loaf of bread each day, but were not to eat "the flesh of quadrupeds" unless they were sick or weak. Benedict also allowed his monks roughly 16 ounces of wine each day or twice that quantity of beer, but also cautioned against drinking too much. Other monastic diets could be more or less stringent than that in St. Benedict's rule. Some monks more ascetic than Benedict ate only gruel and vegetables. One saint ate only mushrooms, and the Carolingian monk Walafrid Strabo recommended a diet that included bread, fish, and wine. Other monasteries sometimes offered more extravagant fare, including quantities of chicken, geese, and cakes.

More extravagant than anything the monks could contemplate were the menus of early medieval kings and nobles. Unlike the monks or the peasants, meat was the mainstay of the diet of kings and aristocrats. In a passage from his life of Charlemagne, Einhard reveals that the preferred means of preparation was roasting, because the great emperor refused to follow doctor's orders to eat boiled meat. Pork, fresh, smoked, or salted, was a popular meat, and beef and mutton were also part of the nobility's diet. Meats were prepared in a variety of ways, including in the form of bacon and sausages. The diet was further supplemented by meat brought in from the hunt, and included rabbit, which was also a domestic food animal. The dishes of the wealthy were highly seasoned with pepper, cumin, cloves, cinnamon, and other spices. Honey was also used for both food and drink, and both beer and wine were popular at the tables of the powerful. The *Capitulare de Villis* of the early ninth century, which regulated management of the royal estates, provides further information on the diet of the Carolingian nobility. Charlemagne ordered that his various estates should be stocked with a large quantity of chickens and geese, which would provide a ready supply of food as well as large quantities of eggs. Cheese, butter, a variety of fruits and vegetables, and fish were also found at the tables of the nobility, and fish was particularly important for seasons of religious fasting. Finally, bread was an important source of calories even for kings and nobles, but it was of the highest quality white bread rather than the coarser grains the peasantry often ate.

The diet of the peasants was clearly the least varied of all the diets of the early Middle Ages, and the diet most dependent on grains as a source of calories. The poor lived on a bare subsistence diet, and a significant portion of their income went to pay for food and drink. The diet of the peasants consisted of porridge or bread, the latter becoming more common as the use of mills increased in the early Middle Ages, made from barley, buckwheat, oats, rye, and several types of wheat. Another important source of calories was beer, the production of which underwent improvement in the Carolingian period with the introduction of hops, which acted as a preservative. Moreover, the beer or ale consumed in this period was quite thick, almost the consistency of soup and practically a meal itself. The diet was supplemented by vegetables that were grown in small gardens by the peasants' homes. Peasants often grew onions, leeks, and cabbages in these gardens. Peas and beans, important sources of protein, were also found in the peasants' gardens; they were grown more extensively after the ninth century as new agricultural techniques were introduced. These legumes improved the nutrition and health of the peasants greatly. The peasants also derived protein from various meats, although not to the same extent as the nobility did. Peasants had access to fish in some local ponds and rivers, and probably also ate some chicken and pork. Indeed, one of the most common images of early peasant life is that of the slaughtering of a pig in midwinter. Thus although it was not without some variety, the peasant's diet was a simple fare, generally involving a simple meal of bread, beer, and stewed vegetables.

See also: Agriculture; Animals; Benedict of Nursia, St.; *Capitulare de Villis*; Carolingian Dynasty; Charlemagne; Einhard

Bibliography

Duby, Georges. *Rural Economy and Country Life in the Medieval West.* Trans. Cynthia Postan. Columbia: University of South Carolina Press, 1968.

Riché, Pierre. *Daily Life in the World of Charlemagne.* Trans. Jo Ann McNamara. Philadelphia: University of Pennsylvania Press, 1983.

Donation of Constantine

One of the most important and well-known forgeries of the early Middles Ages, this document presented itself as issued by the fourth-century emperor Constantine, conferring great power on the pope. The date of composition and the purpose of the *Constitutum Constantini,* or the Donation of Constantine, remain unclear. This uncertainty has led to a variety of interpretations, which often vary as a result of the date assigned to the document's creation. It has been described as a tool intended to support the efforts of the popes to improve ties with the new Carolingian dynasty after the deposition of the last Merovingian ruler, Childeric III, in 751 or following the coronation of Pippin in 754. It has also been seen as a document designed to undermine Byzantine territorial rights in Italy, particularly in light of Byzantine failures to protect the papacy from its enemies, the Lombards. The Donation, the great papal historian Walter Ullmann notes, may have been intended simply to free the papacy from the confines of an antiquated and ineffective Byzantine imperial government framework as part of its long-range program to establish a papal monarchy in Europe. Thomas Noble notes that the document may have served to establish an independent, papal territorial power in central Italy. The Donation, whatever its origin, enjoyed a long career, whether used in defense of or in opposition to papal authority, until proved a forgery by Lorenzo Valla in 1439.

The general consensus among historians is that the Donation was written in the 750s, although some have dated it later in the eighth century and have interpreted its meaning in light of the history of Charlemagne. It was most likely written by a Lateran cleric, possibly with the knowledge of Pope Stephen II, and was associated with the coronation and Donation of Pippin, the first Carolingian king of the Franks. The forgery was based upon legends that had existed in some form or other since the fifth century, legends that told the story of the relations between the Roman emperor Constantine and Pope Sylvester I. The opening section of the false Donation outlines the events associated with Constantine's conversion in the early fourth century. This section of the forgery, which clearly borrows from the legend of Sylvester, includes the story of Constantine being cured of leprosy by Sylvester and then, grateful for this miracle, Constantine accepting instruction in the Christian faith from the pope. Also in this section, Constantine asserts the importance of Rome as the city of the apostles Peter and Paul and as such proclaims the place of its bishop as the ultimate authority in matters of orthodoxy. In the second part, Constantine makes his famed donation to the papacy. Before departing for his new capital in the east, Constantinople, he grants the pope supremacy over the episcopal sees of Antioch, Alexandria, Constantinople, Jerusalem, and all the churches of the world. He also grants temporal authority to the pope and his successors over "Judaea, Greece, Asia, Thrace, Africa, Italy, and various islands" (17). And, most importantly, Constantine bestows on the pope "our palace [the Lateran], the city of Rome and all the provinces, districts, and cities of Italy or of the western regions" (17). This final donation was clearly meant to imply that the imperial dignity in the Western Empire was being passed from Constantine to the pope and his successors and that the popes had the authority to appoint new temporal rulers over the lands of the Western Roman Empire.

Although its origins remain unclear, the later history of the Donation is more definite. The forgery was involved in the struggles between church and state and manipulated by advocates on both sides. In the late ninth century, Frankish bishops inserted the Donation into canon law collections as a means to secure ecclesiastical property rights. In the 11th century emperors and popes passed judgment on the document according to their own political and religious agendas. It was denounced by many leading political figures in the later German empire, including Otto III (d. 1003). Various popes pointed to it to support for their territorial claims in Italy and rights to primacy in the ecclesiastical hierarchy. Indeed, the Donation of Constantine had perhaps even greater influence on political and religious affairs after its composition sometime in the eighth century than it did when it first appeared.

See also: Carolingian Dynasty; Charlemagne; Childeric III; Constantinople; Donation of Pippin; Merovingian Dynasty; Pippin III, Called Pippin the Short; Rome

Bibliography

Dutton, Paul Edward, trans. *The Donation of Constantine.* In *Carolingian Civilization: A Reader.* Peterborough, ON: Broadview, 1993, pp. 13–19.

Henderson, E. F., trans. *Select Historical Documents of the Middle Ages.* Rev. ed. London: George Bell and Sons, 1892, pp. 312–329.

Noble, Thomas X. F. *The Republic of St. Peter: The Birth of the Papal State, 680–825.* Philadelphia: University of Pennsylvania Press, 1984.

Ullmann, Walter. *The Growth of Papal Government in the Middle Ages.* 3rd ed. London: Methuen, 1970.

Donation of Pippin

Traditional name of the oral or written promise made by the Carolingian king Pippin the Short to Pope Stephen II (r. 752–757). The Donation of Pippin was an important step in the establishment of the papal states and in the solidification of the alliance between the pope and the Carolingian kings. Later held to have confirmed the forged document in which Constantine supposedly granted great power to the papacy, Pippin's donation was a grant of land in central Italy, to which the king had no legal claim, to the pope. The promise was made in the context of the papacy's struggle with the Lombard king Aistulf, during which the pope declined support from the Byzantine Empire, and the elevation to the royal throne of the Carolingians. It appeared, therefore, at a critical time in the history of the early Middle Ages and had a significant impact on the history of the papal states.

The Donation of Pippin came into being in the context of the creation of the blossoming papal-Carolingian alliance and in the wake of the coronation of Pippin as king of the Franks. In the face of mounting pressure from the Lombard king

Aistulf, Stephen was forced to find a new protector. Technically still a subject of the Byzantine Empire, the pope received little support from the emperor, who could do little even to protect Ravenna, the imperial capital in Italy. With the fall of Ravenna to Aistulf, the imperial presence in Italy was ended, as was any semblance of imperial protection for Rome. Aistulf's aggression led Stephen to seek aid from Pippin, whose elevation to the kingship owed something to Stephen's predecessor Pope Zachary. The Lombard king's reluctance to yield to Frankish and papal requests to return some of his conquests to Rome forced Stephen to take more drastic action. In January 754, therefore, the pope arrived at the royal palace at Ponthion in the Frankish kingdom, where he was warmly received by Pippin, and remained in the Frankish kingdom until the summer of that year.

In April, Stephen met Pippin at Quierzy (near Soissons, France) and received promises from the king for the restoration of lands in central Italy. This promise, which according to papal accounts included the Exarchate, imperial territory including Ravenna and the surrounding region, and Roman duchy, papal territory in central Italy, is often identified as the Donation of Pippin, but it does not exist in written form and may have been delivered only orally. Whatever the case may be, an alliance formed between the king and pope, which was strengthened in July of that year when Stephen anointed Pippin and his sons Charlemagne and Carloman and declared them the true kings of the Franks.

Although the promise at Quierzy is often seen as the Donation of Pippin, it has been suggested that a later document is the actual donation. This document, the Confession of St. Peter, is a list of cities that submitted to the pope; it was compiled by Pippin's representative following the king's campaigns in Italy. The Confession was made necessary by Aistulf's continued aggression in central Italy and Pippin's invasions in defense of the pope in 755 and 756. After defeating Aistulf a second time in 756 and imposing a peace on him, Pippin sent his supporter, the important abbot of St. Denis Fulrad, to collect the keys of the cities and territories in central Italy. The keys and the list of the cities were then placed on the altar of St. Peter in Rome and thus may constitute the true donation.

The donation, whether the promise of 754 or the document of 756, marked an important moment in the papal-Carolingian alliance and growth of the papal states. It confirmed the pact between Stephen and Pippin and either precipitated or concluded the king's forays into Italy. It was confirmed by Charlemagne in 778 and by Louis the Pious in 817, both of whom sought to strengthen their ties with the pope. The donation also, it should be noted, involved territories that were technically not Pippin's to give. The lands Pippin restored to the pope were imperial territories, and the empire's inability to control them further demonstrated the end of the imperial presence in central Italy. Clearly, the empire's loss benefited both the papacy and the Carolingian dynasty.

See also: Aistulf; Carolingian Dynasty; Charlemagne; Donation of Constantine; Franks; Lombards; Louis the Pious; Pippin III, Called Pippin the Short; Zachary, St.

Bibliography

Davis, Raymond, trans. *The Lives of the Eighth-Century Popes (*Liber Pontificalis*): The Ancient Biographies of Nine Popes from* A.D. *715 to* A.D. *817.* Liverpool, UK: Liverpool University Press, 1992.

McKitterick, Rosamond. *The Frankish Kingdoms under the Carolingians, 751–987.* London: Longman, 1983.

Noble, Thomas F. X. *The Republic of St. Peter: The Birth of the Papal State, 680–825.* Philadelphia: University of Pennsylvania Press, 1984.

Riché, Pierre. *The Carolingians: A Family Who Forged Europe.* Trans. Michael Idomir Allen. Philadelphia: University of Pennsylvania Press, 1993.

Scholz, Bernhard Walter, trans. *Carolingian Chronicles: Royal Frankish Annals and Nithard's History.* Ann Arbor: University of Michigan Press, 1972.

Donatism

Religious schism of North Africa of the fourth and fifth centuries, Donatism adopted a rigorist practice of Christianity and opposed reconciliation with so-called lapsed Christians who were accused of making concessions to imperial persecutors. The Donatists rejected the authority of "lapsed" priests and the validity of the sacraments they offered. The Donatist Church in Africa was a powerful force that found numerous supporters throughout the fourth century including violent extremists known as Circumcellions. Opposition from the imperial authorities and St. Augustine of Hippo helped bring an end to the movement in the fifth century.

The origins of the movement can be traced to the time of the persecutions of the emperor Diocletian (r. 284–305) in the years 303–305. The edict enacting the persecutions ordered the burning of churches and destruction of Christian scriptures. In response, some members of the Christian clergy turned over Bibles and other sacred texts (sometimes the soldiers were given random texts as a means to placate the authorities without surrendering sacred texts) to the Roman authorities to be destroyed. Other Christians staunchly opposed these concessions and refused to surrender the holy books and denouncing those who did turn over the sacred items as *traditores* (betrayers). They further came to believe that the *traditores* among the clergy rendered themselves unworthy of their office and that their personal unworthiness made the sacraments they celebrated invalid. In 304, one group of imprisoned Christians proclaimed that the *traditores* would not gain entry into paradise with the martyrs who suffered during the persecutions.

The schism itself broke out in 311 when the bishop of Carthage, Mensurius, died. His successor Caecilian was consecrated shortly thereafter, but one of the consecrating bishops, according to the Donatists, was a *traditor* and so had lost the authority to participate in the ceremony. Although Caecilian was deposed by a council at Carthage in 312, the emperor Constantine came to support him as the legitimate bishop. The bishop's opponents, now led by Donatus, for whom the movement was named, protested this decision. Further councils in Africa continued to declare in Caecilian's favor, but even more important was the council of Arles in 314, which had been summoned by Constantine and which condemned Donatism. Donatus and his followers, however, remained strong in their opposition to those they believe had betrayed the true church. And Donatus and his followers were not without their successes. In 336, Donatus forced a council to meet to determine if his followers were to be rebaptized, and in 346 he appealed to the emperor Constans (r. 340–350) asking if the emperor would declare Donatus as bishop of Carthage. The emperor did not and unrest associated with the movement led to the exile of Donatus and his followers to Gaul, where Donatus died in 355.

The reign of Julian (360–363), called the Apostate because of his repudiation of Christianity, provided the Donatists the opportunity to reassert themselves in North Africa. Exiles returned and found support among the leaders of North Africa as well as the general lay population. During the course of the fourth century, accounts of the martyrdoms of those who died during the persecutions of Diocletian emerged to support the Donatist cause. Donatist leaders repeated assertions that theirs was the true church and that to become members of that true church Christians would need to be rebaptized. They also repeated their belief that the purity of the sacrament depended on the purity of the priest administering it, defining the extreme rigorist position of the movement that held that the priest must be without sin and rejecting the *traditores* as well as their sacraments and clergy they consecrated.

The resurgence of the movement, however, would not last. Violence associated with the movement and its supporters the Circumcellions and support by leading Donatists of a revolt against Roman rule undermined the popularity of the Donatist Church. The emphasis on purity caused difficulties leading to further schism within the church as questions were raised by members of the church about the sinfulness of its priests. Support for the Donatist position was further undermined by the vigorous attacks launched by the greatest figure of the African church, and one of the most important of all Christian theologians, Augustine of Hippo. Author of a number of treatises against the Donatists, Augustine promoted moral persuasion as well as the coercive power of the state to compel the Donatists back into the Catholic Church. In 405, a council at Carthage requested that the emperor Honorius impose penalties on the Donatists, which he did but in 409 rescinded the order. Despite this grant of toleration, Honorius approved of compelling the Donatists to attend a public debate at a council to be held in Carthage in 411. Representatives of the Donatists attended and faced Augustine in a debate lasting three days, which concluded with the condemnation of the Donatists. Further restrictions against them followed in 414 and in 415 the death penalty was imposed on Donatists. Although no longer a force in Africa, the Donatist Church survived and was only finally destroyed with the arrival of Islam in North Africa in the seventh century.

See also: Augustine of Hippo, St.; Carthage; Circumcellions; Constantine; Honorius

Bibliography

Brown, Peter. *Augustine of Hippo: A Biography*. Berkeley: University of California Press, 2000.

Frend, W.H.C. *The Donatist Church: A Movement of Protest in Roman North Africa*. New York: Oxford University Press, 2000.

O'Donnell, James J. *Augustine*. London: Profile Books, 2005.

Tilley, Maureen. *Donastist Martyr Stories: The Church in Conflict in North Africa*. Liverpool, UK: Liverpool University Press, 1997.

Do-Nothing Kings. *See Rois Fainéants*

E

Ebroin (d. 680)

Frankish mayor of the palace of the Neustrian kingdom of the Merovingians. Ebroin was a powerful figure who dominated politics in the Merovingian kingdom for much of the third quarter of the seventh century. Although deposed for a time in the 670s, Ebroin managed to recover his control of the office of mayor and dreamed of unifying the kingdoms of the Merovingians under his authority—a dream realized by the rival Carolingian dynasty and its leader Pippin of Herstal following the Battle of Tertry in 687. Before his period of disgrace, Ebroin engineered the retirement of Balthild, the Merovingian queen and saint, and, after his return to power, he appointed and controlled several Merovingian kings. His reign as mayor, however, was widely viewed as tyrannical, which led to a fierce rivalry with Pippin and his family, as well as his murder by a frightened noble in 680.

Ebroin rose to power in the wake of the overthrow of the Carolingian pretender Grimoald in the late 650s. Although of unknown family, Ebroin was the most dominant figure at the Merovingian royal court of Balthild and her son Chlotar III (d. 673), and he assumed the office of mayor of the palace for the Neustrian kingdom in 659. In 664 Balthild retired to the monastery she founded at Chelles, possibly because of a coup led against her by Ebroin, whose thirst for power outweighed his sense of loyalty. He then served as mayor, and the real power in Neustria, under King Chlotar until the king's death in 673.

After the death of Chlotar, the kingdom experienced a short period of crisis, which began with the fall of Ebroin and ended with his return to power. At the death of the king, Ebroin, without consulting the other nobles of the kingdom, raised Chlotar's brother, Theuderic III (d. 690/691) to the throne. Ebroin's highhanded act angered the other nobles of the kingdom, who offered the throne to the Merovingian king in Austrasia, Childeric II (d. 675). Ebroin and his king were overthrown, and both were tonsured and placed in a monastery—Ebroin received this punishment only after much pleading by several bishops, who thereby saved his life. But the reign of Childeric over both Austrasia and Neustria was a short and troubled one; not long after his elevation to the Neustrian throne a falling out with some of his key supporters occurred. Moreover, Childeric alienated the Neustrian nobility by his reliance on his loyal Austrasian supporters. He also developed a reputation as a brutal and tyrannical king who violated the rights and traditions of the nobility, actually beating one magnate. The Neustrian nobility, including many of Ebroin's supporters, orchestrated an assassination plot against the king and his wife Bilichild in 675. Their death opened the door for the return of Ebroin and his king Theuderic III to power in Neustria.

Beginning in 675, Ebroin carefully and brutally established his control over the king and kingdom. Although outmaneuvered by a former ally, Bishop Leodegar, at first, Ebroin soon gained control of the king and took the office of mayor of the palace at the expense of his old ally. In fact, Leodegar was one of the many victims of Ebroin's ruthless quest to control all of the Merovingian kingdom. The bishop had his lips, eyes, and tongue cut out and was finally killed in 678 or 679 at Ebroin's order. Although he eliminated a powerful political rival, Ebroin gained little from his brutal treatment of the bishop, whose tomb became a center of miracles shortly after his death. But the bishop was only one of Ebroin's victims, who included other bishops and priests imprisoned or exiled because they had sided with the mayor's rivals. Many members of the nobility also suffered persecution in Ebroin's quest for power. Indeed, not only nobles and bishops in his own region of Neustria but also those in Austrasia were among Ebroin's victims. The most notable, of course, was the king, Dagobert II, who had been promoted in 675 to the Austrasian throne by Childeric's mayor of the palace, Wulfoald. In 679, the king was ambushed by Ebroin and killed, as Wulfoald may also have been, since he is no longer heard of after that time.

By the end of the 670s, Ebroin had made himself master of almost the entire Merovingian kingdom and had nearly reunited Austrasia, Neustria, and Burgundy, the three parts of the Merovingian realm, under the nominal authority of Theuderic. His success, together with the ruthless policies by which it was achieved, inspired great unrest in Austrasia and the opposition of noble families there, led by the early Carolingian Pippin of Herstal. Ebroin's power became even greater in 680, when he decisively defeated Pippin in battle and treacherously murdered Pippin's brother Martin. But Ebroin's triumph was short lived; not long afterward he was murdered by a royal official afraid of being Ebroin's next victim. And not long after the murder, Ebroin's dream of unifying the kingdom was realized by his rival Pippin.

See also: Austrasia; Balthild, St.; Carolingian Dynasty; Merovingian Dynasty; Neustria; Pippin II, Called Pippin of Herstal; Tertry, Battle of

Bibliography

Bachrach, Bernard S. *Merovingian Military Organization, 481–751.* Minneapolis: University of Minnesota Press, 1972.

Fouracre, Paul, and Richard A. Gerberding. *Late Merovingian France: History and Hagiography, 640–720.* Manchester, UK: University of Manchester Press, 1996.

Riché, Pierre. *The Carolingians: A Family Who Forged Europe.* Trans. Michael Idomir Allen. Philadelphia: University of Pennsylvania Press, 1993.

Wood, Ian. *The Merovingian Kingdoms, 450–751.* London: Longman, 1994.

Education and Learning

Traditionally seen as the "Dark Ages," the early Middle Ages were not without their cultural and intellectual achievements. Although these achievements were modest in comparison with the great accomplishments of the ancient world as well as the later medieval world, education and learning did not disappear in barbarian Europe. Even in the worst of times, during the collapse of the Roman Empire and the invasion of various barbarian peoples, education continued, even if only in the monastery schools. Indeed, the monasteries remained the great centers of learning throughout the early Middle Ages and were responsible for preserving many of the great works of antiquity. Moreover, under Charlemagne's direction, a "renaissance" in learning and literature emerged in the late eighth and ninth centuries. Although once thought to have been a shining moment in an otherwise dark time, the Carolingian Renaissance was only the most dramatic example of cultural activity in the early Middle Ages.

The various barbarian peoples that entered the Roman world had their own traditions of education, of course, but these did not focus on the written word. Indeed, theirs was a practical education that emphasized those things necessary for success in tribal society. Many of their educational practices continued even after they settled in the Roman Empire and created their own kingdoms. Boys were taught how to ride, hunt, and use weapons. Girls were taught how to spin and weave wool and how to use the distaff and spindle. These customs continued, but the successors of the Romans also borrowed from the educational practices of the ancient world.

The practices of classical education had a long history in Greece and Rome before the arrival of the barbarians in late antiquity. Education was for boys only and involved the skills necessary for success in the public arena. Consequently, the focus of classical education was on grammar and rhetoric. Boys studied the various parts of speech, grammar and syntax, and rhetoric to speak eloquently and persuasively. Their models were Cicero, Caesar, Quintilian, Seneca, and others, some of whom continued to be the focus of learning after the end of Roman rule in the west. Although it suffered decay as a result of the entry into the empire of various Roman peoples, the classical tradition was preserved. And in the sixth century important transitional figures emerged who embodied the traditions of the past and laid the foundations for later learning. Among the more important figures were two from the early sixth century, Boethius, discussed in his entry, and, especially, Cassiodorus, who compiled two works on sacred and profane letters that encapsulated the best of the Roman and Christian tradition. His work on sacred letters remained at the heart of education for centuries after his death.

Although an important body of learning and pedagogical techniques survived the so-called fall of the Roman Empire, the ancient schools did not. As a result, a new center of education emerged in the early Middle Ages, the monastery. Even though the primary purpose of the monastery was spiritual, education and learning remained an important component of the religious life. Indeed, it was recognized that a good education in Christian letters was essential for the success of the religious life, and monks were required to select a book from the monastery library at least once a year. Consequently, monasteries were centers of book production, as the monks needed to copy the books so that members of the community could read. One of the greatest contributions of the monks was their preservation of many important ancient Christian and pagan classics. They also established schools in the monasteries, based on ancient patterns, to instruct the young boys who were enrolled in the various communities by their parents. It was not only Christian letters that were taught, but classical as well, since the greatest writers of Latin—the language of learning and the Church—were pagan Romans. The most important books of grammar, by the fourth-century grammarian Donatus and the early sixth-century grammarian Priscian, contained a fair sampling of the works of the great classical Roman poets. The traditions of education and learning, therefore, were preserved in the monastic communities of barbarian Europe, and some monasteries, such as Jarrow and Wearmouth in England, were recognized as great centers of learning.

Although he was not the only ruler to promote education and learning, Charlemagne, in the late eighth and early ninth centuries, is perhaps the most noteworthy and influential proponent of learning in the early Middle Ages. He himself, as his biographer Einhard notes, tried mightily to learn to read and write. Another biographer, Notker the Stammerer, noted that the great king would often visit the schools to watch over the progress of the students and would take time to encourage the studious and chastise those who were less than diligent. Moreover, he made learning the center of the reform and renewal of religious life in his great kingdom, issuing the capitulary *Admonitio Generalis* and the Letter to Baugulf to improve learning and the knowledge of Scripture throughout his kingdom. He mandated the construction of schools at monasteries and churches throughout his realm so that the bright young boys of the realm could learn to read and write. His legislation thus encouraged the monks and clergy of the kingdom to teach children who were not members of their religious communities. Charlemagne also encouraged the monasteries to continue their practice of copying important works of Christian and classical Roman literature. Although his renaissance was only marginally successful, his efforts to improve the standard of education and learning in his kingdom demonstrate the importance of education to early medieval rulers.

See also: Admonitio Generalis; Boethius; Capitularies; Carolingian Dynasty; Carolingian Renaissance; Cassiodorus; Charlemagne; Letter to Baugulf

Bibliography

Dutton, Paul, ed. *Carolingian Civilization: A Reader.* Peterborough, ON: Broadview, 1993.

Einhard and Notker the Stammerer. *Two Lives of Charlemagne.* Trans. Lewis Thorpe. Harmondsworth, UK: Penguin, 1981.

Laistner, Max L. W. *Thought and Letters in Western Europe,* A.D. *500 to 900.* 2nd ed. Ithaca, NY: Cornell University Press, 1976.

McKitterick, Rosamond, ed. *Carolingian Culture: Emulation and Innovation.* Cambridge: Cambridge University Press, 1994.

Riché, Pierre. *Education and Culture in the Barbarian West: From the Sixth through the Eighth Century.* Trans. John Contreni. Columbia: University of South Carolina Press, 1976.

Edwin (c. 585–633)

Formidable Northumbrian king from 616 to 633; the first ruler of that kingdom to convert to Christianity. A successful warrior, who may have also possessed a substantial fleet, Edwin extended his authority over Britons and Saxons, according to Bede, and was recognized with the title bretwalda, or ruler over several kingdoms. His stature as a king in England made his conversion important and raised the concerns of other kings, including the pagan Penda and his Christian ally Cadwallon.

Edwin came to the throne in Northumbria after a long exile. The heir to the throne of Deira, Edwin took refuge at the court of a powerful king south of the Humber River. The reigning king in Northumbria, Æthelfrith, demanded his return, but the southern king, Raedwald, refused. The two came to war; Æthelfrith was defeated and killed, and his sons fled into exile. Edwin was welcomed as king of Deira and Bernicia, and eventually succeeded Raedwald as overlord south of the Humber. Indeed, by 626 he was the most powerful figure in England. He married a daughter of Aethelberht of Kent and had contacts with the Merovingian dynasty on the continent. He took possession of the Isle of Man, conquered sections of north Wales, and established a loose confederation, one that foreshadowed more stable and lasting unions. But his invasion of territory ruled by the Britons had dire consequences for his kingdom and his line. He threatened the kingdom of the Briton Cadwallon, the last great native British king. With his pagan ally, Penda of Mercia, Cadwallon launched a counterinvasion of Northumbria in 633. In October of 633, Edwin fought a great battle in Hatfield Chase against Cadwallon and Penda in which he was defeated and killed. Edwin's son Osfrid was killed during the battle while protecting his father. And another son, Eadrid, was forced to submit to

Cadwallon and then was killed by him. Edwin's line was thus destroyed, as was his kingdom and political confederation.

Although he was a powerful king whose authority over much of England foreshadowed later English political organization, Edwin's real importance lies in his conversion to Christianity. Even though the faith did not survive in Northumbria in the generation after his death, Edwin established a significant precedent by his conversion. Edwin's conversion, according to Bede, was accompanied by the miraculous. His wife, Æthelberg, daughter of King Aethelberht of Kent, was a Christian, and when he proposed a marriage alliance, Edwin was told that she could not marry a non-Christian. He said that he would not interfere with her religion and would consider adopting it once he had had the opportunity to examine it. He delayed this conversion until several further events passed. He survived an assassination attempt sent by the king of the West Saxons, and witnessed the birth of a daughter, for which he thanked his pagan gods. Bishop Paulinus assured him that it was prayers to Christ that brought Edwin life and happiness. Edwin declared that only when he was victorious over his attempted murderer would he convert, and shortly thereafter he defeated the West Saxon king. He delayed baptism still, however.

Bede notes that it was a sign offered by Paulinus that finally persuaded the king to convert. While at the court of Raedwald, Edwin, knowing that he was about to be betrayed, had a vision in which he promised a stranger that he would submit to the stranger's teachings if his kingdom were restored to him. The stranger placed his hand on Edwin's head as a sign and shortly thereafter Raedwald was persuaded by his wife to protect Edwin. Later, Paulinus placed his right hand on Edwin's head and asked if he remembered his promise. The final sign convinced Edwin to convert, and on Easter, April 12, 627, he accepted baptism at the hands of Bishop Paulinus. At that moment, Edwin became the first of many later Northumbrian kings to accept Christianity.

See also: Anglo-Saxons; Bede; Merovingian Dynasty; Penda

Bibliography

Bede. *Ecclesiastical History of the English People with Bede's Letter to Egbert and Cuthbert's Letter on the Death of Bede.* Trans. Leo Sherley-Price. Harmondsworth, UK: Penguin, 1991.

Blair, Peter Hunter. *The World of Bede.* Cambridge: Cambridge University Press, 1990.

Geoffrey of Monmouth. *The History of the Kings of Britain.* Trans. Lewis Thorpe. Harmondsworth, UK: Penguin, 1982.

Randers-Pehrson, Justine Davis. *Barbarians and Romans: The Birth Struggle of Europe,* A.D. *400–700.* Norman: University of Oklahoma Press, 1993.

Stenton, Frank M. *Anglo-Saxon England.* 3rd ed. Oxford: Clarendon, 1971.

Whitelock, Dorothy, ed. *The Anglo-Saxon Chronicle.* Westport, CT: Greenwood, 1986.

Einhard (c. 770–840)

Frankish writer and biographer who was a member of Charlemagne's court school. One of the great success stories of Charlemagne's efforts to revive learning in his empire, Einhard is best know for his *Vita Karoli* (Life of Charlemagne), a biography of the great Carolingian emperor. The *Life* is the first biography of a major political figure since antiquity and reveals the debt of Carolingian writers to classical models. Despite its debt to ancient Roman biography, Einhard's work is one of the most important sources for the life of Charlemagne and one of the great works of medieval writing. It is not Einhard's only achievement, however, because he also wrote numerous letters, a theological tract, and an important work of hagiography. Highly interested in architecture, he most likely was the supervisor for the construction of Charlemagne's palace and church at Aachen, the grandeur of which Einhard mentions in his biography.

Born around 770 in the Main Valley to noble parents, Einhard was sent to receive his education at the monastery of Fulda, one of the great centers of learning in the Carolingian realm. In the early 790s, he joined Charlemagne's palace school at Aachen, where he was taught by the greatest of the Carolingian scholars, the Anglo-Saxon Alcuin. He remained at court for a while and earned the friendship of his great hero, Charlemagne. In 806, the emperor sent Einhard to Rome as an ambassador and may have entrusted him with other missions. In 813, Einhard was the first to recommend that Charlemagne make his son, Louis the Pious, coemperor and heir. In the years after Charlemagne's death in 814, Einhard remained at the court of Louis the Pious and was appointed advisor to Lothar, the oldest son of Louis. A lay abbot, Einhard retired from the court in 830 with his wife Imma to the monastery he founded on lands granted by Louis at Seligenstadt. He built a church there as well, where he deposited the relics of the saints Marcellinus and Peter, and he died there on March 1, 840.

Although Einhard had numerous accomplishments in his life, his greatest contribution to medieval Europe was the *Life of Charlemagne.* Despite his assertion that he lacked the skills necessary to write the biography, Einhard's work is one of the most important of the Carolingian Renaissance. His writing reveals the extent of his learning and bears clear echoes of many Roman and Christian Latin writers, including Cicero, Julius Caesar, Tacitus, Orosius, and Sulpicius Severus. His most important debt, however, was to the great Roman writers of the early Roman Empire, Suetonius and Tacitus. Suetonius's *De vita Caesarum* (*Lives of the Caesars*), particularly his life of Augustus, has often been recognized for its influence on Einhard. More recently, *Agricola*, the biography of the Roman noble Agricola by Tacitus, has been suggested as a model of secular biography that provided the format and vocabulary for Einhard's work. But Einhard's work was no slavish copy of Suetonius or Tacitus. It was based also on Einhard's intimate knowledge of his subject. The work addresses the major wars of Charlemagne, his diplomatic activities, and building projects. Einhard provides information on the great ruler's family life, including the king's too strong love of his daughters (whom he would not allow to marry), personal appearance, and personality. Einhard also includes discussion of the imperial coronation of Charlemagne and makes the still controversial statement that had Charlemagne known what was going to happen that Christmas day he would have not gone to church. The life concludes with an extended discussion of Charlemagne's death and includes a copy of his will.

The purpose of the biography and its date of composition remain uncertain, and the former is surely conditioned by the latter. Einhard's life is clearly biased in favor of its subject. He notes in his preface that he must write so as not to allow "the most glorious life of this most excellent king, the greatest of all princes of this day, and his wonderful deeds, difficult for people of later times to imitate, to slip into the darkness of oblivion" (52). He offers only passing criticism of the king, and blames rebellions on the nobles or one of Charlemagne's wives rather than on any action of the king. The work is clearly intended to prove the greatness and virtue of its subject. Beyond Einhard's regard for Charlemagne and sense of obligation,

Einhard and Archbishop Turpin writing the history of Charlemagne, from the *Chroniques de France*, 1494. (Biblioteca Nazionale, Turin, Italy/The Bridgeman Art Library)

it is likely that the work was intended as a commentary on political affairs in the Carolingian Empire after the death of Charlemagne. A letter of 830 establishes that date as the latest it could have been written. And if the biography were written in the late 820s, it was surely a commentary on the difficulties that Louis the Pious faced by that time, as his sons and the nobility began to stir against him. It has also been suggested that the biography was written early in the reign of Louis and within only a few years of Charlemagne's death or even shortly after the death of its subject in 814. Certain internal evidence supports an early composition, and if the work were completed in early 814 or the late 810s it was intended to support the claim of Louis as Charlemagne's divinely ordained heir to imperial power. The biography also helped define the nature of imperial power for the Carolingians, an issue Louis himself pursued. Whether the life was composed in 814, circa 817, or circa 830, it is one of the most important biographies of the Middle Ages, and one that provides an image of the ideal Christian ruler.

See also: Alcuin of York; Anglo-Saxons; Carolingian Dynasty; Charlemagne; Lothar; Louis the Pious; Notker the Stammerer; *Vita Karoli*

Bibliography

Einhard and Notker the Stammerer. *Two Lives of Charlemagne.* Trans. David Ganz. Harmondsworth, UK: Penguin, 2008.

Einhard. *The Translation and Miracles of the Saints Marcellinus and Peter.* In *Carolingian Civilization: A Reader.* Trans. Paul Edward Dutton. Peterborough, ON: Broadview, 1993, pp. 198–246.

Geary, Patrick. *Furta Sacra: Thefts of Relics in the Central Middle Ages.* Rev. ed. Princeton, NJ: Princeton University Press, 1990.

Innes, Matthew, and Rosamond McKitterick. "The Writing of History." In *Carolingian Culture: Emulation and Innovation.* Ed. Rosamond McKitterick. Cambridge: Cambridge University Press, 1994, pp. 193–220.

Laistner, Max L. W. *Thought and Letters in Western Europe, A.D. 500 to 900.* 2nd ed. Ithaca, NY: Cornell University Press, 1976.

McKitterick, Rosamond. *Charlemagne: The Formation of a European Identity.* Cambridge: Cambridge University Press, 2008.

Riché, Pierre. *The Carolingians: A Family Who Forged Europe.* Trans. Michael Idomir Allen. Philadelphia: University of Pennsylvania Press, 1993.

Ermoldus Nigellus (fl. 820s)

Carolingian poet and monk of Aquitaine, Ermoldus Nigellus (Ermold the Black) was an important figure of the Carolingian renaissance in the early ninth century. He wrote a number of poems that depict the realities of contemporary warfare most dramatically and that provide insightful and at times amusing comments about his contemporaries. His work often focusing of historical subjects is steeped in the writings of the ancient Romans, and in this way he reflects one of the main developments of the Carolingian Renaissance. He also wrote two panegyrics to his patron, Pippin, the Carolingian ruler in Aquitaine and son of the emperor Louis the Pious. His most important work, however, is the poem *In honorem Hlodovici imperatoris*. The poem was written around 826 and was intended to restore Ermoldus to the good graces of the emperor. Ermoldus had been exiled for encouraging Pippin to rebel against his father and hoped that the poem honoring Louis would allow him to return.

The poem in four books of 300 couplets provides important historical information about the early reign of Louis and offers effusive praise of the quality and character of the emperor, comparing Louis to the great Christian emperors of Rome and other historical figures who adorned the emperor's palace at Ingelheim. The poem seems to have been successful since Ermoldus was likely recalled to court in 830 and is sometimes identified as Louis's chancellor.

See also: Carolingian Dynasty; Carolingian Renaissance; Louis the Pious

Bibliography

Innes, Matthew, and Rosamond McKitterick. "The Writing of History." In *Carolingian Culture: Emulation and Innovation*. Ed. Rosamond McKitterick. Cambridge: Cambridge University Press, 1994, pp. 193–220.

Laistner, M.L.W. *Thought and Letters in Western Europe, A.D. 500 to 900*. 2nd ed. Ithaca, NY: Cornell University Press, 1957.

Noble, Thomas F.X. ed. *Charlemagne and Louis the Pious: Lives by Einhard, Notker, Ermoldus, Thegan, and the Astronomer*. University Park, PA: University of Pennsylvania Press, 2009.

Eudes of Aquitaine (died c. 735)

A powerful duke of Aquitaine in the late seventh and early eighth centuries, Eudes, or Odo, exploited the weakness of the Merovingian dynasty to assert greater independence from the Franks but faced increasing difficulties preserve this independence because of mounting pressures on both of his frontiers. From Spain to the south, Eudes suffered Muslim raids that increased in number and intensity during his reign as duke. He also endured a challenge from the Frankish kingdoms to the north, as the powerful Carolingian mayor, Charles Martel (r. 714–741), sought to extend his authority into Aquitaine.

Assuming ducal authority in the late seventh century, Eudes most likely inherited the position from his father. By 718 he had involved himself in the civil strife occurring in the Frankish kingdoms—Aquitaine had long been drawn into the Frankish sphere and was a region of great wealth and importance. He joined the Frankish king Chilperic II and his mayor of the palace in the king's struggles against his rival and his mayor Charles Martel. Martel would ultimately triumph in this struggle and then turn his attention to the south. At the same time, however, Eudes was plagued by raids from the Muslims of Spain. They had taken control of much of the Iberian peninsula in the 710s and had begun raiding across the Pyrenees. In 720, they took Narbonne, and in 721 they laid siege to Toulouse. Eudes met them outside the walls of the city and drove them from Aquitaine even though he failed to retake Narbonne. This was not the end to Eudes's problems, as he continued to face pressures from both Islamic Spain and Frankish Gaul. In 725, the Muslims moved back across the Pyrenees, taking Carcassone and moving up the Rhone River and reaching Autun before returning to Spain laden with the spoils of war. These raids were matched by Martel's continued designs on extending his control over Aquitaine. In response to both threats, Eudes arranged a marriage between his daughter and the Muslim leader Othman. This alliance, however, did not resolve the crisis, in part because of Othman's death at the hands of Abd al-Rahman. Muslim raids continued into Aquitaine, according to sources hostile to the duke, Eudes invited them in to assist him against Charles Martel.

Whatever the case, the Muslims laid waste to much of Aquitaine and moved deeper into Christian Europe, forcing Eudes to turn to his Frankish rival, Charles Martel. As a result, Eudes and Charles Martel joined forces and defeated the Muslims at the battle of Tours in 732, a victory that did not end Muslim raids but greatly diminished their threat to Aquitaine and the Frankish kingdom. Although Eudes played a key role in the battle, the real winner was Charles Martel who was heralded throughout Christendom for defeating the Muslims. He took advantage of his victory and further pressured Eudes, who retired to a monastery in 735 and died that year or, possibly as late as 740. His successor was forced to swear fealty to Charles Martel, reducing further the independence of the duchy that Eudes worked so hard to secure.

See also: Aquitaine; Carolingian Dynasty; Charles Martel; Merovingian Dynasty; Tours, Battle of

Bibliography

Riché, Pierre. *The Carolingians: A Family Who Forged Europe*. Trans. Michael Idomir Allen. Philadelphia: University of Pennsylvania Press, 1993.

Euric (c. 420–484)

Visigothic king who ruled over much of southern Gaul (now the south of France) and parts of Spain from his capital at Toulouse. Euric broke a long-standing alliance with the Romans and established an independent kingdom within the boundaries of the Western Empire that was one of the first and most successful successor kingdoms; it had a population of some 10 million people and an area of some 300,000 square miles. A successful warrior, Euric commissioned a legal code, the *Codex Euricianus* (Code of Euric), with the aid of Roman jurist. He was also an Arian Christian and, unlike his predecessors as kings of Toulouse, pursued an anti-Catholic religious policy that alienated his Roman subjects.

Euric seized power over the Gothic kingdom of Toulouse, which had formed as a federate ally of the empire around 418, in 466 when he murdered his brother Theodoric II. The assassination was most likely not over political or religious policy, but rather was a simple power grab by Euric. His thirst for power was further revealed in his relations with the Romans and other barbarian peoples in the coming decades. In the opening years of his reign, Euric negotiated with other barbarians against the Romans and ended the treaty the Visigoths of Toulouse had with the Western Empire. In 468 and again in 472 and 473, Euric sent armies into Spain, where they had great success, capturing cities such as Pamplona and Tarragona to the west and along the coast, respectively.

Ultimately, Euric controlled nearly all of the Iberian peninsula, seizing it from both Roman and barbarian powers. In 469 he sent armies into northern Gaul, and from 471 to 475 he continued the conquest of much of Gaul. By 475, Euric had extended his power across a region that stretched from the Atlantic coast to the Loire and Rhone rivers. His wars to the north included struggles with the Franks, who had already made overtures toward expansion into that region. Euric's power was at its height, and he commanded both land and naval forces; this successful naval command was unique among the unseaworthy Visigoths and reveals the extent of Euric's success. Moreover, many former Roman military leaders had joined Euric's army, which only enhanced his power and reputation. A new treaty between the empire and the kingdom of Toulouse was signed in 475, which recognized the new state of affairs. When Roman government was ended in the Western Empire in 476, Euric waged war against Odovacar, then king in Italy, to force the new power to recognize the Goth's claim in Gaul. And despite aid from barbarian allies of the empire, Odovacar was forced to accept Euric's claims. After creating a great kingdom, Euric died quietly in late 484, and was succeeded by his son Alaric II (r. 484–507).

Along with the creation of a sizeable kingdom in the remnants of the Western Empire, Euric is best remembered for his legal code. Although uncertainty remains about whether the existing code is the one promulgated by Euric, it is certain that in 475 the king issued a series of laws. The code was written in Latin with the help of Roman lawyers, but did not adopt the Roman legal tradition, which was best represented by the codification of Justinian in the next century. Euric's codification did not involve only tribal law, however, but did include royal statutory law. Although not universal tribal law, the *Codex Euricianus,* was, most likely, universal in scope and applied equally to Euric's Visigothic and Roman subjects. The code itself addressed a wide variety of issues, including the use of charters, last wills, lending and borrowing, and other matters concerning relations between Romans and Visigoths. The law code also recognized, for the first time, the institution of private retainers.

In terms of religious policy, as with relations toward Rome, Euric's reign marked a change in Visigothic practice. Unlike his predecessors, who had adopted a policy of tolerating and cooperating with their Catholic Christian subjects, Euric took a harder, less tolerant line. Although to identify his policy as one of systematic persecution of Catholic Christians may be an exaggeration, his attitude toward the Catholic church in his kingdom was hostile. He prohibited the bishops of his realm from communicating with Rome. He prevented the appointment of new Catholic bishops to various sees in his kingdom and banished others, including the archbishop of Bourges. He took steps to restrict the ability of the Catholic church and its clergy to operate freely and was accused of keeping churches deserted. But his opposition to the church moderated somewhat after the empire recognized his territorial conquests. Euric's restrictions on the church were, in part, the result of his inability to incorporate it into the state. Once the political situation eased, so did his oppression of the church associated with the empire. That notwithstanding, his earlier hostility toward the church caused tension between him and his Roman subjects that undermined his ability to govern.

See also: Alaric II; Arianism; Justinian; Odovacar; Visigoths

Bibliography

Bury, John B. *History of the Later Roman Empire: From the Death of Theodosius I to the Death of Justinian.* 2 Vols. 1923. Reprint, New York: Dover, 1959.

Collins, Roger. *Early Medieval Spain: Unity in Diversity, 400–1000.* New York: Longman, 1983.

Heather, Peter. *The Goths.* Oxford: Blackwell, 1996.

Isidore of Seville. *Isidore of Seville's History of the Goths, Vandals, and Suevi.* 2nd rev. ed. Trans. Guido Donini and Gordon B. Ford. Leiden: Brill, 1970.

Thompson, Edward A. *The Goths in Spain.* Oxford: Clarendon, 1969.

Wolfram, Herwig. *History of the Goths.* Trans. Thomas J. Dunlap. Berkeley: University of California Press, 1988.

Wolfram, Herwig. *The Roman Empire and Its Germanic Peoples.* Trans. Thomas J. Dunlap. Berkeley: University of California Press, 1997.

F

Family

As in all societies throughout history, the family was the basic building block of late antique and early medieval society. The structure, definition, and size of families, however, evolved over time, as the nature of society itself changed. That notwithstanding, the family remained an important institution throughout the period, even when the ascetic and monastic movement emerged and challenged conventional family life. Indeed, during the fourth to eighth centuries the family became an even more stable and important institution, and the evolution of marriage customs in the same period further reinforced the structure of the family and its importance in society.

According to Tacitus (c. 56–117), the Roman moralist and historian, the premigration Germanic family was a tight-knit unit. He notes that mothers nursed their own children, who often ran about naked and dirty, which allowed them to develop their bodies fully. Children were raised with minimal pampering and were only married once they had reached maturity. Adultery was rare, according to the Roman writer, and women caught in adultery were severely punished. The importance of the marriage vow and of family was taken very seriously, and women were expected to share in their husbands' labors in the field and even in war. Not only was the nuclear family bound closely together, but the extended family was as well. Members of the family were expected to participate in family feuds, and nieces "are as highly honored by their uncles as by their own fathers" (118). This idyllic picture, which may have more to do with Tacitus's desire to criticize contemporary Roman mores than any desire to reveal the reality of the Germanic situation, bears a grain of truth; the close bonds of the family in later barbarian Europe supports the portrayal in Tacitus of the premigration German family.

The family of the early Middle Ages was shaped not only by premigration Germanic tradition, but also by Roman and Christian traditions. Indeed, as the various Germanic peoples settled in the former Western Empire, they came into contact with Roman legal traditions and Christian views of the family. According to Roman law, the father was the *paterfamilias,* who had complete control over all his children as long as he lived. Although the life-and-death authority once exercised by the Roman father—according to legend, the founder of the Republic, Brutus, executed his own son for the son's betrayal of the city—no longer was in force by the fourth century of the Common Era, the father retained significant power in the family,

which reinforced Germanic tendencies in that regard. Christian teachings emphasized friendship and charity within the family, and Christian theologians strove to
define the importance of marriage, creating the monogamous traditions that shaped
marriage and the family by the eighth century.

In the early Middle Ages, however, the family was in a somewhat fluid state
owing to the various marriage customs of the Germanic peoples. Indeed, loose marital practices allowed for a much broader definition of family than that of a mother,
father, and children. Polygyny was practiced, at least by kings and nobles, into the
eighth century, and all children were welcomed by their father; illegitimate children
even shared in the inheritance. Indeed, Charles Martel was born to an illicit union
and rose to command the Frankish kingdom in the early eighth century. And the
history of Gregory of Tours is filled with the multiple marriages of the Merovingian kings and their numerous concubines and children. This situation changed,
however, under the Carolingian dynasty, which sought to promote monogamous
marriages and thus stabilized family structure.

The family was also an economic unit. Marriages involved exchanges of often
significant amounts of moveable wealth and property and were arranged to promote
the economic interests of both sides. The family household was the center of much
economic activity. It was there that the basic economic activities of the period took
place. Cooking, brewing beer, baking, and spinning were done in the home. Women
also prepared candles, soap, and other necessities for the family, and animal husbandry and farming were performed at this level. And all members of the family
participated in the economic activity of the household. At the head of the household
was the father, and all members of the family were subject to his authority.

It has been customary to maintain that children were raised with little sentimen-
tality or affection. Indeed, it has been suggested that the chances for the survival
of children were so slim that it is likely that little attention was paid to them before they were seven years old or so and that even then they were treated roughly.
Corporal punishment, as contemporary legal codes reveal, was practiced, fathers
could sell their children into slavery, and there is even some indication that infan-
ticide was practiced, as it had been in ancient times. This view, however, has been
challenged, and anecdotes from the histories of Einhard, Gregory of Tours, and
others suggest that there was a great deal of family affection in the early Middle
Ages. Charlemagne, for example, loved his daughters so dearly that he would not
let them marry and always kept them by his side. He would go riding and hunting
with them, and loved them and the illegitimate children they had with members of
the royal court. Moreover, even the most ferocious Merovingian queens, Brunhilde
and Fredegund, revealed their maternal sides quite clearly in the protection of their
children. They struggled mightily against each other to promote the interests of
their sons, and Brunhilde wrote the emperor tearfully seeking his aid in protecting

her daughter, who had been lost in North Africa. The situation of children was also improved by the reforms of the Carolingian dynasty, which strengthened marital practices and family structure.

See also: Brunhilde; Charlemagne; Charles Martel; Einhard; Franks; Fredegund; Gregory of Tours; Marriage; Merovingian Dynasty; Women

Bibliography

Einhard and Notker the Stammerer. *Two Lives of Charlemagne.* Trans. Lewis Thorpe. Harmondsworth, UK: Penguin, 1981.

Gies, Frances, and Joseph Gies. *Marriage and Family in the Middle Ages.* New York: Harper and Row, 1987.

Goody, Jack. *The Development of Family and Marriage in Europe.* Cambridge: Cambridge University Press, 1983.

Gregory of Tours. *The History of the Franks.* Trans. Lewis Thorpe. Harmondsworth, UK: Penguin, 1974.

Herlihy, David. *Medieval Households.* Cambridge, MA: Harvard University Press, 1985.

Riché, Pierre. *Daily Life in the World of Charlemagne.* Trans. Jo Ann McNamara. Philadelphia: University of Pennsylvania Press, 1983.

Tacitus. *The Agricola and the Germania.* Trans. Harold Mattingly. Rev. trans. S.A. Hanford. Harmondsworth, UK: Penguin, 1982.

Wemple, Suzanne. *Women in Frankish Society: Marriage and the Cloister, 500 to 900.* Philadelphia: University of Pennsylvania Press, 1981.

Fastrada (d. 794)

The third wife of the great Carolingian king Charlemagne, Fastrada played a critical role in her husband's reign, according to the biographer Einhard. She was from the eastern part of the Frankish empire, and her marriage to Charlemagne demonstrates the position of women and marriage in the Carolingian kingdom in the eighth century. She also appears in a most negative light in Einhard's biography of Charlemagne.

After the death of Charlemagne's second wife, Hildegard, in 783, the great king married Fastrada. She was the daughter of a powerful east Frankish count, and the marriage between Charlemagne and Fastrada was an important political arrangement, one that reconciled the king to the powerful east Frankish nobility. The marriage produced two daughters, Theoderada and Hiltrude, of whom little else is known. Useful as the marriage may have been politically, Fastrada herself influenced political events, if Einhard is to be believed, less positively. He accused the queen of great cruelty and of influencing her husband to perpetrate actions "fundamentally opposed to his normal kindness and good nature" (76). As a result, Charlemagne faced two conspiracies during his marriage to Fastrada. The first revolt occurred in 785 and involved a number of nobles from the eastern part of the kingdom, and the second involved his favorite bastard, Pippin the Hunchback, in 792. Both revolts were suppressed, and Einhard blames the revolts on Fastrada and her negative influence on Charlemagne. Although Fastrada's exact role in the origins of the two revolts is unclear, it is likely that she had some influence on her husband and, at the very least, played an important role in the creation of marriage alliances in the Carolingian kingdom.

See also: Carolingian Dynasty; Charlemagne; Einhard; Franks; Marriage; Women

Bibliography

Einhard and Notker the Stammerer. *Two Lives of Charlemagne.* Trans. Lewis Thorpe. Harmondsworth, UK: Penguin, 1981.

Collins, Roger. *Charlemagne.* Toronto: University of Toronto Press, 1998.

Halphen, Louis. *Charlemagne and the Carolingian Empire.* Trans. Giselle de Nie. Amsterdam: North-Holland, 1977.

McKitterick, Rosamond. *The Frankish Kingdoms under the Carolingians, 751–987.* London: Longman, 1983.

Riché, Pierre. *The Carolingians: A Family Who Forged Europe.* Trans. Michael Idomir Allen. Philadelphia: University of Pennsylvania Press, 1993.

Scholz, Bernhard Walter, trans. *Carolingian Chronicles: Royal Frankish Annals and Nithard's History.* Ann Arbor: University of Michigan Press, 1972.

Wemple, Suzanne. *Women in Frankish Society: Marriage and the Cloister, 500 to 900.* Philadelphia: University of Pennsylvania Press, 1985.

Fontenoy, Battle of (841)

A major engagement during the civil war between the surviving sons of Louis the Pious, the Battle of Fontenoy was a brutal and bloody struggle. The battle occurred on June 25, 841, and involved the emperor Lothar and his nephew Pippin II of Aquitaine (d. 864) against the kings Charles the Bald and Louis the German. Although the battle was terrible and resulted in the defeat of Lothar, it proved not to be decisive; Lothar continued to struggle against his brothers. However, the outcome of the battle can be described. It was recognized as a significant contest by contemporaries and is memorialized in poetry and in the history of Nithard, a combatant in the battle.

According to Nithard, the battle was the result of fortuitous circumstances for Charles the Bald and Louis the German in late spring 841, as well as of the unwillingness of Lothar to agree to peace. Indeed, Lothar refused to make any concessions to his brothers concerning the government of the empire and refused to limit his powers as emperor. He was bolstered in his defiance by the arrival of his nephew Pippin II, whose troops and opposition to Charles strengthened Lothar's cause. Charles and Louis, however, also enjoyed good fortune when they were able to join their armies together, and Judith, Charles's mother and widow of Louis the Pious, had also recently arrived with a sizeable force.

The growth of the armies on both sides increased tensions between them and made battle between them more likely. Even though contemporary accounts make it seem that war was unavoidable, Charles and Louis attempted to negotiate a settlement and sent peace offers to Lothar on June 23. His refusal forced his brothers to prepare for battle on June 25. According to Nithard, they returned to camp to celebrate the feast day of St. John the Baptist (June 24). This was surely regarded as an omen by the two kings, who sought the judgment of God in battle and knew that the liturgy of the feast of St. John celebrated release and salvation. Charles and Louis then made ready for battle the next day, which they planned to begin at the eighth hour. As Nithard notes, the armies rose at dawn and established their positions, and two hours later the battle began. Both sides fought bitterly, and casualties were heavy. Both Louis and Charles enjoyed success during the battle, and Lothar and his army were forced from the field.

For Charles and Louis, divine judgment had been rendered. They had defeated their brother and secured their positions in the empire. The victory reinforced their alliance, which was confirmed in the Oath of Strasbourg in the next year. The battle also secured Charles's political survival and strengthened his hold on Aquitaine and the western Frankish kingdom, which he claimed as part of his legacy from Louis the Pious. But the battle was not the decisive victory for which Charles and Louis had hoped. Despite the overwhelming defeat he suffered, Lothar managed to continue the war against his brothers and insisted on his authority over the entire empire.

See also: Carolingian Dynasty; Charles the Bald; Judith; Lothar; Louis the German; Louis the Pious; Nithard; Strasbourg, Oath of

Bibliography

McKitterick, Rosamond. *The Frankish Kingdoms under the Carolingians, 751–987.* London: Longman, 1983.

Nelson, Janet. *Charles the Bald.* London: Longman, 1992.

Riché, Pierre. *The Carolingians: A Family Who Forged Europe.* Trans. Michael Idomir Allen. Philadelphia: University of Pennsylvania Press, 1993.

Scholz, Bernhard Walter, trans. *Carolingian Chronicles: Royal Frankish Annals and Nithard's History.* Ann Arbor: University of Michigan Press, 1972.

Franks

A group of West Germanic peoples, the Franks became the most important of all the barbarians to establish a kingdom in the old Roman Empire. In two successive dynasties, the Merovingian and Carolingian, the Franks ruled large sections of Europe from the late fifth to the late tenth century and laid the foundation for medieval and modern France and Germany. They emerged along the Rhine River in two main groups: the Ripuarian Franks along the Middle Rhine, and the more important Salian Franks along the Lower Rhine. Their origins remain obscure, as demonstrated by the uncertain meaning of their name, which has been interpreted to mean "the brave," "the fierce," "the wild," and "the free." The last term may provide the key to the best understanding of their origins as small tribal groups of Germans living along the Rhine who had not been made subject to other barbarian peoples. Whatever their exact origins, the Franks went on to become the most important and influential of the successors of the Roman Empire and boasted a long line of illustrious kings and queens, including Clovis, Clothild, Brunhilde, Fredegund, Pippin the Short, Charlemagne, and Louis the Pious.

The Franks themselves developed the legend that their origins could be traced back to the Trojans, thus giving them an origin as impressive as that claimed by the Romans. This tale was as legendary as that of Rome's Trojan origins, and the Franks appear in history for the first time in the third century, when they exploited the weakness of the Roman Empire and invaded Gaul. They ravaged throughout much of Gaul in the later 250s and even reached the borders of modern Spain. They seized much booty before being defeated by Roman armies. The Franks continued to cause problems for the empire throughout the third century, until the empire managed to settle its own internal crisis. At that point, under the great emperor Diocletian (r. 284–305), the Franks, and many other Germanic invaders, were defeated and settled. The Franks themselves concluded a treaty with the empire that allowed them to settle as *foederati* (federated allies) of the empire.

During the fourth and fifth centuries the Franks maintained a mixed relationship with the Roman Empire. Many Franks served in the Roman armies and rose high in the military and civil ranks of the empire. They often supported the empire during invasions by other peoples and were instrumental in the defense of Gaul. Indeed, they joined with the Romans against the invasion of Attila the Hun and fought against the Huns in the Battle of the Catalaunian Plains in 451, a critical battle in the history of the empire. In the fifth century, however, the Franks also struck back against the empire. In 406, when the Rhine frontier collapsed, the Franks and many other Germanic peoples crossed into the empire to begin carving out territories for themselves. At the same time, a group of Salian Franks located at Tournai began to rise to power. And it was this group of the Salian Franks, under the leadership of the ancestors of the Merovingian dynasty, that rose to predominance; the greatest king of the Merovingian line, Clovis, then gradually established a great kingdom across much of northern Europe.

The Merovingian dynasty lasted from the time of Clovis (r. 481–511) until the time of Childeric III (r. 743–751). The kingdom formed by the kings of this line extended from their traditional homeland across much of modern France. Their success was due, in part, to the conversion of their first king, Clovis, to Catholic Christianity rather than Arian Christianity, which most of the other barbarians chose and which differed from the Catholic Christianity of the Roman population. The dynasty was ultimately replaced by the Carolingian dynasty. The first Carolingian king, Pippin the Short, deposed the last of the Merovingian kings and assumed the throne in 751. He was succeeded by his son, Charlemagne, the greatest of the Carolingian line, who built a great empire, initiated a religious and cultural revival, and was crowned emperor by Pope Leo III on December 25, 800. The dynasty survived until 987.

The Franks, unlike many of their barbarian contemporaries like the Huns, were not horsemen, and their military was comprised mainly of foot soldiers. But like their contemporaries they were nonliterate—literacy and all that accompanies it came only with contact with the Romans. They did have law, or at least custom, which was first codified under Clovis in the Salic law. They also seem to have traded with the Romans, at least in the fifth century, because of the Roman glassware found in many Frankish graves of that period. Grave goods, especially those found at the royal tomb of Tournai, tell us other important things about the early Franks, not the least of which is that they remained devoted to their traditional gods into the late fifth century. Christians buried their dead without material goods, but the Franks buried a variety of goods, including weapons (swords and battle axes), horse heads with their full harness, gold and silver coins, and gold buckles and jewelry. The gold jewelry was typical of Germanic metalwork. There were cloisonné brooches that were made of gold and inlaid with garnets and precious gems. One tomb contained a large number of brooches in the shape of cicadas, which were symbols of eternal life. The buckles and other jewelry were also decorated with designs, often elongated animal designs know as the "ribbon animal style."

See also: Brunhilde; Carolingian Dynasty; Charlemagne; Childeric III; Clotilda; Clovis; Fredegund; Jewelry and Gems; Gregory of Tours; Louis the Pious; Merovingian Dynasty; Pippin III, Called Pippin the Short; Tournai

Bibliography

Bachrach, Bernard S., trans. *Liber historiae Francorum.* Lawrence, KS: Coronado, 1973.

Fouracre, Paul, and Richard A. Gerberding. *Late Merovingian France: History and Hagiography, 640–720.* Manchester, UK: University of Manchester Press, 1996.

Gregory of Tours. *History of the Franks.* Trans. Lewis Thorpe. Harmondsworth, UK: Penguin, 1974.

James, Edward. *The Franks.* Oxford: Blackwell, 1988.

Lasko, Peter. *The Kingdom of the Franks: North-West Europe before Charlemagne.* New York: McGraw-Hill, 1971.

McKitterick, Rosamond. *The Frankish Kingdoms under the Carolingians, 751–987.* London: Longman, 1983.

Wallace-Hadrill, J. M. *The Long-Haired Kings.* Toronto: University of Toronto Press, 1982.

Wolfram, Herwig. *The Roman Empire and Its Germanic Peoples.* Trans. Thomas J. Dunlap. Berkeley: University of California Press, 1997.

Wood, Ian. *The Merovingian Kingdoms, 450–751.* London: Longman, 1994.

Fredegar (fl. c. 642)

Name associated with an anonymous Burgundian chronicler of the mid-seventh century, who is the most important source for Frankish history after Gregory of Tours. The chronicle attributed to Fredegar, traditionally divided into four books, is a composed of various other sources, including Gregory's history, compiled by as many as three authors. Most scholars, however, detect only two authors at work. The important and original section of the work is the fourth book, which chronicles events from 591 to 642. It thus provides important information on the Merovingian kings of the early seventh century as well as on the formative period of the Carolingian family. Sometime in the eighth century Fredegar's chronicle was taken up by another anonymous author, who continued the history to 768, the first year of the reign of Charlemagne.

Little is known of the author or authors of the work, and the name Fredegar is associated with manuscripts of the work only in the 16th century. From evidence in his chronicle, however, it is possible to suggest that Fredegar, or at least the author of the new material on the seventh century, was a Burgundian layman of some standing who was active in the 640s and may have died around 660. He clearly had access to royal archives and to ambassadors from Lombard, Visigoth, and Slavic lands. He also had access to church archives, even though his focus was not that of a cleric. His Latin, in Wallace-Hadrill's words, was "highly individual," and other commentators have said much worse. But the chronicle, especially the fourth book, remains a most important source of information for a pivotal point in Frankish history.

The work itself is mostly derivative, with the exception of the original fourth book. The first three books, or five chronicles depending upon the arrangement of the text, are drawn from a number of earlier chroniclers and historians, with occasional editorial remarks and interpolations by the chronicler. Fredegar included works of St. Jerome, Isidore of Seville, and Gregory of Tours, and other Frankish chroniclers, among others. The fourth book, or sixth chronicle, is Fredegar's own and shows a remarkable knowledge not only of Frankish political life but also of affairs in the Byzantine Empire. Although haphazardly organized and not written on an annual basis as the chronicle format would suggest, the work nonetheless captures a vital moment in the history of the Merovingian dynasty. Fredegar's chronicle begins with the last years of Queen Brunhilde, whom Fredegar clearly dislikes; he must have recorded her grisly demise with some pleasure. His great heroes were Chlotar II, who overthrew Brunhilde, and his son Dagobert I, and it is thanks to Fredegar that we know a good deal about their reigns. It is also in the fourth book of Fredegar's chronicle that the famous legend of Frankish origins appears. According to Fredegar, the Franks were of Trojan origin, a legend that became very popular among the Franks and was probably well known in learned circles in Fredegar's time.

The work was continued in the eighth century, taking up where Fredegar left off and chronicling Frankish affairs in the early years of the Carolingian dynasty, and in the ninth century it became increasingly popular. It remains one of the most important sources of the history of the Frankish kingdoms in the seventh century.

See also: Brunhilde; Carolingian Dynasty; Charlemagne; Chlotar II; Dagobert; Gregory of Tours; Merovingian Dynasty

Bibliography

Laistner, Max L. W. *Thought and Letters in Western Europe, A.D. 500 to 900.* 2nd ed. Ithaca, NY: Cornell University Press, 1976.

Riché, Pierre. *The Carolingians: A Family Who Forged Europe.* Trans. Michael Idomir Allen. Philadelphia: University Press, 1993.

Wallace-Hadrill, John M., ed. and trans. *The Fourth Book of the Chronicle of Fredegar with Its Continuations.* London: Nelson, 1960.

Fredegund (d. 597)

Wife and mother of the Merovingian kings Chilperic I and Chlotar II, respectively, Fredegund was one of the great queens of the dynasty. She was also one of the most ruthless and ambitious Frankish queens, and her rise to power illustrates the flexibility of marriage customs among the Merovingian rulers and the opportunity these customs offered some women. She was probably a slave at court before becoming Chilperic's lover and, eventually, wife. Often motivated by the defense of her husband and children, she surely desired power for her own ends. She is best known, perhaps, for her long feud with a rival Merovingian queen, Brunhilde, and Brunhilde's husband Sigebert. This rivalry and Fredegund's ruthlessness are revealed in all their bloodthirstiness in the pages of the history of Gregory of Tours, whose great animosity toward Fredegund continues to shape historical estimates of the queen.

Fredegund rose to prominence in the Merovingian kingdom because of her relationship with King Chilperic. As a slave, Fredegund became the mistress and, possibly, wife of Chilperic around 566, before his marriage to the Visigothic Spanish princess, Galswintha. Although marriage to low-born women was not uncommon among Merovingian rulers, this custom was abrogated by Chilperic's brother, King Sigebert, who married Galswintha's sister Brunhilde. Jealous of his brother's success, Chilperic arranged a marriage with Galswintha and, according to Gregory of Tours, loved her dearly at first because she brought a large dowry with her. Apparently, Chilperic continued his relationship with Fredegund after his marriage to Galswintha, which led the Visigothic princess to complain bitterly to her husband about her treatment. Chilperic had Galswintha murdered, keeping the dowry, so that he could remain with Fredegund.

Although there is some dispute over the nature of the feud between Fredegund and Brunhilde, it is certain that Fredegund took great pains to protect herself and Chilperic from Brunhilde and her husband Sigebert. When it appeared that Sigebert was about to overwhelm Chilperic in battle and seize his kingdom, Fredegund had her husband's rival murdered. She also attempted to kill Brunhilde on numerous occasions, but repeatedly failed. For example, according to Gregory of Tours, at one point she sent a cleric to kill Brunhilde, but he was discovered and returned to Fredegund, who punished him by cutting off his hands and feet. Despite her best efforts, Fredegund could not strike down her rival, and in fact she was survived by Brunhilde. Of course, Fredegund could claim the satisfaction of causing the death of two of Brunhilde's husbands. Shortly after the murder of Sigebert, Brunhilde married Merovech, the son of Chilperic from an earlier marriage. Merovech and Brunhilde hoped that the marriage would advance their own political agendas, but that hope failed to materialize, as Fredegund and Chilperic hunted down Merovech, who ordered one of his servants to kill him.

Fredegund's murders, however, were not limited to Brunhilde's husbands and were not committed in defense of Chilperic alone. Indeed, according to one contemporary chronicler, Fredegund murdered Chilperic in 584 when the king learned that she was having an affair with one of his advisors. Fredegund also arranged the murder of Chilperic's sons by other wives. She caused the death of Merovech and also ordered the murder of her stepson Clovis, who was allegedly conspiring against his father. These murders were ostensibly committed to protect Chilperic against renegade sons, but they also promoted the interest of Fredegund's sons, especially Chlotar. Although she caused the death of two of his sons, Chilperic found Fredegund to be a useful ally. She not only plotted the murder of his major rival, Sigebert, but also struck against many bishops and nobles who were deemed a threat to Chilperic's power. Ambitious and calculating for her own interests, Fredegund provided valuable services to her husband.

Although she sometimes seemed to promote her own interests beyond all others, Fredegund was nonetheless careful to protect her own children and could react in dramatic and emotional ways to their misfortune. When two of her sons, Chlodobert and Dagobert, were stricken with dysentery, she believed it was divine punishment for Chilperic's new taxation and destroyed the tax registers to save her sons. Their death drove her to great despair and an extended period of mourning. On another occasion, Fredegund tortured and murdered a large number of women in Paris, whom she accused of causing the death of her son Theuderic by witchcraft. To save her son Chlotar when he became seriously ill, Fredegund made a large donation to the church of St. Martin of Tours in the hope that the saint would intervene on behalf of her son. Chlotar, to her relief, survived. She also provided a large dowry for her daughter Rigunth before her daughter's departure for marriage in Spain, and she fell into a terrible rage when she learned that Rigunth had been despoiled of her wealth by her betrothed. Her maternal record, however, is not without blemish. After Rigunth returned from Spain, the two women quarreled constantly, and Fredegund tried to murder her daughter. And she rejected her newborn Samson. She feared she would die and refused to nurse her son, whom Chilperic baptized shortly before the infant died.

After the murder of Chilperic in 584, Fredegund's position was most insecure and she had to use all her talents to preserve her place and secure the succession for her son Chlotar. She took control of Chilperic's treasure, which aided her bid to maintain control for herself and her son. She also continued to attempt assassinations of her rivals, particularly Brunhilde, as well as various nobles and bishops. The most serious challenge came when the paternity of Chlotar was questioned. She managed to rally to her side a large number of nobles and three bishops, who supported the legitimacy of Chlotar and allowed her to assume the regency for her son. She also led armies in battle when her son's part of the kingdom was threatened by rival Merovingians. And despite her life of brutality and ruthlessness, Fredegund died peacefully in 597, reconciled with Guntram, the most important Merovingian king of the time. Her efforts to secure power for herself and her son proved successful, and she even triumphed over her rival posthumously, when Chlotar overthrew and executed Brunhilde in 613. Her career, thus, demonstrates the opportunities that Merovingian marriage customs offered ambitious women and also reveals the importance of family, especially of sons, to Merovingian queens.

See also: Brunhilde; Chilperic I; Chlotar II; Columban, St.; Galswintha; Gregory of Tours; Merovingian Dynasty; Visigoths

Bibliography

Gregory of Tours. *The History of the Franks.* Trans. Lewis Thorpe. Harmondsworth, UK: Penguin, 1974.

James, Edward. *The Franks.* Oxford: Blackwell, 1988.

Lasko, Peter. *The Kingdom of the Franks: North-West Europe before Charlemagne.* London: Thames and Hudson, 1971.

Wallace-Hadrill, J. M. *The Long-Haired Kings.* Toronto: Toronto University Press, 1982.

Wemple, Suzanne. *Women in Frankish Society: Marriage and the Cloister, 500 to 900.* Philadelphia: University of Pennsylvania Press, 1985.

Wood, Ian. *The Merovingian Kingdoms, 450–751.* London: Longman, 1994.

Fritigern (fourth century)

Leader of the Gothic Tervingi (r. 376–380) and rival of Athanaric, Fritigern is best known as the commander of the Gothic armies that destroyed the Roman army led by the emperor Valens at the Battle of Hadrianople in 378. His opposition to Athanaric caused repeated problems for that Gothic judge, whose office, though royal, was of limited power, and led to a division of the Goths in 376. His victory over Valens was a serious, but not fatal, blow to the Roman Empire and caused important changes in the relationship between Rome and the barbarian peoples inside and outside the empire's boundaries.

During the struggles between the empire and Athanaric in the 360s and 370s, Fritigern emerged as a rival to Athanaric and an advocate of a pro-Roman policy. Fritigern, a figure of equal stature to Athanaric among the Goths, rose up against the Gothic ruler after a war with the Romans in the late 360s. Fritigern adopted a pro-Christian stance, and was perhaps supported by the famous missionary Ulfilas, during Athanaric's persecutions in the early 370s. Fritigern's support for the Christians may have been the result of a personal bond with the emperor Valens, who was an Arian Christian. The course of the rebellion remains unclear, it but was probably suppressed by the time of the arrival of the Huns in the mid-370s.

The Hunnish advance afforded Fritigern another opportunity to oppose the rule of Athanaric. The Gothic judge had some initial success against the invaders but was bested in battle by them. Athanaric also lost important territory to the Huns and had his supply lines cut off by them. The devastation caused by war with the Romans and Huns made things extremely difficult for the Goths. In the summer of 376, in response to the crisis brought on by the Huns, Fritigern proposed that the Goths turn to the Romans for help. He persuaded most of Athanaric's followers to abandon their leader and join Fritigern and enter into the empire. Athanaric's long struggle with the Romans made it difficult for him to seek the empire's support, and he withdrew to the Carpathian Mountains. But Fritigern successfully petitioned Valens for support and was allowed to settle in the empire as an ally (*foederatus*) in 376 with some 80,000 Goths. Fritigern had successfully taken control of the Gothic Tervingi, and in the summer of 376 took the fateful step when he and his followers crossed the frontier into the empire.

Fritigern's welcome into the empire was less than enthusiastic, however, and almost immediately difficulties arose, difficulties that brought the Goths and Romans to war. These problems included the incompetence of local administrators to deal with the sudden influx of people and the great number of Goths involved. Although Rome had welcomed barbarian peoples into the empire as allies before, they had never brought so many in at one time. The Goths were expected to serve in the army, farm, and pay taxes, but the services necessary to accommodate them were lacking and for the next two years, Fritigern and his followers operated freely within imperial borders. In 378 Valens and the Western emperor Gratian sent an army of infantry and cavalry of between 30,000 and 40,000 troops to end the threat of Fritigern. Valens, however, seeking a victory without his imperial colleague, moved his troops forward against what he thought were 10,000 warriors, when instead there were roughly 30,000. Despite warnings from Gratian about Gothic battle tactics, despite Fritigern's efforts to reach a peaceful settlement, Valens marched his troops against the Goths near Adrianople in early August.

On August 9, Valens sent his troops forward without food or water in the boiling sun to meet the Goths, who had set fires along the Romans' path. Fritigern still sought to negotiate an agreement, but Roman soldiers, without orders, began a disorganized attack that proved fatal. The counterattack of the Gothic cavalry was rapid and forceful, and when other Goths returned from foraging, the assault on the Romans was made even more terrible. The Romans lost nearly two-thirds of their army at Hadrianople, and most of the casualties were from the infantry, the backbone of the Roman military. Among the dead were generals, unit officers, and the emperor Valens himself.

Fritigern had led his Goths to a smashing victory, but he was unable to exploit the situation and gradually disappeared from view. Although a tragedy for the empire, the Battle of Hadrianople was not the catastrophe it is often seen to be, and it had equally significant consequences for Fritigern. In the wake of the battle, the Gothic leader faced division within his own ranks, and he was unable to restrict the raids for plunder that followed the battle. The Romans, led now by Gratian and Theodosius the Great, took steps to limit the destruction the Goths could cause, steps that included the destruction of a force of Goths in the Roman army. Moreover, an important member of Athanaric's clan joined the Romans and led the opposition to Fritigern, even destroying a large raiding party allied to Fritigern. In response to these steps, the Goths increased Fritigern's royal powers, and he increased the pressure on the empire by extending his raids in Macedonia and northern Greece. He also engineered a plot against his former rival Athanaric that drove the Gothic leader into exile.

Despite these successes, Fritigern's cause was a lost one because of Roman military might and diplomatic skill. Although unable to stop Fritigern, the Romans could at least keep him in check militarily. Athanaric's welcome in Constantinople, together with the lavish funeral he was given there, was a means for the empire to display its compassionate side and identify itself as a friend to all Goths. By 382, when a treaty between Rome and the Goths was signed, Fritigern seems to have disappeared; no mention was made of him in the treaty. On the other hand, Fritigern's original goal for the Goths was achieved, since the Goths became imperial subjects by the terms of the treaty.

See also: Athanaric; Hadrianople, Battle of; Huns; Theodosius; Ulfilas; Visigoths

Bibliography

Ammianus Marcellinus. *Ammianus Marcellinus.* Trans. John C. Rolfe. Cambridge, MA: Harvard University Press, 1971–1972.

Bury, John B. *The Invasion of Europe by the Barbarians.* New York: W. W. Norton, 1967.

Heather, Peter. *The Goths.* Oxford: Blackwell, 1996.

Wolfram, Herwig. *History of the Goths.* Trans. Thomas J. Dunlap. Berkeley: University of California Press, 1988.

Wolfram, Herwig. *The Roman Empire and Its Germanic Peoples.* Trans. Thomas J. Dunlap. Berkeley: University of California Press, 1997.

G

Gaiseric (c. 390–477)

King of the Alans and Vandals from 428 to 477, Gaiseric was one of the more ambitious and cunning of the Germanic peoples who came into contact, or rivalry, with the Roman Empire. Indeed, Gaiseric, an Arian Christian, seemed less impressed with the empire and its traditions than did many of his contemporaries. He was ruthless in his dealings with imperial officials and exploited every opportunity he was offered. After signing a treaty with the empire, Gaiseric proceeded to violate it and took control of all of North Africa. His fleet controlled much of the western Mediterranean, which allowed him to accomplish his most famous, or infamous, feat—the capture and sacking of Rome in 455.

Writing in the sixth century, Jordanes provides a useful description of Gaiseric's physical appearance and personality: "Of medium height, lame from a fall off his horse, he had a deep mind and was sparing of speech" (Bury 1967, 246). Jordanes also notes that Gaiseric hated luxury, was covetous, and had an uncontrollable temper. Rounding out his description of Gaiseric, Jordanes notes, "He was far-sighted in inducing foreign peoples to act in his interests, and resourceful in sowing seeds of discord and stirring up hatred" (246–247). His many talents overshadowed his irregular birth—his mother was a slave, possibly of Roman descent—and enabled him to achieve great success in war. Indeed, he was a most formidable opponent, at least the rival of Attila, if not more dangerous than the king of the Huns. At the very least, Gaiseric carved a more lasting kingdom out of the Roman Empire than did Attila.

Gaiseric's rise to power in the Mediterranean was aided by the turmoil within the government of the Roman Empire. In the 420s the Roman general and military governor in Africa, Boniface, clearly sought to establish himself as ruler of the empire, or at least an independent ruler in Africa. He successfully defeated armies led by Roman commanders sent to bring him to heel. But an army sent under the leadership of the new count of Africa, the Goth Sigisvult, was almost more than Boniface could handle, and the Goth managed to seize the important cities of Hippo and Carthage. To secure his position against Sigisvult, Boniface may have sought an ally in the Vandal leader Gaiseric, and perhaps asked for aid against Sigisvult in exchange for a share of Africa, an exchange that the Vandal accepted. But the chronology of events and the cause of Gaiseric's migration to Africa remain unclear. There is another tradition that authorities in Constantinople invited Gaiseric to

Africa to conquer Boniface. There is also a third version of events that holds that Gaiseric recognized an opportunity when he saw it and moved all the Vandals and Alans under his control, traditionally some 80,000, from their base in Spain to Africa in 429. Whatever the case, Gaiseric's subjects are traditionally held to have included roughly 15,000 warriors, whose swords Boniface or the imperial authorities hoped to use to their advantage but which were used instead against Boniface and Roman authority.

Although the numbers may be exaggerated, Gaiseric led a large enough population from Spain, where his people had been harassed by their traditional enemies the Visigoths as well as the Romans. He moved slowly across Africa and managed gradually, in the course of the 430s, to secure his position there. His first engagement was the siege of Hippo, in May or June of that year. St. Augustine, fearing for his city and near the end of his own life, may have called on Boniface to protect Hippo from the Vandals. But the Roman commander, now in the good graces of the empress Galla Placidia, had little success against Gaiseric, who laid siege to the city for 14 months. Boniface received reinforcements from Constantinople, but they were of little help against Gaiseric, who maintained the siege and defeated imperial armies in engagements outside the city. Although he was forced to call off the siege before the city fell, Gaiseric demonstrated his abilities against Roman armies. Moreover, when Boniface was recalled to Italy, Gaiseric was left alone in Africa. In 435 he settled a treaty with the empire that granted Gaiseric and his Vandals much of North Africa and recognized them as *foederati* (federated allies). Four years later, in the face of continued turmoil, Gaiseric broke the treaty and marched against Carthage, which he took with little resistance.

Gaiseric retained control of his new kingdom until his death in 477 and expanded his authority into parts of the western Mediterranean. His conquests were recognized by a new treaty in 442, which was reinforced by the betrothal of his son Huneric to Emperor Valentinian III's daughter Eudocia. This gain was followed by Gaiseric's efforts to seize control of other parts of the rapidly deteriorated Western Empire and make a statement asserting his place in the western Mediterranean. He may have conspired with Attila and encouraged the Hun to invade Gaul to punish the Visigoths. In 455, Gaiseric invaded Italy and plundered the city of Rome. Although the pope, Leo the Great, sought to stop the attack on Rome, as he had two years earlier in negotiations with Attila, he managed only to extract the concessions that the Vandals would neither burn the city nor indulge in a massacre. Instead, for two weeks Gaiseric and his followers plundered the city, taking thousands of prisoners and much treasure, including statues, gold, precious gems, and important ecclesiastical artifacts.

Gaiseric's assault on the former imperial capital was devastating; it was probably intended as a message that he was the most powerful ruler in the boundaries of the old Western Empire and that had to be taken into account. His conquests in the western Mediterranean included the Balearic Islands, Corsica, Sardinia, and Sicily. He faced repeated attempts to defeat him, including a massive naval attack of more than 1,000 ships that was launched by Emperor Leo I (457–474) in cooperation with the Western emperor in 468. The attack was a disaster for the empire. Gaiseric remained in control, and a peace treaty was finally settled between the Vandal king and the empire in 474. Indeed, over the course of his long reign, Gaiseric managed to create a powerful and impressive successor kingdom in part of the old Western Empire. His military skill and personal drive enabled him to create the most important new political unit in the western Mediterranean, one that lasted several generations before falling to the conquests of Justinian.

See also: Alans; Augustine of Hippo, St.; Attila the Hun; Carthage; Constantinople; Galla Placidia; Huns; Jordanes; Justinian; Rome; Vandals; Visigoths

Bibliography

Bury, John B. *The Invasion of Europe by the Barbarians.* New York: W. W. Norton, 1967.

Cameron, Averil. *The Mediterranean World in Late Antiquity, A.D. 395–600.* New York: Routledge, 1993.

Clover, Frank M. *The Late Roman West and the Vandals.* London: Variorum, 1993.

Randers-Pehrson, Justine Davis. *Barbarians and Romans: The Birth Struggle of Europe, A.D. 400–700.* Norman: University of Oklahoma Press, 1983.

Victor of Vita: History of the Vandal Persecution. Trans. John Moorhead. Liverpool, UK: Liverpool University Press, 1992.

Wolfram, Herwig. *The Roman Empire and Its Germanic Peoples.* Trans. Thomas J. Dunlap. Berkeley: University of California Press, 1997.

Galla Placidia (c. 388–450)

Daughter, sister, and mother of emperors, Galla Placidia played an important role in Roman politics in the first half of the fifth century. The daughter of Emperor Theodosius the Great and sister of Honorius, Galla Placidia is perhaps best known for her marriage to the Visigothic king Ataulf, the brother-in-law and successor of Alaric. Although the marriage was short lived because of Ataulf's death, it offered the possibility of greater union between Ataulf and the empire. Galla Placidia returned to the empire after her husband's death, where she continued to play a role in political life and eventually assumed the regency for her son Valentinian III (425–455).

Galla Placidia was an important figure in the complicated relations between the Romans and Visigoths in the late fourth and fifth centuries. Held at bay by her father, Theodosius, and her brother Honorius's general Stilicho, the Visigoths exploited the emperor's weakness after his murder of Stilicho. In 410, the Visigothic king Alaric sacked the city of Rome, and Ataulf, according to contemporary accounts, captured Galla Placidia himself and took her as a hostage once the Visigoths withdrew from Rome. She remained with Ataulf as his people moved into southern Gaul after the death of Alaric and succession to the throne by Ataulf. The capture of Galla Placidia enraged Honorius and made the establishment of good relations between the two difficult. Even though Ataulf turned over to Honorius a pretender to the throne, Honorius refused to sign a treaty until Galla Placidia was returned. Ataulf, in response, laid waste to imperial territory in southern Gaul.

In 414, a significant step was taken by Ataulf and Galla Placidia that had the potential to change the relationship between the Romans and the Visigoths. In January of that year, in an elaborate ceremony, Ataulf and Galla Placidia were married. The wedding was conducted in the Roman fashion, and Ataulf dressed in the uniform of a Roman general. His wedding gifts to his bride included many of the spoils of the sack of Rome, such as fifty Roman youths dressed in silk each carrying gold and precious gems. According to a contemporary account, Ataulf is supposed to have declared a change of heart in regard to the empire. Rather than seeking to replace Romania with Gothia as he originally intended, Ataulf declared that the "unbridled license" of the Goths would not allow this and therefore he aspired "to the glory of restoring and increasing the Roman name with Gothic vigor" (Bury 1959, 197). This sudden change of attitude was most likely the result of the influence of Galla Placidia, who bore a son in 415, whom they named Theodosius, in honor of his maternal grandfather. The name was a declaration of the legitimacy of the child and staked his claim to inherit the imperial throne. Unfortunately, Theodosius died shortly after birth, and Ataulf was murdered in 416.

Galla Placidia continued to play an important role in Gothic and Roman affairs after the death of her first husband. Ataulf hoped to remain on good terms with the Romans and recommended to his brother that should anything happen to him, Galla Placidia should return to the empire. Although the succession to the throne after the death of Ataulf was tumultuous, Galla Placidia returned to the imperial court on January 1, 417, even though Ataulf's eventual successor, Vallia, was hostile to Rome. On her return, and most likely much to her dismay, Galla Placidia was married to the military commander, Constantius, who was raised to the status of coemperor by Honorius in 421. But the Eastern emperor refused to recognize the new emperor and empress in the west, and Constantius died that same year. Galla Placidia had two children by Constantius, including the future emperor Valentinian III. Her relations with Honorius, however, became strained after her second husband's death, and power struggles ensued between them. She retained the loyalty of her Gothic guard and used them against her brother. She was then banished to Constantinople in 425, where she and her son were welcomed by Emperor Theodosius II (408–450) who had two years earlier spurned her.

On the death of Honorius, Galla Placidia and her son returned to the Western Empire, where she ruled as regent for her young son. She faced numerous challenges during her years as regent, as well as the years following her son's majority, when she continued to exercise influence at court. She was troubled by both imperial politics, especially the rivalry with the powerful general Aëtius, and barbarian peoples, including the Vandals. In the early years of the regency of Valentinian, Galla Placidia's authority was unchallenged. But the successes that Aëtius enjoyed against the various barbarian peoples challenging the Western Empire allowed him to force Galla Placidia to make him her chief military commander in 429. When her son reached his majority, Aëtius's influence increased, even though Galla Placidia managed to replace him with a commander of her choice for a time. The empress's other great challenge came from Gaiseric and the Vandals. During her regency, Gaiseric took advantage of political unrest in Africa and moved there from Spain with his entire tribe of Vandals. Gaiseric managed to take control of much of imperial Africa, but did come to terms with Galla Placidia and signed a treaty in 435. Her last years were spent influencing affairs from behind the scenes and building churches and other public buildings in the imperial capital of Ravenna, Italy.

See also: Aëtius; Alaric; Gaiseric; Honoria; Honorius; Rome; Stilicho, Flavius; Vandals; Visigoths

Bibliography

Bury, John B. *History of the Later Roman Empire: From the Death of Theodosius I to the Death of Justinian.* 2 Vols. 1923. Reprint, New York: Dover, 1959.

Hollum, Kenneth G. *Theodosian Empresses: Women and Imperial Dominion in Late Antiquity.* Berkeley: University of California Press, 1989.

Wolfram, Herwig. *History of the Goths.* Trans. Thomas J. Dunlap. Berkeley: University of California Press, 1988.

Wolfram, Herwig. *The Roman Empire and Its Germanic Peoples.* Trans. Thomas J. Dunlap. Berkeley: University of California Press, 1997.

Galswintha (d. 567)

Spanish Visigothic princess, whose marriage with and subsequent murder by the Merovingian king, Chilperic I, may have caused a terrible blood feud between Galswintha's sister Brunhilde and Chilperic's new wife, Fredegund.

The daughter of King Athanagild (r. 550–568), Galswintha was sought after in marriage by Chilperic after his brother King Sigebert had married Brunhilde.

Sigebert had broken recent Merovingian tradition by seeking marriage with a princess rather than a lowborn woman. His marriage to Brunhilde brought a woman of high status and also a sizeable dowry. Although already married to several women, according to Gregory of Tours, Chilperic sought marriage with Galswintha and promised the king that he would dismiss all his other wives if he were granted his request. Athanagild did so and sent Galswintha with a substantial dowry, just as he had with Brunhilde. Chilperic welcomed and honored his new wife greatly after her arrival at court. Gregory notes that Chilperic loved Galswintha dearly because "she had brought a large dowry with her" (222). To honor her new husband, Galswintha converted from the Arian Christianity practiced in her father's kingdom to the Catholic Christianity of the Merovingians.

Unfortunately the marriage was not to last; Chilperic still loved Fredegund, either a mistress or wife before Galswintha's arrival. He once again began to favor Fredegund, and Galswintha complained bitterly. She claimed that Chilperic showed her no respect and repeatedly asked to be allowed to return home, even if it meant leaving the dowry behind. Chilperic sought to placate her and denied his relationship with Fredegund. In the end, however, Chilperic had one of his servants murder Galswintha so that he could return to Fredegund. He kept the dowry after the murder and faced the rage of Sigebert and the other Merovingian kings.

The murder of Galswintha had serious repercussions for Chilperic and the Merovingian kingdom; civil war broke out shortly after the murder. It is possible that Sigebert was motivated by his wife's grief and anger to attack Chilperic. The bitter struggles between Brunhilde and Fredegund over the next several decades may also have been rooted in the murder of Galswintha. According to Gregory of Tours, God rendered judgment over Galswintha some time after her death by performing a miracle at her tomb. Whatever the exact consequences of the murder of Galswintha were, her life at the Merovingian court demonstrates the flexible nature of marriage among the Merovingians and the uncertain condition of women, no matter what their social rank.

See also: Arianism; Brunhilde; Chilperic I; Chlotar II; Fredegund; Gregory of Tours; Marriage; Merovingian Dynasty; Visigoths

Bibliography

Gregory of Tours. *The History of the Franks.* Trans. Lewis Thorpe. Harmondsworth, UK: Penguin, 1974.

James, Edward. *The Franks.* Oxford: Blackwell, 1988.

Wallace-Hadrill, J. M. *The Long-Haired Kings.* Toronto: Toronto University Press, 1982.

Wemple, Suzanne. *Women in Frankish Society: Marriage and the Cloister, 500 to 900.* Philadelphia: University of Pennsylvania Press, 1985.

Wood, Ian. *The Merovingian Kingdoms, 450–751.* London: Longman, 1994.

Geats. *See Beowulf*

Gelasius, Pope (d. 496)

Possibly of African origins, Gelasius was pope from 492 to 496. His papacy is noteworthy for his defense of Roman authority, Catholic orthodoxy, and the suppression of paganism in Rome. Gelasius is perhaps best known for the so-called doctrine of two swords, which defined the proper relationship between church and state and which was highly influential throughout the Middle Ages.

Upon assuming the papal throne on March 1, 492, Gelasius was faced with the continuing challenge of the Acacian Schism that had erupted during the reign of his predecessor. The schism was begun during the reign of the Emperor Zeno and the patriarch Acacius, who had attempted to quiet religious controversy in the empire but in so doing drifted toward heterodoxy. The emperor himself had issued an edict confirming this apparent error 10 years before the accession of Gelasius. In reaction to the ongoing controversy, Gelasius wrote a letter to Zeno's successor Anastasius defining the nature of the authority of the pope and the emperor: "there are two, august emperor, by which this world is chiefly ruled, the sacred authority of the priesthood and the royal power. Of these the responsibility of the priests is the far more weighty. . .You know, most clement son, that although you take precedence over all mankind in dignity, nevertheless you piously bow the neck to those who have charge of divine affairs." Gelasius asserted the primacy of the priesthood in religious matters and reminded the emperor that it was the pope's responsibility, not the emperor's, to define the faith. Although the two powers were instituted by Christ and were to exist side by side, the priestly authority had the greater duty because it was responsible for the salvation of the soul. Independent in his own sphere, the king or emperor is subordinate to the authority of the priesthood and its greatest representative, the pope. Gelasius asserted both the supremacy of the clergy in the world and the primacy of the papacy in the church.

Along with his letter to the emperor, Gelasius wrote numerous other letters, some 42 are extant as are fragments of some 49 others, and treatises. His many letters, among the most written by a pope up until that point, helped confirm the position of the pope as the arbiter in matters of the faith. According to his official biography, he wrote books against the heretics Nestorius and Eutyches and another two books against the heretic Arius along with a number of hymns and prayers for the sacraments.

As pope, Gelasius sought to ensure the integrity of Rome as a Christian city. In 495, he issued his condemnation of the Lupercalia. An ancient pagan festival, the Lupercalia celebrated the founding of the city and honored the she-wolf who suckled the city's founder. The festival traditionally involved young boys running through the streets naked and striking women and girls to ensure their fertility. In a letter to the Roman senator, Andromachus, an advocate of the festival, Gelasius traced its history and character and pointed out the Lupercalia's failure to protect and purify the city.

See also: Constantinople; Rome; Zeno

Bibliography

The Book of Pontiffs (Liber Pontificalis*): The Ancient Biographies of the First Ninety Roman Bishops to* A.D. *715*. Trans. Raymond Davis. Liverpool, UK: Liverpool University Press, 1989.

Canning, Joseph. *A History of Medieval Political Thought, 300–1450*. London: Routledge, 1996.

Llewllyn, Peter. *Rome in the Dark Ages*. New York: Barnes and Noble Inc., 1993.

Tierney, Brian. *The Crisis of Church and State, 1050–1300*. Englewood Cliffs, NJ: Prentice-Hall, 1964.

Ullmann, Walter. *A History of Political Thought: The Middle Ages*. Harmondsworth, UK: Penguin Books, 1965.

Genevieve, St. (419 or 422–512)

The patron saint of Paris, Genevieve (also known as Genovefa) is best known for her efforts on behalf of the people of Paris and her ties to early Merovingian kings. Born in Nanterre to Severus and Gerontia, simple peasants according to tradition, Genevieve expressed from her youth a desire to live a pious life. In 429, St. Germain of Auxerre and St. Lupus of Troyes preached in Nanterre and encouraged her to take up the life of a nun. She eventually took the veil and on her parents' death moved to Paris to live with her godmother. Although at first criticized by the people of Paris, Genevieve came recognized for her piety and was given charge by the bishop of Paris of a community of virgins. In 451 as Attila and his Huns threatened the city, Genevieve encouraged the people of Paris to stay in their homes and pray for the city. Many believed that it was her intervention that caused Attila to turn away from Paris and move against Orleans.

When the Franks under Childeric laid siege to the city, Genevieve again offered comfort to the people of Paris by arranging the delivery of supplies of food from nearby Troyes to avert starvation. Her efforts on behalf of the city endeared her to the Franks and gained her the devotion of Childeric's son, Clovis, the founder of the Merovingian dynasty. Perhaps under her influence, Clovis founded a convent for her and built a church dedicated to Sts. Peter and Paul. Upon her death in 512,

Genevieve was buried next to Clovis in that church and the miracles that occurred over her tomb led to naming of the church after her.

See also: Attila; Clovis; Huns; Merovingian Dynasty; Paris

Bibliography

McNamara, Jo Ann, John E. Holberg, and Gordon Whatley, eds. *Sainted Women of the Dark Ages*. Durham, NC: Duke University Press, 1992.

Germanic Religion

A collection of beliefs, practices, and heroic tales about the gods, humankind, and nature, Germanic religion was at the core of barbarian culture prior to the conversion of the barbarians to Christianity. Current knowledge of Germanic religion is based on versions of these myths set down in writing long after their original creation; the myths are best preserved in Scandinavian literature because the barbarian peoples of northern Europe were the last to convert to Christianity. Information about Germanic religion is also found in the works of ancient Roman and medieval authors, most notably Julius Caesar, Tacitus, Jordanes, and the Venerable Bede. Evidence from ancient burial sites and other archeological artifacts also provides information concerning early Germanic religious beliefs. The myths and legends of Germanic religion often tell tales of heroic virtues, describe many different gods and their personalities, and outline the ultimate end of the universe. Although the various Germanic peoples that entered the Roman Empire and its successor kingdoms ultimately converted to one form of Christianity or another, it is likely that their understanding of their new faith was much shaped by their traditional beliefs.

According to the classical Roman writer Tacitus, the ancient Germans worshipped many gods who were similar to the gods of ancient Rome. Tacitus notes that the Germans worship Mercury "above all other gods," whom they honor with human sacrifices, probably captured prisoners of war, on high feast days. They also worshipped Hercules and Mars and sacrificed animals to them. These sacrifices to the gods took place, according to Tacitus and later literature, in sacred groves of trees or in wooden temples. Although influenced by his own society's beliefs and practices, Tacitus probably revealed the actual beliefs of the ancient Germans. Archeological evidence supports the widespread veneration of a fire god, and it is likely that Tacitus gave Roman names to deities honored by the early barbarians. His Mercury was probably the god Woden (or Odin) who was the chief of the gods, and Mars and Hercules probably represented the gods Tiwaz, a war god, and Thor, a god of thunder and champion of the gods.

Viking stele from Tjangvide Gotland, ninth century, showing the god Woden (Odin) on his eight-legged horse Sleipnir, assisted by Valkyrie. The structure on the left is believed to represent Valhalla. (© Charles & Josette Lenars/Corbis)

The pantheon of the gods of Germanic religion, however, is much larger than the three main deities mentioned by Tacitus. Indeed, Tacitus himself in another section of his *Germania* describes Nerthus, the earth mother who rides a chariot among the people. She is worshipped in a sacred grove and, as Tacitus reports, is secretly bathed in a lake by slaves after a procession; the slaves are then drowned in the same lake. Tacitus also mentions the Alci, who are compared with the Roman equine gods Castor and Pollux, and Manus, who is the ancestor of all the Germanic peoples. Among other important deities is Balder, or Baldr, who is the subject of one of the great and moving tales of the gods. A son of the chief of the gods, Balder dreamt of his death; his mother tried to protect him by extracting an oath not to harm him from all creatures except the mistletoe. Balder's brother, Hoder, was persuaded to throw a mistletoe dart at his brother, which killed him. Hoder was led to do this by another important god, Loki, a trickster who could change shape and sex at will and who could both deceive the other gods and protect them from trouble. He is sometimes seen as the dark side of the chief of the gods.

Among the lesser gods, there is Heimdall, a rival of Loki; Ullr, an archer deity; and Bragi, a god of poetry and eloquence who has magic runes carved on his tongue. A number of female deities, such as Frigg, the mother of Balder who extracts the oath to protect her son, also appear in various tales, but they receive very little attention. The Vanir is another group of lesser gods, associated with fertility, health, and wealth. Finally, there are various spirits who appear in dreams or are thought to be ancestors who are protecting the family.

Among the many myths of Germanic religion are those that address the ultimate end of individual people as well as the origin and end of the universe. There are various conceptions of the afterlife in Germanic religion. It appears that some believed that life continued after death and was inseparable from the body. The dead lingered for a time, walking among the living and sometimes persecuting them, and sometimes needed to be killed again. There is also evidence from various Norse sagas and archeological finds that suggests the existence of a world of the dead. The practice of ship burials in which the body is placed in a boat, set out to sea, and burned suggests the belief in a world of the dead on the other side of the sea. Other burial sites that include weapons, horses, ships, and other tools of everyday life may indicate the belief in the necessity of these things in the afterlife. Some burial sites seem to be pointing north, which may have been the location of the world of the dead in Germanic beliefs. There was also the belief in an underworld, the hall of Hel, which is the name of both the place and its ruler. It is not a place of punishment but a place where all the dead go, which is surrounded by a great fence to keep out the living. In some texts, the lowest level of Hel is a dark and foreboding place reserved for the wicked. Another place for the dead is Valhalla, which is the heavenly place for heroic warriors killed in battle. The warriors will live in this heavenly hall of 540 rooms until the end of time, feasting at great banquets, going into battle daily, and being restored to health by the next day.

Germanic religion also contains myths of the creation and destruction of the world. As written down in the 13th century, the creation myth was built upon a number of older traditions and is at times contradictory. In the beginning, according to Germanic belief, there was a great void filled with magic forces. Before the emergence of the earth, a number of cosmic rivers and separate worlds emerged, and from one of the rivers the primeval giant, Ymir, was created. He gave rise to a race of terrible giants by sweating them out from under his arms and legs. Ymir was nourished by the milk of a great cosmic cow, who also gave shape to another primeval being, Borr, the ancestor of the gods. Three of Borr's sons, Odin and his brothers, rose up and killed Ymir and created the earth out of his body. His flesh made up the earth, his blood formed the waters of the earth, his hair the trees, his bones the mountains, and his skull, supported by dwarves, was the sky. In the middle of the earth the gods created a land for the first humans, who were created by the gods from two dead tree trunks, and their descendants.

Germanic religion also had a myth concerning the end of the world that is contained in several epic tales from the Middle Ages. Ragnarök, which literally means "fate of the gods," though it is often translated "Twilight of the Gods," is the time of final destruction of the gods and of the world and everything in it. Although the primary account of the Ragnarök was written as the Germanic world was converting to Christianity and was clearly influenced by Christian eschatology, it does reveal important traditional Germanic attitudes toward the fate of the world. In this tale, the movement toward the end begins with the murder of Balder through the machinations of Loki. Although Loki is punished, his acts set in motion the chain of events that will bring about the final cataclysmic struggle. The great wolf, Fenris, breaks his fetters and leads forth the wolves who will devour the sun and moon. Loki too breaks loose and leads the giants and other evil forces against the gods, and a great battle ensues in which all the gods are killed. The sun will then burn out and the stars will sink into the sea as all of existence comes to an end. A new world, however, will rise from the ashes of the old world, new gods and humans will inhabit the world, and Balder and his brother Hoðr will rise again.

Germanic religion gradually faded away, to be preserved only in the later sagas, especially in those of Scandinavia of the 12th and 13th centuries. As a result of the efforts of Christian missionaries from the Roman Empire, the Anglo-Saxon missionary St. Boniface, the great Frankish emperor Charlemagne, and other rulers and missionaries, the barbarian peoples converted to Christianity during the early Middle Ages. The Ostrogoths and Visigoths converted in the fourth century, the Franks in the fifth, the Anglo-Saxons in the late sixth, and other peoples in the ninth and tenth. The last of the Germanic peoples to convert were those of Scandinavia and Iceland, the areas where most of the legends were preserved best.

See also: Anglo-Saxons; Bede; Beowulf; Boniface, St.; Charlemagne; Franks; Ostrogoths; Visigoths

Bibliography

Bede. *Ecclesiastical History of the English People with Bede's Letter to Egbert and Cuthbert's Letter on the Death of Bede.* Trans. Leo Sherley-Price. Harmondsworth, UK: Penguin, 1991.

Dumézil, Georges. *Gods of the Ancient Northmen.* Trans. Einer Haugen. Berkeley: University of California Press, 1973.

Grimm, Jakob. *Teutonic Mythology.* 4 Vols. Trans. James Stevens Stallybrass. London: Routledge, 1999.

Heaney, Seamus, trans. *Beowulf: A New Verse Translation.* New York: Farrar Straus and Giroux, 2000.

Jolly, Karen Louise, *Popular Religion in Late Saxon England: Elf Charms in Context.* Chapel Hill: University of North Carolina Press, 1996.

Jordanes. *The Gothic History of Jordanes in English Version.* Trans. Charles C. Mierow. New York: Barnes and Noble, 1985.

Polomé, Edgar C. *Essays on Germanic Religion.* Washington, DC: Institute for the Study of Man, 1989.

Russell, James C. *The Germanization of Early Medieval Christianity: A Sociohistorical Approach to Religious Transformation.* Oxford: Oxford University Press, 1994.

Tacitus. *The Agricola and the Germania.* Trans. H. Mattingly. Revised trans. S. A. Hanford. Harmondsworth, UK: Penguin, 1982.

Turville-Petre, Edward O. G. *Myth and Religion of the North: The Religion of Ancient Scandinavia.* London: Weidenfeld and Nicholson, 1964.

Gildas (c. 500–570)

A monk and Briton whose history of the Anglo-Saxon invasions of England is the only substantial contemporary account of the fall of late Roman Britain to the invading barbarians. His history is also the earliest source for the deeds that became the basis of the later Arthurian tales, even though Gildas never mentions a King Arthur in his work. Although it does not seem to have been frequently copied in the Middle Ages, his work is important also because it is one of the two sources the great Anglo-Saxon historian Bede used for his ecclesiastical history, and thanks to Bede the name of Gildas was remembered with honor by other historians in the Middle Ages.

Born at around the year 500, the time of the great victory by the British over the invaders at Badon Hill, Gildas wrote his history in the middle of the sixth century, possibly in 547. Gildas's history of the conquest of England is not systematically organized, and includes a collection of quotations of scriptural citations and historical information. It is a bitter tale full of recrimination and reproach. The essential theme of the work by Gildas, one borrowed by Bede in his discussion of the invasion and conquest of England, is that the coming of the Anglo-Saxons was the just punishment by God of people who claimed to be Christian but who indulged in wanton excess and luxury. The conquest of England, for Gildas, began with invasions of barbarians, probably Picts and Scots, and an appeal to the Roman general, Aëtius, for aid, which was not forthcoming. The Britons were able to expel the barbarians but then fell into civil war and further raids. A British ruler, traditionally Vortigern, invited Saxon war bands to aid against other barbarians, and those war bands were subsequently joined by other Saxons against the Britons. The invasions of the Saxons, according to Gildas, laid waste the towns of Briton and destroyed the way of life that had existed.

Gildas's account is not, however, without its heroes, and it is one of these which may have provided the first outlines for the figure of Arthur. Gildas fails to mention Arthur directly, but he only names kings directly who fit into his broader theme that the invasions are divine punishment for the Britons' failure to live as good Christians. Moreover, he does mention one leader on whom the legendary figure of Arthur may be based and a battle that is often listed among those of the legendary king. In 500, the year of Gildas's birth as he tells us, the Britons won a great victory over invading barbarian armies at Mount Badon, a victory that provided England a period of much needed peace that continued at least until the time that Gildas wrote his history. The victor at that battle was the Roman commander Ambrosius Aurelianus, who had reorganized the defense of the Britons, and whose victory was later associated with the deeds of King Arthur.

See also: Aëtius; Anglo-Saxons; Badon Hill, Battle of; Bede; King Arthur; Vortigern

Bibliography

Barber, Richard. *The Figure of Arthur.* Totowa, NJ: Rowman and Littlefield, 1972.

Bede. *Ecclesiastical History of the English People with Bede's Letter to Egbert and Cuthbert's Letter on the Death of Bede.* Trans. Leo Sherley-Price. Harmondsworth, UK: Penguin, 1991.

Blair, Peter Hunter. *The World of Bede.* Cambridge: Cambridge University Press, 1970.

Gildas. *The Ruin of Britain and Other Works.* Ed. and trans. Michael Winterbottom. London: Phillimore, 1978.

Stenton, Frank M. *Anglo-Saxon England.* 3rd ed. Oxford: Clarendon, 1971.

Goor. *See* Alans

Gothic Wars

A major component of the emperor Justinian's effort to reconstitute the Roman Empire, the Gothic Wars lasted from 535 to 561 and were preceded by the emperor's conquest of North Africa. The Gothic Wars were a prolonged and destructive effort that ended with the destruction of the Ostrogothic kingdom and short-lived Byzantine control of the Italian peninsula. Although direct Byzantine control of Italy was undermined beginning in 568, Byzantine influence in Italy lasted into the eight century, and Justinian's conquests shaped cultural, religious, and political affairs in Italy throughout the early Middle Ages.

The first step came with the invasion and rapid conquest of Vandal North Africa. Justinian had originally hoped to secure the aid of the Vandal king, Hilderic, a pro-Roman ruler who had even abandoned Arian Christianity for the Catholic Christianity favored in Constantinople. His overthrow and replacement by Gelimer, who reflected the traditional Vandal hostility toward the empire, forced the emperor to change plans. In 533–534, Justinian's loyal and talented general, Belisarius, led Byzantine armies into North Africa, where he managed to defeat Gelimer and the Vandals. The kingdom was quickly restored to Roman rule, and Belisarius was granted a triumph—the ancient Roman ceremonial parade accorded to victorious generals—through the streets of Constantinople. Gelimer was displayed during the triumph, as were many captive Vandals. The Vandal king was settled on an estate far from the kingdom, and many of the most able Vandal soldiers were enrolled in the Byzantine army and dispatched to the Persian frontier.

Justinian next turned his eyes to Italy, where the great king Theodoric had ruled an Ostrogothic kingdom from the 490s until his death in 526. Theodoric's successors, however, were not his equal, and the kingdom itself was rent by conflict between those who supported an alliance with the empire and those who rejected any ties to the empire or its traditions. Justinian exploited these divisions, especially as they involved Theodoric's daughter and regent, Amalaswintha. According to Procopius, Justinian had more than a diplomatic interest in the beautiful and intelligent princess, and may have desired a marriage alliance with her as a means to claim Italy. Procopius also alleges that Theodora, deeply jealous of Amalaswintha, secretly plotted against her and encouraged the Gothic opposition to kill the princess. Her murder, after Justinian had declared that he would defend the Gothic princess and promised swift punishment should anything happen to her, gave the emperor a pretext to invade Italy. If Procopius is to be believed, the murder came as the result of a letter from Theodora, which assured the Gothic nobles that Justinian would do nothing if they acted against Amalaswintha. It is possible that Justinian and Theodora indulged in a dangerous diplomatic game that led to the death of Amalaswintha, but also provided them the opportunity to restore imperial control over Italy. Whatever the case, Amalaswintha was deposed and murdered, and Justinian used this as the justification for his invasion of Italy.

The war began with a feint into Sicily in 535, which Belisarius quickly conquered. The rapidity of the general's success inspired Justinian to proceed more aggressively in 536, when Byzantine armies marched onto the Italian mainland. Although Belisarius enjoyed early success, the war dragged on for nearly 25 years and caused great destruction to the Italian countryside. The Goths put up a great struggle under different leaders and over two generations, and the Romans of Italy, though they at first welcomed the invaders, proved less open to the restoration of Roman rule and its taxation.

The war proceeded in several phases, at first involving Belisarius, who led the initial campaigns against Witigis, who had married Theodoric's granddaughter and claimed to be the legitimate successor to Amalaswintha and her son Athalaric. Seizing Rome in 356, Belisarius withstood the siege of Witigis and was able to take a further offensive against the Goth who withdrew from Rome hoping to strengthen his position in other parts of Italy. The king's efforts proved ineffective; attempts at finding allies among the Franks and Lombards failed, and his Gothic forces melted away. Witigis also sought to persuade Belisarius to establish himself as ruler in the West, but this backfired and Witigis surrendered to the Byzantine general in 540 who then returned to Constantinople.

In the 540s, however, Justinian and Belisarius faced a greater challenge from the king Totila, who won a series of victories, most notably at Faenza in 541–542, which had the added benefit of attracting new recruits to his army from both the Gothic and Roman population of Italy. Totila also benefited from Justinian's difficulties on the Persian frontier and the emperor's fear of granting Belisarius too many troops because the Goths had offered Belisarius ruling authority in Italy. Building on his early victories, Totila remained in control throughout the 540s. In 546, Totila took Rome after a long siege, which was retaken in the next year by Belisarius who had been returned to Italy in 544. But the Byzantine had little further success against his Gothic rival was recalled to Constantinople in 548. In 549 Witigis in turn took back Rome and captured forts in Tarentum and Rimini. He also built a fleet which attacked Byzantine shipping, ravaged Dalmatia and Epirus, and even captured Sicily. His military and naval successes enabled Totila to attempt a negotiated settlement of the war with Justinian.

Despite the setbacks of the 540s Justinian was unwilling to settle and continued the Gothic Wars throughout the next decade. The emperor had good fortune of his own in the early 550s as he settled affairs with Persia which provided the Justinian the necessary resources to bring the war to a close. The emperor used these resources to undertake a major offensive into Italy through the Balkans, entrusting the campaign to the general Narses. In late June or early July of 552, Narses met Totila in battle at Busta Gallorum, a plain in the northern Apennines. Narses, with a second army of invasion, overwhelmed Totila and his forces. The Goths left 6,000 dead on the field, and Totila was mortally wounded. Repeated efforts over the next few years to push back the Byzantines proved unsuccessful, and from 559 to 560, Narses gradually restored Byzantine authority throughout all of Italy. One final effort was launched in 561, but again the Goths failed, and with that failure, the Ostrogoths passed into extinction. The Italian conquest, however, did not long survive Justinian's death; the Lombards began their conquest of Italy in 568.

See also: Amalaswintha; Belisarius; Constantinople; Justinian; Lombards; Narses; Procopius; Rome; Theodora; Theodoric; Totila; Vandals

Bibliography

Browning, Robert. *Justinian and Theodora*. London: Thames and Hudson, 1987.

Burns, Thomas S. *A History of the Ostrogoths.* Bloomington: Indiana University Press, 1984.

Heather, Peter. *The Goths.* Oxford: Blackwell Publishers, 1996.

Hughes, Ian. *Belisarius: The Last Roman General.* Yardley, PA: Westholme Publishing, 1996.

Llewellyn, Peter. *Rome in the Dark Ages.* New York: Barnes and Noble, 1993.

Procopius *The History of the Wars: Secret History.* 4 Vols. Trans. H. B. Dewing. Cambridge, MA: Harvard University Press, 1914–1924.

Goths. *See* Ostrogoths; Visigoths

Gottschalk of Orbais (c. 803–867/869)

Controversial Carolingian monk and theologian. Gottschalk was a talented theologian whose works provided important interpretations of the teachings of St. Augustine of Hippo. He was involved in two major controversies in his life. The first concerned the practice of child oblation, that is, placing a young child in a monastery before the child is old enough to make its own decision. The second was over his teachings concerning predestination, which were based on the works of Augustine but contrary to the orthodox teachings of the time. The predestination controversy involved a number of leading ecclesiastics in the Carolingian Empire and revealed the increasing intellectual confidence and sophistication of these Carolingian thinkers.

Gottschalk was born in Saxony in 803 and given to the monastery of Fulda as a child by his father. He spent his childhood at monasteries in Fulda and Reichenau under the direction of the abbot and bishop Rabanus Maurus. As an adult, Gottschalk requested that he be released from his monastic vows because he had not taken them personally and because there were no Saxon witnesses to the vow. A church council at Mainz in 829 granted his request, even though it refused to allow him to have the donation made by his father. Rabanus Maurus, however, appealed the decision at a separate church council, and Gottschalk was not released from his monastic vows. He was allowed to join another monastery, and for the next 10 years he was at monasteries in Corbie and Orbais, where he studied the writings of St. Augustine of Hippo. He also was ordained a priest sometime in the 830s, but without the approval of the bishop in the diocese.

In the 840s, he made a pilgrimage to Rome, where he began to preach the views on predestination he had learned from his study of Augustine. He taught that God had foreseen and in fact predestined the salvation or damnation of all people since before the beginning of time, which meant further that Jesus died only for the saved and that the sacraments were valid only for the saved. These views clearly challenged the authority of the church of his day, and the bishops who defended the church's tradition responded harshly to these ideas. Indeed, when word of his teaching reached the Carolingian Empire, his old rival Rabanus Maurus compelled Gottschalk to defend his views at a church council in Mainz in 848. His teaching was condemned at the council, and he was handed over to Archbishop Hincmar of Rheims. At a second council in the following year, Gottschalk was condemned again and was ordered whipped and imprisoned at the monastery of Hautvillers. His writings were burned, his ordination was overturned, and gradually his right to correspond with others was revoked. Despite the severity of his punishment, Gottschalk refused to renounce his ideas and continued to write on the matter and other theological topics until his death. His ideas were condemned at church councils throughout the 850s and 860s, and a number of other Carolingian ecclesiastics wrote treatises against Gottschalk's views. Indeed, the controversy was so great that it attracted the attention of the Carolingian king Charles the Bald, who requested the opinion of a number of ecclesiastics, including John Scotus Erigena.

Gottschalk was also a talented poet, and his surviving poetry confirms our understanding of him as an intelligent and pious man. Although few in number, Gottschalk's poems also reveal the quality and variety of poetry produced during the Carolingian Renaissance. His poetry was especially innovative in its use of rhyme. He wrote a number of religious poems, including poems on the canonical hours and predestination as well as one that was a prayer to Christ. His religious poems demonstrate an awareness of human sinfulness, but also a hope for God's mercy and the mediation of God's Son. He also wrote poems of a more personal nature, including one expressing personal melancholy, and another poem to a friend filled with expressions of love for this friend and praise of God. His poetry, as well as his other writings, reveal the success of Charlemagne's efforts to convert and educate the pagan Saxons.

See also: Augustine of Hippo, St.; Carolingian Dynasty; Carolingian Renaissance; Charlemagne; Charles the Bald; Hincmar of Rheims

Bibliography

Duckett, Eleanor Shipley. *Carolingian Portraits: A Study in the Ninth Century.* Ann Arbor: University of Michigan Press, 1962.

Laistner, Max L. W. *Thought and Letters in Western Europe, A.D. 500 to 900.* 2nd ed. Ithaca, NY: Cornell University Press, 1976.

Marenbon, John. "Carolingian Thought." In *Carolingian Culture: Emulation and Innovation.* Ed. Rosamond McKitterick. Cambridge: Cambridge University Press, 1994, pp. 171–92.

Riché, Pierre. *The Carolingians: A Family Who Forged Europe.* Trans. Michael Idomir Allen. Philadelphia: University of Pennsylvania Press, 1993.

Gregory I, the Great, Pope (c. 540–604)

One of the greatest and most influential of the popes of the early Middle Ages, Gregory, pope from 590 to 604, is also recognized as one of the fathers of the church. Although not the powerful theologian that St. Augustine of Hippo was, Gregory made important contributions to the religious life of the early Middle Ages with his *Dialogues,* which includes a life of St. Benedict of Nursia; his *Pastoral Rule,* guidelines for the proper rule of bishops; and his sermons, many of which took the form of commentaries on books of Scripture. As pope, he corresponded with the kings and queens of the Merovingian Franks; negotiated the difficult relationships between the papacy, the Lombard kings of Italy, and the Byzantine emperor in Constantinople; and reformed papal administration to make it a more effective power in central Italy. He is perhaps best known for the evangelical mission he sent to convert the Anglo-Saxons in England, which also signaled the importance of the barbarian kingdoms to the papacy.

Although little is known of his early life, Gregory was born sometime around 540 to good Christians of the senatorial class, and was the grandson of Pope Felix III. He most likely received a good education, although he knew no Greek and seems to have been little influenced by the classical literature he no doubt read. His learning and family background prepared him for a life of civil service, and in 572 or 573 he was appointed prefect of the city of Rome by the Senate. He held the

Fourteenth-century depiction of the Bavarian princess Theudelinda and her husband the Lombard king Agilulf exchanging presents with Pope Gregory the Great. (St. John Basilica, Monza, Italy/The Bridgeman Art Library)

post until about 574, when he experienced a religious conversion and retired to a monastery he founded on family property and dedicated to St. Andrew. His stay at the monastery was short because the pope, Pelagius II (579–590), called him out of retirement to papal service. He served as the papal representative in Constantinople until 585 or 586, when he returned to act as abbot of his monastery and secretary to the pope. On the death of Pelagius in 590, Gregory was acclaimed pope by the people of Rome, who acted without the consent of the Senate or emperor. He was chosen in large measure because of his administrative skills, which were needed to address the problems brought by excessive rain, flooding, and plague.

Gregory's 14-year pontificate, 590–604, was important for a number of reasons, including his administrative reforms and pastoral activities, which laid the foundation for traditions of the medieval papacy. He asserted the role of the papacy as the main power in Italy and in that role negotiated with Byzantines, Franks, and Lombards. He assumed the old imperial duty of charity and made numerous grants from his private wealth, making monthly donations of food to the poor, daily grants to the sick and infirm, and benefactions to monks and nuns. He assumed the responsibility of restoring public buildings such as aqueducts and churches, and took charge of the defense of the city by appointing military commanders and hiring soldiers. He reorganized papal lands to provide a more secure financial footing for the papacy.

Although an administrative genius, Gregory also established important pastoral practices that guided the papacy for generations to come. In his Pastoral Rule (*Regula pastoralis*), copies of which he sent to numerous bishops, Gregory offers guidelines for the bishop's office. He outlines the character traits needed to be a bishop, the spiritual obligations to a bishop's flock, the duties of teaching and preaching, and the responsibility to set a good personal example. Gregory himself lived by the rules he outlined, thus providing his own example for subsequent popes to follow. An active preacher, Gregory wrote numerous sermons and other works that promoted the cult of the saints, Catholic Christianity over paganism and Arian Christianity, and the monastic life, especially according to the Rule of St. Benedict of Nursia.

Active in church administration and religious life, Gregory faced numerous political challenges in his reign as pope, particularly as a result of the Lombard invasion of Italy in 568. In the generation before Gregory's ascension to the papal throne the Lombards had made great strides in the conquest of Italy and had undermined the ability of the emperor in Constantinople or his representative in Ravenna to defend the pope effectively. They also devastated the famous monastery of Benedict at Monte Cassino, thus demonstrating the weakness of the empire and the necessity for the pope finding alternate means of protection. The situation for Gregory worsened in 593 when the new Lombard king, Agilulf, came to power and resumed hostilities. He attempted to negotiate a peace settlement with Agilulf, but was hampered by Constantinople's desire for war with the Lombard king. At one point, Gregory bought peace from Agilulf at the price of 500 pounds of gold and finally managed to secure peace in Italy, despite the Byzantines, in 598. Not only did Gregory work to secure peace with the Lombards, but he also sought to convert them from Arian to Catholic Christianity. He was a frequent correspondent of Theudelinda, the wife of Agilulf, who was a Catholic and was encouraged to convince her husband to convert. At the very least, Gregory's correspondence with Theudelinda brought the return of papal territories and numerous churches from Agilulf, even though the Lombards converted to Catholic Christianity only at the end of the seventh century.

Gregory also regularly corresponded with the Merovingian kings and queens during his reign, and his most important correspondent was the powerful queen Brunhilde. He wrote her because of his concern with improprieties in the Frankish church, particularly the practice of simony (the buying or selling of church offices). To obtain reform in the church, Gregory made concessions to Brunhilde; most importantly, he granted her request that the see of Vienne be elevated to the status of metropolitan bishopric. Little progress was made in the reform of the Frankish church, but an important relationship was established that foreshadowed the relationship of the Franks and the popes in the eighth century. Gregory's correspondence with Brunhilde had one significant result, however. According to Gregory, Brunhilde, whom the pope asked to support the missionary Augustine of Canterbury, was more responsible for the success of the mission to England than anyone but God.

Perhaps more than anything, Gregory is best known for that mission to convert the Anglo-Saxons of England in 596. According to the English historian Bede, Gregory had the idea of converting the English even before he became pope. One day while shopping in the market place Gregory saw a group of handsome boys for sale as slaves. He asked where they came from and was told from Britain. He inquired further if they were Christian and of what race they were. He was told that they were not and that they were Angles. He declared that it was appropriate that they were Angles because they had "angelic faces" (100) and that they must be rescued from the error of paganism. Gregory asked the pope to send him as a missionary to convert the English, but he was forbidden to go because he was needed in Rome.

Once he became pope, however, Gregory revived the idea of an evangelical mission to England, and sent St. Augustine and a number of missionaries to undertake the conversion of the English. To ensure the success of the mission, Gregory wrote to Brunhilde for support of the missionaries on their journey and to the English king

Aelle to allow the establishment of the mission in England. Gregory continued to write to the English king, encouraging him to accept the faith, and also to Augustine, encouraging him in his mission. In the generation after Augustine the English converts fell back into paganism, but the mission to England did ultimately succeed, and an important relationship was established between England and Rome, one that had important consequences when Anglo-Saxon missionaries returned to preach on the continent.

Gregory's reign was important in the history of the papacy and in the history of early medieval Europe. His administrative reforms and pastoral regulations improved the standing of the papacy in Italy and set the standard for religious life and practice for popes and bishops. His correspondence with barbarian kings and queens left a great legacy and marked the beginnings of a shift in papal policy from east to west. Although Gregory remained a loyal subject of the emperor in Constantinople, he recognized the importance of the barbarian rulers of the west, and his contacts with them led to increasingly close ties between Rome and western rulers over the next century and a half, culminating in the formal alliance of the Franks and popes in the eighth century.

See also: Anglo-Saxons; Augustine of Canterbury, St.; Augustine of Hippo, St.; Bede; Brunhilde; Constantinople; Lombards; Merovingian Dynasty; Ravenna, Rome

Bibliography

Bede. *Ecclesiastical History of the English People with Bede's Letter to Egbert and Cuthbert's Letter on the Death of Bede.* Trans. Leo Sherley-Price. Harmondsworth, UK: Penguin, 1991.

Colgrave, Bertram, ed. and trans. *The Earliest Life of Gregory the Great, by an Anonymous Monk of Whitby.* Lawrence: University of Kansas Press, 1968.

Evans, Gillian R. *The Thought of Gregory the Great.* Cambridge: Cambridge University Press, 1988.

Gregory the Great. *Saint Gregory the Great: Dialogues.* Trans. Odo John Zimmerman. New York: Fathers of the Church, 1959.

Herrin, Judith. *The Formation of Christendom.* Princeton, NJ: Princeton University Press, 1989.

Llewellyn, Peter. *Rome in the Dark Ages.* New York: Barnes and Noble, 1996.

Markus, Robert A. *Gregory the Great and His World.* Cambridge: Cambridge University Press, 1998.

Meyvaert, Paul. *Benedict, Gregory, Bede and Others.* London: Variorum Reprints, 1977.

Paul the Deacon. *History of the Lombards.* Trans. William Dudley Foulke. Philadelphia: University of Pennsylvania Press, 1974.

Richards, Jeffrey. *Consul of God: The Life and Times of Gregory the Great.* London: Routledge and Kegan Paul, 1980.

Straw, Carol. *Gregory the Great: Perfection in Imperfection.* Berkeley: University of California Press, 1991.

Gregory II, Pope (669–731)

Gregory II was one of two popes in the eighth century who were involved in a revolution in papal policy that led to the establishment of an alliance between the papacy and the Carolingian dynasty and the rupture of relations with the Byzantine Empire. Although it was his successor, Pope Gregory III, who made formal overtures to the Carolingian mayor of the palace and effective ruler of the Franks Charles Martel and the later pope Stephen II who formalized the relationship, the conditions that required the diplomatic revolution were set in Gregory II's reign. His difficulties with both the Lombard king and the Byzantine emperor, as well as the papacy's growing connections with the Frankish kingdom, laid the foundation for a closer association in the coming generation.

Gregory's pontificate (715–731) revealed the growing tensions with the Byzantine Empire and growing connections with the barbarian kingdoms in a number of ways. One of the most important examples of the increasing ties with the west was Gregory's relationship to Boniface, an important Anglo-Saxon missionary with great influence among the Franks, who possessed the devotion to Rome shared by the English since their conversion to Christianity. Boniface's visits to Rome reinforced the Franks' interest in the papal city and brought Roman liturgical and administrative reforms to the Frankish church and newly converted areas of Saxony. In 719, Boniface visited Rome for the first time and swore allegiance to the pope before going to preach among the pagans of central Germany. Three years later in 722, Boniface returned to Rome to receive episcopal consecration from Gregory. He also swore an oath of allegiance to Gregory in preparation for his mission to convert the Saxons and reform the Frankish church. Gregory's own correspondence reveals that he saw the mission as an extension of the authority of the Roman church. Boniface's mission and dedication to Rome and Gregory's support of the mission was an important step in strengthening ties between Rome and the Frankish kingdom.

Gregory also faced serious challenges in Italy of the kind that ultimately led to a break between Rome and Constantinople. In 712, a new Lombard king, Liutprand, ascended the throne and renewed the Lombard effort to unify Italy. Although the Lombards had converted to Catholic Christianity at the end of the seventh century, they did not let spiritual concerns interfere with political ambitions and were thus still eager to take control of all Italy, including territories controlled by the papacy. The papacy's traditional ally against the Lombards, the Byzantine Empire, was, however, powerless to assist Gregory in his struggles with Liutprand. Moreover, the emperor, Leo III, the Isaurian, had instituted a religious policy of iconoclasm (banning and eventual destruction of icons with images of Jesus, Mary, and the saints) without the approval of the pope. Leo further alienated the pope and people of Italy with his administrative reforms, which increased the burden of taxation on Italy.

Gregory was placed in an awkward position by the actions of the Lombard king and the Byzantine emperor. He attempted to restrain Liutprand and also remain loyal to Leo. In the 720s, for example, he negotiated successfully with Liutprand for the return of papal territory that had been seized by the Lombard king. Gregory also kept Liutprand from marching on Rome, and instead welcomed him into the city to pray at St. Peter's and make an offering of his cloak, sword, breastplate, and crown to the apostle Peter. The pope also sought to restrain the worst assaults on imperial rule by the people of Rome and refused to support a rival emperor. Gregory realized that his only support against the unreliable Liutprand was the emperor, but the pope's activities clearly established a new relationship between Rome and Constantinople. No longer was the pope a subject of the empire but an ally, and once the empire proved unable to help, later popes turned to a more reliable supporter in the kingdom of the Franks.

See also: Boniface, St.; Carolingian Dynasty; Charles Martel; Constantinople Gregory III; Iconoclastic Controversy; Leo III, the Isaurian; Liutprand; Lombards; Rome

Bibliography

Davis, Raymond, trans. *The Lives of the Eighth-Century Popes* (Liber Pontificalis): *The Ancient Biographies of Nine Popes from* A.D. *715 to* A.D. *817.* Liverpool, UK: Liverpool University Press, 1992.

Herrin, Judith. *The Formation of Christendom.* Princeton, NJ: Princeton University Press, 1987.

Llewellyn, Peter. *Rome in the Dark Ages.* New York: Barnes and Noble, 1971.

Noble, Thomas F. X. *The Republic of St. Peter: The Birth of the Papal State, 680–825.* Philadelphia: University of Pennsylvania Press, 1984.

Paul the Deacon. *History of the Lombards.* Trans. William Dudley Foulke. Philadelphia: University of Pennsylvania Press, 1974.

Riché, Pierre. *The Carolingians: A Family Who Forged Europe.* Trans. Michael Idomir Allen. Philadelphia: University of Pennsylvania Press, 1993.

Gregory III, Pope (d. 741)

Mid-eighth-century pope (r. 731–741) who sought aid from the Carolingian mayor of the palace and effective ruler of the Franks, Charles Martel, to resolve the crisis brought on by the failure of Byzantine power in Italy and the continued encroachments on papal territory by the Lombards. Although Charles Martel was unable to aid the pope because of his long-standing friendship and political alliance with the Lombard king Liutprand, Gregory's diplomatic initiative marked a significant step in the history of the papacy and the Carolingian family. The pope's effort moved the papacy further into an alliance with the Frankish rulers of the west and further from the Byzantine emperor in Constantinople. It also laid the foundation for the alliance struck in the 750s between the popes and the Carolingian mayor of the palace and later king Pippin III the Short.

Gregory inherited a number of problems from his predecessor, Gregory II, including difficult relations with the Lombards and with the Byzantine emperor. In fact, the situation between Rome and Constantinople worsened in the opening year of Gregory III's reign as pope. In response to the emperor Leo III's policy of iconoclasm (the prohibition and eventual destruction of images of Jesus, Mary, and the saints) the new pope summoned a council in Rome to denounce the emperor's religious policy. The council asserted the growing independence of papal Rome from imperial Constantinople and was followed by Gregory's ambitious program of construction and renovation in Rome, a program that promoted the cult of images. Leo III's reaction is not altogether clear, but he did introduce a series of administrative reforms shortly after the council that may indicate his displeasure. He restructured taxation policy in Italy, reorganized the method of military recruitment, and withdrew a number of churches in Sicily from Roman jurisdiction.

Despite the increasing sense of alienation between Rome and Constantinople, Gregory continued to look at the emperor as his main source of protection against his enemies in Italy. The main rival of the popes was the Lombard king Liutprand, who had revived the traditional Lombard goal of unifying Italy. Liutprand, either because of illness or an agreement with Gregory II or probably both, had restrained his assault against Rome and papal territory in central Italy in the 730s. Unfortunately, several actions by Gregory III forced Liutprand back into action. During Liutprand's illness, his nephew, Hildeprand, was made coregent, and Byzantine commanders in Italy struck against the Lombards. When Hildeprand counterattacked, the Byzantine commanders were supported by Gregory III. The pope also sought further support from Lombard powers in southern Italy, the dukes of Beneventum and Spoleto. This alliance and the attacks against the Lombards in the north roused Liutprand to action against the pope and his allies. Liutprand's offensive put the pope in very straitened circumstances. The Lombard king took several papal cities in central Italy and captured the duchies of Beneventum and Spoleto for a time. The pope was powerless to stop the king and was now without allies in southern Italy or in the Byzantine capital in Italy, Ravenna, which Liutprand had recaptured. And the emperor himself could not be relied on for help.

In the face of extreme crisis in 739–740, Gregory took the initiative and contacted Charles Martel. He in fact wrote to the Carolingian mayor of the palace twice during the years 739–740 seeking aid against the advances of Liutprand. It is likely that Gregory had little hope that anything positive would ensue from the correspondence, because the pope surely knew of the friendship that had existed between the two rulers since 725. If he was unaware of that personal tie, he could not have been unaware of Liutprand's military assistance to Charles in 739 against the Muslims. But that notwithstanding, the pope wrote to Charles. He was possibly persuaded to do so by the Anglo-Saxon missionary Boniface, who had received protection from the Carolingian mayor. Indeed, Charles's support for Boniface was highly regarded by Rome, and the activities of Boniface may have increased Rome's prestige among the Franks. Moreover, Gregory's second letter, in 740, was couched in language and combined with gifts—keys to the tomb of St. Peter, a link from St. Peter's chain— that were intended to gain the most favorable response possible from Charles Martel. The second letter and, especially, the gifts may have inspired Charles to aid the pope. Although there was no official reaction from Charles, who relied upon his alliance with Liutprand, it is possible that when he returned the ambassadors he sent his own ambassadors, who mediated between Gregory and Liutprand. Whatever the case, Liutprand made no attacks on Roman territory from 739 to 742, possibly as a result of a request by Charles Martel.

Although it is possible that Gregory's diplomatic initiative bore no immediate fruit, it was significant in itself. It marked a crucial step in the papacy's disengagement from its ancient alliance with the emperors in Constantinople and their representatives in Ravenna. It was also an important moment in the establishment of an independent papal power in central Italy and an important attempt to limit the Lombard advance. Gregory's effort also set the stage for the establishment of a formal alliance between the pope's successors and Charles Martel's son, Pippin III the Short in the 750s.

See also: Boniface, St.; Carolingian Dynasty; Charles Martel; Constantinople; Gregory II, Pope; Iconoclastic Controversy; Leo III, the Isaurian; Liutprand; Lombards; Pippin III, Called Pippin the Short; Rome

Bibliography

Davis, Raymond, trans. *The Lives of the Eighth-Century Popes* (Liber Pontificalis): *The Ancient Biographies of Nine Popes from A.D. 715 to A.D. 817.* Liverpool, UK: Liverpool University Press, 1992.

Herrin, Judith. *The Formation of Christendom.* Princeton, NJ: Princeton University Press, 1987.

Llewellyn, Peter. *Rome in the Dark Ages.* New York: Barnes and Noble, 1971.

McKitterick, Rosamond. *The Frankish Kingdoms under the Carolingians, 751–987.* London: Longman, 1983.

Noble, Thomas F. X. *The Republic of St. Peter: The Birth of the Papal State, 680–825.* Philadelphia: University of Pennsylvania Press, 1984.

Paul the Deacon. *History of the Lombards.* Trans. William Dudley Foulke. Philadelphia: University of Pennsylvania Press, 1974.

Riché, Pierre. *The Carolingians: A Family Who Forged Europe.* Trans. Michael Idomir Allen. Philadelphia: University of Pennsylvania Press, 1993.

Gregory of Tours (c. 538–594)

Bishop of Tours from 573 until his death in 594, Gregory came from an illustrious Gallo-Roman family that included powerful political and religious figures. His father, Florentius, was a member of the senatorial class, and ancestors on both his paternal and maternal side were bishops of Clermont-Ferrand, Langres, and Tours. Gregory entered the priesthood at a young age, dedicated his life to the service of the church and the saints, and, despite weak connections with the town, became bishop of Tours in 573. Even though he had limited connections with Tours, he was devoted to St. Martin, whose cult was centered in Tours. Gregory ruled as bishop for the last two decades of his life, during a time of great political strife between the grandsons and great-grandsons of the Merovingian king Clovis, including a violent feud between the queens Brunhilde and Fredegund and between their husbands. Although a successful bishop and staunch advocate of the cult of St. Martin of Tours, Gregory is best known as the author of the *Histories in Ten Books,* commonly known as *The History of the Franks.* The work contains a famous and influential portrait of Clovis, the founder of the Merovingian dynasty, and the tale of his descendants throughout the sixth century. This great work also includes extensive discussion of Gregory's time as bishop—seven of ten books of the *Histories* address this period—and reveals important information on the social, cultural, and, especially, religious life of the Frankish kingdoms in the sixth century. Gregory also wrote eight books on miracle stories, a life of the church fathers, lives of various saints and martyrs, *Commentary on the Psalms,* a preface for a collection of church masses, and a work on liturgical masses.

Gregory, originally Georgius Florentius, was born on November 30, 538, to Florentius, a Gallo-Roman senator, and his much younger wife, Armentaria, who also was of senatorial lineage, in the Auvergne in the town now called Clermont-Ferrand. Although quite expansive about the many dukes, senators, bishops, and saints in his ancestry, Gregory offers few details in his writings about his own life. It is likely that his father died while Gregory was still quite young, and certain that his education was taken over by his relatives, especially his maternal uncle Bishop Nicetius of Lyons and paternal uncle Bishop Gallus of Clermont-Ferrand. Like his uncles and many of the ancestors of whom he was so proud, Gregory was marked for the religious life. He became a priest in 543, entered a choir school in Lyons for further instruction, and became a deacon in Lyons in 563. Moreover, his family connections introduced Gregory to many of the important saints of Gaul, including St. Julian of Brioude, whose relics once cured Gregory's brother Peter, and, most importantly, St. Martin of Tours, whose relics cured Nicetius of a terrible sore on his face. Devotion to the cult of the saints, especially St. Martin, remained an important aspect of Gregory's life.

Gregory himself benefited from saintly intervention. While on pilgrimage once, he was cured of a headache, and after his election as bishop of Tours in 573 the saints intervened to confirm his place as bishop. His election was controversial because the people of the town knew Gregory, who spent his time away from the region, only slightly. Shortly after arriving in Tours, Gregory placed the relics of St. Julian near those of St. Martin, an act that was followed by a brilliant flash of light. On the following day, he took the relics on procession, and a resident of the town declared that Martin had invited Julian to Tours, which was understood to mean that Martin wished Julian's spiritual son, Gregory, to be bishop. Although this event secured his place as bishop of Tours and the support of St. Martin, Gregory faced the challenge of surviving as a bishop despite the tumultuous politics of the Frankish kingdom.

Gregory faced numerous challenges as bishop from various Merovingian kings and queens, especially from Chilperic. Indeed, at the very outset of his tenure as bishop, Gregory tangled with Chilperic over rights of sanctuary and the marriage of the king's son, Merovech, to Brunhilde, the main rival to Chilperic and his wife Fredegund. At a council in Paris in 577, Gregory stood up to Chilperic and defended the fellow bishop who had performed the marriage ceremony for Merovech and Brunhilde. In 580, Chilperic nearly exiled him because of false allegations that Gregory intended to transfer authority to another Merovingian ruler. He also struggled with Chilperic over theological matters; he threatened the king with the wrath of God and the saints because Chilperic issued a charter denying the Catholic teaching that there were three persons in the Trinity. In the 580s, Gregory faced difficulties with Kings Guntram and Childebert. But his ability to weather these storms raised his prestige among the Merovingian kings and nobles as well as the people of his diocese. He became an important mediator between the various kings of the Franks, who indulged in civil war throughout much of Gregory's reign as bishop. At one point, he negotiated an important agreement between Childebert and Guntram. In 590 he received gifts from Fredegund, who was most likely hostile to Gregory because he assumed his position with the support of Brunhilde, and he was among those chosen to settle a dispute in the convent of St. Radegund, a member of the royal line, in Poitiers.

Although active in Merovingian politics and the religious life, Gregory wrote extensively; he is best known for his history, much of which is devoted to events in Gregory's own day. The work is divided into 10 books; it begins as a chronicle of world history. The first book tells the story of Adam and Eve, and continues with the history of the ancient Jews, the birth of Christianity, and the introduction of Christianity into Gaul. The next two books cover the history of Christianity and the late Roman Empire in the third to the fifth centuries, and the rise of the Merovingian kingdom of the Franks and its greatest leader, Clovis. The third book takes the history of the kingdom into Gregory's time, and the remaining books are a detailed study of the kingdom in Gregory's lifetime.

Although appearing somewhat episodic and chaotic, Gregory's work offers a view of history that suggests human existence is by nature chaotic and that only the divine is orderly. Whatever Gregory's methodology was, his history of his own time is a most valuable resource; it includes important portraits of the many kings and queens he knew and dealt with, including Chilperic, Fredegund, and Brunhilde. Drawing on the Bible and the works of Jerome, Eusebius, Orosius, and other important Christian historians and writers, Gregory's work pays attention to the miraculous and is concerned with the moral and religious undertones of history. Its view of kingship is shaped by the teachings of the Hebrew Scriptures, and Gregory's famous portrait of Clovis as king reveals the notion that the king must do God's work. The *Histories* also provides a number of contemporary letters, in full or part, from Gregory, St. Remigius, and other bishops; a copy of Radgund's letter of the foundation of her monastery in Poitiers; and excerpts from histories by Renatus Frigeridus and Sulpicius Alexander that have not otherwise survived. Along with his numerous writings on the saints and their miracles, Gregory's *Histories* provides important insights into the history of the late sixth century and, especially, the beliefs and practices of an influential, aristocratic bishop.

See also: Brunhilde; Chilperic I; Clovis; Fredegund; Merovingian Dynasty; Martin of Tours, St.; Sigebert

Bibliography

Goffart, Walter. *The Narrators of Barbarian History (A.D. 550–800): Jordanes, Gregory of Tours, Bede, and Paul the Deacon.* Princeton, NJ: Princeton University Press, 1988.

Gregory of Tours. *The History of the Franks.* Trans. Lewis Thorpe. Harmondsworth, UK: Penguin, 1974.

Gregory of Tours. *Gregory of Tours, Glory of the Martyrs.* Trans. Raymond Van Dam. Liverpool, UK: Liverpool University Press, 1988.

Gregory of Tours. *Gregory of Tours, Glory of the Confessors.* Trans. Raymond Van Dam. Liverpool, UK: Liverpool University Press, 1988.

Gregory of Tours. *Gregory of Tours: Life of the Fathers.* 2nd ed. Trans. Edward James. Liverpool, UK: Liverpool University Press, 1991.

Laistner, Max L. W. *Thought and Letters in Western Europe, A.D. 500 to 900.* 2nd ed. Ithaca, NY: Cornell University Press, 1976.

Nie, Giselle de. *Views from a Many-Windowed Tower: Studies of Imagination in the Works of Gregory of Tours.* Amsterdam: Rodopi, 1987.

Van Dam, Raymond. *Saints and Their Miracles in Late Antique Gaul.* Princeton, NJ: Princeton University Press, 1993.

Wallace-Hadrill, John M. *The Long-Haired Kings.* Toronto: University of Toronto Press, 1982.

Wood, Ian. *The Merovingian Kingdoms, 450–751.* London: Longman, 1994.

Grimoald (c. 615–657)

Early leader of what became the Carolingian dynasty. Grimoald's ambition nearly destroyed the family and sent it to the political wilderness until its restoration to power by Grimoald's nephew, Pippin II of Herstal. The son of Pippin I of Landen—Pippin had established the family's early prominence through an alliance with Arnulf of Metz and their combined support of Chlothar's rebellion against Brunhilde—Grimoald assumed the office of mayor of the palace in Austrasia on his father's death in 640. But Grimoald dreamed of greater power than that of mayor and had his son adopted into the Merovingian family. His son actually assumed the throne for a time, but in the end Grimoald's plan failed and nearly ruined the family's fortunes.

Assuming leadership of the family at his father's death, Grimoald was a popular and ambitious figure. He sought the office of mayor of the palace, which his father had held, but which was now held by Otto, the tutor of King Sigebert III (d. c. 656). Grimoald's opportunity came during the revolt of Radulf, duke of Thuringia. Joining the king and other nobles in the battle, Grimoald displayed courage and ingenuity that won the king's favor. Sigebert's army was decisively defeated by Radulf, and the king himself survived only because he was rescued by Grimoald. Rising in royal favor, Grimoald took the opportunity to strike out against Otto, arranging his assassination, and then taking his place as mayor of the palace in Austrasia. According to contemporary accounts, Grimoald held the region in tight control and was recognized as ruler of the realm. His success was due both to his own skill and the king's youth.

As mayor of the palace, Grimoald managed to accumulate great power and undertook a number of policies that continued to be pursued by later generations of the Carolingian family. As Pippin's son, Grimoald possessed numerous estates, an important source of wealth and power. His landed wealth allowed him to establish monasteries, which became sources of both political and spiritual support. By establishing monasteries, Grimoald could place political allies in positions of power with the ability to command even greater amounts of land and wealth that they could use on Grimoald's behalf. He continued to support these monasteries with his own wealth or that of the king after their foundation. Moreover, he persuaded his mother, Itta, to establish a monastery where she could retire. She established three churches on her property near the monastery and dedicated one of them to St. Peter. Her activities brought her into contact with St. Peter's successor, the pope in Rome; thus Grimoald and his mother laid the foundation for the relationship between the Carolingians and the pope that was so important to the family's success.

Grimoald also was an active supporter of Irish missionaries, who, along with the monks of the monasteries he founded, surely prayed for Grimoald and his family.

He also benefited from another family connection. His residence as mayor was at Metz, where his father's ally and Grimoald's uncle Arnulf of Metz was buried. A powerful aristocrat and bishop, Arnulf was recognized as a saint shortly after his death. The spiritual power of the saint enhanced the reputation of Grimoald's family, and Grimoald's own ties to the church of Metz were strengthened when he successfully supported the appointment of his relative, Chlodulf, the son of Arnulf, as bishop of Metz.

His success as mayor of the palace, and the power he acquired in that role, may have inspired Grimoald to take an even more ambitious step at the death of King Sigebert in 656. The king, who died at the age of 26, owed his life to Grimoald, and because of his youth he was dominated by the powerful mayor. Although still young, Sigebert was most anxious to have a male heir, but he met at first with no success. According to some contemporary accounts, Grimoald took advantage of the king's anxiety to convince Sigebert to adopt Grimoald's own son, Childebert, as the king's heir. When the queen produced a male heir, Dagobert II (d. 679), it appeared that Grimoald's plans for the succession of Childebert the Adopted, as he is known, were ruined. Indeed, Sigebert changed his plans and entrusted Dagobert's education to his trusted ally Grimoald. But the mayor preferred the advancement of his family to loyalty to the Merovingian line, and he orchestrated the deposition of Dagobert and the promotion of Childebert as king.

After Sigebert's death, Grimoald had Dagobert tonsured as a monk and taken to Ireland. Childebert was made king in his place, and the moment of the triumph of the Carolingian family seemed to have arrived. But the nobles of Neustria and their king Clovis II (d. 657) were not willing to accept the usurpation and lured Grimoald into a trap. He was captured and executed, probably in 657. His son Childebert, however, survived the death of his father and reigned until 662. He may have survived because of the death of Clovis and the youth of Clovis's heir, Chlotar III (d. 673). In 662, Childebert's reign came to an end for reasons unknown, and he was replaced by Clovis's son Childeric II (d. 675). Grimoald's coup, therefore, was a terrible failure, and it pushed the family out of power until the time of Pippin of Herstal. Although the Carolingian family successfully usurped the throne in the eighth century, they were unable to do so in the time of Grimoald, whose attempt nearly destroyed the family.

See also: Arnulf of Metz, St.; Austrasia; Balthild, St.; Brunhilde; Carolingian Dynasty; Chlotar II; Ebroin; Merovingian Dynasty; Neustria; Pippin I, Called Pippin of Landen; Pippin II, Called Pippin of Herstal

Bibliography

Bachrach, Bernard S. *Merovingian Military Organization, 481–751.* Minneapolis: University of Minnesota Press, 1972.

Fouracre, Paul, and Richard A. Gerberding. *Late Merovingian France: History and Hagiography, 640–720*. Manchester, UK: University of Manchester Press, 1996.

Gerberding, Richard, A. *The Rise of the Carolingians and the "Liber Historiae Francorum."* Oxford: Clarendon, 1987.

James, Edward. *The Franks*. Oxford: Blackwell, 1991.

McKitterick, Rosamond. *The Frankish Kingdoms under the Carolingians, 751–987*. London: Longman, 1983.

Riché, Pierre. *The Carolingians: A Family Who Forged Europe*. Trans. Michael Idomir Allen. Philadelphia: University of Pennsylvania Press, 1993.

Wood, Ian. *The Merovingian Kingdoms, 450–751*. London: Longman, 1994.

Gundobad (d. 516)

Important king of the Burgundians (r. c. 480–516) and leading figure in the early post-Roman world, Gundobad was a lawgiver and frequently involved with the major kings of his day. He was the nephew of the Roman general and power behind the throne, Ricimer, and was involved in Roman service for a while. As king of the Burgundians, Gundobad was involved with the Franks and Ostrogoths, concluding marriage alliances with the kings of those peoples. He also, according to the sixth-century historian Gregory of Tours, considered converting from Arian Christianity to Catholic Christianity, and even if he did not convert, the Catholic faith was an important tradition in his family, as demonstrated by his niece Clothild.

One of several brothers of the royal family, Gundobad was also a high-ranking figure in the Roman military and a strong supporter of his uncle Ricimer, the leading figure in the Western Empire. He fought with his uncle against the Vandals and succeeded him as the chief military officer of the Western Empire from 472 to 474. He fell from favor when a new emperor took the throne in the west, and fled north to his family's homeland, where he became king by about 480 and shared rule with his three brothers for the next decade. By the early 490s, two of his brothers had died, and according to Gregory, Gundobad murdered one of his brothers, Chilperic II, the father of Clothild. Although he may not have killed Chilperic, who may have died of natural causes, Gundobad was a leading power; he invaded Italy while Theodoric the Great was at war with Odovacar, the Germanic king who deposed the last Roman emperor in the West, to seize some territory. Theodoric was forced to expel the Burgundians and make territorial concessions to them. To improve their relationship, Theodoric and Gundobad forged a marriage alliance, in which one of Theodoric's daughters married Gundobad's son Sigismund in 496 or 497. Despite the marriage, the relationship between the two kings remained tense, in part because of the alliance that existed between the Burgundians and the Franks.

The relationship between the Burgundians and the Merovingian Franks, however, was also one that was often strained because of the ambitions of the two kings, Gundobad and Clovis. According to Gregory, a source of the tension between them came from Clothild, the wife of Clovis and niece of Gundobad. Gregory notes that Gundobad killed Clothild's father, but granted permission for her to marry the Frankish king, and she ultimately convinced her sons to avenge her father's death. Clovis himself made war on Gundobad. According to the historian of the Franks, Clovis was invited by Gundobad's brother Godigisel to join him against Gundobad about the year 500. When Clovis invaded, Gundobad called on his brother, who arrived but switched to Clovis's side during the battle, which forced Gundobad to flee. Unable to capture Gundobad, Clovis withdrew and left a detachment to support Godigisel, who was then defeated by an alliance of Gundobad and the Visigoths from Spain. Gundobad grew stronger and stopped payment of tribute to Clovis, who was forced to maintain his alliance with the Burgundian because of the threat of the Alemanni to the Franks. Indeed, Gundobad joined with Clovis against the Alemanni and the Visigoths when Clovis went to war against them and suffered because of this alliance. In the settlement of these contests, which drew the attention of Theodoric, Gundobad lost territory and weakened the kingdom.

Although he was not the most successful military leader, Gundobad was an important lawgiver. Around the year 500, Gundobad codified the laws of the Burgundians in the *Lex Gundobada* or *Liber constitutionem* (Book of Constitutions). The law was a compilation of traditional Burgundian tribal laws in Latin that applied to Gundobad's Burgundian subjects, issued in its final form by Gundobad's son Sigismund in 517. It included important sections on settlement patterns and distribution of land to the Burgundians and also contained a number of royal edicts. When issued by Sigismund it was joined by a collection of laws that concerned the Roman subjects of the Burgundian kings. The *Lex Gundobada* remained an important and influential legal code long after the destruction of the Burgundian kingdom, lasting into the ninth century, and is Gundobad's most important legacy.

See also: Arianism; Burgundian Code; Burgundians; Clotilda; Clovis; Franks; Gregory of Tours; Merovingian Dynasty; Law and Law Codes; Odovacar; Ricimer; Sigismund, St.; Theodoric the Great

Bibliography

Drew, Katherine Fisher, trans. *The Burgundian Code: The Book of Constitutions or Law of Gundobad and Additional Enactments.* Philadelphia: University of Pennsylvania Press, 1972.

Gregory of Tours. History of the Franks. Trans. Lewis Thorpe. Harmondsworth, UK: Penguin, 1974.

Randers-Pehrson, Justine Davis. *Barbarians and Romans: The Birth Struggle of Europe, A.D. 400–700.* Norman: University of Oklahoma Press, 1983.

Wolfram, Herwig. *The Roman Empire and Its Germanic Peoples.* Trans. Thomas J. Dunlap. Berkeley: University of California Press, 1997.

Wood, Ian. *The Merovingian Kingdoms, 450–751.* London: Longman, 1994.

Guntram (c. 535–592)

King of the Merovingian Franks, grandson of the great king Clovis, and favorite ruler of the bishop and historian Gregory of Tours, Guntram ruled over Burgundy, one of the kingdoms of the Franks, during a particularly tumultuous period in Merovingian history. Although at odds at times with his brothers, Guntram often sought to keep the peace and generally sought to promote unity and family interests rather than foment civil war and division. Despite differences with Fredegund, the wife of his brother Chilperic, he put personal interests aside to protect her son and his nephew, Chlothar II. He was also supportive of the church in his kingdom, and he was believed able to perform miracles by some of his contemporaries. Although he won the favor of church leaders because of his endorsement of religious reform, Guntram's piety could sometimes be a liability because it kept him from instilling fear in his subjects or rivals.

Guntram came to power on the death of his father, Chlotar I, in 561. He was joined by his brothers Charibert I, Chilperic, and Sigebert, with whom he came into conflict with over the division of Chlotar's kingdom. Traditionally, each of the sons of a Merovingian king would inherit part of the realm, a custom that in Guntram's generation caused great difficulty of the family. The conflict between the brothers was worsened, perhaps by the death of Charibert, certainly by the rivalry that also existed between Brunhilde, a Visigothic princess and the wife of Sigebert, and Fredegund, the wife of Chilperic. Guntram often found himself in the middle of the conflict between his brothers and between their wives, but he bore the brunt of his brothers' aggression. In 568, for example, Sigebert invaded Guntram's share of the kingdom and attempted to seize the city of Arles. Guntram and his armies were able to repel the invasion, and Sigebert lost many of his soldiers as they crossed the Rhone River after being turned away in their assault on Arles. In the 570s, the brothers once again came into conflict. In 573 a dispute broke out between Guntram and Sigebert that grew into a wider conflict involving all the brothers and their allies. Sigebert called on his allies among the Avars and faced an attack by Chilperic, who had formed an alliance with Guntram. Despite their combined might, Guntram and Chilperic were no match for Sigebert, and Guntram made peace with Sigebert in 575. Indeed, Sigebert seemed the most powerful of the three brothers and was on the point of eliminating Chilperic when Chilperic managed to assassinate his brother.

The death of Sigebert changed the landscape of the Merovingian kingdoms and altered the relationship of Guntram with the surviving members of his family. Chilperic once again became the aggressor in the family, and Guntram sought to protect his own interests and those of his nephew Childebert II (d. 596), successor of Sigebert. Chilperic struck quickly to seize cities belonging to Childebert, and Guntram took steps to protect his nephew and ensure his position as king. Although Guntram and Childebert had a falling out in the early 580s and Childebert joined with Chilperic, the two kings, Guntram and his nephew, remained in good terms after their falling out and remained allies against Chilperic until Chilperic's murder in 584. Once again the death of his brother altered Guntram's position in the kingdom. At first, Guntram was suspicious of the paternity of Chlotar II, Chilperic's son by Fredegund and his heir. Fredegund was reluctant to have the child baptized, which would have made Guntram the godfather, and she kept Chlotar from Guntram. As a result, Guntram became skeptical of Fredegund's claim that Chilperic was Chlotar's father. Ultimately, Fredegund and Guntram became reconciled, and Guntram remained Chlotar's defender until Guntram's death in 592. It should also be noted that Guntram's defense of family interests was not limited to the sons of his brothers. He was a staunch defender of his nieces, who were married or betrothed to Visigothic kings. He took a keen interest in the fate of Ingunde, who married the rebel Hermenegild, and was active in the failed negotiations over the marriage between Reccared and Chlodosind. Indeed, in both cases Guntram attacked Visigothic territory, unsuccessfully, in defense of family interests.

Guntram's struggles with his brothers and in defense of family interests were complicated by turmoil in his own kingdom. The most dangerous episode for Guntram was the invasion of the pretender Gundovald (d. 585), who claimed that he was one of Chlotar I's sons and therefore had a right to the throne. Gundovald's claims were supported by other Merovingian kings, but failed to bring him a share in the kingdom, and so he departed for Constantinople until the early 580s. In 582 or 583 he made his first attempt to return to the kingdom. Although that attempt failed, he returned again in 584 and gathered much support. A number of important supporters of Guntram, including his chief military officer and nobles loyal to Guntram's ally and nephew Childebert II, supported Gundovald's attempt to claim the throne and joined his army. Guntram managed to suppress the attempt and capture or kill the disloyal followers as well as the pretender.

Although some members of the kingdom did not fear Guntram because of his piety, the king gained the respect and support of the church and its bishops in the Frankish kingdoms. He often corresponded and even dined with the bishops, especially Gregory of Tours. The king was well known for his acts of charity. He also helped end an outbreak of an epidemic by his actions, which were more like those of a bishop than a king. He called his subjects together in a church and ordered them to eat and drink only bread and water and to keep prayer vigils. His prescription ended the outbreak, according to Gregory of Tours. Also, Gregory records the story of Guntram's miracle. As Gregory notes, a woman whose son was seriously ill with a fever "came up behind the King . . . [and] cut a few threads from his cloak" (510). She steeped the threads in water, which she then gave to her son who was immediately cured. Guntram was for Gregory the ideal Christian king; he was devoted to God, supported the interests of his family, and sought to keep the peace in the Merovingian kingdoms.

See also: Brunhilde; Chilperic I; Chlotar II; Clovis; Franks; Fredegund; Gregory of Tours; Hermenegild; Merovingian Dynasty; Reccared I; Visigoths

Bibliography

Bachrach, Bernard S. *Merovingian Military Organization, 481–751.* Minneapolis: University of Minnesota Press, 1972.

Gregory of Tours. *History of the Franks.* Trans. Lewis Thorpe. Harmondsworth, UK: Penguin, 1974.

James, Edward. *The Franks.* Oxford: Blackwell, 1988.

Lasko, Peter. *The Kingdom of the Franks: North-West Europe before Charlemagne.* New York: McGraw-Hill, 1971.

Wallace-Hadrill, J. M. *The Long-Haired Kings.* Toronto: University of Toronto Press, 1982.

Wemple, Suzanne. *Women in Frankish Society: Marriage and the Cloister, 500 to 900.* Philadelphia: University of Pennsylvania Press, 1981.

Wood, Ian. *The Merovingian Kingdoms, 450–751.* London: Longman, 1994.

Hadrian I, Pope (d. 795)

Roman noble and pope (r. 772–795), Hadrian was an important figure in the birth of the Papal States and an important ally of the Carolingian ruler Charlemagne. The pope contributed to Charlemagne's renewal of church and society and supplied law and liturgical models that helped the king reform affairs in his realm. He also welcomed the king to Rome twice as a pilgrim. Moreover, Hadrian presided over the final separation of the papacy from the Byzantine Empire, its long-time protector, and strengthened the alliance with the Carolingians. The pope contributed also to the strengthening of the Papal States and the demise of the Lombard kingdom. His appeal to Charlemagne for aid against the Lombard king Desiderius led to the Carolingian king's invasion and destruction of the Lombard kingdom. Hadrian's invitation also led to the greater involvement of the Carolingian dynasty in Italian affairs.

According to the *Liber Pontificalis* (Book of the Popes), Hadrian was a "very distinguished man, sprung from noble ancestry and born to influential parents" (123). He was, the official biography notes further, "elegant and most decorous of manner, a resolute and strenuous defender of the orthodox faith, his homeland and the flock entrusted to him" (123). He was raised by his uncle Theodatus, a powerful figure in Roman lay and religious circles, because his parents died while Hadrian was still young. The *Liber Pontificalis* records that from his youth, Hadrian was a pious and devout person who spent much time in prayer and praise of God. He lived a chaste life and was generous to the poor. His piety was noticed by Pope Paul I (r. 757–767), who made him a cleric and gave him an important office in the Roman church. Hadrian also served Paul's successor, Stephen III (r. 768–772), who also employed Hadrian in important positions in the church of Rome. His service brought him the favor of the people of Rome and election to the office of pope on the death of Stephen III.

Along with a number of internal political difficulties, which he effectively resolved, Hadrian's greatest challenge upon his elevation to the papal throne was the protection of the Papal States from the lingering Lombard threat. Indeed, the internal tensions that existed at Rome were related to Italian political affairs, as some factions in Rome were still friendly to the Lombard king, Desiderius. The papacy, during the reign of Stephen II (752–757), had confirmed its alliance with the Frankish Carolingian dynasty, however, and Hadrian continued that policy and was supported by the pro-Frankish faction in Rome. The situation was complicated by affairs in the Frankish kingdom, as its rulers Charlemagne and Carloman found themselves on the point of civil war and Charlemagne himself married the daughter of Desiderius. The death of Carloman ended one crisis, but his widow and children fled to Italy and the protection of Desiderius, whose daughter was repudiated by Charlemagne in 771–772.

The situation only improved slightly for Hadrian with the death of Carloman; he still faced an aggressive Desiderius, who sought to expand Lombard control in Italy and see Carloman's sons elevated to the kingship. Hadrian sent emissaries to Desiderius noting the pope's willingness to negotiate matters with the Lombard king, but also demanding the return of several key cities that the king had recently conquered. Desiderius refused the pope's request and even threatened to invade Roman territory, but withdrew from the border when Hadrian threatened to excommunicate him. Desiderius's continued hostility to Rome led Hadrian to seek aid once and for all from the Frankish king. He petitioned Charlemagne, after first giving Desiderius one last chance, to fulfill the obligations his father, Pippin the Short, had undertaken toward Rome. The Carolingian king willingly invaded Italy at the pope's request in 773 and defeated his Lombard rival in 774, who was besieged in his capital of Pavia for six months before submitting.

While the siege was proceeding, Charlemagne journeyed to Rome as a pilgrim to celebrate Easter and was welcomed by the pope, who sent an official delegation to meet the king some 30 miles from the city. Indeed, Hadrian accorded Charlemagne full honors as patrician, the title that had been bestowed on his father Pippin. The pope also welcomed the king on the steps of St. Peter's, and the two established a personal friendship that lasted until Hadrian's death in 795, despite the occasional tension caused by their competing claims to authority in Italy. Not only did the two forge a lasting friendship at that time, but they also renewed the political alliance the papacy had established under Charlemagne's father. The exact terms of the political discussions that took place between Charlemagne and Hadrian at their first meeting, however, remain vague and uncertain. According to the *Liber Pontificalis,* Charlemagne confirmed the donation of his father, the so-called Donation of Pippin which granted the papacy extensive lands in Italy, in full and deposited it on the altar of St. Peter. But this is a later and uncertain tradition and may not signal Charlemagne's exact intentions in regard to Italy and papal territory at that time. At the very least, Charlemagne did end the Lombard threat, with the exception of occasional raids on Roman territory from the Lombard duchies of the south, and established himself as king of the Lombards after his final victory over Desiderius.

Hadrian and Charlemagne remained close friends and important allies for the next two decades, and the pope provided further aid to the Carolingian ruler. In 780, Charlemagne made his second visit to Rome, where he was once again welcomed by Hadrian. On Easter, Charlemagne's son, Pippin (775/756–781), was baptized by the pope, who was also his baptismal sponsor. Hadrian, at Charlemagne's request, anointed the king's sons, Louis the Pious as king of Aquitaine and Pippin as king of Italy. Pippin established himself as king in Pavia, the old Lombard capital, and acted as his father's representative in Italy and did his will. Indeed, the establishment of Italy as part of the growing Carolingian Empire and the introduction of Carolingian authority in the peninsula remained a source of tension between Hadrian and Charlemagne. But the pope had little recourse, and his anointing strengthened the already powerful dynasty.

Although Charlemagne and Hadrian found themselves at odds at times over political and religious issues, they did find common cause in their opposition to the Spanish heresy of Adoptionism, which maintained that Christ was the son of God by adoption. Hadrian was also an important contributor to Charlemagne's religious reforms and sent him a copy of church law that the king could apply to the Frankish church. On the other hand, they found themselves in dispute over the second Council of Nicaea in 787. The empress Irene had invited representatives of the pope to attend the council, which repudiated Iconoclasm and restored the Byzantine tradition of the veneration of icons (religious images). Charlemagne and his advisors, as a result of a faulty translation of the decisions of the council, attacked the council. Despite religious and political differences, Charlemagne and Hadrian remained on good terms, and the king was greatly saddened at Hadrian's death and, according to Einhard, wept as if he had lost a brother. When he died in 795, Hadrian had presided over an important period in the history of the papacy and in relations between the Carolingians and Rome. He was succeeded by Pope Leo III, who further developed the alliance with the Carolingians.

See also: Adoptionism; Carloman, King of the Franks; Carolingian Dynasty; Charlemagne; Desiderius; Donation of Pippin; Einhard; Franks; Irene; Leo III, Pope; *Libri Carolini*; Lombards; Louis the Pious; Pippin III, Called Pippin the Short; Rome

Bibliography

Christie, Neil. *The Lombards: The Ancient Langobards.* Oxford: Blackwell, 1995.

Davis, Raymond, trans. *The Lives of the Eighth-Century Popes* (Liber Pontificalis): *The Ancient Biographies of Nine Popes from A.D. 715 to A.D. 817.* Liverpool, UK: Liverpool University Press, 1992.

Einhard and Notker the Stammerer. *Two Lives of Charlemagne.* Trans. Lewis Thorpe. Harmondsworth, UK: Penguin, 1981.

Halphen, Louis. *Charlemagne and the Carolingian Empire.* Trans. Giselle de Nie. Amsterdam: North-Holland, 1977.

Llewellyn, Peter. *Rome in the Dark Ages.* New York: Barnes and Noble, 1993.

Noble, Thomas X. F. *The Republic of St. Peter: The Birth of the Papal State, 680–825.* Philadelphia: University of Pennsylvania Press, 1984.

Riché, Pierre. *The Carolingians: A Family Who Forged Europe.* Trans. Michael Idomir Allen. Philadelphia: University of Pennsylvania Press, 1993.

Scholz, Bernhard Walter, trans. *Carolingian Chronicles: Royal Frankish Annals and Nithard's History*. Ann Arbor: University of Michigan Press, 1972.

Hadrianople, Battle of (378)

Major battle between Roman imperial armies and rebellious Gothic armies; traditionally regarded as an important step in the "fall" of the Roman Empire. The battle was a dramatic victory for the Visigoths, who destroyed the imperial force and killed the emperor of the Eastern Roman Empire, Valens. Although they inflicted a catastrophic defeat on the Romans, the Visigoths were unable to take advantage of their victory and were forced to come to terms with the great Roman emperor, Theodosius. The victory of the Visigoths at Hadrianople did cause a change in the relationship between Rome and the barbarians, however, despite the Visigoths' inability to capitalize on their victory.

During the course of the migrations of peoples during the later fourth century, increasing pressure was placed on the Roman frontiers. This was due in part to the aggressive nature of the Huns, whose movement westward had either absorbed or displaced numerous settled peoples. Among these peoples was a group that later came to be known as the Visigoths. Their traditional homeland had been devastated and could no longer support them, and the Huns proved too great a threat to the Visigoths. A new leader, Fritigern, seized power and declared that he would save his people by fleeing into the Roman Empire. By the year 376, when Fritigern petitioned for entry, the absorption of foreign peoples was nothing new for Rome, which accepted them on the condition that they lay down their arms, submit to Roman authority, pay Roman taxes, work the land, and serve the Roman military. Other peoples had done this, and Fritigern's Goths were admitted on these conditions, but the number of people admitted, which Bury placed at 80,000 or more, and the incompetence of the local administration opened the way for disaster.

The Goths flooded across the border in numbers too large for the local military forces to keep order, and the Goths simply overran them. The emperor Valens was occupied with the Persian frontier and requested aid from his Western counterpart, Gratian. Over the next two years the Goths operated freely in the Balkans as the emperors prepared to march against them. In 378 both Valens and Gratian were ready to crush the Goths, and Valens assembled an army of infantry and cavalry of between 30,000 and 40,000 troops. Gratian too mobilized a sizeable force, but he faced a threat from the Alemanni, which he successfully overcame, that detained him from joining Valens. The Eastern emperor was all the more anxious to win a great victory over the barbarians after Gratian's victory over the Alemanni. He moved his troops forward to meet Fritigern's Goths, which reconnaissance numbered at 10,000 warriors, but which was actually three times that number. Despite warnings from Gratian, who had witnessed at first hand the new battle tactics of the Goths, Valens proceeded. In early August he marched his troops against the Goths near Hadrianople, and Fritigern sent messengers to treat with Valens. On August 5 and again on the day of battle, August 9, Fritigern sought to negotiate with the emperor, but without success. While Fritigern sent messengers, Valens sent his troops forward without food or water in the boiling sun to meet the Goths, who had set fires along the Romans' path. As negotiations were beginning, Roman soldiers, without orders, began the attack that proved fatal to the Roman force. The Roman attack was disorganized, and the counterattack of the Gothic cavalry was rapid and forceful. Units of Gothic cavalry returned from foraging to join the fray and made the assault on the Romans even more terrible. A cavalry unit then attacked the Roman left flank, and the Gothic foot soldiers made a ferocious push on the Roman center. The Roman cavalry fled, abandoning the Roman infantry, which was quickly surrounded and cut to pieces by superior Gothic forces. The Romans lost nearly two-thirds of the army at Hadrianople, and most of the casualties were from the infantry, the backbone of the Roman military. Among the dead were generals, unit officers, and the emperor Valens himself, who was either killed by an arrow or wounded and then burned to death when the building he was taken to was set on fire by the Goths.

Although Ammianus declared it the worst loss since Rome's defeat at Cannae and a tragic defeat for the empire, the Battle of Hadrianople was not a military turning point nor especially catastrophic for the empire. The Goths had a golden opportunity to do permanent harm to the empire after their victory, but they failed to follow it up with an aggressive assault on the empire's cities or armies. Moreover, the arrival of the new emperor, Theodosius, provided the empire with much needed support, and together with the Western emperor, Gratian, he was able to force the Goths to terms within a few years of the defeat in 378. Fritigern's victory, however, did force the Romans to come to terms with the Goths and settle them in Roman territory as subjects of the empire. And it was the descendants of these Goths, under the leadership of Alaric, who caused such great disturbance in the early fifth century. The Battle of Hadrianople also contributed to the triumph of Catholic Christianity, because the death of the Arian Christian Valens seemed to be God's judgment, and the new emperor Theodosius ultimately declared Catholic Christianity the official religion of the empire.

See also: Alaric; Ammianus Marcellinus; Fritigern; Huns; Theodosius the Great; Visigoths

Bibliography

Ammianus Marcellinus. *The Later Roman Empire (A.D. 354–378).* Trans. Walter Hamilton. Harmondsworth, UK: Penguin, 1986.

Bury, John B. *The Invasion of Europe by the Barbarians.* New York: W. W. Norton, 1967.

Heather, Peter. *The Goths.* Oxford: Blackwell, 1996.

Wolfram, Herwig. *The Roman Empire and Its Germanic Peoples.* Trans. Thomas J. Dunlap. Berkeley: University of California Press, 1997.

Helena, St. *See* Women

Heliand

An epic poem of the ninth century of some 6,000 lines, the *Heliand* (Old Saxon: "Saviour") is, perhaps, the oldest work of Germanic literature. Its main theme is the life of Christ and provides the story of the Gospels in the Saxon language. According to a Latin preface first published in the 16th century, a version of the Gospel was compiled at the order of either Louis the Pious (778–840) or Louis the German (d. 876) in the native Saxon language to complete the conversion of the Saxons to Christianity. Drawing on an early Latin Gospel commentary as well as works by the Venerable Bede and Hrabanus Maurus's commentary on the Gospel of Matthew, the unknown Saxon poet composed an epic poem of great power. Although telling the Gospel story, the context of the life of Christ is distinctly Germanic. Christ is a ruler who is joined by his loyal vassals, the Apostles, to found a kingdom. His disciples depict Germanic virtues and are reward by arm bands.

The marriage at Cana is depicted as a great banquet, and the feast of Herod is described as a drinking bout. The author of the *Heliand* did incorporate the core teachings of the Gospels, notably a version of the Sermon on the Mount, to ensure that the new Saxon converts truly got the word. The poem, which survives in only four manuscripts, was composed in alliterative verse, which was popular with the early Germanic peoples.

See also: Bede; Hrabanus Maurus; Louis the German; Louis the Pious; Saxons

Bibliography
Murphy, G. Roland, trans. *The Heliand: The Saxon Gospel.* Oxford: Oxford University Press, 1992.

Hengist and Horsa (mid-fifth century)

Brothers who, according to the history of Bede and the *Anglo-Saxon Chronicle,* led a band of Anglo-Saxon mercenaries to England at the request of a British ruler. Rather than aiding the native Britons, they conquered them and established a

Death of Hengist and the destruction of his army, ca. 1470–1480. From *Premier volume des et nouvelles chroniques d'Angleterre*, Roy 15 E IV, Folio No: 120 (detail). (The British Library Board)

kingdom. Bede also notes that they were descendants of Woden, "from whose stock sprang the royal house of many provinces" (56).

Following the Roman withdrawal from Britain in 410, the native British population faced raids from the Picts and Scots to their north. Unable to defend themselves from these invaders, the British, led by Vortigern, sought out mercenaries to help them. Vortigern invited a band of Angles and Saxons under the direction of Hengist and his brother Horsa to expel the invaders. In exchange for their assistance the mercenaries were promised the Isle of Thanet. In 449 Hengist and Horsa arrived with three shiploads of warriors to fight off the invaders from the north. Having successfully defeated the northerners, Hengist and Horsa turned their mercenaries against their employers and began their own invasion of Britain. In 455 Hengist and Horsa fought a battle against Vortigern. Horsa was killed in the battle, but Hengist defeated Vortigern and took over the kingdom of Kent. Hengist and his son Æsc fought several other battles against the Britons in the course of their conquest of Kent. In 465 they defeated the Britons and killed 12 British chieftains, and in 473 they fought another battle in which they overwhelmed the British and forced them to flee from the battlefield. Although the date of his death is unknown, Hengist may have ruled Kent for much of the next 15 years. According to the *Anglo-Saxon Chronicle*, Æsc became king in 488 and reigned over Kent for the next 24 years.

See also: Anglo-Saxons; *Anglo-Saxon Chronicle*; Bede; Vortigern

Bibliography

Bede. *Ecclesiastical History of the English People with Bede's Letter to Egbert and Cuthbert's Letter on the Death of Bede.* Trans. Leo Sherley-Price. Harmondsworth, UK: Penguin, 1991.

Blair, Peter Hunter. *The World of Bede.* Cambridge: Cambridge University Press, 1990.

Geoffrey of Monmouth. *The History of the Kings of Britain.* Trans. Lewis Thorpe. Harmondsworth, UK: Penguin, 1982.

Howe, Nicholas. *Migration and Mythmaking in Anglo-Saxon England.* New Haven, CT: Yale University Press, 1989.

Stenton, Frank M. *Anglo-Saxon England.* 3rd ed. Oxford: Clarendon, 1971.

Whitelock, Dorothy, ed. *The Anglo-Saxon Chronicle.* Westport, CT: Greenwood, 1986.

Heptarchy

A term, literally meaning seven kingdoms, used in Anglo-Saxon history to describe the political structure of early medieval England. The term is derived from remarks made by Bede concerning the nature of the political organization of England in the eighth century. It came into more general use among scholars in the 16th century. Although it became popular among scholars in the 19th century and still occasionally appears, it is generally not used by contemporary scholars.

The term heptarchy was used to describe a hypothetical confederacy of the Anglo-Saxon kingdoms of early medieval England, especially for the period from the sixth to the ninth centuries. It refers to the seven kingdoms that had been established by the Anglo-Saxon invaders and their descendants: East Anglia, Essex, Kent, Mercia, Northumbria, Sussex, and Wessex. Although in some ways a useful designation because it reveals the basic structure of early English political organization, the term fails to convey the variety in political institutions, size, and importance of the various kingdoms. It implies an equality of status among the kingdoms that seldom if ever existed. The kingdoms of Mercia, Northumbria, and Wessex were certainly more powerful than the other kingdoms and at times exercised dominion over them. Essex often lost power in political struggles with the other kingdoms and may have disappeared before the coming of the Vikings, the time traditionally considered the end of the heptarchy.

There were also subkingdoms, such as Deira (the region made famous by Pope Gregory the Great's encounter with Anglo-Saxon slaves in the Roman market), that were as powerful as some of the seven kingdoms of the heptarchy. The term also suggests a static relationship between the various kingdoms that fails to take into account the disappearance of some of the seven or the ebb and flow of political power among the various kingdoms. Although heptarchy is a convenient term to describe the political make up of Anglo-Saxon England, it is a term that conveys a false impression of the Anglo-Saxon kingdoms of England and is best relegated to history's trash heap.

See also: Aethelberht I of Kent; Alfred the Great; Anglo-Saxons; Bede; Mercia; Wessex

Bibliography

Bede. *A History of the English Church and People.* Trans. Leo Sherley-Price. Harmondsworth, UK: Penguin, 1981.

Bassett, Steven, ed. *The Origins of Anglo-Saxon Kingdoms.* Leicester, UK: Leicester University Press, 1989.

Sawyer, Peter H. *From Roman Britain to Norman England.* 2nd ed. London: Routledge, 1998.

Stenton, Frank M. *Anglo-Saxon England.* 3rd ed. Oxford: Clarendon, 1971.

Hermenegild (d. 585)

Spanish Visigothic prince and coregent with his father Leovigild and brother Reccared, Hermenegild led an unsuccessful revolt against his father. The rebellion may have been inspired by Hermenegild's conversion to Catholic Christianity from the Arian faith of his father. According to some accounts, his conversion and rebellion brought about his murder in 585, after the rebellion had been put down. Although his efforts ultimately failed, his conversion foreshadowed that of his brother, and with Reccared's conversion the Visigothic kingdom of Spain converted to Catholic Christianity.

Hermenegild played an important role in his father's reign before his rebellion in 579. The firstborn son of Leovigild, Heremenegild surely had a part to play in his father's conquests in Spain. In 573, Leovigild made his two sons coregents, thus granting them royal authority and marking them as eventual heirs to his power. Indeed, Hermenegild's elevation most likely reveals Leovigild's intention to establish a royal dynasty. Hermenegild also played a significant role in his father's diplomacy. In 579 Hermenegild married the Merovingian princess Ingunde, the daughter of powerful Brunhilde, a Visigoth herself, and the Frankish king Sigebert. The marriage was surely a recognition of the importance of good relations between Leovigild's family and the Merovingian dynasty, as well as of the growing power of Leovigild. Of course, the marriage complicated relations between the two dynasties after the revolt and then murder of Leovigild.

Despite his earlier importance, Hermenegild rebelled in 579. The exact cause of the revolt, however, remains uncertain. The sources and chronology of events are a bit confused, and it remains unclear whether Hermenegild converted before or after his revolt began. According to some accounts, Hermenegild was driven to accept Catholic Christianity by his young—she was 12 at the time of the marriage—but determined wife. Hermenegild's stepmother and grandmother of Ingunde, Goiswinth, may have persecuted the young girl and pressured her to convert to Arian Christianity from the Catholic faith practiced by the Merovingians. To establish peace at court, Leovigild sent his son and daughter-in-law to southern Spain, which Hermenegild governed for his father. In southern Spain, Hermenegild came under the influence of Leander, the older brother of the famous encyclopedist Isidore of Seville. Leander is also identified as the agent of Hermenegild's conversion, and it is while he was in the south that Hermenegild both revolted and converted, in whatever order. What is of importance is that Hermenegild did convert and was probably influenced to do so by both his wife and Leander.

Whether he converted before or after the rebellion broke out, Hermenegild used his conversion as justification for the rebellion and declared that he had revolted because of religious persecution. To guarantee the success of his uprising, Hermenegild undertook furious diplomatic negotiations with a number of peoples. He forged alliances with those conquered by his father. He also found support from the Suevi, who committed to him for both political and religious reasons. The Suevi, a Germanic tribe who had established a kingdom in northwestern Spain and had been defeated by Leovigild in 576, had converted to Catholicism during the previous generation. He also found allies among the relatives of his wife, the Catholic Merovingians. He sought the support of the emperor in Constantinople and found a great friend and ally in Pope Gregory the Great. Although he found much support against Leovigild, the only effective aid came from the Suevi; both the Merovingians and the Byzantines were involved in internal and external military difficulties at the time.

The course of the revolt went poorly for Hermenegild. It broke out in 579, and the tide turned by 582 when Leovigild struck back hard at his son and his allies. The Suevi were defeated by Leovigild in 583 and forced to withdraw their support and recognize Leovigild's authority over them. Hermenegild withdrew to Seville, which fell after a lengthy siege in 584. Hermenegild then moved to Córdoba, where he was welcomed by the Byzantine commander of the town. But this support was not long lasting; the imperial commander quickly settled a treaty with Leovigild that returned the city to the Visigoth in exchange for 30,000 pieces of gold. Abandoned by the Byzantines, who withdrew with Ingunde and their son, Hermenegild sought refuge in a church in the hopes of negotiating with his father. Leovigild had mercy on his rebellious son. He demanded that Hermenegild renounce his royal title in exchange for his life and accept exile to Valencia. He moved in the next year, 585, to Tarragona, where he was murdered in the same year.

Hermenegild's conversion pointed the way of the future for the Visigoths in Spain, but it found him little support from Catholic Christians after his revolt failed. With the exception of Gregory the Great, most contemporary writers had little good to say about Hermenegild. The pope recognized Hermenegild as a martyr to the faith and implicated Leovigild in the murder, but this view finds little support from Gregory's contemporaries, and the Roman and Visigothic population of Spain seem to have held that the revolt was the result of Hermenegild's ambition and not his conversion. Some Merovingian kings sought revenge for the death of Hermenegild, and Guntram invaded Visigothic territory in defense of Ingunde. But Gregory of Tours found little good in the revolt, saying of Hermenegild, "Poor prince, he did not realize that the judgment of God hangs over anyone who makes such plans against his own father, even if that father be a heretic" (375). Notwithstanding this verdict on his revolt, his conversion was vindicated by the successful conversion of Visigothic Spain by Reccared.

See also: Arianism; Brunhilde; Gregory I, the Great, Pope; Gregory of Tours; Isidore of Seville; Leovigild; Merovingian Dynasty; Reccared I; Toledo; Visigoths

Bibliography

Bury, John B. *History of the Later Roman Empire: From the Death of Theodosius I to the Death of Justinian.* 2 Vols. 1923. Reprint, New York: Dover, 1959.

Collins, Roger. *Early Medieval Spain: Unity in Diversity, 400–1000.* New York: Longman, 1983.

Gregory of Tours. *History of the Franks.* Trans. Lewis Thorpe. Harmondsworth, UK: Penguin, 1974.

Heather, Peter. *The Goths.* Oxford: Blackwell, 1996.

Isidore of Seville. *Isidore of Seville's History of the Goths, Vandals, and Suevi.* 2nd rev. ed. Trans. Guido Donini and Gordon B. Ford. Leiden: Brill, 1970.

Thompson, Edward A. *The Goths in Spain.* Oxford: Clarendon, 1969.

Wolfram, Herwig. *History of the Goths.* Trans. Thomas J. Dunlap. Berkeley: University of California Press, 1988.

Wolfram, Herwig. *The Roman Empire and Its Germanic Peoples.* Trans. Thomas J. Dunlap. Berkeley: University of California Press, 1997.

Hincmar of Rheims (c. 806–882)

Archbishop of Rheims from 845 until his death in 882, Hincmar was one of the leading religious figures of the Carolingian empire in the ninth century and an important ally and supporter of King Charles the Bald. Hincmar was also a noted canonist, theologian, and scholar whose works represent the achievements of the Carolingian Renaissance of the ninth century. As archbishop, Hincmar was involved in a number of ecclesiastical and political controversies during his reign.

Born to a prominent family, Hincmar was sent early to the monastery of St. Denis where he was professed a monk and obtained the best education available. He was guided in his early years by the Abbot Hilduin, who also introduced Hincmar to the leaders of Frankish government and society. When the abbot was made royal chaplain to Louis the Pious in 822, Hilduin brought Hincmar with him to court where the young cleric made a favorable impression. Hincmar also had the opportunity to witness the function of Carolingian government and the operations of the imperial court at first hand, an opportunity that would serve him well in his later years as an advisor to Carolingian rulers. Following the revolt of Lothar in 830, Hilduin was sent into exile for backing the rebel and was joined in his exile by his devoted student Hincmar. And it may have been Hincmar's ties to Louis that helped arrange his abbot's return to good graces.

On the death of Louis in 840, Hincmar supported Charles the Bald in the Carolingian ruler's struggles to maintain his authority in the Carolingian Empire against his brothers. His support was rewarded by Charles who bestowed upon Hincmar the abbacies of Notre Dame de Compiegne and Saint-Germer de Flyin 840, and in 845 the king helped secure the office of archbishop of Rheims for Hincmar. The archbishop continued to support Charles throughout the king's reign, most notably in 858 when Charles' half-brother, Louis the German, invaded. It was Hincmar who defended Charles' authority as king and helped organize the defense of the West Frankish kingdom against the invader. Two years later, Hincmar played an important role at the peace negotiations between the two Carolingian kings. Perhaps related to his support for his king was Hincmar's opposition to the divorce of Lothar II, the king of Lotharingia, which led to the composition of one of Hincmar's more important works, *De divortio Lotharii*. Whether motivated by politics or not, Hincmar supported Charles' designs on Lotharingia and on the death of Lothar in 869, Hincmar secured Charles' succession to the throne and crown Charles king at Metz. Following Charles' death in 877, Hincmar served as advisor to the late king's successors and composed *De Ordine Palatii* (On the Order of the Palace), an important commentary on the duties of a king and on the structure of government, for Charles' son Caroloman.

Hincmar was involved not only in the great political developments of the kingdom but also in several ecclesiastical affairs. In 848, he was engaged in the predestination controversy initiated by the teachings of Gottschalk of Orbais, whose works the archbishop condemned in a treatise of his own. He also participated in the council that formally condemned Gottschalk's teachings. Hincmar was also a zealous defender of the interests of the archbishopric of Rheims and of his authority as archbishop. From the very beginning of his reign as archbishop, Hincmar fought for the rights of his church. His predecessor, Ebbo, who had been deposed as a result of his role in the revolts against Louis the Pious, had alienated episcopal property and improperly consecrated clergy, and Hincmar fought these ordinations and worked hard to regain the lost property. He later came into conflict with the bishop of Soissons over episcopal rights, which involved frequent reference to the pseudo-Isidorian Decretals, a recently forged collection of church canons attributed to the early popes, by both Hincmar and his adversaries. Although Hincmar was defeated in this contest, he successfully asserted his authority over his nephew, Hincmar bishop of Laon, and secured the rights of Rheims as the archiepiscopal see.

Active in secular and ecclesiastical politics, Hincmar was also a noted scholar. Along with the *De Ordine Palatii* and treatises condemning Lothar's divorce and Gottschalk's teachings, Hincmar wrote important canonical works on the rights of an archbishop as well as a number of poems, capitularies, letters, sermons, and biblical commentaries. He was also a historian and hagiographer, continuing the Annals of Bertin and composing a life of St. Remigius (d. 533), the founder of Hincmar's see and patron saint of Rheims.

See also: Carolingian Dynasty; Carolingian Renaissance; Charles the Bald; Gottschalk of Orbais; Louis the German; Lothar; Louis the Pious; Saint-Denis, Abbey of

Bibliography

Duckett, Eleanor Shipley. *Carolingian Portraits: A Study in the Ninth Century*. Ann Arbor: University of Michigan Press, 1961.

Nelson, Janet L. *Charles the Bald*. London: Longman, 1992.

Riché, Pierre. *The Carolingians: A Family Who Forged Europe*. Trans. Michael Idomir Allen. Philadelphia: University of Pennsylvania Press, 1993.

Honoria (mid-fifth century)

Empress and Augusta, Honoria was a member of one of the great imperial lines. Her grandfather was the emperor Theodosius and her brother was Valentinian III. She was also the daughter of Constantius III and Galla Placidia, the domineering and ambitious empress whom Honoria was most like. Honoria's life was one of intrigue and scandal, and she herself suffered the consequences of dynastic policy.

Although little is known of her early years or even the date of her death, Honoria had a remarkable impact on the fate of the Western Empire in the first half of the fifth century. She most likely joined her family on their trip to Constantinople in 423 and returned with them to the Western Empire in 424. Her image appears in a number of mosaics of the 420s, and she was described in a poem, extant only in a fragment, that celebrated the imperial family. In 426, when her brother assumed the imperial dignity, Honoria was proclaimed Augusta. Honoria is most notorious, however, for her attempted marriage alliance. For a time, Honoria held a position of prestige at court, but when her nieces were born Honoria's status declined. In response to this loss of status, Honoria, with her lover the imperial steward Eugenius, plotted the murder of her brother in 449. The plot was discovered, and Eugenius was cruelly executed. Valentinian decided that it was time to secure a safe and sober marriage for her sister, proposing she marry the rich but uninspiring senator Flavius Bassus Herculanus. Honoria, of course, had other ideas and in 450 sent the eunuch Hyacinthus with a ring and money to Attila the Hun asking that he rescue her from a dull and dreary marriage. Attila, believing this was a marriage proposal, demanded that Honoria and half the Western Empire be turned over to him or he would invade the empire to secure his bride.

In response to these demands, Valentinian had Hyacinthus tortured and killed and would have killed Honoria herself had their mother, Galla Placidia, not intervened. Attila sent a further embassy again demanding his bride and equal share of the empire or face invasion. Demands for Honoria may have been the justification for Attila's long-desired invasion of the empire in 451, which resulted in the Battle of the Catalaunian Plains, and a second invasion that reached Rome itself in 453. Attila's goals of conquest of empire and acquisition of his betrothed failed on both occasions, and Honoria was left to a dismal fate—possibly marriage to the Herculanus and certainly to fade into obscurity after the death of her hero.

See also: Attila; Catalaunian Plains, Battle of the; Galla Placidia; Huns; Rome; Theodosius the Great

Bibliography

Bury, John B. *History of the Later Roman Empire: From the Death of Theodosius I to the Death of Justinian.* 2 Vols. 1923. Reprint, New York: Dover, 1959.

Hollum, Kenneth G. *Theodosian Empresses: Women and Imperial Dominion in Late Antiquity.* Berkeley: University of California Press, 1989.

Wolfram, Herwig. *The Roman Empire and Its Germanic Peoples.* Trans. Thomas J. Dunlap. Berkeley: University of California Press, 1997.

Honorius (384–423)

Son of the emperor Theodosius the Great and brother of the eastern emperor Arcadius, Honorius, in full Flavius Honorius, ruled the Western Empire in the early fifth century and presided over the beginning of the final demise of the empire in the west. His reign was troubled by uneasy relations with his own subordinates, especially Stilicho, and with Germanic leaders like the Visigoth Alaric. During Honorius's reign, the borders of the empire were breached on several occasions and Italy itself suffered invasion numerous times. His reign also witnessed the sacking of the city of Rome for the first time in 800 years, and even though it was no longer the capital, Rome's violation came as a profound and disturbing shock to the empire. His weakness and poor judgment were especially detrimental to the fate of the empire and worsened an already difficult situation.

The early years of his reign were marked by the guardianship of Stilicho, a Vandal-Roman general who had been his father's commander-in-chief, and the struggle with Alaric. Although occasionally allowing him to escape, Stilicho stood as the empire's firmest defense against the invasions of Alaric and his Visigoths. Sometimes caught in the competition between Honorius and his brother Arcadius, Stilicho remained loyal to the emperor and served him well. He benefited from this service by rapid promotion and close proximity to the imperial house, even marrying his daughter to Honorius. The emperor, however, came eventually to tire of Stilicho and became critical of his general's stewardship. To protect the imperial heartland against Alaric, Stilicho withdrew imperial troops from Britain and the frontiers. Even more serious, though, was the general's failure to defend the empire against the invasion of Italy by Radagaisus and his army of Ostrogoths during the first decade of the fifth century. Although Stilicho defeated the Ostrogoth, the devastation that Radagaisus caused in the north unsettled many. Moreover, Stilicho's efforts to secure the succession to the throne by the marriage of his son to Honorius's sister Galla Placidia alienated the emperor even more. In 408, when Arcadius died, Honorius was persuaded to allow Stilicho to go to Constantinople to guarantee the succession of Honorius's nephew. In Stilicho's absence, Honorius was persuaded that Stilicho had actually gone to place his own son on the throne. As a result, Honorius ordered the arrest and immediate execution of Stilicho, whose end came on August 22, 408.

Honorius had eliminated Stilicho, but he had only exacerbated the real problems of the empire. Indeed, Alaric, the greatest threat faced by the Western Empire, remained at large, but now Stilicho, who had had at least some success against Alaric, was no longer around to restrict Alaric's activities. Even worse, the wanton massacre of many of the German troops that had supported Stilicho provided Alaric another opportunity to invade Italy. In 408, Alaric marched into Italy and eventually reached Rome, no longer the capital but still a symbol of the empire. For the next two years, Honorius and his generals were involved in complicated negations with Alaric. Although making numerous concessions and ultimately demanding only settlement for his followers, Alaric was repeatedly rebuffed by Honorius. Indeed, Honorius refused the most favorable terms Alaric offered and suffered the consequences, the sack of the city of Rome. This event, which clearly shook the confidence of the empire, demonstrates the incompetence of Honorius. After their assault on Rome, the Visigoths most likely moved into southern Italy before heading north and settling in Gaul. The failures of Honorius thus contributed to the dismemberment of the Western Empire and the emergence of the first Germanic successor states.

Honorius also suffered a personal embarrassment in the sack of Rome; his sister, Galla Placidia, was kidnapped by Alaric's successor, Ataulf. She ultimately married her Visigothic captor, and both of them hoped to produce an heir to the imperial throne that would unite Visigoths and Romans. Ataulf's murder, however, ended this dream, and Honorius successfully negotiated for her return in 416, in exchange for his support of the Visigoths. Honorius then married his sister to one of his generals, a marriage that produced the heir, Valentinian, in 419.

In his remaining few years, Honorius remained relatively inactive and in so doing caused few problems for the empire. His death in 423 was the occasion for dispute over the succession, which ultimately fell to Valentinian under the regency of Galla Placidia. The reign of Honorius was clearly a low point for the empire. He presided over the withdrawal of troops from England and the frontiers, which allowed barbarian tribes to enter and begin to carve up the Western Empire. He eliminated his most important general, while not taking the steps necessary to get rid of his greatest enemy. He also presided over the sack of Rome, an event that heralded the imminent collapse of the Western Empire.

See also: Alaric; Arbogast; Galla Placidia; Ostrogoths; Rome; Stilicho, Flavius; Theodosius the Great; Vandals; Visigoths

Bibliography

Burns, Thomas S. *Barbarians within the Gates of Rome: A Study of Roman Military Policy and the Barbarians, ca. 375–425 A.D.* Bloomington: University of Indiana Press, 1994.

Bury, John B. *History of the Later Roman Empire: From the Death of Theodosius I to the Death of Justinian.* 2 Vols. 1923. Reprint, New York: Dover, 1959.

Bury, John B. *The Invasion of Europe by the Barbarians.* New York and London: W. W. Norton, 1967.

Claudian. *Claudian's Fourth Panegyric on the fourth consulate of Honorius.* Ed. and trans. William Barr. Liverpool, UK: Liverpool University Press, 1981.

Heather, Peter. *The Goths.* Oxford: Blackwell, 1996.

Wolfram, Herwig. *The Roman Empire and Its Germanic Peoples.* Trans. Thomas J. Dunlap. Berkeley: University of California Press, 1997.

Zosimus. *New History.* Trans. Ronald T. Ridley. Canberra: Australian Association for Byzantine Studies, 1982.

Huneric (d. 484)

The son and successor of the great Vandal king, Gaiseric. Huneric's rule (r. 477–484) is best known for its persecutions of Catholic Christians in his kingdom. But he also attempted to preserve his father's legacy and maintain the power and place of the Vandal kingdom in North Africa. Before his rule as king, Huneric was involved in his father's diplomacy and was betrothed to and eventually married an imperial princess. His reign, however, was relatively short, especially when compared with that of his father, and his efforts to solidify and unify the kingdom remained unfinished because of his death.

When Huneric came to the throne at his father's death in 477, he was already advanced in years. He was probably 66 years old, and although little is known of his life before he ascended the throne, Huneric probably was involved in the affairs of the kingdom during his father's reign. At the very least, it is known that Huneric was involved in diplomatic affairs. In 442, to guarantee a treaty with the Western Empire, Huneric was sent to Ravenna, the imperial capital, as a hostage and stayed there for three or four years. He was also betrothed to the Eudocia, the daughter of Emperor Valentinian III. She was quite young at the time of the engagement and the marriage had to wait some 10 years. Moreover, Huneric was already married, but Gaiseric did not let such details interfere with diplomacy—he accused Huneric's Visigothic wife of attempting to poison him, cut off her nose and ears, and returned her to Visigothic Spain. The betrothal and eventual marriage with the imperial princess were clearly important concerns in Gaiseric's relations with the imperial government in Italy, which were obviously more significant than his relations with the Visigoths. These ties were unsettled, however, before Huneric actually married Eudocia. Before marrying Huneric, she married the son of her father's successor, which may have prompted Gaiseric's invasion and sack of Rome. Huneric captured his betrothed and married her in 456.

The marriage itself did not last, but it did produce one and possibly two sons. In 457, Eudocia bore Hilderic, and perhaps another son within the next few years. But Huneric and Eudocia were poorly matched, particularly in religion. There was, of course, the great difference in age, with Huneric probably some 28 years older than his wife. Furthermore, she was a devout Catholic, and he was an aggressive Arian who persecuted Catholics. As a result she left her husband in 472 and fled to Jerusalem, where she spent the rest of her days.

Once on the throne in 477 Huneric paid far less attention to affairs with Rome and instead sought to unify the kingdom and ensure that his son would succeed him as king. To guarantee his son's succession he needed to eliminate rivals from within his own family, particularly the sons of Gaiseric's brothers. According to an agreement within the ruling family, the eldest son of any of Gaiseric's brothers or nephews was to inherit the throne, and Hilderic was the third oldest of that generation. In 481, Huneric launched a bloody purge of his brothers and nephews to secure his son's succession. The effort failed, however, because he failed to capture or kill the two nephews who were ahead of Hilderic, and it was those nephews who actually did take the throne from 523 to 530. Huneric's other domestic initiative was an equal failure. He attempted to unify the kingdom by imposing Arian Christianity on all his subjects. In 483 he passed an anti-Catholic edict, and in 484 issued a formal law against Catholic Christianity. He actively persecuted the Catholics in his kingdom and found support for this from the Arian bishop of Carthage. But to contemporaries his efforts seemed to inspire divine displeasure; his kingdom suffered famine in the summer of 484, and Huneric himself died of a mysterious and horrible disease in 484.

See also: Alans; Arianism; Gaiseric; Jordanes; Justinian; Pope Leo I the Great; Ravenna; Rome; Vandals

Bibliography

Bury, John B. *The Invasion of Europe by the Barbarians.* New York: W. W. Norton, 1967.

Clover, Frank M. *The Late Roman West and the Vandals.* London: Variorum, 1993.

Randers-Pehrson, Justine Davis. *Barbarians and Romans: The Birth Struggle of Europe,* A.D. *400–700.* Norman: University of Oklahoma Press, 1983.

Victor of Vita: History of the Vandal Persecution. Trans. John Moorhead. Liverpool, UK: Liverpool University Press, 1992.

Wolfram, Herwig. *The Roman Empire and Its Germanic Peoples.* Trans. Thomas J. Dunlap. Berkeley: University of California Press, 1997.

Huns

Nomadic steppe people who were skilled horsemen and great warriors and who challenged the power of the Roman Empire in the late fourth and fifth centuries. Although the Huns were never a direct threat to the existence of the empire, they did create great difficulties for Rome and won a number of battles against imperial armies. They both served in the Roman military against invaders and were themselves invaders. The Huns also may have caused such great terror among various Germanic tribes along Rome's periphery that their advance led to the Germanic migrations (or barbarian invasions) of the fourth and fifth centuries. They created a great empire under their greatest leader, Attila, which collapsed shortly after his death.

The origins and early history of the Huns remain obscure and uncertain. The ancients offer a number of views of their origins. The historian Ammianus Marcellinus said that they came from the "ice-bound north," suggesting, therefore, that they had Finno-Ugrian roots like the 10-century invaders, the Magyars who settled in Hungary. Other sources describe them as a Turkic people, or as a new wave of Scythians, Iranian horsemen who disappeared in the second century. A popular modern view of the Huns places their origins on the frontiers of ancient China. According to this view, the Huns can be associated with the Hsiung-nu (the name Huns thus would be a corruption of the Chinese word for "common slaves"), northern neighbors of the Chinese until the second-century AD. The Hsiung-nu had long harassed the Chinese and inspired the erection of the Great Wall to protect the Chinese from their powerful neighbors. Kept in check by the great Han dynasty, the Hsiung-nu turned their attention elsewhere and eventually moved westward, with dire consequences for those in their way. As attractive as this last view is, it has met with increasing skepticism. It is likely that the Hunnish nation, like that of the other barbarian peoples, was not ethnically homogenous but made up of a number of peoples. At the very least, it is clear the Huns were a nomadic steppe people of Eurasia, who absorbed Alans, Goths, and other peoples as they swept into the Roman Empire.

The ancient sources also reveal certain physical and sociocultural characteristics of the Huns. According to the historian of the Goths, Jordanes notes that the Huns prepared their meat by placing it between the horse and saddle and "cooking" it as they rode. Moreover, up until the time of Attila, and to a lesser degree his predecessor Ruga, the Huns lacked a central ruling authority. As a nomadic people shepherding their flock from pasture to pasture, they were migratory and organized under tribal chieftains who were hierarchically ranked. The Huns themselves were organized by families and larger clan units, with families living together in one tent, six to ten tents forming a camp, and several camps forming a clan. Kinship, rather than kingship, was the most important institution among the Huns until the time of Attila, and even then it remained an important institution. Indeed, even Attila, the greatest ruler of the Huns was not recognized as a sacred king. The Huns were skilled horsemen and equally skilled in the use of the composite bow, a bow made of different materials that were glued together and reinforced by strips of sinew. The ancient sources also reveal the funeral rites, at least for exalted figures like Attila. His body was borne into an open field, where it was laid to rest in a tent of the finest Chinese silk. A ceremony called the *strava* then took place around the body, during which the Huns rode around the tent, chanting a dirge, tearing out their hair, and gashing their faces. He was then buried in a three-layer coffin of gold, silver, and iron and much wealth was placed in the grave with him. The slaves who prepared Attila's tomb were killed so that its whereabouts would remain unknown.

The Huns, whatever their exact origins, first arrived in Europe in 375 and helped initiate the so-called migration of peoples. It should be noted, however, that although the arrival of the Huns and their allies among the Gepids, Rugians, and others caused great turmoil and forced the movement of the Goths, a generation passed before the Huns were politically mature enough to exploit the situation in the empire and along its frontiers. Nonetheless, the arrival of these terrifying warriors on horseback did destabilize the balance along Rome's frontier.

The Huns' advance included the conquest of the Alans along the Don River—and the Huns were ruthless overlords who kept their subject peoples from seceding—which brought them and their allies from among the subject Alans into contact with the Ostrogothic kingdom of Ermanaric. The exact size of the army of the Huns remains in doubt, but it is likely that they fought a series of successful battles against Ermanaric. The Gothic king then took his own life, a sacrifice to the gods for the safety of his people that proved ineffective. The failure of Ermanaric and his successor led to the absorption of much of Ermanaric's nation by the Huns. Some Goths, however, escaped subjugation by seeking the protection of the emperor, Valens, and requesting admission to the empire as *foederati* (federated allies). This was perhaps the most serious consequence of the Huns' first contact with the Germanic peoples living along Rome's frontier. The settlement of the Goths in the empire had disastrous consequences; in 376 the Goths fought a major battle at Hadrianople that resulted in the death of the emperor and the weakening of the empire.

A generation passed, however, before the Huns themselves raised the banner of war and conquest again. In the last decade of the fourth century, Hunnish raiders once again began striking at the frontiers of the empire and at the Germans living on either side of that frontier. During the winter of 394–395, the Huns simultaneously attacked the Balkan provinces of the empire and, moving across the Caucasus, Asia Minor. The advance was stopped by a Visigothic count, Tribigild, whose success inspired his demands for reward from the imperial government. When the emperor refused, Tribigild rebelled, in 399, and another Visigoth in the service of the empire, Gainas, was sent to put down the rebellion. Gainas quickly rallied the large number of Visigoths in the Roman army to his side, and then he too rebelled. His campaign was much more serious than that of Tribigild; he aimed to establish himself as the power behind the throne in Constantinople. Gainas met success early and even occupied the city of Constantinople for a time. He was, however, expelled from the capital, and as many as 7,000 of his followers were massacred during the withdrawal. But Gainas, remaining undaunted, attempted to establish a kingdom north of the Danube and sacrificed the Roman soldiers in his control to the god of the Danube to ensure success. At this point the Huns, led by the first known Hunnish king, Uldin, met the Visigoth and his army. The two armies fought several battles. Uldin ultimately triumphed; Gainas died in battle on December 23, 400, and the Hunnish king sent his rival's head to Constantinople. The imperial government lavished gifts on Uldin and established a treaty with him.

The treaty proved a great benefit to the empire when a wave of Goths and other peoples spread into the empire in 405, possibly the result of increasing pressure from the Huns themselves. Uldin, however, honored the treaty with Rome when the Gothic leader Radagaisus invaded the empire. Although it was the Roman military commander Stilicho who defeated Radagaisus, he was able to secure his victory because of the support of Uldin's Huns. Although he was only one of several Hunnish rulers at the time, Uldin's association with Rome set the stage for Roman-Hunnish relations for much of the next generation. Roman military commanders, such as Stilicho and Aëtius, employed Hunnish soldiers, and made alliances toward that end with other Hunnish kings, such as Charaton. The Huns aided Roman generals against invading barbarians and against internal rebels during this period, and also solidified their position along the Roman frontier, possibly in the Carpathian mountain region.

During the opening decades of the fifth century, the Huns underwent transformation. As they moved into the Carpathians and also across Illyria, the Huns shed some of their earlier social and political structures. They became less pastoral and migratory and more dependent upon the agricultural produce of their subject peoples. They also undertook raids to acquire the livestock they no longer husbanded themselves. With settlement came changes in their political organization, as the old tribal structure of hierarchically ranked chieftains was gradually replaced by a smaller number of kings and, eventually, a sole king who ruled the Hunnish peoples and their subject folk.

In the 420s, Attila's uncles Octar and Ruga ruled the Huns as kings and shaped them into a more unified people. Ruga, the senior partner, was particularly important to the formation of the Huns and helped establish the foundation for his nephew's success. As king, Ruga oversaw important changes in the relationship of the Huns and the Roman Empire. In 433, the leading general of the West, Aëtius, feared for his position and life and turned to the Huns for assistance. He negotiated a treaty with Ruga and returned to the Western Empire with strong Hunnish military support that enabled him to reestablish his power and, in fact, increase his authority. The relationship with Aëtius was surely an aid to Ruga and his Huns, who also were involved with the Eastern Empire. Ruga staged raids on the Eastern Empire and threatened the capital of Constantinople. He was the first leader of the Huns to extract tribute from the Eastern Empire, imposing a treaty on Constantinople involving annual payments of 350 pounds of gold. Although this was not a significant amount, it did suggest a changing balance of power and the increasing self-confidence of the Huns and their king. Ruga also demanded the return of Hunnish soldiers who had deserted to imperial armies, and failure to return them, Ruga declared, would be a violation of the treaty between the empire and the Huns.

Ruga's death occurred before he could resolve the disagreement over the return of Hunnish soldiers, which would be addressed by his successors, his nephews Attila and Bleda. The Huns continued to enjoy success against the empire under Attila and Bleda. In 435, they negotiated a new treaty with Rome that doubled the annual tribute and required the return or ransom of Hunnish deserters. In the early and mid-440s, Hunnish power continued to expand at Rome's expense. The violation of the treaty Attila had signed led to an invasion of the empire that involved the razing of a number of cities by the Huns, who also threatened the city of Constantinople. Attila's invasion led to another treaty with the empire that increased the annual tribute to 2,100 pounds of gold and a one-time payment of 6,000 pounds of gold. At this point, fortunes turned for the Huns, who no longer appeared so fearsome to their enemies. Bleda was blamed for this and was assassinated by his brother, who now became the sole ruler of the Huns.

Attila quickly resumed hostilities against the empire, ravaging the Balkans, and reestablishing his position. In 450 he turned his attention to the Western Empire, perhaps because of a marriage proposal from the emperor's sister, Honoria. He invaded with a huge force, numbering between 300,000 and 700,000 soldiers according to contemporary sources, made up of Huns and various subject peoples and allies. Despite a sizeable force, Attila met several setbacks at the hands of Aëtius and his equally mixed army of Romans and Germans, setbacks that included the failure to take the critical city of Orleans. Aëtius and Attila fought a terrible and bloody battle on the Catalaunian Plains. At one point things were going so badly for the Huns that Attila prepared to commit suicide. But the Huns rallied and left the battlefield in orderly fashion, and they were not pursued by the Roman armies— wounded, the Huns would have fought on ferociously, and Aëtius needed the Huns too much to destroy them. Attila pressed on and invaded Italy in 452 for a second time. The invasion began more favorably for the Huns, until they met Pope Leo the Great, who persuaded Attila to withdraw, which he did. According to sacred tradition, Saints Peter and Paul and a host of angels and saints supported Leo and forced Attila's departure. Another explanation for Attila's withdrawal is that his army was being decimated by plague. Attila refused to relent and planned a great invasion of the Eastern Empire in 453, but his death on his wedding night put an end to those plans.

With the death of Attila, the Roman Empire breathed more easily. Although he never threatened the empire's existence, Attila posed a great challenge that did serious damage to the empire and its allies. Unfortunately for the Huns, but fortunately for everyone else, Attila had no successor that was his equal. His numerous sons failed to provide a united front and were unable to overcome the challenge raised by the various subject peoples, particularly the Gepids. In 454 the Huns and their allies were decisively defeated by an ethnically diverse army, similar to those that had fought for and against Attila, at the Battle of Nedao. Attila's oldest son, Ellac, died at Nedao, but other sons continued the struggle and were defeated and killed by 469. The empire of the Huns collapsed, and rival Germanic peoples carved out new kingdoms in its place. The Western Roman Empire, too, did not survive long after the death of Attila and the collapse of his empire. Within a generation of his death and the disappearance of his empire, various Germanic peoples had moved into the Western Empire and brought about its fall.

See also: Aëtius; Alans; Ammianus Marcellinus; Attila the Hun; Hadrianople, Battle of; Honoria; Jordanes; Ostrogoths; Rome; Visigoths

Bibliography

Bury, John B. *History of the Later Roman Empire: From the Death of Theodosius I to the Death of Justinian.* Vol. 1. 1923. Reprint, New York: Dover, 1959.

Heather, Peter. "Goths and Huns, c. 320–425." In *The Late Empire, A.D. 337–425, vol. 13, The Cambridge Ancient History.* Eds. Averil Cameron and Peter Garnsey. Cambridge: Cambridge University Press, 1998, pp. 487–537.

Lot, Ferdinand. *The End of the Ancient World and the Beginnings of the Middle Ages.* Trans. Philip and Mariette Leon. New York: Harper Torchbooks, 1961.

Reynolds, Susan. "Our Forefathers? Tribes, Peoples, and Nations in the Historiography of the Age of Migrations." In *After Rome's Fall: Narrators and Sources of Early Medieval History.* Ed. Alexander Callander Murray. Toronto: University of Toronto Press, 1999, pp. 17–36.

Thompson, Edward A. *A History of Attila and the Huns.* Oxford: Clarendon, 1948.

Thompson, Edward A. *The Huns.* Oxford: Blackwell, 1995.

Wolfram, Herwig. *The Roman Empire and Its Germanic Peoples.* Trans. Thomas J. Dunlap. Berkeley: University of California Press, 1997.

I

Iconoclastic Controversy

A century long religious dispute that shook the Byzantine Empire, the Iconoclastic Controversy addressed one of the fundamental religious practices of the eastern empire and had important repercussions for the relation of church and state in the empire and the relationship between papal Rome and imperial Constantinople. Initiated by an imperial decree in the early eighth century that abolished the practice of the veneration of images, the controversy finally ended in the mid-ninth century with the restoration of the practice.

The tradition of Christian religious art and the depiction of Jesus and Mary and the saints stretched back to before the age of Constantine, and churches routinely included images of sacred personages. Icons, images of saintly persons, were intended as a means of educating the faithful but were also understood as having a direct connection with the saint they represented. This belief that the icon served as a conduit to the saint in heaven contributed to the growing popularity of venerating images, which were often the site of miracles such as a bleeding or crying icon. The growing popularity of icon veneration the seventh and eighth centuries attracted the attention of those who held that the veneration of images was little more than idolatry and formally condemned by Scriptures. It also inspired the composition of theological treatises providing a defense of the popular understanding of the nature of the icons.

During the reign of the emperor Leo III the Isaurian (r. 717–41), the question of the acceptability of the veneration of icons emerged in the empire. Leo himself opposed the practice and officially banned the practice in 727. His motivations are not completely clear and may have been a mix of personal religious belief and the dictates of the Mosaic code along with animosity toward the monks and priests who benefited from the practice and posed a potential political rival to the emperor. Whatever the case, Leo assumed that he was exercising his prerogative as emperor to implement the ban and found support for his policy from natural and military disasters which seemed to Leo to convey divine disfavor of the practice of the veneration of icons. The emperor also had the support of the army for his iconoclastic policy but was strongly opposed by the monks. This resistance forced Leo to take harsher measures in the 730s, attacking the monasteries and even ordering the destruction of images. His son and successor Constantine V (r. 741–54) took the policy of iconoclasm even further and more aggressively smashed icons and harassed monks, whom he may have forced to marry and to shave off their beards. The policy of iconoclasm was given official ecclesiastical sanction under Constantine when it was approved at the Council of Hiereia in 754 and for the next two decades following the council the persecution of the supporters of icons and the destruction of icons reached its greatest height.

Despite its formal acceptance by the army and ecclesiastical hierarchy, the policy of iconoclasm faced resistance at Rome and in the Byzantine Empire. Pope Gregory III (r. 731–741) denounced Leo's policy, criticizing the emperor for usurping the papal prerogative to define matters of the faith and specifically rejecting the terms of iconoclasm. Gregory undertook an extensive building program in Rome that supported the traditional use of images in response to Leo's policy, and the dissension over iconoclasm may have contributed to Gregory's efforts to seek a new protector in the Carolingian mayor Charles Martel. Along with opposition from Rome, elements within the Byzantine Empire were resistant to the new policy. Although Leo's son Constantine V was an ardent iconoclast, his son, Leo IV (775–780), and his son's wife, Irene, were not. And it was Irene who overturned the policies of Constantine V and Leo the Isaurian. In 787, she and her son, the emperor Constantine VI, presided over the Second Council of Nicaea, which restored the veneration of icons to its respected place within the Byzantine church. The council received the blessing of Pope Hadrian I (772–795) and was attended by two of his representatives as well as a large number of bishop, monks and priest from throughout the empire. Nicaea's decisions were recognized as ecumenical, binding on all Christians, and were to be accepted by all those subject to Hadrian's authority. The leader of the largest church in Europe, Charlemagne, did not accept Nicaea's decisions. Representatives of Charlemagne's Frankish church were not invited to the council, and its decisions were repudiated by the Carolingian church. In the Caroline Books (*Libri Carolini*), Theodulf of Orléans, with the possible help of the great Anglo-Saxon scholar and missionary Alcuin of York, and working from a flawed copy of the decrees of the council, provided the official response of the Carolingian church to Irene's Council of Nicaea. Theodulf offered a sophisticated view of art in his work, even though it failed to accurately address the defense of images announced at Nicaea. The Frankish response, however, had little effect in Constantinople, and the veneration of icons was once again officially approved and popularly practiced throughout the empire.

Following series of military setbacks and in the face of Islamic proscriptions of images, a second wave of iconoclasm broke out in the empire from 815 to 842. In 815 the first of three iconoclastic emperors, Leo V the Armenian (r. 813–820), presided over a council that once again banned the veneration of icons and deposed the patriarch of Constantinople and appointing a new patriarch that supported iconoclasm. The same divisions emerged in Byzantine society that had existed during the first phase of iconoclasm with the army generally supporting the emperor and the monks opposing iconoclasm. Iconoclastic policies were supported by Leo's successors Michael II (r. 820–829) and, especially, Theophilos (r. 829–842), who banned veneration of icons and actively persecuted supporters of icons. Theophilos's widow, Theodora, however, was declared regent and almost immediately restored the practice of the veneration of icons. She deposed the sitting patriarch and appointed Methodius as patriarch of Constantinople who presided over a church ceremony on the first Sunday of Lent in 843 that anathematized iconoclasts and honored the defenders of icons. The ceremony continues to be celebrated in the Orthodox Church in the Triumph of Orthodoxy.

See also: Charlemagne; Charles Martel; Gregory III, Pope; Irene; Leo III, the Isaurian; *Libri Carolini*; Theodulf of Orléans

Bibliography

Barber, Charles. *Figure and Likeness: On the Limits of Representation in Byzantine Iconoclasm.* Princeton, NJ: Princeton University Press, 2002.

Chazelle, Celia. *The Crucified God in the Carolingian Era: Theology and Art of Christ's Passion.* Cambridge: Cambridge University Press, 2001.

Noble, Thomas F. X. *Images, Iconoclasm, and the Carolingians.* Philadelphia: University of Pennsylvania Press, 2009.

Pelkian, Jaroslav. *Imago Dei: The Byzantine Apologia for Icons.* Princeton, NJ: Princeton University Press, 2011.

Irene (c. 752–802)

Empress, imperial regent, and even emperor herself (r. 797–802), Irene was an important and powerful figure at the Byzantine court in the late eighth and early ninth centuries. Irene was able to exercise great influence, in part not only because of the premature death of her husband, Leo IV (r. 775–780), but also because of her own talents and ambition. Like all emperors, Irene was active in religious, political, and military policies. She was in diplomatic contact with the great Carolingian ruler Charlemagne and even attempted to arrange a marriage alliance with the Carolingian. Her involvement in religious policy seriously strained relations with the church of Charlemagne. Her political ambitions also had serious repercussions in the Frankish world, particularly when she usurped the imperial throne from her son and gave Charlemagne's advisors a further justification for encouraging Charlemagne to take the imperial title.

At the death of the iconoclastic emperor, Constantine V in 775, Leo IV succeeded to throne with his wife, Irene. With the early and unexpected death of Leo, Irene was thrust into great prominence in the Byzantine Empire as the regent for her young son Constantine VI (r. 780–797). Throughout the 780s, Irene was the guiding force in the empire and introduced important new policies that were often contrary to those of her predecessors, the most dramatic of which was overturning the policy of iconoclasm. Unlike Leo III, Constantine IV, and, to a lesser degree, Leo IV, Irene favored the veneration of icons as an integral part of religious life and practice in the Byzantine Church. Consequently in 787, with her son, Irene presided over the Second Council of Nicaea. This council officially reversed the iconoclastic policies of the previous three generations and restored icons to a respected place in the church. The council was ecumenical— its decisions were binding on all Christians—and was attended by a large number of bishops, monks, and priests from the Byzantine Empire. It also boasted two representatives of the pope, Hadrian I (772–795), whose presence confirmed the universal nature of the council. The pope's legates returned to Italy with the decisions of the council, which were to be accepted by the churches under Hadrian's authority. Indeed, the Council of Nicaea achieved two goals that undermined recent imperial policy: the abolition of iconoclasm and improvement in relations with the west.

Irene's good relations with the pope established at the council were part of a broader effort on her part to improve relations with the leaders of Western Europe. Her efforts to improve relations with western leaders, however, achieved only partial success, and the council at Nicaea was both a high point and a low point in her efforts to secure better relations with western leaders. Although she gained the good graces of the pope, Irene lost the good relations she had secured earlier in the decade with the most important leader in Western Europe, Charlemagne. At the outset of her regency, in 781, Irene sought to arrange a marriage alliance with the great Carolingian ruler. Charlemagne was clearly pleased by the proposed marriage between his daughter, Rotrude (d. 839), and Irene's son and the future emperor, Constantine. The children were quite young at the time, ages six or seven and eleven, respectively, but this would have been a marriage alliance of great importance, at least to the Carolingian ruler, who saw the prestige of the association with the imperial throne in Constantinople. The marriage, however, never came to be, and relations between Charlemagne and Irene worsened before the end of the 780s.

Irene's support of the Lombard duke Arichis, whom she promised to grant the rank of patrician in return for his obedience, surely angered the great Carolingian, who sought to establish his authority over much of Italy. Even more serious damage was done to Carolingian–Byzantine relations by the council in 787. Although representatives of the pope were invited, no representatives of the Carolingian church, the largest church in Western Europe, were invited. This slight enraged the great king and gravely harmed relations between Charlemagne and Irene. Indeed, in response to the council, Charlemagne commissioned an answer to the perceived errors of Irene's council. The Caroline Books (*Libri Carolini*) were written by Theodulf of Orléans, with some possible aid from Alcuin, to denounce the veneration of icons promoted by Irene. Based on faulty translations of the acts of the council, the Caroline Books were a bitter denunciation of Irene's policy as heresy and a statement of the orthodoxy of the Carolingian church.

Although Irene's relationship with the greatest power of Western Europe was seriously damaged by the late 780s, she spent most of the decade strengthening the empire. She had success quieting the unrest brought on by Leo the Isaurian's religious policy, as well as some success defending the frontiers of the empire. In 790, however, she faced a serious internal rival—her own son. In that year, Constantine, in full manhood by now and recently married to a Byzantine noble's daughter, sought to end his mother's excessive influence and assert his own authority. Irene was sent into internal exile from 790 to 797, and Constantine ruled as sole emperor. His reign was not the most successful, however; he faced military setbacks against Arab and Bulgarian armies on the empire's eastern and northern frontiers. He also divorced his wife to marry a woman at court, which caused great scandal in Byzantine society. His military failures and personal scandals undermined confidence in him and allowed for the return of his mother. On August 15, 797, she launched a successful coup, and she had Constantine arrested and blinded in the very room of his birth. Even though he probably survived the blinding, he was now rendered unfit to rule, and Irene ruled as emperor until 802, when she was overthrown.

Although she did not rule as emperor for long, her usurpation was not without significant consequence, at least in Western Europe. Indeed, her impact in the Byzantine Empire during her sole reign was not great, but her usurpation had important repercussions for Charlemagne and his court scholars. Already in the 790s Charlemagne's advisors had spoken of him in imperial terms, noting that he was a great conqueror who ruled over much of the old Western Roman Empire. Many of Charlemagne's advisors denounced Irene's actions, declaring that a woman could not rightfully hold the office of emperor. In a famous letter in 799, Alcuin noted that "the governor of that empire has been deposed by his own circle and citizens." For Alcuin, therefore, as for others around Charlemagne, the imperial throne was vacant because a woman claimed to hold it. Irene's deposition of her son and usurpation of the throne was used as a further justification for Charlemagne himself to claim the title of emperor. And, although the exact meaning for all involved remains unclear, Charlemagne was crowned emperor of the Romans by Pope Leo III on December 25, 800. Irene's ambition and failure in relations with Western Europe played some role in that great event.

See also: Alcuin of York; Carolingian Dynasty; Charlemagne; Hadrian I, Pope; Iconoclastic Controversy; Leo III, the Isaurian; Leo III, Pope; *Libri Carolini*; Rome; Theodulf of Orléans

Bibliography

Davis, Raymond, trans. *The Lives of the Eighth-Century Popes* (Liber Pontificalis): *The Ancient Biographies of Nine Popes from A.D. 715 to A.D. 817.* Liverpool, UK: Liverpool University Press, 1992.

Herrin, Judith. *The Formation of Christendom.* Princeton, NJ: Princeton University Press, 1989.

McKitterick, Rosamond. *The Frankish Kingdoms under the Carolingians.* Longman: London, 1983.

Obolensky, Dmitri. *The Byzantine Commonwealth: Eastern Europe, 500–1543.* New York: Praeger, 1971.

Riché, Pierre. *The Carolingians: A Family Who Forged Europe.* Trans. Michael Idomir Allen. Philadelphia: University of Pennsylvania Press, 1993.

Sullivan, Richard. *Heirs of the Roman Empire.* Ithaca, NY: Cornell University Press, 1974.

Irminsul

An important shrine of pagan Saxon religion, the Irminsul (Saxon: "mighty pillar" or "great pillar") was believed to be a great pillar that supported the heavens and was an important symbol of Saxon political and religious independence. It may have been a representation of Yggdrasil, the cosmic tree or tree of life found also in Scandinavian traditions. Constructed out of a tree trunk and possibly containing an idol, the Irminsul was most likely the focus of Saxon religious rites and was also a sign of Saxon power as it advanced against the Christian Franks. Established near the fortress of Eresburg on the river Lippe, the great pillar was erected in territory recently conquered by the Saxons and may have been built to celebrate Saxon military victories. Its importance to the Saxons and sacred character is evident from the large hoard of gold and silver that was stored at the Irminsul. The centrality of the Irminsul to Saxon religious and political identity is confirmed by Charlemagne's Saxon campaign in 772. The opening of a protracted struggle that would last until 804, the invasion sought to stop Saxon attacks on the Carolingian realm and to introduce Christianity to the Saxons. On this first campaign, as the Royal Frankish Annals note, Charlemagne seized the fortress of Eresburg and destroyed the Irminsul, collecting the vast store of gold and silver that was held at the shrine.

See also: Anglo-Saxons; Charlemagne; Carolingian Dynasty

Bibliography

Scholz, Bernard Walter. *Carolingian Chronicles: Royal Frankish Annals and Nithard's History.* Ann Arbor: University of Michigan Press, 1972.

Isidore of Seville (c. 560–636)

Spanish bishop and author of numerous works, Isidore was one of the greatest scholars of the early Middle Ages; his work was influential and popular, both in Spain and the rest of Europe. Only the work of Augustine of Hippo, among authors before 800, was copied more often than the work of Isidore. His most important work, the *Etymologies,* was an encyclopedia of all knowledge at the time and was an important reference work for scholars for generations to come. He also wrote works of history and biography as well as a commentary on the Bible and works on Christian doctrine. His work of history was highly nationalistic and portrayed the Visigothic kingdom of Spain in most glorious light as a great Christian kingdom and as the rival and worthy successor of the Roman Empire.

Little is known of his life outside of his great literary output. He was probably born at Carthagena, which was in Byzantine hands at the time, before his family moved to Seville. His older brother, who was a great influence on him, St. Leander (d. 599 or 600), was an active figure in Visigothic religion and politics. Leander influenced the conversion of Hermenegild, a Visigothic prince who led an unsuccessful revolt against his father, and then Reccared I from Arian Christianity to Catholic Christianity. Leander was also bishop of Seville and an advocate of the monastic life. Considering Leander's support for monasticism, it is possible that Isidore himself was a monk. Although Isidore himself did write a rule for monastic life, it is uncertain whether he was a monk. He was most likely put on the path of the religious life while he was young, whether or not he became a monk. He probably was made a deacon and priest as soon as legally possible and eventually succeeded his brother as bishop of Seville at Leander's death in 599 or 600.

As bishop, Isidore was elevated to the national stage and most likely influenced affairs in the Visigothic kingdom, even if this influence was not as great as that of his brother. Although he performed the normal daily duties as bishop, he also corresponded with the Visigothic kings and seems to have been quite close to King Sisebut (612–621), who was an active supporter of intellectual and cultural life in Spain. In his correspondence with kings, bishops, and other clergy, Isidore cultivated a new model of kingship, promoted the concept of the Visigothic kingdom as the ideal Christian state, denigrated the Byzantine Empire, and denounced the Visigothic kings' attempts to convert the Jews of Spain to Christianity. He also presided over two important church councils in Seville in 619 and at the Fourth Council of Toledo in 633. The council at Toledo especially was of great significance and reinforced the values of Isidore by defining the proper behavior of the clergy, the proper teachings of the Catholic faith, and the ideals concerning the Visigothic kings and kingdom.

Although most likely an important figure in Spain, Isidore is best known for his literary works. His most important and influential work was the *Etymologies* (*Etymologiarum sive originum libri XX*), which is extant in over 1,000 manuscripts and was probably found in most monastic libraries in the Middle Ages. Unfinished at his death and completed by one of his disciples, the *Etymologies* was a compendium of all knowledge of the ancient world. Isidore drew from Augustine of Hippo, Jerome, Cassiodorus, Pope Gregory the Great, and Virgil, among other classical and Christian authors, in the preparation of his great encyclopedia. His approach was linguistic, and he opened each entry with the derivation of the word being treated. These derivations were often quite fanciful, so much so that these explanations have often prevented recognition of the value of the material included. The *Etymologies* covered a wide range of topics, including the seven liberal arts (grammar, rhetoric, dialectic, arithmetic, geometry, music, and astronomy), medicine, law, books of the Bible, angels, saints, men, animals, fabulous monsters, the universe, agriculture, war, ships, dress, food, drink, and furniture. The *Etymologies* thus treated all branches of knowledge, and it was intended as a tool for scholars to use; the rise of scholarship in Spain following Isidore's death suggests that it was successful in that regard.

Isidore wrote a number of other secular works. He wrote a second learned treatise, *De natura rerum* (On the Nature of Things), which was widely popular; it discusses the sun, moon, and planets, as well as earthly natural phenomena, including the Nile River, earthquakes, and the sea. Its purpose was to provide an explanation of nature to rival that offered by popular astrology. He also wrote several works of history, including a world history (*Chronica mundi*), a biographical guide of illustrious people (*De viris illustribus*), and the very important *History of the Goths, Vandals, and Suevi*. His works of history are important sources for the understanding of the history of the Visigoths; for his own time, they were also a means to glorify the Visigoths. In his *History of the Goths*, he praises the Goths of Spain, and portrays the Gothic kingdom as the true successor of the Roman Empire, which is now subject to the Goths. He also criticizes the Byzantine Empire and declared its greatest emperor, Justinian, a heretic. Like his other works, all Isidore's historical writings were very popular in Spain, and the *Chronica* and *De viris* were found in libraries throughout Europe.

Along with his numerous secular works of literature, Isidore wrote a number of religious works. His work borrows from many important church fathers, most important among whom for Isidore were Augustine and Gregory the Great. He wrote a rule for monastic life that borrowed from Augustine and Gregory and, probably, from St. Benedict of Nursia. A practical guide, the Rule of Isidore, among other things, encouraged the monks to read Christian works and to take books out of the library, read them, and return them each day. He also wrote the *Sententiae*, a moral and pastoral guide for clergy that was very influential, exists in hundreds of manuscripts, and provided a source book for many later collections of church law. He was the author of a commentary on the books of the Hebrew Scriptures, as well as a polemical treatise against the Jews (*De fide catholica contra fide Iudaeos*). This treatise, which was influenced by Augustine, reveals one of the darker aspects of medieval Christian civilization. The work is hostile to the Jews and encourages the conversion of Jews to Christianity as a means to bring about the final age of humankind. Conversion of the Jews would also contribute to the complete integration of Visigothic Spain and enable it to reach its most glorious potential. Despite his hostility to the Jews, Isidore's legacy includes an important body of written work that had a generally positive influence on the development of culture and society.

See also: Arianism; Augustine of Hippo, St.; Gregory the Great; Hermenegild; Justinian; Reccared I; Toldeo; Visigoths

Bibliography

Cohen, Jeremy. *Living Letters of the Law: Ideas of the Jew in Medieval Christianity.* Berkeley: University of California Press, 1999.

Curtius, Ernst Robert. *European Literature and the Latin Middle Ages.* Trans. Willard R. Trask. 1953. Reprint, with a new epilogue by Peter Goodman. Princeton, NJ: Princeton University Press, 1990.

Herrin, Judith. *The Formation of Christendom.* Princeton, NJ: Princeton University Press, 1987.

Isidore of Seville. *History of the Goths, Vandals, and Suevi.* 2nd rev. ed. Trans. Guido Donini and Gordon B. Ford. Leiden: Brill, 1970.

King, P. D. *Law and Society in the Visigothic Kingdom.* Cambridge: Cambridge University Press, 1972.

Laistner, Max L. W. *Thought and Letters in Western Europe, A.D. 500 to 900.* 2nd ed. Ithaca, NY: Cornell University Press, 1976.

Riché, Pierre. *Education and Culture in the Barbarian West: From the Sixth through the Eighth Century.* Trans. John Contreni. Columbia: University of South Carolina Press, 1976.

Thompson, E. A. *The Goths in Spain.* Oxford: Clarendon, 1969.

Wolfram, Herwig. *History of the Goths.* Trans. Thomas J. Dunlap. Berkeley: University of California Press, 1988.

Ivories

Ivory was a popular and important medium in early medieval art; carved ivories served a variety of artistic purposes. Ivory was frequently used for liturgical objects and also for book covers and reliquaries. Ivory was also used for more secular objects, including small boxes and combs. Early medieval artists borrowed from classical models for their works and often created beautiful and high-quality pieces. Continental artisans had access, even though restricted and limited in quantity, to elephant ivory from Africa, although they also used animal bones and teeth and whalebone. Anglo-Saxon artisans, however, had no access to elephant ivory, and their "ivories" are often made of whalebone or walrus tusk.

Ivory was a popular material for artists in the Roman Empire, and elephant ivory could be obtained by artists with little difficulty. But after the fall of the empire in the west, this commodity became harder to come by until the ninth century, when the Carolingians expanded trade. Despite the scarcity of ivory, even under the Carolingians, the art form continued to be popular, and imperial models continued to influence artists. Ivories continued to appear throughout the post-Roman world and are found among the treasures of the Merovingians. Ivory carving was frequently used to produce religious items, and ivory carvers employed simple tools similar to those of the woodworker. The ivories were often polished or painted and were often placed with metalwork and jewels in the finished product.

Under the Carolingians ivory carving flourished again and reflected the Carolingian interest in Roman imperial models. Carolingian ivory workers created small boxes and combs, but more frequently produced book covers, which borrowed from classical models or were patterned after contemporary manuscript illuminations. They were often used to adorn psalters, the Gospels, and other books of Scripture and therefore often depict scenes from the life of Christ, including his birth, Crucifixion, and Resurrection. One example from Metz that was commissioned by the bishop Drogo (d. 855), Charlemagne's son, depicts the Temptation of Christ along with a number of episcopal rites. The borders of the ivory covers are sometimes decorated with a geometric design or leaf pattern.

Tenth-century ivory and metal book cover depicting
Christ as Pantocrater. (Elio Ciol/Corbis)

Anglo-Saxon artists, although forced to find an alternate source of "ivory," produced high-quality works made of whalebone and, particularly from the 10th century, morse teeth (walrus tusk). Some early examples of whalebone ivory carving include a writing tablet that was decorated with carved interlace design and carved panels of winged beasts, and eighth-century Northumbrian crosses, which have similar carved animals. There are also examples of small boxes or caskets of carved whalebone, but, as with all whalebone items, there are not very many of these items because of the limited durability of the whalebone. There are more numerous examples of Anglo-Saxon carvings in morse. Like the Carolingian artists, Anglo-Saxon ivory carvers often created book covers that included designs from the life of Jesus or other religious images.

See also: Anglo-Saxons; Barbarian Art; Charlemagne; Carolingian Dynasty; Carolingian Renaissance; Merovingian Dynasty

Bibliography

Beckwith, John. *Ivory Carvings in Early Medieval England.* London: Harvey Miller, 1972.

Hubert, Jean, Jean Porcher, and Wolfgang Fritz Volbach. *The Carolingian Renaissance.* New York: George Braziller, 1970.

Lasko, Peter. *The Kingdom of the Franks: North-West Europe before Charlemagne.* New York: McGraw Hill, 1971.

Lasko, Peter. *Ars Sacra, 800–1200.* 2nd ed. New Haven, CT: Yale University Press, 1994.

Neese, Lawrence. *Justinian to Charlemagne: European Art, 565–787: An Annotated Bibliography.* Boston, MA: Hall, 1987.

Randall, Richard H., Jr. *Masterpieces of Ivory from the Walters Art Gallery.* New York: Hudson Hills, 1985.

J

Jarrow. *See* Benedict Biscop

Jerome (347–420)

A Christian priest, theologian, and Doctor of the Church, St. Jerome is best known for his elegant Latin edition of the Bible, the Vulgate, which became the standard text of the Bible throughout the Middle Ages. Active in both Rome and the east, Jerome was a master of the Latin and Greek languages and wrote numerous commentaries, treatises, and letters that helped shape the traditions of eastern and western theologies. Jerome was also an important figure in the ascetic movement and in the growth of monasticism.

Jerome (Eusebius Sophronius Hieronymus) was born in 347 in Stridon (near modern Ljubljan, Slovenia) in the Roman province of Dalmatia. His father Eusebius, a member of a wealthy Christian family, first educated his son at home and then sent him to study in Rome where he was taught by the great pagan grammarian Donatus. While in Rome in the 360s, Jerome learned Latin and some Greek and was baptized a Christian. In the 370s Jerome traveled extensively, visiting Antioch and other cities in the eastern empire. In 373, while in Calchis, two of his travelling companions died and Jerome himself fell ill. It may have been at this point that Jerome had his famous dream in which Jesus visited him and condemned him for being more Ciceronian than a Christian. Taking up the ascetic life, he then dedicated himself to the study of the scriptures and sacred learning and may have begun the study of Hebrew. In 378 he was ordained a priest and then continued his travels, visiting Constantinople before settling in Rome for a time in the 380s. While in Rome he served as secretary to Pope Damasus (382–385) and surrounded himself with a group of women, notably the widows Marcella and Paula, devoted to ascetic life. He also began work on the translation and revision of the Bible into Latin, which would serve as the starting point for his greatest contribution, his Latin Vulgate Bible, as well as works on matters of the faith such as the defense of the virginity of Mary. His staunch defense of the ascetic life and condemnation of paganism and luxurious and immoral living among Christians earned Jerome numerous enemies, who questioned Jerome's relations with the wealthy widows in his circle. Following the death of Damasus,

Jerome left Rome for good and visited Antioch, Egypt, and Palestine before settling in Bethlehem where he adopted the life of a hermit. He was joined by Paula, who helped support Jerome financially, and other pious women he had met in Rome. Spending the rest of his life in the Holy Land, Jerome wrote extensively and founded a monastery, several convents for women, and a school for boys. He died on September 30, 420 and was buried at Bethlehem. His relics were later translated to Rome.

Although important for his advocacy of celibacy and the monastic life, Jerome's greatest contributions to late antique and early medieval society were his numerous literary works. His many writings are characterized by a fierce passion in defense of his beliefs and an elegant Latin style that helped shape the literary language of the Middle Ages. His works include controversial and personal letters, commentaries on Daniel and many other books of the Old and New Testaments, saints' lives, and lives of illustrious men. He also was a strong defender of Catholic orthodoxy and wrote a harsh polemical work against the Pelagians, who emphasized the freedom of the will over the grace of God in matters of salvation, as well as a work against the teachings of Origen (184/185–253/254). A skilled linguist, adept in Latin, Greek, and Hebrew, Jerome translated the chronological tables of Eusebius into Latin. His most influential work, however, was his translation and edition of the Bible, which drew from Latin, Greek, and Hebrew texts and became the standard text of the Bible for much of the Middle Ages.

See also: Antioch; Monasticism; Rome

Bibliography

Brown, Peter. *The Body and Society: Men, Women, and Sexual Renunciation in Early Christianity.* New York: Columbia University Press, 1988.

Kelly, J.N.D. *Jerome: His Life, Writings and Controversies.* London: Gerald Duckworth and Company, 1975.

Rebenich, Stephen. *Jerome.* New York: Routledge, 2002.

Williams, Meghan Hale. *The Monk and the Book: Jerome and the Making of Christian Scholarship.* Chicago: University of Chicago Press, 2006.

Jewelry and Gems

In the early Middle Ages the various barbarian peoples that settled in the remnants of the Western Roman Empire left an important artistic legacy in the metalwork they created. Sophisticated and attractive works in gold and silver were created for both secular and religious purposes. Originally employed for personal adornment, the techniques for creating jewelry and metalwork were later employed to create sacred and liturgical objects. These creations were so highly valued that the fine for the murder of a metalworker was three times that of a peasant and twice that of a blacksmith. The discovery of numerous artifacts at archeological sites like Tournai demonstrates the creativity and talent of these early medieval artisans and the quality of their creations.

As the various Germanic tribes made contact with the Roman Empire, they brought their own traditions with them, which merged with those of the empire. During the migration period, the barbarian peoples were already forging jewelry and other metalwork. The practice of jewelry making predates contact between Romans and barbarians, but came to be influenced by contacts with the empire. The Visigoths and Lombards especially were influenced by imperial models of jewelry. Close contact with the empire shaped metalworking patterns, and Visigoths and Lombards imitated Byzantine models and received gifts of jewelry and metalwork from Constantinople. A third people, the Franks, particularly under the Merovingian dynasty, showed less influence from Rome and a greater reflection of traditional Germanic models.

Early medieval artisans crafted a variety of jewelry and metalwork for their noble patrons. There was a wide range of jewelry made of silver and gold and encrusted with precious gems that was worn by the barbarian peoples of early medieval Europe. Rings and earrings were commonly worn, as were buckles, pins, necklaces, bracelets, arm bands, and brooches. The jewelry of gold and silver was often decorated with amethyst, pearls, emeralds, garnets, and other precious stones. Cameos were also popular among the barbarian peoples. One of the most popular pieces of jewelry was the fibula, a type of brooch used to hold a cloak or other article of clothing together. The fibula came in a variety of styles, including the gold disk fibula developed by the Merovingians in the seventh century, which remained an essential part of clothing until the 13th century. Fibulae in the shape of birds or eagles, often worn in pairs, constituted another popular design. The various techniques used to create personal jewelry were employed for religious purposes as well, in the creation of chalices, reliquaries, crosses, and related items. The skills used to design gold and gem jewelry were also applied to the creation of book covers for the important manuscripts in monastic or royal libraries.

The jewelry and other metal items used for personal adornment or for religious purposes were created by highly skilled artisans. The designs of the jewelry fell into one of several categories. The patterns of some pieces were simply abstract and geometric in design. Other pieces used an animal pattern in the decoration of the metalwork and jewelry. The animal style is generally classified as Style I or Style II. Style I placed animal parts and compact animals in an abstract or decorative pattern in the metalwork; it is recognized as a northern European style that spread into France in the sixth century. Style II, or the ribbon animal style, originated in Lombard Italy and spread northward. It employed animal figures in elongated, intertwined, continuous, and symmetrical patterns. Also popular was the use of cloisonné, the practice of setting garnets or other jewels or glass in gold compartments or bands that were then soldered to a metal base.

Saxon brooch from south London, England, early sixth century. Square-headed brooches were almost universal in early medieval Europe. The square at the top held a hinged pin, while the cross shape at the bottom concealed the pin's clasp. The bridge between these parts held the gathered folds of cloak or tunic. (Museum of London/The Bridgeman Art Library)

Many of these practices and styles continued into the Carolingian period. But as the research of Genevra Kornbluth shows, the Carolingian period was also one of innovation, especially in the handling of gemstones. A number of quality gems were produced by Carolingian artists, demonstrating the great variety in Carolingian art; they were produced as a result of royal and noble patronage. Carolingian artists also introduced a new technique in the production of gems. They did not use the carving tools of the Roman and Byzantine Empires; instead, they used a round drill that was fitted with a rotating ball or wheel. The gems they produced were of high quality and unique in that they were not influenced by Roman imperial precedents.

See also: Barbarian Art; Carolingian Dynasty; Clothing; Clovis; Lombards; Merovingian Dynasty; Tournai; Visigoths

Bibliography

Hubert, Jean, Jean Porcher, and Wolfgang Fritz Volbach. *Europe in the Dark Ages.* London: Thames and Hudson, 1969.

Kornbluth, Genevra A. *Engraved Gems of the Carolingian Empire.* University Park, PA: Pennsylvania State University Press, 1995.

Lasko, Peter. *The Kingdom of the Franks: North-West Europe before Charlemagne.* New York: McGraw Hill, 1971.

Neese, Lawrence. *Justinian to Charlemagne: European Art, 565–787: An Annotated Bibliography.* Boston, MA: Hall, 1987.

Ross, Marvin, and Philippe Verdier. *Arts of the Migration Period in the Walters Art Gallery.* Baltimore, MD: Walters Art Gallery, 1961.

Jews and Judaism

Late antiquity and the early Middle Ages was a critical period in the history of Jews and Judaism for both positive and negative reasons. It was the period in which the Jews suffered tremendous persecution at the hands of Romans and barbarians but also enjoyed periods of prosperity and were welcomed by the world around them. During the late Roman and early medieval period some of the key texts and institutions that formed Rabbinical Judaism were established and some of the key texts and institutions that were central elements of Christian antisemitism were also established. The developments that affected the life of the Jews and their faith in late antiquity and the early Middle Ages left a profound lasting impact on the Jewish people and the world around them.

The history of the Jews in late antiquity and the early Middle Ages was in many ways shaped by two significant events: the destruction of the Second Temple in 70 CE by the Romans and the conversion of the emperor Constantine to Christianity in 312. The destruction of the Temple reinforced trends already in existence among the Jews, notably the emergence of the synagogue as the center of prayer and worship and the dispersion, or Diaspora, of the Jews throughout the Mediterranean world. With the destruction of the Temple, furthermore, the need for the priests who served there was eliminated and a new figure, the rabbi, took prominence in Jewish worship. Along with new leaders and institutions, a series of texts were compiled that would transform Judaism. The first of these texts, and the first of the texts of rabbinical Judaism was the Mishnah. Compiled in 200 CE by Judah ha Nasi, the Mishnah was the codification of and commentary on the Oral Law that had been delivered to Moses. The Mishnah, in turn, would be the starting point for two later texts, the Palestinian and the Babylonian Talmud. Completed between 550 and 650, the Babylonian Talmud, far more important and influential than Palestinian Talmud, includes commentary on the Oral and Written Law, legal debates, stories concerning important rabbis and sages that provide guidance to everyday living for Jews.

As the Jews spread throughout the empire and developed their faith they faced a Roman population that was at best uncertain how to deal with them and at worst openly hostile. The animosity toward the Jews and Judaism worsened after Constantine's conversion to Christianity in the early fourth century. As the first Christian emperor, Constantine set a number of important precedents for his successor, and among those was his treatment of the Jews. In 315, shortly after taking control of the western half of the empire, Constantine issued a law that imposed the death penalty on Jews who attacked Christians and forbade conversion to Judaism. His opposition to Judaism was asserted further in a letter to the churchmen meeting at Nicaea in 325. The emperor denounced the Jews as a wicked and blind people and encouraged the church to separate itself as much as possible from them. With the exception of the emperor Julian the Apostate (r. 361–363), Constantine's successors built upon his precedent and imposed increasing restrictions on the Jews. In Roman law, the Jews were forbidden from serving in the military or in civil government, were prohibited from serving as lawyers or witnesses against Christians in court, and could not own Christian slaves. They lost control of their own affairs with the abolition of the office of patriarch, were not allowed to proselytize or build synagogues, suffered restrictions on the public celebration of major religious festivals, and were forced to follow Christian laws on marriage. Finally, in the sixth century, imperial policy toward the Jews was codified in the great legal reform of the emperor Justinian, whose *Body of Civil Law* incorporated the anti-Jewish legislation of his predecessors and omitted any legislation that recognized Judaism as a licit religion.

Imperial policy was reinforced during the fourth and fifth centuries by canon law and works of polemic by the church fathers and other Christian authors. In the Council of Elvira (306), church leaders restricted Christian contact with Jews, forbidding Christians from marrying and even eating with Jews. Legislation from councils at Nicaea (325), Antioch (341), and Laodicea (434) prohibited Christians from celebrating Passover with Jews and kept Christians from honoring the Jewish Sabbath. Other councils barred Christians from accepting gifts from Jews or accepting hospitality from Jews and restated laws preventing Christians from marrying or having sexual relations with Jews. As the church developed its own laws against the Jews, John Chrysostom, Ambrose of Milan, and other church leaders created a theological image of the Jews that identified them as killers of Christ, followers of the devil, and enemies of God. A less virulent but equally influential view was forged by Augustine of Hippo, who recognized the important role Jews had played in the plan of salvation and maintained that they should stand as witness to the truth of Christianity until the end of time.

The worst aspects of Roman and Byzantine law and practice toward the Jews was emulated by the Visigoths in Spain where close ties between the kings and bishops led to restrictions on the Jews in both secular and religious law. The Jewish community in Spain was an old one and predated the arrival of the Visigoths. Settling in Spain as early as the first century of the Common Era, the Jews of Spain had assimilated to Roman society and fulfilled a variety of roles—merchants, farmers, landowners, professionals. Early church legislation in Spain restricted contact between Christians and Jews, outlawed ownership of Christian slaves by Jews, and forbade Christians from asking Jews to bless their fields, which suggests that all those things happened and that the Jews formed an important and accepted minority in Spain. In the late sixth and seventh centuries, however, attitudes began to change, and the kings and bishops of Spain began to persecute the Jews. Anti-Jewish legislation was far reaching and alienated the Jews who remained in Spain. The Visigothic kings, often presiding over church councils held in the central city of Toledo, renewed earlier restrictions of Jewish liberties and contact with Christians and imposed even harsher restrictions such as prohibiting Jews from holding public office, forcing baptism of Jews, curtailing marriage rights, enslaving Jews, and confiscating their property. In 636, King Chintilla effectively exiled the Jews by proclaiming that no unbaptized persons could reside in Spain, and although late seventh-century kings allowed the Jews back into Spain they continued to enforce increasingly harsh anti-Jewish legislation.

Life for the Jews of Spain improved dramatically following the Muslim conquest of much of the Iberian Peninsula in the early eighth century. Muslim success was, in part, due to the aid offered by the Jews who surely believed that their situation could only improve if the Visigoths were defeated. Applying traditions that existed throughout the Islamic world, the Muslims of Spain established the Jews as a protected minority which were burdened with various restrictions on their liberties and were expected to pay a special tax (*jizyah*). These restrictions were accompanied with protections of Jewish position in society and the restrictions themselves were at times ignored. The Jewish community thrived under Islamic rule and, at times, even found their services demanded at court. The Jews were granted their own leader, the patriarch or *nasi,* who represented the Jews before Muslim officials and presided over Jewish affairs and collected the *jizyah*. The Jews were granted their own religious courts to resolve disputes within the Jewish community. They also assumed key economic positions as merchants and bankers and, especially, doctors. Jewish scholars also performed the valuable service of translator. Their knowledge of Greek allowed them to translate the writings of Aristotle and Galen and other ancient thinkers as well as ancient Greek medical and scientific treatises into Arabic.

The harsh treatment the Jews endured in Visigothic Spain also found expression in Frankish Gaul under the Merovingian dynasty, but under the Carolingians the Jews enjoyed a period of relative prosperity and even acceptance, often living side by side with their Christian neighbors and speaking the same language. Although only gradually entering the northern parts of the Carolingian realm, the Jews were an important minority in the Aquitaine and other parts of the south, notably the town of Narbonne that included a large and important Jewish community. The first Carolingian king, Pippin the Short (r. 751–768), issued a series of edicts (*praecepta*) that granted important rights to the Jews. He confirmed their access to Roman and Jewish law and granted them rights to their own, especially religious, courts. The Jews were also permitted to own land and, in a significant break from Roman and church law, were allowed employ Christian servants in their homes and on their property. The precedent sent by Pippin was continued and expanded by his illustrious successor, Charlemagne (r. 768–814). Along with preserving the edicts of Pippin, Charlemagne issued new laws that made freeborn Jews subject to military service (testimony to the equal status Jews had with freeborn males; military service was mark of prestige) and extended Jewish property rights. In 809, he removed restrictions on Jews from serving as witnesses in court and implemented a new oath to be sworn by Jews in court and allowed Jews to swear their oath on the Torah, rather than the Christian Bible. Carolingian rulers in the ninth century continued this pattern of toleration of the Jews. Jews were exempted from paying certain tolls and taxes, were granted the power of political authority (*bannum*), and were allowed to convert pagan slaves to Judaism. Laws were passed prohibiting markets from being held on the Jewish Sabbath, and charters were granted binding the Jews closely to the Carolingian emperor.

Although the policy of toleration faced strong opposition from church leaders and gradually eroded in the 10th century, it benefited both the Carolingians and the Jews in the eighth and ninth centuries. Under the Carolingians, the Jews prospered economically. They were essential figures in the Carolingian economy as landowners and agriculturalists, and even more importantly, the Jews were great international merchants who had extensive contacts throughout the Islamic world. Jews from the Carolingian empire traded furs, timber, and, especially, swords with merchants in the Middle East and returned with musk, camphor, cinnamon, silks, and textiles. The Jews were also important figures in the highly lucrative trade in slaves, a popular commodity in both the Christian and Islamic worlds. Along with their economic and commercial success, the Jews enjoyed a degree of political power. Jews served at Charlemagne's court as advisors and ambassadors, playing a key role in Charlemagne's embassy to the great Abbasid caliph Harun al-Rashid. Jews also ran royal mints and served as tax collectors, judges, and administrators even exercising power over Christians. During the reign of Charlemagne, Jews played an important role in the defense of Aquitaine, defending Narbonne against an attack from the Muslims of Spain in 793 and participating in campaigns against Barcelona in 802 and Tortosa in 805. Finally, the Jews shared in the general cultural renaissance of the period promoted by Carolingian rulers. Jewish scholars and sages helped develop Jewish liturgy, composed hymns, and adapted the Order of Prayer to local conditions. They also wrote important religious commentaries and exegetical works as well as philosophical and scientific works and religious and secular poetry in Hebrew. Rabbis in the Carolingian empire provided guidance for everyday life for Jews and wrote to the masters of the schools of Babylon to resolve more difficult problems, which increased the importance of the Babylonian Talmud for European Jews and shaped their understanding of Jewish belief and practice for generations to come.

See also: Ambrose of Milan, Augustine of Hippo, St.; Carolingian Dynasty; Charlemagne; Constantine; Justinian; Merovingian Dynasty; Pippin; Visigoths

Bibliography

Bachrach, Bernard. *Early Medieval Jewish Policy in Western Europe.* Minneapolis: University of Minnesota Press, 1977.

Cohen, Mark R. *Under Cross and Crescent: The Jews in the Middle Ages.* Princeton, NJ: Princeton University Press, 1994.

Fredriksen, Paula. *Augustine and the Jews: A Christian Defense of Jews and Judaism.* New York: Doubleday Religion, 2008.

Glick, Leonard B. *Abraham's Heirs: Jews and Christians in Medieval Europe.* Syracuse, NY: Syracuse University Press, 1999.

Marcus, Jacob R. *The Jews in the Medieval World a Source Book: 315–1791.* Cincinnati, OH: Hebrew Union Press, 1999.

Poliakov, Léon. *The History of Anti-Semitism: From the Time of Christ to the Court Jews.* London: Elek Books, 1965.

Riché, Pierre. *The Carolingians: A Family Who Forged Europe.* Trans. Michael Idomir Allen. Philadelphia: University of Pennsylvania Press, 1993.

Roth, Norman. *Jews, Visigoths, and Muslims in Medieval Spain.* Leiden: Brill Academic Publishers, 1994.

Rutgers, L. V. *The Jews of Lat Ancient Rome.* Leiden: Brill Academic Publishers, 1995.

Schwartz, Seth. *Imperialism and Jewish Society: 200 B.C.E. to 640 C.E. (Jews, Christians, and Muslims from the Ancient to the Modern World)*. Princeton, NJ: Princeton University Press, 2004.

Stow, Kenneth R. *Alienated Minority: The Jews of Medieval Latin Europe*. Cambridge, MA: Harvard University Press, 1992.

John Scottus Erigena (fl. 845–879)

The most original and perhaps greatest of all Carolingian Renaissance scholars, John Scottus Erigena was a highly controversial thinker whose influence lasted long after his death and whose thought aroused opposition into the 12th century. John Scottus was actively involved in a theological controversy during his stay in the Carolingian Empire, but remained a close friend and advisor of the West Frankish king Charles the Bald. He was also the only Carolingian scholar with more than superficial knowledge of Greek, and this knowledge contributed to his production of a number of highly original works.

Little is known of his life, including the dates of his birth and death, although there is some indication that he was born around 810 and lived into the 870s. It is certain, though, that he was from Ireland, as his name implies, and left his homeland for the Carolingian realm at some point in the 830s. At some point after his arrival in the Frankish kingdoms, John Scottus came to the attention of the western Carolingian king Charles the Bald. He is mentioned as being at the court of Charles, who came to appreciate the Irishman's genius, in the year 843, but may have been known before that. John was recognized by contemporaries in the Carolingian kingdom as a holy man even though he was never consecrated as a priest or monk. He was also noted for his knowledge of Greek, which he most surely acquired before his arrival in the kingdom of Charles the Bald. His learning attracted the attention, not only of the king, but also the archbishop of Rheims, Hincmar.

It was Hincmar who invited John to participate in the controversy that had recently erupted over the teaching of Gottschalk of Orbais concerning predestination, which had already attracted the attention of Carolingian bishops like Hincmar and Rabanus Maurus. John's response, however, *De divina praedestinatione* (On Divine Predestination) was as controversial as the original teachings of Gottschalk. The Irish scholar rejected Gottschalk's double predestination and argued that souls were predestined to salvation, suggesting that evil, sin, and Hell were not real. His position was judged heretical by his contemporaries and condemned, but John Scottus survived because Charles the Bald remained his loyal supporter. He remained at the royal court until his death and while there wrote a great deal of poetry, in Greek and Latin, that celebrated the victories of the king and honored religious holy days.

He also was commissioned by Charles to translate the works of pseudo-Dionysius the Areopagite, an unknown author who wrote influential works of mystical theology around the year 500, from Greek into Latin. He was working on a commentary on the Gospel of John at the time of his death.

The most important and influential of John Scottus's works was the *Periphyseon,* or *De divisione naturae* (On the Division of Nature). Drawing on his knowledge of the Latin and Greek fathers of the church and Christian Neoplatonic thought, John Scottus created a highly sophisticated theology, which developed some of the ideas of his earlier works. In his discussion of the nature of God and his creation, John divided and classified all of creation but argued that God was incomprehensible and could not be put into any category. His work posed a serious challenge to his contemporaries, who had difficulty understanding it and thought it heretical. But the work survives in numerous manuscripts, attesting to its popularity, and exercised great influence on theologians in the 10th century and beyond.

See also: Carolingian Renaissance; Charles the Bald; Gottschalk of Orbais; Hincmar of Rheims

Bibliography

Laistner, Max L. W. *Thought and Letters in Western Europe,* A.D. *500 to 900.* 2nd ed. Ithaca, NY: Cornell University Press, 1976.

Marenbon, John. "Carolingian Thought." In *Carolingian Culture: Emulation and Innovation.* Ed. Rosamond McKitterick. Cambridge: Cambridge University Press, 1994, pp. 171–92.

Nelson, Janet. *Charles the Bald.* London: Longman, 1992.

Van Riel, Gerd, Carlos Steel, and James McEvoy, eds. *Iohannes Scottus Eriugena: The Bible and Hermeneutics.* Leuven: Leuven University Press, 1996.

Jordanes (sixth century)

Historian of the Goths, Jordanes has left the primary record for the early history of the Gothic people. Although probably less reliable and less complete than the now lost history of the Goths by Cassiodorus, Jordanes's history, *De origine actibusque Getarum* (On the Origins and Deeds of the Getae), is the earliest narrative source for the history of the Goths. Like the history of the later polymath, Isidore of Seville, Jordanes's work was intended to glorify the Goths and justify their authority over the Romans.

Little is precisely known of the life of Jordanes, including the exact dates of his birth and death. His movements remain uncertain, but a few matters about his life can be pieced together from his surviving writings. He identifies himself as being of Gothic descent, and in the early sixth century he served as a notary to the

Ostrogothic king of Italy, Theodoric the Great, who became one of the great heroes of his history. An Arian Christian, as most Goths were, Jordanes converted to Catholic Christianity at some point in his life, and some scholars have identified him with a contemporary bishop of the same name. This identification, as with most things, remains uncertain. It is generally held that he wrote his history in Constantinople around 550, but he may also have lived in one of the empire's provinces along the Danube River.

His most important work, commonly known as the *Getica,* has long shaped our understanding of the origins of the Goths and the end of antiquity. Jordanes was among the first to declare that the Roman Empire came to an end in 476 with the deposition of Romulus Augustulus, and the *Getica* chronicles the history of the Goths from the origins of the people until Jordanes's day. Although a distillation of the much larger history of the Goths by Cassiodorus, Jordanes's history was based upon oral traditions drawn from the Goths themselves as well as a wide range of other classical sources. The work is divided into four main sections: a geographical introduction, the history of the united Goths, the Ostrogoths, and the Visigoths and separate histories of the united Goths, and others. The work covers the reign of Theodoric the Great and other matters treated by contemporary Latin and Greek sources, but it alone treats the earliest history of the Goths. Indeed, it is this material that is the most important and controversial.

The model of Gothic history established by Jordanes has long been a point of debate among historians. According to Jordanes, the Goths originated in Scandinavia and then moved south and east, where they came into contact with some of the greatest civilizations of antiquity. Eventually the Goths divided into two main groups, Ostrogoths and Visigoths. Modern scholarship has undermined many of the claims Jordanes made, demonstrating his errors and identifying the influence of Roman anthropology on his understanding of the character of the Gothic people. Archeological research, however, has confirmed some of Jordanes's claims, and as a result most scholars treat his work cautiously, neither completely rejecting it nor accepting it without reservation. The *Getica* also contains information about some of the most important figures in late antiquity (e.g., Alaric, Attila the Hun, Justinian, Theodoric the Great) as well as on the movements of barbarian peoples other than the Goths, including the Huns and Vandals. It describes the great Battle of the Catalaunian Plains and the funeral of Attila the Hun.

Jordanes wrote a second work on the history of the Roman people, commonly known as the *Romana.* This too was a compilation based on another lost history and was probably written in Constantinople at around the same time as the *Getica.* It surveys the history of Rome from its legendary founding by Romulus to the age of the emperor Justinian. It is generally a less valuable and less interesting survey.

See also: Arianism; Attila the Hun; Cassiodorus; Catalaunian Plains, Battle of the; Huns; Justinian; Ostrogoths; Theodoric the Great; Vandals; Visigoths

Bibliography

Goffart, Walter A. *The Narrators of Barbarian History (*A.D. *500–800): Jordanes, Gregory of Tours, and Paul the Deacon.* Princeton, NJ: Princeton University Press, 1988.

Jordanes. *The Gothic History of Jordanes in English Version.* Trans. Charles C. Mierow. New York: Barnes and Noble, 1985.

Laistner, Max L. W. *Thought and Letters in Western Europe,* A.D. *500 to 900.* 2nd ed. Ithaca, NY: Cornell University Press, 1976.

Riché, Pierre. *Education and Culture in the Barbarian West: From the Sixth through the Eighth Century.* Trans. John Contreni. Columbia: University of South Carolina Press, 1976.

Wolfram, Herwig. *The Roman Empire and Its Germanic Peoples.* Trans. Thomas J. Dunlap. Berkeley: University of California Press, 1997.

Judith (c. 800–843)

The second wife of Louis the Pious and the mother of Charles the Bald, Judith was an important figure in Carolingian political affairs in the early ninth century. She was her husband's trusted advisor, especially after the death of Benedict of Aniane in 821. The birth of her son Charles and her strenuous efforts on his behalf have traditionally been seen as contributing to the collapse of the Carolingian Empire. At the very least, she was accused a variety of crimes by her husband's enemies and suffered a number of indignities at the hands of her stepsons, especially Lothar. She survived these insults to see her husband and son triumph over their enemies, as well as to see her son succeed to the throne, along with his half brothers Lothar and Louis the German, after the death of Louis. She also developed a reputation as a patron of letters and learning.

After the death of his first wife in 818, Louis the Pious was encouraged, despite his reputation, to marry again to save himself from the temptations of the flesh. According to the *Royal Frankish Annals,* he married Judith "after looking over many daughters of the nobility" (Scholz 1972, 105). She was a member of a powerful and important noble family, whose alliance seemed likely to benefit Louis, and she was also recognized by contemporaries for her beauty and intelligence. She and Louis were married in February 819, and two years later they had their first child, Gisela. She bore Louis a son on June 13, 823, the future king and emperor, Charles the Bald. At the time Louis had three sons from his first marriage and had also already established a plan of succession in which his oldest son, Lothar, was to share the imperial title with him and succeed as sole emperor on his father's death. Louis's two other sons shared in the inheritance as subordinate kings of parts of the Carolingian Empire. The birth of Charles and the need to find a place in the succession for him eventually led to some difficulty.

From the time of her son's birth until 829, Judith worked to find a share in the succession plan for Charles. At first Louis found help from Lothar, who agreed to protect his young stepbrother. But this situation did not last, and Judith herself found little comfort in the promises of Lothar. According to Nithard, Lothar consistently sought to undermine the agreement with his father. Judith and Louis were not unaware of this and found an able ally in Louis's trusted supporter Bernard of Septimania, an association that later came back to haunt Judith. Bernard proved a capable ally for both Louis and Judith, and he helped stabilize the southeastern frontier of the empire. Louis felt secure enough with the support of Bernard and Judith to alter the plan of succession in 829 to include Charles.

The change in the succession proved almost fatal for Judith and Louis; Louis faced two major revolts in the 830s that nearly ended his reign. His older sons, led by Lothar, rebelled against Louis in 830 and 833–834. In reaction to the changed settlement of 829, and with the support of the so-called imperial party of bishops, the older sons of Louis revolted against their father, with Lothar eventually taking charge. Numerous allegations were made against Judith, including sorcery and adultery with Bernard of Septimania, who was himself married to Dhuoda, a noblewoman and the author of a famous manual on the duties of a prince addressed to her son. Judith was forced to take the veil, and Louis and Charles were held by Lothar. But Louis quickly recovered, and the rebellion was put down. Judith was recalled from the convent and swore a solemn oath of purgation, thereby establishing her innocence before a great council of the nobles and bishops of the realm. Judith and her husband, however, had not seen the last of their troubles; a second and more serious revolt broke out in 833. Once again, Louis's older sons revolted, in part because of the new division of the empire forged after the first revolt. Judith again was dispatched to a convent, and Louis was forced to resign his office. Again, Louis was able to restore himself to power, and again Judith was called to his side and restored in a great ceremony.

For most of the remaining decade of her life, Judith witnessed the triumph of her husband and son, bittersweet as those victories may have been for her. She ruled with Louis until his death in 840. In 837 she persuaded Louis to restructure the succession to power that Charles might receive an inheritance, and Louis granted his son a kingdom that included much of modern France. She also helped restore good relations between Lothar and his father and stepbrother. In 839, Lothar returned from Italy, was brought back into the good graces of his father, and granted a sizeable portion of the empire as his legacy. Lothar also agreed to aid and support his godson Charles, who promised aid and support in return. Not only did Judith consolidate her position and that of her son, she also, according to some accounts, exacted vengeance on her enemies. Despite these successes, Judith also witnessed the outbreak of civil war after her husband's death. Although she helped her son secure his position in his part of the empire and witnessed the marriage of her son, Judith was sent into retirement at Tours by that same son, who also seized her lands from her. She, no doubt, was consoled by her son's successes, and died on April 19, 843, shortly after her "retirement."

Best known for her important role in her husband's reign, Judith was also a patron of the arts and education. She sponsored several works by important Carolingian scholars, including a work of history and biblical commentaries. Among those who received her patronage was Rabanus Maurus, who dedicated biblical commentaries on the books of Judith and Esther to her and praised her learning, wit, and desire to imitate holy women. Walafrid Strabo, who was made tutor for Charles the Bald from 829 to 838 by Judith, described Judith as pious, loving, and clever. She may also have been responsible for the establishment and expansion of her husband's court library.

See also: Benedict of Aniane; Bernard of Septimania; Carolingian Dynasty; Charles the Bald; Dhuoda; Lothar; Louis the German; Louis the Pious; *Royal Frankish Annals*

Bibliography

Ferrante, Joan M. "Women's Role in Latin Letters from the Fourth to the Early Twelfth Century." In *The Cultural Patronage of Medieval Women.* Ed. June Hall McCash. Athens: University of Georgia Press, 1996, pp. 73–105.

Halphen, Louis. *Charlemagne and the Carolingian Empire.* Trans. Giselle de Nie. Amsterdam: North-Holland, 1977.

McKitterick, Rosamond. *The Frankish Kingdoms under the Carolingians, 751–987.* London: Longman, 1983.

Nelson, Janet. *Charles the Bald.* London: Longman, 1992.

Riché, Pierre. *The Carolingians: A Family Who Forged Europe.* Trans. Michael Idomir Allen. Philadelphia: University of Pennsylvania Press, 1993.

Scholz, Bernhard Walter, trans. *Carolingian Chronicles: Royal Frankish Annals and Nithard's History.* Ann Arbor: University of Michigan Press, 1972.

Ward, Elizabeth. "Caesar's Wife: The Career of the Empress Judith, 819–829." In *Charlemagne's Heir: New Perspectives on the Reign of Louis the Pious.* Ed. Peter Godman and Roger Collins. Oxford: Clarendon, 1990, pp. 205–27.

Wemple, Suzanne. *Women in Frankish Society: Marriage and the Cloister, 500 to 900.* Philadelphia: University of Pennsylvania Press, 1981.

Julian the Apostate. *See* Ammianus Marcellinus

Justinian (c. 482–565)

One of the greatest emperors in Byzantine history, Justinian made profound and lasting imprint on the course of the empire's subsequent development. Famed for his marriage to the actress and courtesan, Theodora, whose reputation has been permanently darkened by the sixth-century Byzantine historian Procopius,

Justinian influenced much of Byzantine law, religion, and art and architecture. His codification of the law, involvement in religious disputes, rebuilding of Constantinople, and building programs elsewhere in the empire provided the foundation for later intellectual, legal, and cultural development. Many of his achievements were accomplished with the support of Theodora, whose strength helped Justinian at times of crisis and whose death left the emperor less effective than he had been earlier in his reign. His most ambitious effort, however, was the reconquest of the west and reunification of the empire under his authority. His wars in Italy, more destructive than any of the barbarian invasions of the peninsula, led to the successful restoration of Byzantine power in Italy and the destruction of the kingdom of the Ostrogoths, but at a great cost. And the success was only short lived; three years after Justinian's death, Italy was overrun by the Lombards. Byzantine influence lasted for several generations, but the effort was ultimately a failure. Justinian's overall legacy is marked by great successes and failures.

Rising to power as the nephew of the reigning emperor Justin (r. 518–527), Justinian—originally Petrus Sabbatius and later Flavius Petrus Sabbatius Justinianus—first reached Constantinople in 495 to receive an education. Later, when his uncle took power, he joined Justin in the capital and played an important role in government. He was rewarded by promotion as well as with a special dispensation to marry Theodora, which was necessary because members of the senatorial aristocracy could by law not marry anyone who appeared on the stage. Justin made his nephew caesar in 525 and coemperor in 527. Hardworking, dedicated, with a limited ability to delegate authority, Justinian dominated affairs in Constantinople for the next 40 years.

Justinian reached a major turning point early in his reign when he faced the Nika Revolt in 532. Although a number of Justinian's initiatives had already been started before that date, they were only completed after the revolt, and therefore his survival of the rebellion was critical. The revolt broke out over the arrest of the leaders of two rival factions in Constantinople—factions often in conflict with each other that led to rioting. This arrest brought the factions together against the government of Justinian. The rebellion was so severe that it nearly toppled the emperor, who was on the verge of fleeing the city with members of the imperial court. Theodora, however, gave an impassioned speech that persuaded her husband to stand his ground. He then gave the order for a detachment of barbarian mercenaries to enter the city and put down the revolt. According to contemporary accounts, the barbarians entered the hippodrome, the arena in which the rebels concentrated, and massacred 30,000 people. The leaders of the rebellion were also executed, and Justinian remained in firm control of the empire.

There were two immediate consequences of Justinian's suppression of the revolt: the completion of the reform and codification of Roman law and the rebuilding of the city of Constantinople. Indeed, one of the most pressing needs the emperor faced after the Nika Revolt was the restoration of the city after the great destruction caused by the rebellion. Along with aqueducts and number of public buildings, Justinian built a great new church, the Hagia Sophia. This became the imperial church, standing as the head of all churches in the empire and binding all Christians in the empire together. It was also a repository and model for late imperial art and asserted the close association between politics and religious beliefs in the empire. Its lavish decoration, including mosaics and different colored marble, and massive structure inspired Justinian to declare "Solomon, I have outdone thee!" when he first saw the completed church. Like a new Solomon, Justinian also was a great lawgiver, and he was able to complete the codification of the law he began in 529. The *Corpus Iuris Civilis* (Body of the Civil Law) was compiled by the jurist Tribonian and several commissions organized by Justinian or Tribonian; upon completion it was organized in four main sections: the Code of Justinian, the Digest, the Institutes, and the Novels. The codification of the law was intended not only to organize the law, which had been in a confused state, but also to create a bond of unity in the empire in the same way that the Hagia Sophia was designed to do.

Justinian's activities in law and building were those of the traditional Roman emperor, and indeed he saw himself in that tradition. As a result, he also saw it as his duty to rule over a united empire that included the old Roman heartland of Italy and Rome, the ancient capital. Therefore, beginning in the 530s and continuing for some two decades, Justinian's armies undertook the reconquest of parts of the old Western Empire. The first and almost incidental step in this process was the conquest of Vandal-controlled North Africa. Although long settled in North Africa and with a tradition of hostility toward Rome, the Vandals had expressed a new openness toward the empire and the Vandal king, Hilderic, had even converted to Catholic from Arian Christianity. But Hilderic's overthrow forced a change of plans for Justinian who entrusted the invasion to his great and loyal general Belisarius, who began his campaign in June 533. Seemingly unaware of the invasion and clearly unprepared, the Vandals and their king Gelimer put up feeble resistance before fleeing in disarray. As a result of this lightening quick invasion, the Vandal kingdom collapsed and the Vandals as a people were absorbed by the larger Roman and Berber population.

The dramatic and rapid victory in Africa also had the consequence of opening the way to Italy, where internal political turmoil among the ruling Ostrogoths offered Justinian with the opportunity to intervene there as well. The murder of the pro-Roman queen, Amalaswintha, provided the necessary justification for an invasion of the old imperial heartland in 535. Unlike the African campaign, however, the war in Italy was a protracted and brutal conflict. Early victories by Belisarius were followed up by a successful counteroffensive by the Gothic king Totila in the 540s. Challenges on Justinian's eastern frontier undermined his efforts in Italy as did his fear of an over-mighty Belisarius, who was recalled, and the resentment of the Italians over the return of imperial taxation. The final phase of the Gothic Wars was led by Narses, who replaced Belisarius. The new commander led Byzantine soldiers to a smashing victory over Totila at the battle of Busta Gallorum in 552 and continued the solidification of Byzantine control of Italy during the 550s, bringing the wars to a close in 561. Unfortunately for the Byzantines, their success was short lived as the Lombards took control of much of the Italian peninsula beginning in 568.

Justinian's reign was thus a pivotal one for both the Eastern and Western Empire. He oversaw the codification of the law, which actually ended by having greater influence on later medieval and modern Europe than on the Byzantine Empire, and a massive building program in Constantinople and Italy that laid the foundation for later Byzantine and medieval European art. His conquest of Italy restored imperial rule to the peninsula, destroyed the Ostrogothic kingdom, and brought the existence of the Ostrogothic nation to an end. The conquest, however, failed, and direct Byzantine rule ended with the Lombard invasion. A Byzantine presence continued for several generations in Italy, however, and the competition between the Byzantines and Lombards caused Italy further difficulties. The conquest also came at great cost for the empire, as did all of Justinian's activities, and his successors proved less suited to the challenges at hand than did Justinian.

See also: Amalaswintha; Belisarius; Code of Justinian; Constantinople; Gothic Wars; Lombards; Narses; Ostrogoths; Procopius; Rome; Theodora; Theodoric the Great; Vandals

Bibliography

Barker. John W. *Justinian and the Later Roman Empire.* Madison: University of Wisconsin Press, 1960.

Browning, Robert. *Justinian and Theodora.* London: Thames and Hudson, 1987.

Burns, Thomas S. *A History of the Ostrogoths.* Bloomington: Indiana University Press, 1984.

Bury, John B. *History of the Later Roman Empire: From the Death of Theodosius I to the Death of Justinian.* 2 Vols. 1923. Reprint, New York: Dover, 1959.

Cassiodorus. *The Variae of Magnus Aurelius Cassiodorus.* Trans. S.J.B. Barnish. Liverpool, UK: Liverpool University Press, 1992.

Heather, Peter. *The Goths.* Oxford: Blackwell, 1996.

Llewellyn, Peter. *Rome in the Dark Ages.* New York: Barnes and Noble, 1993.

Maas, Michael, ed. *The Cambridge Companion to the Age of Justinian.* Cambridge: Cambridge University Press, 2005.

Procopius. *The History of the Wars; Secret History.* 4 Vols. Trans. H. B. Dewing. Cambridge, MA: Harvard University Press, 1914–1924.

Treadgold, Warren. *The History of the Byzantine State and Society.* Stanford, CA: Stanford University Press, 1997.

Ure, Percy N. *Justinian and His Age.* Harmondsworth, UK: Penguin, 1951.

Watson, Alan. *The Digest of Justinian.* Philadelphia: University of Pennsylvania Press, 1997.

Wickham, Chris. *Early Medieval Italy: Central Power and Local Society, 400–1000.* Ann Arbor: University of Michigan Press, 1981.

K

Kells, Book of

Along with the Lindisfarne Gospels, the Book of Kells (formally known as Dublin, Trinity College, MS 58) is one of the greatest examples of Insular style manuscript illumination and book production. Produced in a monastery in Iona or Kells, the book's home for much of the Middle Ages, in the eighth or ninth century, the Book of Kells is a lavishly illuminated work containing the complete Gospels of

Chi-Rho page from the Gospel of Saint Matthew, from the Book of Kells, ca. 800. The Book of Kells is an illuminated manuscript of the Gospels that is considered a masterpiece of the Hiberno-Saxon style. (Jupiterimages)

Matthew, Mark, and Luke and the Gospel of John to John 17:13, based mainly on the Vulgate of St. Jerome. Along with the Gospel texts, the Book of Kells contains a list of Hebrew names, summaries of the Gospels, biographies of the Evangelists, and a canon table that lists the divisions of the Gospels.

Written in Insular majuscule with occasional use of minuscule letters, the Book of Kells contains the greatest number of highly decorated initial letters and is best known for its program of illuminations. The work contains a broad array of brilliant colors, including blue, red, purple, green, lilac, pink, and sienna. There are numerous full page illuminations in the manuscript that depict the Virgin and Child, the Arrest of Jesus, and the four Evangelists and their symbols. Along with the large illustrations, the Book of Kells includes marginal illustrations of humans and animals, zoomorphic designs, interlaced chains, and the decorated initials.

See also: Lindisfarne Gospels; Monasticism

Bibliography

Farr, Carol Ann. *The Book of Kells: Its Function and Audience.* Toronto: University of Toronto Press, 1997.

Meehan, Bernard. *The Book of Kells: An Illustrated Introduction to the Manuscript in Trinity College Dublin.* London: Thames and Hudson, 1994.

Pulliam, Heather. *Word and Image in the Book of Kells.* Dublin: Four Courts Press, 2006.

King Arthur

Semilegendary hero and king of the Britons who defended England from Anglo-Saxon invaders in the fifth or sixth century and who traditionally fought 12 battles, including the great Battle of Badon Hill (*Mons Badonicus*) in 516. The legendary figure of Arthur is possibly based on a historical person, who has been identified as one of a broad range of figures, including a professional mercenary, a late Roman military commander, a Welsh duke, and an Irish king in Scotland. He is best known, however, through the tales of romance composed on the basis of the old legends in the high and late Middle Ages by Geoffrey of Monmouth, Thomas Malory, and others that describe the adventures of Arthur and Merlin, Lancelot and Guinevere, and their home, the fabled Camelot.

The origins of the legend can be found in the descriptions of invasion-era England by Gildas in the sixth century and Nennius in the ninth century, as well as in the comment of an anonymous early medieval Welsh poet who says of a certain warrior that he "was not Arthur." Although Gildas does not name his hero, he seldom does name names in his history, and he does describe the victory at Badon Hill and the brief recovery of the fortunes of the Britons after the battle—key elements in the later fame of Arthur. Nennius identifies his hero as Arthur and lists 12 battles, including Badon Hill and Camlann where Arthur died, that the great hero fought against invading Saxon armies. Although two of the battles have been located geographically and probably did occur, the other 10 battles have not been located and may not have occurred, or least as Nennius described them. It is from these simple beginnings that the full-scale legend evolved in Welsh and later English sources. It was a legend of great popularity that, at the same time, made any English prince named Arthur suspect in the eyes of the ruling monarch.

Some scholars claim to have identified Camelot, the most famous landmark of the legend of Arthur. As early as the 15th and 16th centuries, Cadbury Castle in South Cadbury, Somerset, was recognized as Camelot. In the 1960s excavations discovered early fortifications that could be associated with a historical Arthur and also unearthed foundations of a church and numerous objects of everyday use of high quality. Although some scholars accept this as Arthur's castle, others reject it and argue that the documentary record of an active warrior does not support his association with the structures found at Cadbury.

See also: Anglo-Saxons; Badon Hill, Battle of; Gildas; Nennius

Bibliography

Alcock, Leslie. *Arthur's Britain: History and Archeology,* A.D. *367–634.* Harmondsworth, UK: Penguin, 1971.

Barber, Richard. *The Figure of Arthur.* Totowa, NJ: Rowman and Littlefield, 1972.

Geoffrey of Monmouth. *The History of the Kings of Britain.* Trans. Lewis Thorpe. Harmondsworth, UK: Penguin, 1996.

Gildas. *The Ruin of Britain and Other Works.* Ed. and trans. Michael Winterbottom. London: Phillimore, 1978.

Malory, Sir Thomas. *Le Morte d'Arthur.* Ed. Norma Lorre Goodrich. New York: Washington Square Press, 1966.